THE PRO-WAR MOVEMENT

A VOLUME IN THE SERIES
Culture, Politics, and the Cold War
EDITED BY
Christian G. Appy

OTHER TITLES IN THE SERIES

James T. Fisher, *Dr. America: The Lives of Thomas A. Dooley, 1927–1961*

Daniel Horowitz, *Betty Friedan and the Making of "The Feminine Mystique": The American Left, the Cold War, and Modern Feminism*

Tom Engelhardt, *The End of Victory Culture: Cold War America and the Disillusioning of a Generation*

Christian G. Appy, ed., *Cold War Constructions: The Political Culture of United States Imperialism, 1945–1966*

H. Bruce Franklin, *Vietnam and Other American Fantasies*

Robert D. Dean, *Imperial Brotherhood: Gender and the Making of Cold War Foreign Policy*

Lee Bernstein, *The Greatest Menace: Organized Crime in Cold War America*

David C. Engerman, Nils Gilman, Mark H. Haefele, and Michael E. Latham, eds., *Staging Growth: Modernization, Development, and the Global Cold War*

Jonathan Nashel, *Edward Lansdale's Cold War*

James Peck, *Washington's China: The National Security World, the Cold War, and the Origins of Globalism*

Edwin A. Martini, *Invisible Enemies: The American War on Vietnam, 1975–2000*

Tony Shaw, *Hollywood's Cold War*

Maureen Ryan, *The Other Side of Grief: The Home Front and the Aftermath in American Narratives of the Vietnam War*

David Hunt, *Vietnam's Southern Revolution: From Peasant Insurrection to Total War*

Patrick Hagopian, *The Vietnam War in American Memory: Veterans, Memorials, and the Politics of Healing*

Jeremy Kuzmarov, *The Myth of the Addicted Army: Vietnam and the Modern War on Drugs*

Robert Surbrug Jr., *Beyond Vietnam: The Politics of Protest in Massachusetts, 1974–1990*

Larry Grubbs, *Secular Missionaries: Americans and African Development in the 1960s*

Robert A. Jacobs, *The Dragon's Tail: Americans Face the Atomic Age*

Andrew J. Falk, *Upstaging the Cold War: American Dissent and Cultural Diplomacy, 1940–1960*

Jerry Lembcke, *Hanoi Jane: War, Sex, and Fantasies of Betrayal*

Anna G. Creadick, *Perfectly Average: The Pursuit of Normality in Postwar America*

Kathleen Donohue, ed., *Liberty and Justice for All? Rethinking Politics in Cold War America*

Jeremy Kuzmarov, *Modernizing Repression: Police Training and Nation Building in the American Century*

Roger Peace, *A Call to Conscience: The Anti–Contra War Campaign*

Edwin A. Martini, *Agent Orange: History, Science, and the Politics of Uncertainty*

THE PRO-WAR MOVEMENT

Domestic Support for the Vietnam War and the
Making of Modern American Conservatism

Sandra Scanlon

UNIVERSITY OF MASSACHUSETTS PRESS
Amherst and Boston

Copyright © 2013 by University of Massachusetts Press
All rights reserved
Printed in the United States of America

ISBN 978-1-55849-62534-018-4 (paper); 017-7 (hardcover)

Designed by Sally Nichols
Set in Palatino
Printed and bound by Thomson-Shore, Inc.

Library of Congress Cataloging-in-Publication Data

Scanlon, Sandra.
The pro-war movement : domestic support for the Vietnam War and the making of modern American conservatism / Sandra Scanlon.
  pages cm. — (Culture, politics, and the Cold War)
Includes bibliographical references and index.
ISBN 978-1-62534-017-7 (hardcover : alk. paper) — ISBN 978-1-62534-018-4 (pbk. : alk. paper) 1. Vietnam War, 1961–1975—Political aspects—United States. 2. Conservatism—United States—History—20th century. 3. Public opinion—United States—History—20th century. 4. United States—Politics and government—1961–1963. 5. United States—Politics and government—1963–1969. 6. United States—Politics and government—1969–1974. I. Title.
DS559.62.U6S33 2013
959.704'31—dc23
2013009435

British Library Cataloguing-in-Publication Data
A catalogue record for this book is available from the British Library.

To Dónal and Liam

Contents

Acknowledgments   ix
Abbreviations   xiii

Introduction
Conservatives and the Vietnam War   1

1. No Substitute for Victory
The Beginnings of a War   17

2. The Loyal Opposition?
The Push for Victory, 1965–1968   43

3. Conservatives for Nixon
The Domestic Politics of Vietnam, 1968–1969   72

4. From Victory to Honor
Making Peace with Withdrawal, 1969–1972   125

5. The Search for a New Majority
Popular Support for the War   184

6. Tell It to Hanoi
Student Pro-War Campaigns   242

7. Snatching Victory
The Endings of a War   289

Conclusion
Defining the Vietnam War   328

Notes   343
Index   389

Acknowledgments

Completing this book presented me with the opportunity to travel across the United States in search of source materials and inspiration, to connect with people who remembered and loathed the Vietnam War in multitudes of ways, and to engage with scholars on two continents who continue to debate the meaning of the war and its political legacies. The sleepless nights notwithstanding, it has been a tremendously rewarding experience. I began work on this project while a graduate student at the University of Cambridge. Tony Badger was a source of constant encouragement, and I thank him most sincerely for his intellectual support. John Thompson led the graduate research seminar at which I first articulated the ideas contained in this book. He pushed me to reconsider my approach and my early conclusions and offered a wonderfully thought-provoking research environment. The seminar was also the source of dear friendships, and I thank Alex Goodall, Gabriella Treglia, Kate Dossett, David Milne, Catherine Callard, and Joel Isaac for their comments on my early work.

Bob Brigham became an adviser at this time and later a valued colleague and friend at University College Dublin. I thank him for his continued advice on this project. My current and former colleagues at UCD, Oxford University, the University of Sheffield, and the London School of Economics and Political Science were sources of inspiration and comfort. I especially thank Steven Casey, Daniel Scroop, Andrew Heath, Simon Middleton, and Stephen Tuck. The School of History and Archives at UCD continues to provide a stimulating academic home. My graduate students, past and present, helped shape the way I think about the relationship between domestic politics and foreign policy, and I am especially grateful to Ciarán Murphy. I have discussed my thoughts about the Vietnam War and American conservatism at much-valued research seminars, and I thank Fabian Hilfrich, Jarod Roll, Gareth Davies, William Mulligan, Arne Westad, John Kirk, Kendrick Oliver, and Elizabeth Tandy Shermer for their invitations and feedback. Robert Mason and Iwan Morgan graciously asked me to participate in a conference on the making of the Republican majority during the 1960s and 1970s. My chapter in their collection, *Seeking a New Majority: The Republican Party and American Politics, 1960–1980* (Nashville: Vanderbilt University Press, 2013), deals with some of the issues and ideas that are part of this book, and I appreciate their editorial advice and intellectual support. In 2008 I was fortunate in being asked to participate in the Society for American Foreign Relations first summer institute at Ohio State University. Robert McMahon and Peter Hahn created a richly inspiring atmosphere, and each of the institute's fellows helped me to take my work in new directions.

Writing American history from Europe remains an expensive task, and I owe a deep debt of gratitude to several organizations. The Gates Cambridge Trust funded my doctoral studies, while travel grants from the Sara Norton Trust, Peterhouse College, and the British Association for American Studies allowed me to spend extended periods in the United States. The Roosevelt Study Center in the Netherlands was a wonderful local resource, and I appreciatively acknowledge the center's financial grants. I was awarded postdoctoral funding by the Irish Research Council for the Humanities and Social Sciences, while the John F. Kennedy Library Foundation and the Lyndon Baines Johnson Library Foundation generously supported my visits to their archives. I thank their staffs for their considered guidance. My special appreciation goes to the staff of the Hoover Institution Archives, whose knowledge of the Institution's collections seems boundless and who offered great conversation throughout my stay at Stanford. I am also grateful to the staffs of the Nixon Presidential Materials, the Library of Congress Manuscript Reading Room, the Manuscripts and Archives Division at Yale University Library, the Arizona Historical Foundation, and the Strom Thurmond Center at Clemson University, for their valued assistance.

Clark Dougan, Chris Appy, Carol Betsch, Mary Bellino, and Lawrence Kenney at the University of Massachusetts Press deserve my unreserved gratitude for their dedication to the production of this book and for their encouragement and guidance. I also thank the reviewers for their important contributions to the development of the manuscript.

To my parents, Fergus and Marguerite, I humbly offer my deepest appreciation for their constant encouragement and enduring trust. Their faith in the power and beauty of a university education reminds me of the privileges that I continue to enjoy every day. It is perhaps only now that I fully understand the sacrifices they made in supporting me. They enjoyed punting on the Cam, evenings in the Eagle, and lunch in Central Park, but such ventures were small recompense. I also thank my brothers, Conor and Barry, for reminding me of life beyond this research. My grandmother Patricia Twohig inspired my childhood interest in the past by telling stories of her service in the Women's Auxiliary Air Force during the Second World War. She laid the basis for my enduring love of history, and this book is offered in her memory.

I dedicate this book to my husband, Dónal Mac Nioclóis, who has been on this journey with me from the very start. He patiently spent many hours waiting for me to emerge from libraries and discovered more than he ever wanted to know about politics and war. His dedication made my work possible. Our son, Liam, was born just as this project was completed. In its final months, he has been my inspiration.

Abbreviations

ACU	American Conservative Union
AFL-CIO	American Federation of Labor and Congress of Industrial Organizations
AFV	American Friends of Vietnam
ARVN	Army of the Republic of Vietnam (South Vietnamese Army)
ASC	American Security Council
ASG	Association of Student Governments
AWP	Americans for Winning the Peace
CACC	Christian Anti-Communist Crusade
CCPFV	Citizens Committee for Peace with Freedom in Vietnam
CRNC	College Republican National Committee
DRV	Democratic Republic of Vietnam (North Vietnam)
JBS	John Birch Society
MIA	missing in action
NSA	National Student Association
NSCVV	National Student Coordinating Committee for Victory in Vietnam
PAVN	People's Army of Vietnam (North Vietnamese Army)
POWs	prisoners of war
PRC	People's Republic of China
UAW	United Automobile Workers
VIVA	Victory in Vietnam Association (1966–69), Voices in Vital America (1969–)
VFW	Veterans of Foreign Wars
YAF	Young Americans for Freedom

THE PRO-WAR MOVEMENT

INTRODUCTION

Conservatives and the Vietnam War

In 1980 the Veterans of Foreign Wars (VFW) broke with an eighty-year-old precedent and endorsed a presidential candidate. Four weeks after winning the Republican presidential nomination, Ronald Reagan delivered an address to the VFW's annual convention in Chicago. Reagan's address was typically impassioned and politically astute. Seven years had passed since U.S. troops had left the field of battle in Vietnam, and Reagan condemned the social and political divisions the war had helped create in America. Decrying partisan divisions over foreign policy, he called for unity in order to make America great and to keep it at peace. He declared the need "to unite people of every background and faith in a great crusade to restore the America of our dreams." Reagan implicitly declared the need to put aside the political and cultural divisions wrought by America's experiences during the Vietnam War. He therefore adopted the culturally powerful emphasis on national healing that was particularly evident in Vietnam veterans' calls for unity in honoring their service. Reagan had decided to belatedly use the term *noble cause* in a speech that was intended to focus primarily on the importance of resurrecting popular faith in the U.S. armed services. But his tone made clear and indeed reflected the pro-war position he had adopted throughout the Vietnam War. He declared that it was time to candidly acknowledge the simple reality of the Vietnam experience: "It's time we recognized that ours was, in truth, a noble cause." The United States had come to the rescue of a "small country newly free from colonial rule [which] sought our help in establishing self-rule and the means of self-defense against a totalitarian neighbor bent on conquest."[1] U.S. policy may have been misguided at times, according to Reagan, but it had always been based on America's commitment to its allies and to freedom and democracy. In essence, the cause was entirely in keeping with America's core values.

Reagan's skill and his appeal to the VFW audience lay not in his ability to recite, however eloquently, conservatives' long-stated belief that the Vietnam War was an essential part of America's Cold War struggle against the spread of totalitarian communism. His skill lay in his ability to relate the idea of supporting those Americans who served in Vietnam to endorsement of his interpretation of the war's meaning. As was the case during the Vietnam era, Reagan conflated the disparate issues of the war's aims, the means of fighting the war, and patriotic support of those who served into a single whole.

By 1980 there was a strong consensus within the conservative movement that the alleged lessons of Vietnam related to how the war was fought, not to the principles on which U.S. intervention had been based. This reflected the wartime activism of intellectual conservatives and conservative politicians in both parties in favor of expanded military measures. The failure of the United States to win the war, they argued, resulted from the government's refusal to allow the military to win. Society, furthermore, had failed to understand the important sacrifices made in the effort to support South Vietnamese freedom, largely because of the failure of the administration of President Lyndon Johnson to articulate these interests and because of biased reporting on the part of the news media. In his attempt to appeal directly to his VFW audience, Reagan incorporated the Vietnam experience into a longer tradition of American heroism and implicitly tied support for the troops to support for the war's noble goals: "We dishonor the memory of 50,000 young Americans who died in that cause when we give way to feelings of guilt as if we were doing something shameful, and we have been shabby in our treatment of those who returned." There seemed to be hope, however. Following the dedication ceremony for the Vietnam Veterans Memorial at the National Cathedral in 1982, Reagan commented that people were finally beginning to realize that the war was a "just cause."[2] He later used the dedication ceremony for the Tomb of the Unknown Soldier of Vietnam at Arlington National Cemetery, on May 28, 1984, to reiterate the themes that the war was noble and that Americans had insufficiently praised veterans of the war. Rather than acknowledge the flaws in the decisions of policymakers of the 1950s and 1960s, Reagan argued that the war had been necessary. Its loss, he claimed, resulted from a purely American failure to sufficiently support the troops and allow the military the autonomy to pursue a more forceful military campaign and initiate extensive bombing of the Democratic Republic of Vietnam (North Vietnam).

Reagan's depiction of the war was certainly well received among its intended audience, but its wider reception was more ambivalent. Reagan's own advisers recognized that it was "politically problematic and divisive." Among the mainstream media, responses were divided. Some charged that Reagan had reopened the wounds of Vietnam by reigniting domestic debates about the purpose of the war, while others applauded his "courage and frankness."[3] Reagan's statement at the VFW convention was enlightening and novel only to the extent that he had been willing to publicly broach the Vietnam issue. It reflected neither a departure from his largely consistent position on the war, nor an attempt to rationally consider the foreign policies that had underpinned U.S. engagement or the factors that had contributed to the failure of the American endeavor. In raising the issue at the VFW convention, Reagan intended not to provoke debate or to re-ignite the fires of division that had helped fan his own celebrity during the 1960s. His was an endeavor based on the principle of undermining debate, of achieving the aim to "Bring Us Together" set forth by Richard Nixon during the acrimonious presidential election of 1968. As in 1968, Reagan's vision of unity did not involve acceptance of the arguments put forth by the anti-war movement. Yet the complexities of popular memories of the Vietnam War and the varied responses to defeat precluded the possibility that he would be able to simply declare the war a moral victory. Indeed, conservatives' postwar claims that victory could have been achieved if alternative military measures had been introduced served only to polarize opinion. Among many Americans who recalled the years of warfare, this argument also appeared somewhat naïve. In large measure, however, Reagan's speech represented the climax of a long process by which supporters of the war had attempted to reframe the popular debate regarding Vietnam into a simple question of patriotism, specifically, patriotic support for those Americans who served in Vietnam and those prisoners and missing men figuratively held by the Vietnamese enemy.

This patriotic campaign helped generate a revisionist culture, one that was prevalent in films, television series, memoirs, and certain scholarly approaches to the war and that reached its zenith in the mid-1980s. More accurately, Reagan's attempt to invigorate patriotic passions by promoting positive interpretations of Vietnam reflected the then-dominant theme of the older pro-war sectors. By emphasizing the nobility of veterans' service, Reagan employed means reminiscent of those used by both the Nixon administration and conservative leaders in their wartime efforts to stimulate a populist surge in favor of the war. As had been the case during the war, Reagan's motivation extended beyond rallying patriotic fervor. He intended to secure justification of the war effort and of those who had most vociferously endorsed it, coupled, yet again, with the aims of strengthening conservatives' conception of foreign policy priorities and limiting détente. The populist drive was simply a means of achieving more important political and social goals.

Reagan may have enjoyed increasingly popular support during the 1960s and early 1970s, but leading conservative politicians had not, in fact, been particularly successful in rallying broad popular support for the Vietnam War at that time. As the enigmatic governor of California, Reagan certainly utilized public frustrations with student, anti-war, and civil rights protests to rally support. But he was ideologically committed to the Vietnam War as a symbol of America's challenge to communism. In this respect he was more committed to selling the national security imperatives on which intervention had been based than on simply pushing a patriotic agenda. This view reflected that of intellectual conservatives and the leading conservative figures in the Republican Party. The American effort in Vietnam afforded important opportunities to conservatives to demonstrate their fervent anticommunism. Conservatives did organize large-scale rallies to demonstrate support for the war, and these events represent a significant part of this story. Such rallies gave coherence to diverse conservative interest groups, contributed to the organization of the conservative movement, and recruited new devotees to the cause. Conservative youth groups such as Young Americans for Freedom (YAF) established pro-war drives on campuses across the country, which helped exacerbate the differences between those who identified with the pro- and anti-war positions. The goal of victory in Vietnam was not secured, but U.S. failure and the war's apparent futility provided impetus to the more important conservative objective of highlighting the government's failure to deal successfully with the communist menace and thereby helped highlight the dangers of détente.

The more successful efforts to rally support for the war and demonstrate opposition to the anti-war movement were not orchestrated by conservative political activists, however. Indeed, by 1970 the conservative leaders' demand for outright victory in Vietnam held little political or popular legitimacy. Social conservatives had already let go of their already limited commitment to the war and focused their attention on dealing with domestic social ills. Grassroots activists who organized pro-war drives did not identify specifically with the conservative movement. They concentrated on promoting opposition to the anti-war movement, and it was their message of national unity and support for the troops and American values that succeeded in garnering widespread popular backing. Many of these activists explicitly denounced partisan and ideological affiliations. They promoted support of the president, even as both the Johnson and Nixon administrations continued to endorse the policies of limited war that conservatives continually challenged as ineffective. Nonetheless, their efforts helped legitimize conservatives' postwar interpretation of Vietnam as a noble cause.

During the period of the Vietnam War conservative leaders were largely preoccupied with trying to impact government policy and focused less attention on attempting to sway public opinion. In this respect, there was a clear distinction between conservative intellectuals and movement leaders on the one hand and conservative politicians on the other. Yet the two groups were not mutually exclusive entities. Sen. Barry Goldwater of Arizona acted as a figurehead for the amorphous conservative coalition, and grassroots activists identified with the onetime presidential hopeful. Goldwater's rhetoric and policy positions were also informed by the ideas that emanated from the intellectual conservative community. Yet Goldwater and his fellow conservatives in Congress were far more concerned with prompting public support for the Vietnam War than their counterparts in organizations such as the American Conservative Union (ACU). The ACU was founded in late 1964 by activists who had spearheaded the effort to draft Goldwater for the Republican presidential nomination. The most prominent conservative journal, *National Review,* demonstrated little interest in mounting a popular drive to enhance public support for the war. Its focus was squarely on pushing the Johnson and Nixon administrations to abandon the supposedly failed policies of limited warfare. The ACU and *National Review* focused almost exclusively on the security imperatives mandating U.S. intervention and military victory in Vietnam during the early years of the war and remained committed to highlighting security factors as the rationale for continuing and, indeed, winning the war.

Such conservatives reluctantly acknowledged the significance of public opinion as political and popular factors undermined the government's commitment to Vietnam. The growth of the anti-war movement was a clear target for conservative condemnation; its radical elements allowed conservative leaders to claim that opposition to the war was unpatriotic and helped create an alliance, however fragile, between conservatives and elements of the public still committed to the war. As wider segments of the public openly turned against the war after 1967, this alliance became stronger. Conservatives did not initially welcome the temptation to emphasize patriotic themes at the expense of national security considerations. But the temptation became irresistible and politically vital, particularly given the popularity of the patriotic drives sponsored by organizations like the American Legion and the Veterans of Foreign Wars (VFW) and the popular salience of campaigns associated with concern for prisoners of war, which reached their zenith in 1970–72. Within the conservative community, it was politicians who were the first to embrace these patriotic themes. They argued that anti-war protestors gave comfort to the enemy, which prolonged the war, and urged war-weary Americans to remain faithful to the president and his efforts to successfully end the war.

There were wide divisions within the conservative movement regarding Vietnam, however. Social conservatives had always been less committed to the war; their focus on domestic issues took precedence over the struggle in Southeast Asia, and when they looked abroad their attention was focused on the more significant threats posed by the Soviet Union and China. In light of the failure of the United States to utilize escalated military measures, they were the more likely conservatives to argue for immediate withdrawal. Intellectual conservatives were loath to endorse patriotic themes at the expense of national security factors and were unimpressed with the Republican administration's employment of such techniques to boost support for the war effort. Nonetheless, social conservatives welcomed the opportunity to use the war issue to denigrate liberals as unpatriotic, and intellectual conservatives ultimately recognized the power of harnessing populist perspectives on anti-war protestors and support for prisoners of war. The conservative movement as a whole thereby succeeded in allying itself with a populist, patriotic interpretation of the war that became widely accepted in the aftermath of American defeat. During the late 1970s conservative politicians found little popular traction for their arguments that the United States could easily have won in Vietnam. As Reagan's successful employment of the noble cause argument made clear, however, it was possible to rally broad swathes of the American population behind the idea that at the very least America's intentions had been honorable. Despite the great differences in the ways in which various conservatives spoke of the meaning of Vietnam during the conflict, their postwar consensus that it was a noble endeavor enabled conservative politicians to relate to the wider public. Their success was in no small part built on a legacy established by a wide variety of groups that had petitioned in support of the Vietnam War during the war years.

Patriotic campaigns in support of the Vietnam War emerged as soon as it entered the public consciousness. Many such initiatives were organized by conservative groups and echoed standard anti-communist rallies that had been commonplace since the late 1940s. Others focused on supporting President Johnson's policies of limited war in Southeast Asia. In terms of numbers, however, the most significant rallies promoted the theme of supporting the troops in Vietnam. The most dramatic demonstration of large-scale support for Americans serving in Vietnam occurred on May 13, 1967, when a parade lasting more than nine hours marched on Fifth Avenue in New York City. Organized under the banner "We Support Our Boys in Vietnam," the parade was also labeled an Americanism pageant, a pro-war rally, and a demonstration of faith in government. The diversity of aims and the catchall nature of supporting the troops were intended by organizers to avoid commentary on the war itself. Marchers and spectators were urged, rather, to unite in admiring and endorsing the dutiful commitment of those serving the United States in Vietnam. It was hoped that by such means Americans could put the divisions of the war to one side and unite as citizens. That the organizers were committed to such aims is clear. That they also supported the cause for which the United States was involved in Vietnam and were committed to bringing the conflict to a successful conclusion, if perhaps mainly to honor the sacrifice of those fighting and dying in Vietnam, is also beyond doubt. Writing to Gen. William Westmoreland, the Support Our Boys in Vietnam Parade Committee stated the group's purpose succinctly: "The real heart of America is behind you all the way, and it's time it showed its true colors to the world."[4]

Parades of this nature were repeated in New York City in 1969 and on a smaller scale across the United States throughout much of the war. They culminated in a Welcome Home Parade in New York City in 1973, which was designed as a symbolic sign of gratitude to all those whose service had supposedly been insufficiently appreciated by the American public and news media. These events failed to promote conservatives' core goals regarding Vietnam and were often initiated by individuals and groups wishing to simply counter anti-war arguments. As such, this story is one of diverse agencies. Not all of those who campaigned in favor of supporting the troops or the president's foreign policies were ideologically committed to the war. The pro–Vietnam War movement reflected varied perspectives on the war as well as competing political affiliations. A unifying issue was one of culture and American identity. Supporters of the war or the troops deemed anti-war dissent potentially treasonous and harmful to American society. Activism in favor of the war, conversely, fostered traditional practices and values that were understood to promote national pride and unity, as evidenced by the prominence of community pageants, candlelight vigils, and military-style parades. Such concerns went beyond fears of international communism and reflected divergent opinions on the best means of understanding and expressing American identity. Indeed, the populist focus on supporting the troops and prisoners of wars highlighted the extent to which traditional appeals to Cold War paradigms had limited salience by the early 1970s. Conservatives remained more intent on emphasizing the international implications of a hasty withdrawal from Vietnam but succeeded in fostering a powerful political association between their continued support of the war and American patriotism. In the postwar political environment, conservatives demonstrated that they had ably learned the public opinion lessons of Vietnam.

A key aim of this book is to explore the journey that led conservative activists to gain public support for their postwar interpretations of Vietnam. The conservative movement did not succeed in securing its core goals in Vietnam, that is, to achieve military victory by encouraging the administration to abandon its policies of limited war. But this is not to suggest that conservatives did not help shape the course of the war; during the Johnson years they limited the president's ability to act unilaterally in formulating policy in Vietnam and fanned the emergence of a credibility gap by questioning the veracity of the White House's claims that progress was being made. President Johnson's inability to achieve public unity on Vietnam devastated his presidency and helped bring an end to the era of Democratic dominance. This failure was certainly not caused simply by conservative antagonism toward the administration's handling of the war, but hawks' constant attacks on the president deepened domestic division and popular confusion. Conversely, during the administration of President Nixon, leading conservatives supported the Nixon Doctrine and his policies of withdrawal and negotiation that brought an end to direct American engagement. Like Johnson, Nixon was concerned by the potential of a widespread conservative backlash against his policies and took steps to avoid such an outcome. He sought to win conservatives' support while also working to undermine their political power by redefining the meaning of victory in Vietnam. As such, conservatives helped shape the ways in which these two administrations sold their policies to the public.

The conservative movement was also changed by the war. New alliances were formed and new voices gained prominence within the broad conservative movement. Divisions among conservatives over the importance of the war and the value of maintaining public support for administration policies, however, highlighted the weaknesses of the conservative political alliance. The popular salience of campaigns undertaken by veterans and by student and grassroots organizations to frame the war as a question of patriotism, rather than an urgent matter of national security, challenged the power of conservatives' arguments. They helped, however, to forge tenuous alliances between such groups, many of which associated with the Democratic Party, and the evolving conservative movement. This story therefore traces four distinct areas: conservative efforts to alter administration policy in favor of military victory; grassroots initiatives to support the war and counter anti-war activism and popular defeatism; administration initiatives to maintain conservative and public support for Vietnam strategies; and divisions among conservatives. Ultimately, each of these issues impacted the identity of the conservative movement, allowing social issues to become part of conservatives' conception and presentation of foreign policy debates.

The role of domestic issues in determining the course of U.S.

policy in Vietnam cannot be underestimated. Historians have long noted the significance of domestic politics in influencing the ways in which presidents present their foreign policies to the public. The actual impact of domestic politics on foreign policy is more contentious and has invited extended debate among scholars of international relations. Recent studies of the Cold War demonstrate that a realist perspective that denies the relevance of popular opinion in international affairs is limited. It misjudges the cultural, personal, and ideological influences on policymakers and distorts the relevance of the electoral process on the timing of foreign policy decisions.[5] The partisan character of foreign policy is explored in Colin Dueck's analysis of the Republican Party and in Andrew Johns's examination of the Republican Party and the Vietnam War. Dueck in particular notes how foreign policy preferences and a distinctly hard-line perspective on international affairs influenced the development of the party from the late 1950s.[6] Johns contends that domestic debates over the Vietnam War shaped the ideological character of the Republican Party and helped enhance conservative domination of the party.[7]

Julian Zelizer and Robert David Johnson demonstrate the importance of discarding a purely presidential synthesis in understanding the development of U.S. foreign policy and the creation of the Cold War national security state. While Congress, particularly the House of Representatives, invariably prioritized domestic issues, its role in the making of foreign policy cannot be summarily dismissed. President Harry Truman relied on the support of key advocates across party lines, most notably the Republican senator Arthur Vandenberg of Michigan, to gain backing for his bold foreign policy initiatives. Truman was obliged, moreover, to present his plans for expanding the role of the United States in world affairs in almost cataclysmic terms in order to win over members of Congress who were reluctant to appropriate funds for his policies and wary of enhancing presidential authority in foreign affairs. As Johnson notes, congressional activism was conditioned by individual foreign policy philosophies and personal activism. It was not, therefore, constant throughout the Cold War, and its zenith was in large part conditioned by the American experiences of the

Vietnam War. Still, both Johnson and Zelizer demonstrate that the president's ability to rely on congressional support when it came to international affairs was by no means guaranteed.[8]

As this book will demonstrate, partisan politics influenced congressional responses to both Johnson's and Nixon's handling of the Vietnam War. Despite a deserved image as the loyal opposition, Republicans took major steps during the Johnson administration to make political gains from the Vietnam War. Democrats, both liberal and conservative, were far more willing to openly oppose the continuation of the war once it became Nixon's war. Partisanship was also greatly enhanced as a consequence of the war. Intraparty divisions characterized both parties during the war. They helped fracture the New Deal coalition established during the Franklin D. Roosevelt years and resulted in the Democratic Party's abandonment of core tenets of the Cold War consensus. The Republican Party, meanwhile, experienced extensive divisions over the Vietnam War. Anti-war Republicans played a vital role in challenging the domestic consensus on Vietnam but ultimately found themselves in the minority within the party. Conservatives became convinced that shared economic values were insufficient to sustain the Republican coalition. Their strong ideological commitment to the Vietnam War and opposition to détente fostered greater determination to take control of the Republican Party, an endeavor in which they were successful.

The conservative movement was (and still is) made up of diverse interests and distinct factions. Explanations for the rise of conservatism have been similarly distinct, presenting analyses that focus on the creation of a political movement during the Draft Goldwater drives in 1960 and 1964, the backlash against civil rights and racial integration, the emergence of a discernible suburban culture that encouraged local activism and embraced small government, and the stimulation of business interests in opposition to organized labor and the economic policies of New Deal liberalism.[9] Historians of modern conservatism do not disregard this competition among conservative interest groups, but, as Zelizer comments, they have perhaps exaggerated the coherence of conservatism as a political force.[10] Conservative activists did not succeed in eliminating their differing goals, social and cultural priorities, or policy preferences any more than liberals did. At times even the movement's self-proclaimed leaders sought to exaggerate their policy differences with fellow conservatives in order to enhance their own image as the responsible face of modern conservatism. This was most evident in William F. Buckley's long-standing effort to purge the John Birch Society (JBS) from the movement, which was realized only when the far-right group questioned the utility of U.S. engagement in Vietnam in 1965. Throughout much of the 1960s, however, conservative political activists sought unity and a form of right-wing political consensus that would result in the creation of a new political majority.[11] It may have been impossible to reach consensus on the philosophical and policy priorities that the conservative movement as a whole should pursue. It was certainly impossible to eradicate liberalism as a viable, entrenched part of the American political and cultural landscape. But it was possible to forge a political alliance that allowed conservatives to dominate the Republican Party.

As I show in this book, foreign policy debates played a central role in helping to create this important consensus and thereby unite conservative political activists. Anticommunism was not the only factor that stimulated the reemergence of conservatism as a powerful political force. It was, nonetheless, an enormously powerful component in energizing grassroots activists and in unifying conservatives in active support of single-issue campaigns.[12] The Vietnam War acted as just such a unifying force for conservatives during much of the war. It allied intellectual conservatives committed to a more hard-line foreign policy with social conservatives angered by the moral degeneracy they associated with the anti-war movement and the broader questioning of America's moral standing in the world. The pro-war stance rallied conservatives under a single banner. The longevity of the war took a toll on the conservative movement and challenged basic conceptions of the utility of direct engagement by the United States abroad. Divisions among conservatives over the Vietnam War were certainly not inconsequential. By the final years of the war, such differences fostered hostility between allies such as Goldwater and John Ashbrook. But the war's longevity also helped maintain a veneer of unity that became part of conservatives' broader identity. While they might disagree over the necessity of maintaining the struggle in Southeast Asia in the face of wider security threats revived by détente, conservatives of all traits could agree on their shared opposition to the arguments of the anti-war movement. It was, in fact, the anti-war movement's moral challenge to American anticommunism that served to preserve conservative unity on the controversial topic of the Vietnam War. In the postwar environment, it was the continued frustration with the anti-war movement that propelled conservatives to unify behind an alternative understanding of the war's legacy for Americans.

The conservative leadership represented the dominant force in the tenuous pro-war alliance by the late 1960s and early 1970s. They had not been the drivers of U.S. military intervention in Vietnam, yet they remained committed to the anticommunist struggle in Southeast Asia for some time after their liberal counterparts abandoned the effort. More ideologically committed to a demonstrative and symbolic victory over expansionist communism than perhaps any other group, conservative leaders promoted victory in the war long after the government relinquished this objective. They hoped the war might delegitimize the dominance of liberal interventionism in foreign policymaking in favor of a more fervent and unqualified anticommunism. This effort was characteristic of the modern conservative movement as a whole, but it was dominated by the so-called *National Review* circle. These Goldwaterite conservatives represented the segment of the postwar conservative alliance that was both the most prominent and the most able, at least during the 1960s, to claim the mantle of conservative leadership. Ideological and practical disagreements continued to challenge conservatives' organizational efforts, but *National Review*'s attempts to formulate a common foreign policy for conservatives met with considerable success during the late sixties. This was in large part owing to the editors' attempts to combine ideological prescription, grassroots sentiment, and political objectives in responding to specific foreign policies. The *National Review* circle displayed a nuanced understanding of the domestic political and international factors influencing administration policy. They incorporated and reflected the ideas of conservative Republicans such as John Tower, Reagan, and Strom Thurmond and were thus more obviously influential during the war than grassroots activists. It was this group of conservatives that worked most fervently and astutely to secure influence in the Republican Party.

While acknowledging the prominent role of international considerations in determining the policies of conservative leaders and organizations, historians of the conservative movement have thus far paid little attention to the movement's complex relationships with the administration of President Nixon and grassroots supporters of the Vietnam War. Opposition to the Johnson administration's Vietnam policies rallied conservatives and enhanced activists' association with the Republican Party. The era of the Nixon administration proved a more contentious period, however, and the war's long, slow ending proved more problematic for the conservative movement than its beginning. By failing to understand the relationship between the conservative movement and the Vietnam War, one fails to understand the political trajectory of this movement. By failing to understand popular reactions to the war, one misinterprets the reasons for popular reactions to the war in succeeding decades. Reagan's messages of hope and pride regarding the Vietnam War were not simply cathartic; they reflected ideas popularly held throughout much of the conflict.

Chapters 1 and 2 explore conservatives' early commitments to U.S. military intervention in Southeast Asia and their drive for a military victory there between 1964 and 1965. Nixon's drive for the Republican nomination and the presidency, discussed in chapter 3, was vociferously supported by many conservatives who believed his personal reputation in regard to the Cold War would forestall defeat in Vietnam. Conservative support for Nixon's policies regarding Vietnam during 1969 and 1970 helped legitimize Nixon's overall foreign policy, particularly as it related to the much-vaunted Nixon Doctrine. Divisions within the conservative movement, discussed in chapter 4, undermined leaders' abilities to respond with more than tepid threats of reduced political support when Nixon's phased withdrawal increasingly came to resemble a unilateral retreat. Popular backing of Nixon's Vietnamization policy, as analyzed in chapter 5, further reduced conservatives' willingness to challenge the president on Vietnam. Chapter 5 examines grassroots campaigns in support of the war and the initiatives undertaken by armed forces and patriotic groups to garner public backing for the causes of freedom and victory in Vietnam. The Nixon White House attempted to manage public opinion and to control these independent campaigns but ultimately failed in these endeavors. An early version of the noble cause thesis of the Vietnam War influenced both administration and conservative rhetoric and was characteristic of the policy stance assumed and promoted by Republicans like Goldwater and Reagan.

As the most demonstrably activist component of the conservative alliance, YAF proved a vital force in harnessing youthful activism for the conservative cause. Their attempts to foster student support for the Vietnam War often met with considerable disappointment, but nonetheless underlined the complexity of students' attitudes toward the war. YAF was by no means the sole standard-bearer of student support for the war, however. The Victory in Vietnam Association and the College Republican National Committee offered distinct rationales for supporting the war. Chapter 6 considers the extent to which these diverse groups succeeded in uniting to promote a common cause. In many respects, student support for the war, often expressed as opposition to the New Left, elucidates wider societal responses to the anti-war movement. Reduced student support for a victory policy, which coincided with popular war weariness, further illustrates the challenges facing pro-war leaders and contributed much to their ultimate calls for withdrawal from Vietnam.

Conservative leaders were not always preoccupied with military solutions for successfully concluding the Vietnam War, but they consistently preferred such means and, during the final year of the war, offered support to Nixon only when negotiation was coupled with overwhelming displays of military strength. This book is an examination of the journey conservatives made from denouncement of Johnson's limited war policies to acceptance of the final settlement of the Vietnam War in 1973, and the role this journey played in defining the modern conservative movement.

CHAPTER 1

No Substitute for Victory

The Beginnings of a War

> Make no bones of this. Don't try to sweep it under the rug. We are at war in Vietnam.
>
> —Barry Goldwater, speech on accepting the Republican presidential nomination, July 1964

> The key to a successful defense of Southeast Asia is to make it clear to the Asian Communists that we will not allow them to limit "wars of liberation" to our side of the line. We must be willing, and give concrete evidence of our willingness, to extend our "war of liberation" into the enemy camp.
>
> American Security Council, *Guidelines for Cold War Victory*, September 1964

As Sen. Barry Goldwater triumphantly accepted the Republican Party's nomination for president in 1964, a great many of the Republicans who crowded into San Francisco's Cow Palace stood jaded. Many were exhausted by the last-minute campaign to stem the unexpected tide of Goldwaterite strength. Others were tired simply from their efforts in the four-year campaign to see Goldwater nominated and from the prospect of a difficult election battle. The potential, or even actual, American war in Vietnam did not prove to be a prominent feature of the debate that consumed the Republican Party during this period. This was hardly surprising, given the great many other issues on which Republicans publicly expressed their differences. Gov. Mark Hatfield of Oregon delivered a keynote address that was widely cheered but also booed by spectators. In challenging extremism, he denounced the "venom of hate" he claimed characterized such conservative organizations as the John Birch Society (JBS). In denouncing Democrats' records on Laos, Cuba, Berlin, and Vietnam, he echoed conservatives' claims that the administration of President Lyndon Johnson feared "telling us what our foreign policy is" and lamented that "American boys are dying in a war without a name."[1]

Despite later efforts by Hatfield to vociferously oppose the Vietnam War, the Republican Party as a whole did little to prevent the Democrats' greater commitment of material, men, and national will to Vietnam during 1964 and 1965.[2] Sen. Everett Dirksen, who was minority leader, consistently backed the president's policies throughout this period, which was characteristic of the stance adopted by most within his party.[3] Those most responsible for nominating Goldwater did much, indeed, to create the environment in which it was difficult to repudiate or accept as unnecessary the commitments made and sustained by successive administrations since Harry Truman first provided financial support for the effort by France to regain its colonies in Indochina. As President John F. Kennedy found his administration's Vietnam policies floundering during 1963, Republicans pushed for a more concerted effort to meet the communist challenge in Southeast Asia. Articulating a theme that would become commonplace during the Johnson administration, Rep. Robert Wilson, a Republican from California, denounced Kennedy's polices for having "done nothing but back down, give in, retreat, and lose ground before Communism." He also hinted that the Kennedy administration's failure of will was contributing to the deaths of "hundreds and perhaps thousands" of Americans.[4] While Republicans may have been ideologically divided over the Vietnam War during 1964, therefore, the dominant image was one of support for a more concerted military campaign. Such a campaign, they argued, would secure victory against the communist insurgency plaguing the government of the Republic of Vietnam (South Vietnam) and indicate that the government was using all means to support those Americans serving in the region.

Conservative political activists were conflicted over Vietnam during 1964 and indeed for much of the war. On the one hand, their perspective on the international ambitions of the Soviet Union and its use of wars of national liberation convinced them of the importance of directly meeting the communist insurgency in South Vietnam. Their inaccurate belief that this campaign was being solely directed by the communist government of North Vietnam led them to push for military attacks against Hanoi. Yet this was not the war of conservatives' choosing, and their concern that it distracted public attention from more serious threats such as Cuba impacted the extent of their early commitment to the emerging conflict. In no small part, conservatives' limited emotional commitment to Vietnam was determined by the perception that this was Johnson's war.[5] In spite of these conflicted perspectives on the war, the opportunity to directly challenge communist expansion trumped a deep hostility to Johnson's understanding of international relations and the Cold War.

Indeed, Johnson's pursuit of limited war in Southeast Asia opened political opportunities for both Republicans and the wider conservative movement. Desperate to escape the connotations of extremism and radicalism associated with right-wing politics, conservatives associated with *National Review* and the American Conservative Union (ACU) saw in Vietnam a chance to push for a stronger anticommunist foreign policy without attracting unwarranted claims that they were warmongers. William Rusher, the publisher of *National Review* and one of the driving forces behind the original campaign to draft Goldwater for the Republican presidential nomination, would later argue that such conservatives should "all start using the term 'responsible conservatives'" to describe themselves. "I have been promoting the phrase 'responsible conservatives' for some years, and find it has enormous advantages," he wrote. "It raises by implication the image of others who must of necessity be the 'irresponsible conservatives'" and "liberals often find it irresistible, even though they hate themselves in the morning. Finally, I think it accurately describes the situation."[6]

This considered attempt to dispel the politically debilitating association with an extremist foreign policy agenda was furthered by U.S. engagement in Vietnam. The initial rally-'round-the-flag campaigns in support of President Johnson's interventions in Vietnam were celebrated by conservatives as signs of the public's recognition of the fundamental significance of championing a strong foreign policy. The "responsible conservatives" quickly became the most powerful advocates of an unambiguous military victory and used popular anxieties regarding the war's limited progress to challenge Democrats' handling of the struggle against communism. Before engagement in Vietnam, conservatives had appeared extreme in their calls for a more determined and militarized U.S. foreign policy. During the war, however, their calls for military success seemed considerably more reasonable and politically powerful. As Ronald Reagan simply stated at a rally in San Diego during his gubernatorial run in 1966, a "suspicion prevails" that American troops "are being denied the right to try for victory in that war."[7] During the Johnson administration, conservatives at *National Review* continued to push their demand for a more determined anticommunist foreign policy. They fully recognized that they could use their campaign of opposition to the government's handling of the war not only to enhance this goal but also to secure greater political control of the Republican Party.

Anticommunism on the Right

Vietnam was not a particularly prominent topic of discussion in conservative journals until the coup against Ngo Dinh Diem in November 1963. Conservatives were not therefore at the forefront of the push into Southeast Asia. During 1962 and 1963, advocates of a more uncompromising anticommunist foreign policy looked principally to Cuba as the test case for engaging in so-called small wars of liberation. Fidel Castro's apparent embrace of the Soviet Union emboldened conservatives' claims that the communist regime on the island posed a direct threat to American national security. Conservative activists at *National Review*, *Human Events*, and the American Security Council (ASC) argued that Cuba afforded the most promising means for the United States to actively push back the frontiers of communism. Not only was the island within America's direct sphere of influence, but public opinion might easily be brought to bear to support military intervention. The Kennedy administration's resolution of the missile crisis only heightened conservatives' animosity to the president's Cuba policies. The crisis furthermore convinced them that the Soviet leadership had played a game of chance in placing the missiles on Cuba but would not intervene directly to stop an American sponsored attempt to overthrow the Castro regime. *Human Events* published a series of scathing assessments of the situation in Cuba and maintained that neither the missile crisis nor the moral issue of U.S. failure to aid subjugated peoples had been resolved.[8] This is not to suggest that conservatives did not pressure the Kennedy and Johnson administrations to extend further aid and commitment to Vietnam; they did so both directly and indirectly as part of a concerted and continuous campaign of pressure for a hard-line policy toward the Communist world.

Strident anticommunism served conservative leaders' broader social and political goals, including the effort to "bolster capitalism, militarism, and moral traditionalism."[9] Early historians of modern conservatives exaggerated the significance of anticommunism as the defining issue of the post-1945 right. They failed to fully recognize the power of grassroots conservatives' social and economic perspectives on civil rights and the government's pursuit of broader social equality.[10] But the importance of shared interpretations of the threat posed by international communism served an important function in prompting conservative activists to seek greater political power and unified activism. Sen. Robert Taft's star as the guardian of American conservatism waned as conservative intellectuals felt obliged to abandon any adherence to isolationism. As David Farber notes, Taft played a pivotal role in harnessing postwar conservatives' opposition to the New Deal and the radicalism of organized labor. He was not, however, particularly well suited to the nation's preoccupation with the twin threats of Soviet power and domestic communist subversion. Faced with the dominance of domestic anticommunism during the period of McCarthyism, "Taft battled to stay relevant and to reshape his conservative beliefs to fit the nation's needs."[11] Intellectual conservatives, on the other hand, were becoming increasingly worried about communism. The conservative alliance opposed isolationism as the basis of U.S. foreign policy not simply because of the circumstances of the Cold War. Although opposed to entangling alliances such as U.S. involvement in the United Nations, they promoted the necessity of the United States assuming a leadership role in international affairs, necessitated by its position of overwhelming power. Despite being united on the import of the American role in the world, throughout the postwar period conservative activists were forced to labor under the divisions caused by ideological debate between traditionalists and libertarians.

People like Buckley, James Burnham, Frank Meyer, the publisher of *National Review,* and Rusher sought to promote conservative ideas among intellectuals and elite political actors. Yet they also wanted to establish a politically viable conservative political consensus, which would appeal to wider sections of the electorate. Conservatives at *National Review* realized that ideological tensions proved fruitful in furthering debate, but they also understood the debilitating political effects stemming from the divisions between the pure libertarian ideals of people like Frank Chodorov and the more traditionalist conservatism sponsored by Russell Kirk. Kirk's rejection of utopian ideology and libertarianism was more influential and evident in the formula that *National Review* promoted for establishing unity among conservatives.

Meyer wrote a column titled "Principles and Heresies," which regularly explored the philosophical basis of conservatism in the Cold War era. In the early 1960s he focused on the unifying significance of anticommunism and articulated a new solution to the differences between libertarians and traditionalists known as fusionism. Fusionism did not in fact resolve conservatives' internal differences, but it did become a defining characteristic of the movement's identity during the 1960s. Meyer had been a socialist during his youth and later an active communist. He left Princeton University to study at Oxford University, where he earned a BA in 1932, and then pursued a PhD at the London School of Economics (LSE). His communist activism led to his expulsion from the LSE, where he had violated the School's ban on communist organizations by selling the left-leaning magazine he founded, the *Student Vanguard*. Meyer was subsequently deported from the United Kingdom in June 1934 on the back of his communist activism. Following service in the army during the Second World War, he completely abandoned his communist sympathies. His rejection of communism led him to embrace conservatism wholeheartedly, which distinguished him from other former communists who embraced New Deal liberalism and established a commitment to the Democratic Party.[12] Meyer's hatred of his former ideology assumed a crusading nature, characterized by apocalyptic rhetoric and constant reference to the threat to Western civilization posed by liberalism and the international communist conspiracy. Predominantly libertarian in his political outlook, Meyer also promoted the achievement of a truly virtuous society, one of the principal ideological bases of the traditionalist perspective. Meyer's libertarian ideals did not dissuade him from the view that international communism, not domestic liberalism, posed the most imminent threat to American political freedom.[13]

Meyer's fusionism, a term that was coined by Buckley's brother-in-law, L. Brent Bozell, was first explored in his book of essays *In Defense of Freedom*, published in 1964. He distilled the idea in an article of 1964 titled "What Is Conservatism?" This was the formula by which Meyer combined conservatives' anti-statist views and moral traditionalism with militant anticommunism. The philosophy had mainly practical origins, born in part from the political experiences of conservatives in the early 1960s and in part from the recognition that a more coherent theoretical framework was required if the movement was to avoid the factionalism that had haunted its earlier forays into politics. Meyer's article was a distillation of the already implemented cooperative methods and ideas that had begun with the creation of *National Review* in 1955 and that climaxed with the Draft Goldwater drives of 1960 and 1964. It soon became the active philosophy of the *National Review* circle and the ACU.

The ACU, founded in the wake of Goldwater's electoral defeat, marked a turning point for the conservative leadership in terms of its cooperative political efforts and was heavily allied with *National Review, Human Events,* and YAF. Furthermore, YAF was influenced by the ideological and practical influences of Buckley and Rusher. The ACU's founding members included Meyer and Rusher, who chaired the committee on political action. Other directors included Stefan Possony of the Hoover Institution, who chaired the committee on foreign and military policy, the Texas political activist Peter O'Donnell, the playwright and novelist John Dos Passos, the conservative author John Chamberlain, and the journalist Jameson G. Campaigne. Espousing a determined faith in the traditional values of the American republic and promoting "an economic system based on private property and directed by a free, competitive market," the ACU made abundantly clear its dedication to opposing international communism. The United States and indeed "the civilization that illuminated it" was "mortally threatened by the global Communist revolution." The ACU denied the possibility of peaceful coexistence with communism and extolled the virtues of using "any means expedient" to avoid becoming enslaved by communist expansion. American military superiority and the exertion of relentless pressure were required to defend the United States and to "advance the frontiers of freedom."[14]

The ACU's emphasis on anticommunism and Meyer's promulgation of fusionism led to disquiet among certain quarters of the conservative movement. The eminent libertarian Murray Rothbard, who described Meyer as a dear friend and mentor, was among the leading critics of fusionism. He later argued that Meyer's obsession with anticommunism had the practical effect of favoring "U.S. imperialism and of all-out military statism in the U.S." Rothbard further claimed that Meyer's "devotion to the global crusade against communism and the Soviet Union" ensured that "the Enemy for him and for the conservative movement, was not statism and socialism but communism." Consequently, he argued, "it was under Frank's theoretical and strategic aegis that the conservative movement rushed to welcome and honor any species of dangerous socialist so long as they were certifiably anti-communist or anti-Soviet."[15] Conservatives at *National Review* were deeply concerned about the unbridled growth of the national security state and avowedly criticized liberals' policies in relation to civil rights, education, welfare and other areas of social reform as bordering on socialism. But Rothbard's frustrations reveal the truth that many conservatives associated with the Republican Right and *National Review* were prepared to adopt any and all measures, including those contrary to individual freedom and conservative economic doctrine, in order to focus on opposing international communism. Despite the continued ideological divisions among conservatives, Meyer succeeded in articulating a practical philosophy that functioned as a source of unity and helped define the identity of the conservative movement during the 1960s. Despite the protestations of individuals such as Rothbard, anticommunism became a powerful symbol of unity within the conservative movement and allowed the *National Review* circle to assume a position of public prominence and political leadership.

Buckley was keen to associate the journal with the conservative wing the Republican Party by supporting Goldwater's presidential bids and, perhaps more important, by helping to legitimize conservatives' domestic and foreign policies. Buckley stated that the purpose of *National Review* was "to articulate a position on world affairs which a conservative candidate can adhere to without fear of intellectual embarrassment or political surrealism."[16] As part of this effort, Buckley was eager to sideline the radical, or Far Right, elements of the conservative movement associated with the JBS and such populist organizations as the Christian Anti-Communist Crusade (CACC), founded by the Australian physician Fred Schwarz. Robert Welch, the eccentric candy manufacturer who founded the JBS, espoused an antigovernment doctrine more extreme than that supported by the Republican Right and *National Review*. Welch angered the *National Review* circle principally because of his neo-isolationist foreign policies and his tirade against President Dwight Eisenhower in the late 1950s in which he accused the president of consciously aiding international communist expansion. Welch's comments were made in a series of statements and articles published in *American Opinion,* the publication funded by the JBS. In 1959 he synthesized his views on Eisenhower in a book, *The Politician,* but toned down his assertions that the president had consciously acted in support of communist expansion. He based his criticisms of postwar U.S. foreign policy on each administration's failure to act decisively and militarily to undermine the Soviet military buildup and to achieve unambiguous success in such areas as Korea and Eastern Europe. While such views may have accorded with those of *National Review* activists in certain respects, Welch's outrageous accusations and his resort to isolationism as the basis of U.S. foreign policy earned the hostility of the "responsible Right." Indeed, his accusations were met with condemnation by hard-liners in the Republican Party such as House Minority Leader Gerald Ford of Michigan.

Many prominent conservatives were associated with the JBS and believed that it served an important role in disseminating conservative ideas and publications. The group had helped rally activists in support of Goldwater's 1960 and 1964 presidential bids and it functioned as a centralizing body for the many self-declared freedom groups that had developed at the grassroots. Michelle Nickerson astutely notes the extent to which Welch built the JBS on the "organizational infrastructure" established by local anti-communist and antiliberal groups in cities such as Los Angeles. JBS leaders "saw their organization as its own movement," and this movement "rested upon a grassroots networking pattern that was already expansive." Women, Nickerson writes, were particularly important in organizing conservatism groups and maintaining their momentum during the early 1960s.[17] Simply writing the JBS out of the conservative movement was therefore not a straightforward task, and in many respects Buckley's goal revealed his limited understanding of how the conservative movement was developing in local communities. Goldwater had rejected appeals from Buckley and Burnham, among others, to denounce the JBS as early as 1962. Recognizing the organization's role in disseminating conservative publications and the organizational function of JBS chapters in voter registration and campaign drives, Goldwater feared that a rejection of the group would undermine the organizational structure of the emerging conservative political movement. Nonetheless, conservative leaders were determined to limit any association with Welch's foreign policy views. This stance was underscored at a meeting to organize the ACU when the activists adopted a statement which read, "The directors of the ACU take a view of world affairs substantially at variance with that taken by Mr. Robert Welch in his most publicized writings. Under the circumstances, the leadership of the ACU will be wholly distinct from that of the John Birch Society." Jonathan Schoenwald accurately notes that the ACU's public statement relative to the JBS "sounded suspiciously like Buckley's doing."[18] JBS members were not, however, inclined to simply adopt Welch's foreign policy ideas writ large. As Lisa McGirr's study of conservative activists in southern California demonstrates, the JBS provided a forum for anticommunist activism but also served as a loose network of like-minded activists rather than a strict ideological organization.[19]

Leading conservatives' rejection of the JBS was born primarily of their fears that the group's official pronouncements were politically embarrassing and even dangerous. By this time, conservatives at *National Review* and among the Republican Right had also come to terms with the political necessity of accepting containment as the basis of United States foreign policy. In the immediate postwar period, Burnham expressed conservatives' dismay at the Truman and Eisenhower administrations' embrace of a foundational policy, which did not offer the opportunity to liberate the captive nations of Eastern Europe. He charged that containment was not only immoral and certain to weaken the resolve of peoples currently experiencing pressure from communist influence, but also likely to embolden the Kremlin's expansionist crusade. Conservatives' early emphasis on the morality of American foreign policy became a key issue during the Vietnam War and reflected their early hostility to the amoral pursuit of international equilibrium or stability.

Burnham was described as the individual who "more than any other . . . supplied the conservative intellectual movement with the theoretical formulation for victory in the cold war."[20] He never abandoned his belief that containment was immoral, but he altered his position on the policy following the Hungarian revolution of 1956. *National Review* joined the Eisenhower administration and Western governments in condemning the suppression of the antigovernment uprising that broke out across Hungary on October 23. The journal also denounced the Eisenhower administration for its feeble attempts to bring pressure to bear on the Soviet Union. *National Review* signed up to the Hungary Pledge, which was issued by the conservative anticommunist group, the American Friends of Captive Nations. The pledge stated that the Soviet Union had once again demonstrated its isolation from the "moral community" and promised to avoid any relations—economic, political, social, or cultural—with the Soviet regime, which had freely condoned the "Hungarian massacre."[21] Burnham believed Hungarians had been influenced by American promises of liberation and charged that the administration had effectively abandoned the rebels to their miserable fate. The event caused him, however, to fully realize that the Eisenhower administration had no intention of pursuing any kind of liberationist policy. He was obliged to reconsider the means by which conservatives could ensure victory in the Cold War and thereby concluded that mainstream political success was essential. Conservatives, he insisted, could not continue to be shut out of policymaking circles. In December 1956 Burnham urged conservatives to come to terms with reality and acknowledge that the military policies needed for a policy of liberation were unattainable in light of the "liberal-humanitarian abstractions that now preside over the President's mental processes." Burnham's views were not welcomed at *National Review* but his argument was simply the articulation of what many conservative leaders already understood—that liberation via military means was unrealistic as a genuine foreign policy objective. Conservative intellectuals, as they became more politically active, quietly accepted Burnham's position and acknowledged that liberation was a morally preferably but politically implausible goal. The majority of the Republican Party, furthermore, did not favor liberation.[22] While conservative activists like Goldwater were willing to push for a more forceful foreign policy, Colin Dueck remarks on the Republican leadership's tendency to "reaffirm hard-line cold war stands overseas while supporting and deferring to the president in moments of crisis."[23]

Conservatives may have continued to characterize containment as defeatist, but they no longer openly rejected it. In accepting containment, however, they promoted the necessity of engaging in smaller wars that would result in a rollback of communist influence. In essence, they continued to reject the idea of mutual coexistence. Burnham continued to emphasize the hegemonic ambitions of the Soviet Union. He built on the ideas of scholars like Possony and Robert Strausz-Hupé of the University of Pennsylvania, who coauthored *International Relations in the Age of Conflict between Democracy and Dictatorship*, which was published in 1950. Both Possony, who was a member of the ASC, and Strausz-Hupé, who in 1955 founded the rightward leaning Foreign Policy Research Institute, were well respected within the conservative community and had various organizational links with conservative activists. Somewhat concerned by the label right wing, they did not subscribe to the consciously conservative activism espoused by *National Review*. Strausz-Hupé in 1962 denied that the ideological links between the People's Republic of China (PRC) and the Soviet Union were sufficiently strong to overcome pragmatic differences or the power struggle between the two states. Although divergences existed regarding certain matters of foreign policy and on the presentation of policy prescriptions, the *National Review* circle of conservatives and prominent figures such as Possony and Strausz-Hupé complemented one another in arguing that the war would continue until one side, the Soviet Union and its clients, or the other, the United States as the only powerful alternative, won.[24]

This perspective was aptly represented in Goldwater's manifesto for modern conservatism, *The Conscience of a Conservative* (1960), which was ghostwritten by Bozell, Goldwater's former speechwriter, at the behest of the conservative broadcaster Dean Clarence Manion. The book reflected Goldwater's views and championed conservative perspectives on economics, civil rights, and the appropriate role of the federal government, social policy, and unsurprisingly, international relations. The book concluded with a call to arms and made plain the simple choice available to conservatives concerned about their liberty in the face of unprecedented international threats. The communist, Goldwater charged, was on the offensive and "will invite us in local crisis after local crisis to choose between all-out war and limited retreat; and will force us, ultimately, to surrender or accept war under the most disadvantageous circumstances." Yet such a future was not foreordained. Americans could still "summon the will and the means for taking the initiative, and wage a war of attrition against them—and hope, thereby, to bring about the international disintegration of the Communist empire." Both courses ran the risk of inciting war, but only a war of attrition offered "the promise of victory." Americans who cherished their freedom more than their lives would not find the choice difficult to make.²⁵

Like Goldwater, Meyer believed that victory over communism was possible and maintained that it would be achieved by forcing the "Communist personality" to realize the false promises of communism. He claimed that by debunking communist myths, Americans could destroy the "foundations" on which the communist's "life was built."²⁶ This focus on the need to undermine communist illusions was shared by Burnham, who viewed his column as a means of educating people on two major themes, namely, that the Soviet Union and the United States were in reality at war and that every Soviet move was aimed at achieving its long-term goal of world domination.²⁷ Mass anticommunist organizations such as CACC echoed the vital importance of alerting the American people to the dangers posed by international communism and the need to oppose all semblance of socialist influence in government, popular culture, and daily life. Yet at *National Review* promoting domestic understanding of the communist threat served primarily as a means of highlighting the international ambitions of the Soviet Union. In order to debunk Soviet myths, it was necessary for the United States to challenge communists' use of wars of national liberation and in fact engage in its own process of "liberating" the American people from fear of involvement in small wars.

Vietnam was not a pronounced concern to conservatives in 1960. But their view of communism's advance through the utility of local crises informed their opinion that the United States should continue to support the anticommunist government in Saigon. This presumed local crisis could not be ignored if the United States wished to avoid continuous decline, any more than nuclear deterrence could be recognized as viable if American policymakers openly stated that nuclear weapons would never be used. Kennedy's failure, as deemed by conservatives, to promote an anticommunist agenda during the Laos crisis and the outcome of the Cuban missile crisis served only to exacerbate the magnitude of Vietnam in the administration and among conservatives alike.

The Push into Southeast Asia

Conservatives discussing U.S. policy in Vietnam before 1964 continued to do so in the context of thwarting Soviet and Chinese expansion. Vietnam was not considered in isolation but was understood as another possible instance in Kennedy's foreign policy that was likely to result in failure. In many respects conservatives were more concerned with highlighting the potential failure of U.S. policy in Southeast Asia than in actively protecting Vietnamese freedom. This stance emphasized one of the main divisions among leading conservatives. Activists associated with the old China lobby, the most notable of whom was the former congressman Walter Judd, demonstrated deep philosophical and emotional commitments to South Vietnam. The China lobby represented the section of the Republican Party that had long held that the heart of the Cold War battleground was in Asia. American failures in China and Korea heightened the importance of Vietnam for such activists, and their position was furthered by long-term supporters of Ngo Dinh Diem in both parties.[28] Forming a determined Vietnam lobby, this group may have been influenced and even dominated by conservatives, but its perspective was quite distinct from that advanced by *National Review*.[29] The Vietnam lobby championed support for Saigon as a vital part of U.S. foreign policy; economic and military aid must be continued despite the limited gains made by the anticommunist regime to establish order and stability. *National Review*, on the other hand, did not prioritize Vietnam during this period. It represented an important battleground in the Cold War but was not recognized as the most vital area of contention. As a result, *National Review* conservatives attacked the Kennedy administration's Vietnam policy but demonstrated only a limited commitment to offering policy solutions for Southeast Asia. In 1963 they had other things on their minds, the most notable of which was Cuba, ninety miles from the Florida coast.

Aghast at the administration's hesitance in using force during the Bay of Pigs invasion and the neutralization of Laos, conservatives feared the implications for American credibility that would result from the United States agreeing to a test ban treaty. George Nash has argued that "as conservatives surveyed world crises in the late 1950s and the 1960s, one fundamental fact seemed paramount: the continuous, implacable assault on the West by messianic, revolutionary Communism."[30] Accepting the belief that the United States was losing the Cold War, conservatives at *National Review* emphasized the paramount importance of U.S. military supremacy and saw Vietnam as an opportunity to forestall the communist wave of success. They also recognized that the Kennedy administration's failure to secure its goals in Vietnam offered the opportunity to attack the president's wider foreign policies. They were not alone. As Andrew Johns comments, each of the three most prominent Republican presidential candidates, Nixon, Nelson Rockefeller, and Goldwater, sought ways to take political advantage of Kennedy's mistakes in South Vietnam. "As the election campaign [of 1964] got under way," Johns notes, "bipartisan support for the administration's foreign policy broke down further."[31]

The Kennedy administration's focus on an apparent Sino–Soviet split, the significance of which was vociferously denied by conservatives, heightened the relevance of Southeast Asia because conservatives feared the government intended to relax its restrictions on trade and contact with the PRC. Emphasizing the role of the PRC in facilitating and encouraging the communist insurgencies in Southeast Asia, conservative activists called for military escalation of the American effort in Vietnam during the final year of the Kennedy administration. In January 1963 *Human Events* charged that the administration was pursuing a no-win policy and was repeating the mistakes of Korea in failing to attack the enemy's sanctuaries in North Vietnam, China, Cambodia, and Laos. Rejecting isolationist opposition to American involvement in the Korean War, these new nationalist (or interventionist) conservatives charged that the problem in Korea had not been with objectives but with the means employed to secure these goals. More important, the Truman administration's justification of intervention in Korea failed to convince the American people of the magnitude of the stakes involved.[32] The powerful symbol of Gen. Douglas MacArthur's removal from his command served to highlight conservative claims that the war had not been fought with sufficient commitment to victory. Neither, according to conservatives, had it been fought on the basis of a moral crusade against communist expansion. Objections regarding the Korean War, however, were largely based on its outcome. Judd, who became the leading figure in support of a strong U.S. commitment to nationalist China, argued that Korea stood before Americans as a "painful object lesson of the results of a half-settlement."[33] The Cold War in Asia thus became a focus of the conservative movement from the late 1940s. This, in some part, reflected the military's preference for a Pacific-first policy during the Second World War. It was also conditioned by American missionaries' experiences of working in China and their shock at the religious implications of the communist revolution of 1949. Taking a strong line in Asia was therefore deemed essential in order to demonstrate America's strategic and moral commitment to protect the region and indeed liberate those in communist captivity.

Such understandings of the importance of Asia impacted conservatives' policy preferences for Vietnam in 1963. Interpreting the Pentagon's preferences, *Human Events* declared that the "only solution [in Vietnam] ... is either bombing the sanctuaries or eliminating them through other means." By taking such measures and "choking off these supply centers" the United States might in fact "prevent escalation."[34] While not advocating the direct introduction of troops, therefore, conservative activists continued to argue for an intensified American role in combating the communist insurgency in Vietnam. In doing so they maintained that the United States could not restrict itself to targeting the campaign in South Vietnam and rejected the supposition that the situation could be interpreted as a civil war or one irrelevant to U.S. national security. The "Viet Nam ... peril point" could not, they claimed, be resolved through a policy of American "tolerance and pretty-please."[35]

By advocating that the administration adopt escalation in Vietnam, conservatives intended to subject the basic rationale of liberal foreign policy to scrutiny: "Only strength and willingness to use it are deterrent facts respected by policy-makers in the Kremlin."[36] Goldwater asserted that American leaders had failed to deal with the problem of power and its uses since 1945, further contending that American military supremacy had kept and would continue to keep international peace but only if such power was maintained and applied to all relations with other states. To conservative leaders it was the failure to understand and use its power which had led to such losses as Korea, Cuba, and Laos, indeed to the increasingly weak position of the United States in the protracted war with international communism. And it was within this context, the view that the United States was losing the Cold War, that the meaning of Vietnam was evaluated.[37]

While a subtle shift toward acceptance of containment as the basis of U.S. foreign policy was discernible among conservative intellectuals and opinion makers, vocal opposition to the concept and practice of limited war remained dominant. In reality the move toward containment prefigured further confusion rather than a resolution of conservatives' uncertainties about the fighting of small wars. In rejecting limited war, associated with the failure to sufficiently implement one's military and diplomatic power, conservatives offered only an obscure, sometimes narrowly defined means of achieving victory. In this regard they relied on specific measures of military escalation and intimidation but failed to coherently establish the long-term effects of such policies as the bombing of sanctuaries and the cutting of supply routes.

Demands for escalation, however, increased dramatically following the military coup against Diem. Claiming that the Kennedy administration could not have been an "innocent bystander" in the coup, the right-leaning *Chicago Tribune* asserted that U.S. military officials had not been opposed to the Diem regime and charged that "liberal correspondents" in Saigon had continued the propagandist drive that had undermined Chiang Kai-shek and Fulgencio Batista.[38] A subsequent article in *Human Events* detailed the "inglorious role" of the United States in the overthrow of Diem and concluded, "The only sure thing in Vietnam today is that the United States has set an extremely controversial precedent by encouraging, for the first time in our history, the overthrow in time of war of a duly elected government fighting loyally against the common Communist enemy."[39] Republicans like Rep. Melvin Laird and Rep. Gerald Ford warned that the Kennedy approach lacked strength and direction and pushed for the administration to adopt a "more muscular approach" to defeating the communist insurgency.[40] Conservatives began to talk of Vietnam not simply as another instance of American failure to act decisively or even as simply a proxy war in the wider conflict with the Soviet Union. For conservatives Vietnam was the next, perhaps the last, test of American will and credibility. It was, Goldwater later remarked, "as close as Kansas or New York or Seattle" in "the mileage of peace and freedom."[41] Success, as surely as loss, in Vietnam would reverberate throughout the world.

It is disingenuous to maintain that conservatives argued in favor of either securing victory in Vietnam or withdrawing all aid and military support, although some grassroots conservatives and anticommunist activists did employ such rhetoric. It had appeal as a rhetorical tool for far right figures in their efforts to undermine the liberal administrations in Washington and to focus attention on the primacy of domestic anticommunism. Schwarz's CACC used Vietnam to demonstrate that so-called anticommunists in government were no more committed to victory over communism than their Soviet counterparts. From 1960 the CACC was based in southern California and was part of a nexus of right-wing organizations that promoted a virulent form of anticommunism in that region. Schwarz, furthermore, was the author of a widely read text titled *You Can Trust the Communists (To Be Communists)*, which repeated the long-standing conservative argument that communists could not be trusted in any form of negotiation. The government's failure to pursue a strategy of outright victory, activists like Schwarz claimed, limited the relevance of Vietnam to the anticommunist crusade.

Phyllis Schlafly, the formidable conservative activist who wrote several texts on foreign policy during the 1960s, also questioned the meaning of Vietnam. According to her biographer Donald Critchlow, she "originally opposed sending American troops to Vietnam" and later "maintained that the Vietnam War was a Soviet-engineered distraction designed to weaken America's defense capability."[42] As the Vietnam War progressed, Schlafly became more and more focused on social issues and in 1967 founded the Eagle Trust Fund in order to raise money for conservative interests. Both Schwarz and Schlafly focused on building grassroots support for their initiatives and were dedicated to educating the American people about the dangers of communism and liberalism. Their limited attachment to the Vietnam War demonstrates the fractured nature of the conservative movement's interpretations of the importance of the conflict. In many respects such limited commitment was conditioned by a widespread interpretation of the conflict as Johnson's war. For social conservatives this often led to a rejection of the endeavor as another example of liberals' soft approach to communist expansion. For conservatives in the Republican Party and for those associated with *National Review,* the recognition that this was Johnson's war led to more complex responses. On the one hand, they championed the importance of the anticommunist crusade in Southeast Asia and pushed for widespread popular backing of the war effort. On the other hand, they realized the political gains to be made by attacking the Democratic president's failure to secure victory.[43]

Despite social conservatives' limited commitment to Vietnam, conservatives in the Republican Party and those at *National Review* consistently pushed for military escalation throughout 1964. Others within the party called for escalation, but they added the proviso that if the United States failed to win soon, they should pull out. In May, Rep. William Broomfield of Michigan introduced a resolution that amounted to a win-or-get-out strategy. Gov. William Scranton of Pennsylvania endorsed this idea when he stated, "We've either got to win the war in South Viet Nam in due time—or else forget it, lose it."[44] Goldwater and his supporters, however, always maintained that the war simply had to be won; there was no alternative. There was certainly a political motivation underlying the constant focus on Johnson's failure to secure the regime in South Vietnam. But the push for escalation was also based on foreign policy considerations and anxiety over the implications of military failure. In July *Human Events* supported the line that because of Johnson's failure to extend the war beyond Vietnam through bombing campaigns, the United States might be forced to increase troop levels in South Vietnam. The journal took the opportunity to charge that the New Frontier's policies had been catastrophic for South Vietnam, most notably because of the State Department's collusion in overthrowing the legitimate ruler of the country, President Diem. The Johnson administration's pursuit of "no-win" war had simply deceived the American people about America's role in the region. As the editors at *Human Events* wrote, the "truth is we are already at war.... We may have to enlarge the war effort there for precisely the reason that our dangerous 'no-win' policies have allowed the Communists to come to the brink of inflicting an overwhelming defeat upon the United States."[45] Goldwater's presidential platform left little ambiguity regarding Vietnam: "We will move decisively to assure victory in South Viet Nam."[46] He ignored the clear signs of French and British wariness about U.S. military intervention.[47] Instead, Goldwater claimed that "no responsible world leader suggests that we should withdraw our support from Viet Nam," and he committed the United States to learning the lessons of Korea: "In war there is no substitute for victory." Goldwater concluded by asserting, "Peace in Asia depends on our strength, and on our purpose to use that strength to achieve peace. Nowhere in the world today is there a clearer road to peace through strength than in Viet Nam."[48]

Conservative leaders were not ambiguous about their preferred means of securing victory in Southeast Asia, although the extent to which such measures could ensure victory was misguided. On the eve of the Republican National Convention, Goldwater simply stated that he would hand the management of the war over to the Joint Chiefs of Staff and say, "Fellows, we made the decision to win, now it's your problem."[49] During the presidential campaign Goldwater's calls for military escalation in Vietnam led the journalist Howard K. Smith to question him about realistic options for stopping supplies from reaching North Vietnam via China. Goldwater's response reflected his continued focus on the use of American airpower: "Well, it is not as easy as it sounds because these are not trails that are out in the open. I've been in the rain forests in Burma and South China. You are perfectly safe wandering through them as far as an enemy hurting you. There have been several suggestions made. I don't think we would use any of them, but defoliation of the forest by low yield atomic devices could well be done. When you remove the foliage, you remove the cover."[50] He added that it could be done "in a way that would not endanger life," and in response to Smith's concern that such action might spark a war with China, Goldwater stated, "You might have to.... Either that, or we have a war dragged out and dragged out. A defensive war is never won."⁵¹ Goldwater's words provoked public outrage among liberals and fueled their claims that a Goldwater presidency would result in uncontrolled war. As he continued to assert that he had not advocated the use of nuclear weapons, Goldwater implicitly rejected their use in Vietnam.

Conservatives' military options with regard to Vietnam were based on the principle that the war should not be limited to South Vietnam. Rather, it should automatically be extended to North Vietnam, and conservatives denied that its extension into either Laos or Cambodia would escalate the conflict to include direct superpower rivalry. "Red China," Goldwater maintained, would not take the "suicidal" step of entering the war. Indeed, China was "bluffing." He also questioned the rationale that extending the war would invite Soviet intervention to defend its ally, claiming that the Soviet Union "would hardly invite its own destruction as a nation by using nuclear weapons in *any* cause except the defense of its own soil." Nuclear exchange was therefore "not even likely, let alone probable, although the United States has allowed the specter of it to inhibit any firm diplomacy since World War II."⁵² Conservatives argued that military escalation would not only improve the situation in Vietnam, but also deter further communist aggression. During the debates over the Gulf of Tonkin Resolution, which conservative Republicans wholly supported, Sen. Strom Thurmond cautioned that the administration must use the event as an opportunity to abandon its "purely defensive posture in favor of a 'win policy' in Vietnam." This was the time for "victory, not stalemate."⁵³

Much of the specifics of conservative policies for Vietnam were garnered from the strategies advocated by the ASC, a think tank and lobbying organization founded in 1955 and committed to a hard-line foreign policy. In September 1964 the ASC's military committee, which included such hard-liners as Gen. Albert Wedemeyer and Adm. Chester Ward, put forth a strategy for victory. "The cheapest and quickest way to win the war in South Viet Nam," the ASC purported, "is to begin with one or more of the privileged sanctuaries like North Viet Nam and Communist-held parts of Laos." The report continued, "If these countries could be neutralized and cut off as a base of supply and sanctuary for the Viet Cong, both the military and the all-important psychological atmosphere in South Viet Nam could be transformed. . . . It is often forgotten that the logistics problem of fighting a major war in Laos is far more formidable to the Communists than ourselves."[54] Despite such claims, the report did not offer a detailed analysis of how or why it was more difficult for the communists to fight in Laos. Indeed, the Kennedy administration had already concluded that Laos was an especially unfavorable location for fighting an insurgency.[55] Conservatives nonetheless remained buoyant about the prospects of military victory. In commenting on the ASC's report, Kirk averred that such action could "cut the Ho Chi Minh Trail and thus cut off supplies to the Communist guerrillas in South Viet Nam."[56]

Calls for the implementation of an enhanced bombing campaign against North Vietnam only escalated once the United States had dispatched greater resources to the area; in January 1965 Holmes Alexander warned that Vietnam was beginning to "look like Cuba" because of a lack of American resolve in using its air force. Alexander castigated the administration's reliance on a ground war, comparing the situation to that of the Bay of Pigs. He argued that what stopped the United States from using the necessary force to secure victory was fear: "Fear of nuclear war, fear of world opinion, fear of doing something wrong. Fear, of course, is the instinct for self-preservation. It may at times have lengthened the lives of men and nations, but it is probably true that courage has saved more lives than cowardice, and it certainly has made for better lives." He concluded, "We have never been quite the same country since the Bay of Pigs. And now it appears we are making the same craven mistakes in Viet Nam."[57] From early 1965 conservatives demanded that the United States use its air force and navy to destroy the war-making potential of North Vietnam by attacking targets such as Hanoi and Haiphong harbor, on the supposition that the insurgency in the South would subsequently cease.

Conservatives had few hopes that the Johnson administration

would seek the victory policy in Vietnam that they deemed essential to American credibility. They offered broad support in Congress when the president requested passage of the largely uncontroversial Gulf of Tonkin Resolution in August 1964 and were buoyed by the bombing of torpedo bases and an oil storage facility that had been initiated in response to two alleged attacks on US ships off the North Vietnamese coast. They were soon disheartened, however, by the president's emphasis on the reciprocal nature of the bombing campaigns, by which the United States justified its airstrikes as direct responses to specific actions by Hanoi, rather than as a consequence of the North Vietnamese government's wholesale support of the southern insurgency. Conservatives were, moreover, outraged by the limitations imposed on the military's choice of targets. Speaking only weeks after passage of the resolution, Goldwater charged that Johnson had endangered the lives of American pilots by warning Hanoi that patrol boat installations off the North Vietnamese coast were to be bombed. Goldwater referred to the fact that Johnson's televised announcement of the bombing came an hour and a half before the planes hit their targets. He rejected the administration's defense that this measure had been specifically designed to warn the North Vietnamese and the Chinese that the United States planned only a limited attack. Goldwater made his remarks on his first day of campaigning outside Washington since winning the presidential nomination and reflected the extent to which Vietnam remained a political issue. "This administration," he charged in front of a large crowd of supporters in Springfield, Illinois, "has shown little skill when negotiating with Communists. Now it appears they have as little skill when fighting with Communists."[58]

Goldwater might well have directly accused his rival of trying to make political use of Vietnam by timing the presidential address to coincide with the optimum time for domestic television viewing, but such charges against the president were not without political risks. By challenging Johnson's policies conservatives ran the risk of being accused of holding unpatriotic views. Indeed, this possibility was heightened when Johnson's early initiatives in Vietnam resulted in positive popular responses. But the public at large did not demonstrate a very strong emotional attachment to the emerging American war in Vietnam. In part this was the result of the administration's efforts to avoid a debate on the war, which Johns accurately attributes to fears of a right-wing backlash against the policies of limited war.[59] Yet if the public was not pushing for abandonment of the Saigon regime, there were few calls for escalation along the lines that conservatives recommended. The *New York Times* warned in September that the deteriorating political situation in South Vietnam might offer room for Goldwater to continue his attacks on the soft policies being pursued by Johnson. Yet its analysis that such a crisis might rally the public behind the president was more prescient.[60] Goldwater did not let up in his attacks on the president, charging in late October that Johnson's Vietnam policies were those "of drift, of deception, and of defeat."[61] In many respects, however, he was speaking to the converted. Conservatives continued to champion his calls for escalation as the only means of securing victory, and grassroots activists used the Vietnam issue to stress Democrats' limited commitment to anticommunism. But the broader public maintained its faith in Johnson's strategies. The concern with appearing unpatriotic certainly impacted the ways in which conservative Republicans voiced their disquiet about the administration's handling of the war, leading them to emphasize the benefits of simply allowing the military to fully control the war in recognition of the sacrifices made by Americans serving in Southeast Asia.

The wider conservative movement was less restrained and accused the administration of failing to understand the international significance of the Vietnam War. They would continue to make such claims for the remainder of Johnson's presidency. In early 1965 their accusations appeared less relevant given the Johnson administration's escalation of the conflict through the initiation of Operation Rolling Thunder, the large-scale bombing of North Vietnam that began in February. Johnson enjoyed widespread support of the familiar rally-'round-the-flag variety. Patriotic groups and veterans' organizations concentrated on organizing campaigns that endorsed the president rather than ones that engaged with conservatives' demands for further escalation. Nonetheless, Vietnam posed an opportunity for the conservative movement: it offered the possibility of legitimizing and popularizing their hardline foreign policies, but only so long as the war remained broadly uncontroversial at home.

CHAPTER 2

The Loyal Opposition?

The Push for Victory, 1965–1968

> We have committed our prestige as a great nation....
> What we *must* do is instill in ourselves and our allies a determination to win this crucial war—and *win it decisively*. We must recognize that we are in a life-and-death struggle that has repercussions far beyond Vietnam, and that victory is essential to the survival of freedom.
>
> Richard Nixon, August 1964

> We are the peace party because we understand victory.
>
> Barry Goldwater, October 1967

Intellectual conservatives and political activists wasted little time in questioning the policies of the Johnson administration. This distinguished them from most within the Republican Party, who remained largely silent on the Vietnam War because of the widely held view that challenging the popular president at this time would backfire politically. In the run-up to the midterm elections in 1966 Republicans preferred to allow Democrats to question the president's policies rather than enter the political fray themselves.[1] Sen. John Tower was among the few Republican legislators who bucked this trend: by mid-1966 he openly attacked the president's handling of the war. On the basis of his frequent visits to Vietnam he deduced that the only way to "negotiate a reasonable peace with honor" was through the use of greater force against North Vietnam.[2] The majority of Republicans were less hostile toward the White House. In many respects, therefore, Johnson enjoyed greater support for his Vietnam policies among Republicans than he did among his fellow Democrats.

The degree to which Johnson feared right-wing attacks on his failure to win in Vietnam remains controversial. The president certainly exaggerated the degree to which conservatives were focused on Vietnam prior to the escalations of 1964 and 1965. Conservative Republicans, furthermore, appeared poised to attempt to make political gains from *any* policy that Johnson pursued in Southeast Asia. One of Johnson's foreign policy advisers, Francis Bator, has since argued that the president pursued war in Southeast Asia in order to gain political support for his domestic policy agenda.[3] Johnson too suggested that victory in Vietnam was essential to the success of his Great Society. Writing to George Ball, he argued that the "great black beast for us is the right wing. If we don't get this war over soon they'll put enormous pressure on us to turn it into an Armageddon and wreck all our other programs."[4] Yet Johnson's personal commitment to Vietnam was deeper than such statements imply, and his ability to keep conservative Democrats in line was substantial during 1964. As Goldwater's campaign indicated, Republicans were likely to make political use of any setback in Vietnam. Given Johnson's resounding political success in 1964, however, it is not unreasonable to argue that he could have withstood the pressure to escalate in the face of the habitually weak regimes in Saigon. Once escalation occurred, Johnson found that his room for maneuver was reduced, and his administration came under intense pressure from conservatives within his own party. Johnson may indeed have feared the right, but his escalation of the war in Vietnam silenced their demands for only a brief time. The war, in fact, provided new opportunities for conservatives to gain political traction from their attacks on the administration's weak foreign policy.

Johnson's greatest source of concern during 1965 was from Democratic hawks, those whom Secretary of Defense Robert McNamara referred to as the "heavier bombing boys" because of their vocal opposition to the administration's implementation of a brief bombing pause in December 1965. They included Johnson's close confidante, the powerful southern conservative Sen. Richard

Russell of Georgia. The former secretary of the air force, Sen. Stuart Symington of Missouri, was also a determined supporter of the greater use of airpower to defeat the enemy in Vietnam. This perspective was shared by several prominent southern Democrats in the House of Representatives, including Bob Sikes of Florida, Olin Teague of Texas, John McClellan of Arkansas, and Mendel Rivers of South Carolina. One of the most powerful southern Democrats of the era, Sen. John Stennis of Mississippi, consistently advocated greater bombing of North Vietnam during the Johnson years. While southern Democrats may have dominated among the heavier bombing boys, they were not alone. Sen. Thomas Dodd of Connecticut enthusiastically backed this cause, as did Sen. Howard Cannon of Nevada and Rep. Wayne Hayes of Ohio. These advocates of escalated bombing had not necessarily been at the forefront in pushing for U.S. intervention in Southeast Asia, but McClellan articulated their shared belief that American failure at this point would undermine the international and moral credibility of the United States: "To get out now would be surrender and an admission of guilt, of [U.S.] aggression."[5] By 1966, indeed, the stark divisions among Democrats over the war and foreign policy issues were becoming increasingly obvious and politically detrimental. Republicans also divided over the war, but these intraparty divisions did not create the same degree of political instability. If both Democrats and Republicans called on the administration to escalate the fighting in Vietnam during 1965 and 1966, it was conservatives who voiced the most consistent argument for dramatically altering military policy in Vietnam. They were also more critical of the administration's efforts to sell the war to the American people.

In 1965 one of the first actions of the newly formed American Conservative Union (ACU) was to put forward its prescription for fundamentally altering policy in Vietnam and for winning the war. Charging that the United States did not have "a clear-cut objective of ending the war on our terms," that very few people understood U.S. strategy, and that "it is generally believed, and not without reason, that the United States lacks the will to win," the ACU attacked the Johnson administration for its failure to "discourage further Communist aggression, let alone compel North Vietnam (and whoever else might be involved in the present Communist aggression) to cease and desist." The ACU presented the case for winning in Vietnam in global terms, challenging the administration and the American people to recognize that the "cost of a loss of the war, whether through military defeat, withdrawal, or a Laos-type face-saving negotiation, is prohibitive." Failure in Vietnam, the organization charged, would simply result in the resumption of hostilities "on other fronts on a greater scale at greater disadvantages." Reminding Americans of the Soviet Union's determination to make use of wars of national liberation, the ACU warned of the importance of dispelling the doves' charge that Vietnam "cannot be won." Such an acceptance of American limitations would only embolden the Soviet Union to initiate new "guerrilla centers" in areas such as Africa and Latin America. South Vietnam was, in addition, of inherent strategic value, according to conservatives, and as "a principal 'rice bowl' of Asia," played a critical role in "Communist plans of conquest." Echoing President Eisenhower's articulation of a domino effect, the ACU charged that the fall of South Vietnam would immediately widen the conflict to other parts of Southeast Asia, while "the Philippines, Australia, New Zealand, Taiwan, Korea, Okinawa, and Japan would be in the line of direct pressure from the expanding circle in the Western Pacific."[6]

Sent to all the directors and members of the advisory assembly, a virtual who's who of the conservative movement, for consideration and comment, the March draft of the statement on Vietnam attracted some criticism. Adm. Thomas Lane, who was retired from the navy and an activist with several conservatively oriented and patriotic organizations, was a frequent columnist for *Human Events*. Lane denied the efficacy of the ACU's stated military policy. He claimed, "We don't need U.S. infantry divisions nor as many advisors as we have on the ground now" and added that the U.S. strikes against North Vietnam that had recently been initiated by the Johnson administration "represent not a correction . . . but an extension of the erroneous policy of recent years" because the strikes are designed to "preserve the stalemate and produce a climate favorable for negotiations." Lane's primary concern was that consideration of negotiations suggested that the

United States sought "something less than the independence of S[outh] Vietnam."⁷ Lane's criticisms, however, did not fundamentally challenge the ACU's preferred policies; both relied on attacking the enemy's sanctuaries and opposed a negotiated settlement. The ACU, in fact, echoed Lane's claim that the "present air strikes are not sufficient to secure the borders" of South Vietnam and that they "tend to preserve the stalemate." Negotiation, according to the ACU, should not be regarded as the end goal: "The war aims of North Vietnam are not open to negotiation," so concessions by the United States "would simply acknowledge that aggression pays."⁸

Conservatives echoed the pleas of prominent military leaders in calling for the initiation of a full-scale bombing campaign against North Vietnam. President Johnson was urged to remind Hanoi of its obligation under international law. The administration should also recognize that legitimate military targets included "any location used as support for combat operations or a location which is of tactical significance to the outcome of the actual battle." By leaving these areas untouched, the administration was allowing the enemy to create sanctuaries that they could reliably expect to remain free from attack. While generally dismissive of international treaties, particularly those reached with communist states, conservatives used the issue to highlight North Vietnam's intransigence and unreliability. Given "the Communist warfare of 'indirect' aggression," the ACU claimed, the administration needed to attack the "supply lines on which weapons and troops move on the battlefield." Also consistent was the demand that North Vietnam be given an ultimatum and a warning to cease its support and control of the insurgency in South Vietnam. Once this was rejected, the United States should waste no time in responding with air strikes, a naval blockade, and an amphibious attack against North Vietnam. Displaying little faith that Hanoi would ever comply with American terms for peace, the ACU concluded, "If the response of North Vietnam is not to cease aggression but to step up the war, the intensity of our military measures must increase, up to and including the elimination of the Hanoi Communist dictatorship."⁹

The ACU contended that negotiations with North Vietnam would serve no purpose other than to further weaken South Vietnam.

They concluded, therefore, that the only viable policy option was to engage in measures that would oblige North Vietnam to desist in its engagement in the southern campaign of conquest. Determined to emphasize this point on a popular level, pro-war groups concentrated on several specific military endeavors. They emphasized the enemy's use of the so-called Ho Chi Minh Trail to move men and supplies freely from North Vietnam to the south. The enemy's undisturbed use of its sanctuaries constituted the background for hawks' most fundamental proposition: the destruction or blocking of Haiphong harbor.

Demands for escalated military measures became more specific as the U.S. military commitment to Vietnam intensified. As noted, such demands were not limited to the ranks of the conservative movement. Reporting on a visit he made to Vietnam in December 1965, Senator Symington proclaimed that it "would seem that we are attacking the least important most, the more important targets less and the most important not at all." Displaying a similar faith in the efficacy of aerial attacks as Republican conservatives, Symington agreed "with some leading military authorities that a real air effort to knock out important military targets, instead of periodic attacks on targets of far less importance such as bridges, barracks, and buses, would eliminate the necessity of sending thousands of additional ground troops to South Viet Nam."[10] Shortly afterward, Symington claimed that the entire Joint Chiefs of Staff (JCS) sanctioned additional military measures, including the closing of Haiphong harbor.[11]

Speaking before the Senate Foreign Relations Committee in March 1966, the former congressman Walter Judd called for the bombing of war and power plants, oil tanks, and other sites of military significance in North Vietnam's prosecution of the war. He asked, "Why not openly announce to North Viet Nam and the world a list of military targets that are going to be destroyed sometime in the next few weeks or months?"[12] Judd denied that such action would lead to the deaths of many civilians and displayed a similar faith in the efficacy of bombing petroleum, oil, and lubricant sites and other industrial targets, a course of action then being demanded by hawkish figures in the Johnson administration. This policy was favored by both National Security Adviser Walt Rostow and the JCS.

When bombing was finally extended, however, it seemed to do little to dampen conservatives' animosity toward the administration's policy. In November 1966 Goldwater wrote of his impending visit to Vietnam, charging that what he had heard from Vietnam "is not encouraging."[13] His visit in January 1967 led him to conclude, in a letter to YAF, that "it is a disturbing picture." Goldwater did offer praise for Johnson when the administration released new bombing targets in February 1967. Writing in June, Goldwater admitted that the president "has been doing the right things for the last month or two." He was referring to U.S. air attacks on North Vietnamese airfields, which began on April 24, 1967, the air battles above Hanoi and Haiphong in April and May, and the interception of North Vietnamese troops moving into South Vietnam from Cambodia in May.[14] Judd likewise applauded Johnson's recent policies in writing to Nixon in December 1967. He urged Republicans not to become "so misguided as to adopt a dove position and start attacking the President for his having, however belatedly, finally started doing some of the things in Vietnam that we were advocating years ago."[15] Goldwater's praise for and faith in Johnson was scant: "I am not so sure he is going to keep it up."[16] Adm. Ulysses S. G. Sharp, Commander in Chief Pacific from 1964 to 1968, explored the prospect of destroying the North's war-making potential in his writings. Sharp publicly advocated the initiation of an intensified bombing campaign as early as 1964, and he was referenced by the American Security Council (ASC) in its promotion of such policies. Sharp's most widely distributed critique of the war was published by *Reader's Digest* in May 1969, but this article represented merely a distillation of his frequently expressed policy preferences.[17] In the absence of the implementation of far greater military measures, perhaps the total abandonment of limited war, conservatives like Goldwater would never endorse the policies of the Johnson administration. The apparent weakness of limited war was symbolized by the administration's failure to attack Haiphong harbor.

The harbor tied the Vietnam War to Soviet expansionism in both physical and symbolic terms. Buckley charged that "the failure of the U.S. Government to interdict the flow of material to North Vietnam from the Soviet Union is perhaps the major act of masochistic sentimentality in the post-war period." Estimates of the "Soviet contribution to the material effort of the North Vietnamese and the Viet Cong" were, according to Buckley, "never any lower than 60% and they go as high as 90."[18] According to a report commissioned by the ASC in 1967 to propose a course to expedite the successful conclusion of the war, the Soviet Union provided approximately $1 billion worth of military aid to North Vietnam, a substantial contribution against the $100 million furnished by China by overland routes. Charging that the failure to block supplies entering Haiphong harbor had "already condemned thousands of American servicemen to be killed by Soviet weapons and ammunition freely delivered through Haiphong," the ASC prophesied that "every month of further delay is, in effect, condemning hundreds of additional U.S. fighting men to death."

The ASC proposed six distinct means of blocking the harbor. The first and most widely supported among hawks was to bomb the port following the provision of "adequate warning . . . to the Soviets and to any other nations likely to have vessels in the harbor." Several less destructive measures also existed, including mining the sea and river approaches to the harbor, a measure that would simply echo the little-publicized enemy mining of Saigon harbor; a "declaration of contraband" by the United States; a classic blockade of the entire North Vietnamese coast, "a most effective measure of employing U.S. sea power and air power"; an amphibious landing in the Haiphong area, "which would also force North Vietnam to re-deploy some of its forces from South Vietnam to the North"; and, finally, making the harbor impassable for oceangoing vessels by purely physical obstructions such as sunken ships. This final task, the panel argued, could be achieved by scuttling two medium-sized ships, an operation that could be implemented by the South Vietnamese if necessary.[19] Reference to the South Vietnamese indicated the ASC's early association with handing sensitive or controversial operations over to the South Vietnamese armed forces, a policy that was not necessarily the preferred option but that was designed to overcome the supposedly politically motivated restrictions on

American forces. Johnson's unwillingness to attack Haiphong became, in the hawks' estimation, a symbol of his administration's failure to understand the nature of warfare in Vietnam and its international importance.

The ASC continued its challenge to administration policy in February 1968 by publishing an article titled "Carrying the War to North Vietnam: Time to Strike the Red River Dike System." Goldwater's personal copy of the article was underlined in several key places, each highlighting the dramatic impact of an attack on the dike system, which prevented the Red River from flooding the rice-producing delta around Hanoi. Underlined was the key argument: "Attack or even threat of an attack on these water systems could measure the war's duration in months instead of years." Even modest dike cuts and leaflet drops warning the local inhabitants and government of impending American action would result in a "morale-cracking tremor" throughout North Vietnam. The author concluded by declaring this a "bloodless, humane method of attaining a solution to the problem of shortening the war."[20]

Conservatives, while predominately concentrating on attacking North Vietnam and its sanctuaries, responded as well to the administration's policies in the South. Reluctant to wholly reject the search-and-destroy policies developed by military leaders in Washington and Vietnam, conservatives pushed for the development of anticommunist guerrilla groups to hunt down and destroy National Liberation Front insurgents. Such groups were also recommended by YAF for use in other third world and developing countries.[21] *National Review* heralded the policies of the British insurgency expert Sir Robert Thompson, arguing that Britain's campaign against communist rebels in Malaya had depended on transforming the armed forces to fight the enemy on similar terms. Buckley, writing in 1966, urged any reader "who at this late date is not aware of the pattern of Communist insurgency" to examine Thompson's book *Defeating Communist Insurgency*, which catalogued the communists' policy of "wholesale murder."[22] Focusing perhaps too much on the similarities of the Malayan and Vietnamese cases, conservatives attributed the administration's failure to quash the insurgency in the South on its failure to adopt the method of the enemy.

The emphasis on altering policy in the South included such issues as land reform and cooperation with local leaders. Yet even as many in the conservative movement became disillusioned with the succession of governments in Saigon, they remained reluctant to pressure the government to reform. Such demands would, it was argued, not only weaken the morale of the Saigon regime but also detract from the primary aim of the United States: defeating the North Vietnamese, Soviet-sponsored war of aggression on the Republic of Vietnam. As William Rusher asserted repeatedly, the United States was not in Vietnam "to impose democracy" or "even to *save* democracy."[23] The international threat of communism took precedence over the nature of the government in Vietnam and was reflected in the military options demanded by conservative activists.

Yet conservatives increasingly dwelled on humanitarian issues, and within the hawkish conservative community claims abounded that ending the war by swift military action was more humane than prolonging the stalemate. This change in focus reflected popular anxieties over the war's apparent brutality and was a response to the ideas promoted by grassroots activists who worked to promote support for the war. Such a position relied heavily on the assumption that the war could indeed be ended within a short period of time— within two weeks if "proper targeting" were adopted, according to Goldwater—and on North Vietnam's complete control of the war in South Vietnam.[24] Neither position required an immense conceptual leap for conservatives committed to the efficacy of strategic bombing and convinced of the monolithic communist role in Vietnam. Neither were they immune to the political opportunities afforded by the promotion of a policy that promised to bring to a decisive end a stalemated, increasingly unpopular war.

Conservatives were not alone in calling for escalation. The scope of hawkish demands was extended by hearings held by the Senate Armed Services Committee's Preparedness Investigating Subcommittee (SPIS), chaired by Sen. John Stennis. The hearings began in August 1967 and were in no small measure designed to counter the anti-war line that had dominated the Senate Foreign Relations Committee hearings, which were chaired by Sen. J. William Fulbright and had begun in 1966. Johnson had long feared a right-wing attack on his failure to win the war, and indeed evidence of conservatives' halfhearted support for limited war had been evident since the early days of U.S. military involvement in Southeast Asia. Despite the benefit of support for the war emanating from hawks within both parties, by 1967 conservatives in Congress posed a real threat to the president's credibility and limited his room for maneuver. Stennis and his supporters believed that the American people were not necessarily opposed to the war in Vietnam but were frustrated by the lack of military progress since 1965. Their views were shared by senior military officials. As Joseph Fry properly notes, the JCS "recognized correctly that the American people needed to be told forthrightly that the nation was at war." The JCS believed that the public needed to recognize, furthermore, the costs of war, which would include the mobilization of reserves and the enhanced deployment of troops in order to do more than simply "stave off defeat." Senator Russell echoed this line of argument, stating in 1966 that "we cannot afford to let this war drift on and on as it is now." The current military strategy might, he claimed, "bring the Vietcong to their knees" after ten or twelve years, "but the American people are going to be very unhappy about it."[25] In the face of civilian challenges to these measures, the JCS focused ever more on extending the permitted military targets for aerial bombardment. Stennis adopted this line of argument in the hearings held by the SPIS.

The SPIS hearings drew extensive news coverage and helped enhance the legitimacy of conservatives' long-held arguments that the war could be won in the air over North Vietnam. Several prominent military figures testified that military victory was still a possibility and that the Johnson administration should desist in its pursuit of policies of gradually escalating the fighting while seeking a compromise, negotiated settlement. The hearings thereby gave a voice to those who directly challenged the anti-war argument that the war could not be won at costs acceptable to the United States. Such arguments exacerbated the divisions between hawks and doves and prolonged, rather than resolved, debates about how best to proceed in Vietnam. By late 1967 it was indeed evident that the American people were increasingly frustrated with the slow pace of progress and the mounting evidence that the war was stalemated. Maintaining popular support for the war therefore became a pivotal goal of the broad pro-war movement, despite conservatives' preferred policies of exhorting the administration to escalate the bombing.

The Vietnam Lobbies

Conservative policies regarding Vietnam were influenced by concurrent campaigns to promote patriotic support for the war. Such campaigns became increasingly prominent during 1967, but they built on ideas promoted by pro-Vietnam activists since the 1950s. The American Friends of Vietnam (AFV) understood the American effort in Vietnam as an experiment in nation building and was concerned primarily with promoting government support of the Diem regime and popular affiliation with the people of South Vietnam. The AFV, termed the Vietnam Lobby by the historian Joseph Morgan, was officially founded in 1955 but its origins stretched back to 1950, when Diem gained the backing of U.S. State Department officials, political activists, journalists, and clergymen.[26] The AFV promoted the image of Diem as a nationalist committed to social and economic reform and determined to undermine any communist insurgency. Support of Diem was based on postwar theories of development and modernization of postcolonial states, theories that in practice relied upon Third Force nationalist leaders who rejected both colonialism and communism. Morgan argues that by the time it became clear that Diem would not follow American goals for reform, "America had already committed itself deeply to the survival of his regime."[27]

While the AFV's rationale for supporting South Vietnam differed in many respects from that of conservatives, the organization's activism influenced the terms by which conservatives promoted backing for the war. This was particularly true with regard to the AFV's and *National Review*'s emphasis on the Catholic fervor imbuing the anticommunist struggle in South Vietnam. The language employed by such prominent supporters of Diem as Cardinal Francis Spellman of New York was echoed by the AFV and Catholic intellectuals, including Buckley. In 1966 Buckley said that as a "Christian, I consider it fantastic to urge acquiescence in a Communist takeover, or on the grounds of 'conscience' to recommend an entire population to the superintendence of the Viet Cong."[28] Cardinal Spellman, who was vicar general of the armed forces and one of the Church's most prominent exponents of the war, argued that it was "a war for civilization" and charged that "less than victory was inconceivable."[29] This religious or humanitarian rationale for supplying U.S. aid to South Vietnam encouraged popular support for the war, especially after its escalation in 1965. While popular affection for the South Vietnamese was insufficient to generate mass support for the war, the patriotic campaign demanded by religious figures, government officials, veterans' groups, and conservatives proved sufficiently powerful to affect popular responses to the war. Concern for the Vietnamese, however, was never as powerful as campaigns that focused on American servicemen.

Veterans' groups promoted support for the war in the guise of patriotic and dutiful encouragement of those serving their country in Vietnam. Pro-Vietnam activists understood that employing patriotic campaigns could prove more powerful than more intellectual rationales for engaging in Vietnam. Although conservative leaders had been reluctant to overtly associate religious fervor and patriotism with U.S. policy in Southeast Asia, their determination to avoid an image of extremism or exaggerated hawkishness pushed them to adopt some of the measures proving successful with the public. This did not result in conservative leaders establishing specific patriotic programs, but it did lead to their unprecedented promotion of such programs employed by others and altered their language regarding Vietnam.

The *National Review* circle was keen to distance the conservative political leadership from the image of extremism following Goldwater's presidential campaign, and *National Review* in particular wished to purge the JBS from the movement. This division on the Right predated the Vietnam War but came to a head when the JBS's publication *American Opinion* announced in 1965 that the society opposed continued American involvement in Vietnam.[30] Robert Welch argued that the war was part of a Soviet effort to entangle the United States in a debilitating war, and he claimed that if American leaders were serious about meeting this challenge they would immediately employ the means necessary to win. Such views corresponded to a certain extent with those of conservative hawks. His prescription of withdrawal most certainly did not.

It is difficult to ascertain the extent to which Welch's opinion informed that of the JBS members, for many of the JBS's loose membership were also involved in patriotic and veterans' organizations that continued to support the war. Dean Clarence Manion, one of the most celebrated figures associated with the JBS, continued to urge popular support for the war, albeit with limited approval of the administration's policy, throughout this period. He did not break his affiliation with the JBS over the Vietnam issue, intimating that acceptance of Welch's opinions on foreign policy was not universally recognized as a condition of membership in the organization. *National Review*'s decision to run a front-cover story followed by fourteen pages of analysis wholly denouncing the organization led in the interim to a fall in sales and advertising. The falloff, however, was largely because of the journal's wholesale denunciation of the JBS, a policy opposed by Rusher and feared by Goldwater, not because most followers of the JBS endorsed the organization's call for withdrawal from Vietnam.

The promotion of a patriotic campaign by conservatives was encouraged by the demonstrative efforts of local organizations and by more national campaigns. The fear of appearing overtly pro-war inhibited individual or group efforts in support of Vietnam. Thus the theme of supporting the troops resonated with Americans who were reluctant to assume the tactics of anti-war protesters. But individual acts of support for the troops in Vietnam, undertaken by "Young Republicans and Young Democrats; by Lions, Moose, Elks and Masons; by the American Legion, the Jewish War Veterans, the VFW, DAR; by church groups, women's clubs, PTAs, the Junior Chamber of Commerce, and Boy Scouts; by garden clubs, labor unions, and 4-H groups; by local newspapers and television stations," cannot be entirely separated from support for the war itself.[31] Activities like blood drives, gift programs, and pro-war and pro-government rallies became more prevalent as anti-war sentiment became increasingly vocal and explicit. Yet it would be false to assume that open expressions of support for the American effort in Vietnam were undertaken merely because of social and moral rejection of the aims and methods of the radical Left. Rather, they should be viewed as manifestations of faith in some or all of the goals for which the United States was fighting in Vietnam: for example, belief that Americans were defending the independence of a weaker people; that they were extending democracy and protecting that of the United States; and that the war was a latent means of undermining the Soviet threat. Many Americans may have had difficulty fully articulating why the war in Vietnam was directly related to American security, a factor indicated by YAF's constant focus on educating people about the real meaning of the war, with the result that emphasizing support for the troops and for the government became the most relevant means of confirming American involvement in Southeast Asia.

The most dramatic exhibition of support for U.S. troops serving in Vietnam took place in May 1967 with the mammoth rally We Support Our Boys in Vietnam. Raymond Gimmler, a New York Fire Department chief, a veteran of the Second World War, and an active member of the East Rockaway division of the American Legion, probably would not have conceived of the idea of organizing a large-scale patriotic parade of this nature had it not been for his disgust at the "peaceniks" and "anti-Americans" protesting the war. Gimmler was evidently motivated by a desire to strike back at the ever-growing anti-war protest movement. Opposition to the war had been evident since its earliest days. As early as August 1964 a rally to protest the Johnson administration's military policies in Vietnam was broken up by police in New York City. Organized by the May 2nd Movement, the demonstration's two named speakers, "who had long been active in leftish causes," were individuals who were reported to have traveled to Cuba, which resulted in one of them being called before the House Un-American Activities Committee. A ban on such protests in this area had been imposed since 1962, and seventeen people were arrested. The *New York Times* reported that demonstrators chanted their opposition to "Fascist cops" and carried signs reading, "Stop Johnson's War Against the Vietnamese People" and "Send Troops to Mississippi—Not to Vietnam."[32] The student-dominated and leftist sympathies of the demonstrators characterized early accounts of anti-war demonstrations, which served to highlight their marginal relationship to mainstream public opinion. By 1967 the marginality of dissent was questionable, given the hearings into the Vietnam War overseen by the Senate Foreign Relations Committee and the publication of *The Arrogance of Power*, a widely read book written by the committee's chairman, Senator Fulbright. Large-scale public demonstrations against the war remained the purview of radical elements of the anti-war movement during this period, however. Dissent over the war was therefore often equated with disorder and challenges to traditional conceptions of American patriotism. This perspective was certainly reflected in the goals of Gimmler's rally.

Gimmler petitioned the American Legion to endorse his planned parade and established an organizing committee. The committee issued a statement of purpose that attested to their goal of gaining maximum support for the demonstration in favor of U.S. engagement in Vietnam: "Peace is not the issue—all sane men are for peace. Our purpose is to morally support our servicemen in the field." The committee maintained that it was not taking a position on the administration's policy and did not deny the right of those who opposed the war to protest against it. Yet it also made clear that the parade was designed to challenge "attacks on our nation and the impression given to the world of a people who oppose their country. Above all we are striving to assure our fighting men in Vietnam that they have the full respect, love, prayers and backing of the American People." The committee was convinced that its efforts represented the "*authentic* voice of the American people."[33] The goal of ensuring that as many Americans as possible would unite behind the parade's core message of national unity led the committee to avoid any ideologically narrow or partisan connotations. But the parade was repeatedly portrayed as an antidote to the anti-war demonstration that had taken place in New York City on April 15, 1967, the scene of a much-publicized burning of the American flag. Gimmler's aim was to refute anti-Americanism while also highlighting the association of such behavior with the anti-war movement, implicitly relating patriotism with support for the government's objectives in Vietnam.

Gimmler and his associates, while contributing a great deal to the organization and promotion of the event, relied heavily on the legitimating sponsorship of the American Legion. The legion's financial contribution as well as its resources in the area of mass distribution of information immensely aided the group's activities. Having accepted the parade committee's request to distribute information about the event, the New York Veterans of Foreign Wars (VFW) informed its post commanders of the "mammoth Patriotic Parade," giving its full blessing to the event. The commander of the VFW's New York Department, Herbert Brian, made clear to Gimmler, however, that the VFW "has for a number of years conducted a program for the very same purposes," likening the parade to the VFW's Loyalty Day, a campaign inaugurated when the VFW "first chased the Communists off the streets of New York." Indeed, organizations like the VFW regularly referenced the similarities between the contemporary anti-war movements and earlier groups considered un-American. The parade was therefore described as an opportunity for "every loyal American to demonstrate his loyalty to the Government of the United States and its institutions."[34] The issue of fidelity to America served as a powerful rhetorical tool for those committed to the causes for which the United States was engaged in Vietnam, even when the causes were reduced to such matters as basic anti-communism and the protection of American values. Despite some concerns among VFW members about the trajectory of government policy in Vietnam, the significance of demonstrating loyalty to one's country during wartime prevented the organization from openly questioning the administration's strategy. The focus on public loyalty also had the effect of creating a substantial antithesis toward anti-war protest.

On May 13 tens of thousands of people marched down Fifth Avenue in a parade that lasted almost nine hours. The *New York Times* estimated that seventy thousand people, in a "forest of American flags" and "stirred by martial music," marched in the parade.[35] The organizing committee argued, however, that the Police Department had earlier estimated that twice as many people were involved. The

Public Broadcasting Service provided live coverage of the parade for thirteen hours, which was later used by the parade's committee and the American Legion to create a documentary. The conservative Freedoms Foundation at Valley Forge awarded the filmmakers a prize in 1968, which enabled the committee to reproduce and widely disseminate the documentary among patriotic and conservative youth groups.

Conservative groups attempted to co-opt the allegedly apolitical parade. The event found a welcome sponsor in the New York Conservative Party, a political organization founded in 1962 that ran candidates in local and state elections, one of whom was Buckley when he ran as a mayoral candidate in New York City in 1965.[36] Promising that notable conservative leaders, including Buckley and Kieran O'Doherty, a founder of the New York Conservative Party, were to attend the parade, the party's poster urged citizens to "counteract the vicious anti-American spectacle" of the April antiwar demonstration.[37] The Conservative Party's stance with regard to the Vietnam War, which corresponded with that of conservatives such as those at *National Review,* furthered the already widespread belief that the parade was a demonstration of faith in the objectives the United States was fighting to achieve in Vietnam. The national board of YAF followed suit, requesting that its chapter chairmen in the area of New York send Victory in Viet Nam buses to the parade. In promoting the event, YAF's *Action Line,* which was distributed by members for public consumption, urged more than mere attendance at the parade and support of the troops. They asked attendees to "to write their Congressman, U.S. Senators, and President Johnson [asking them] to take all necessary steps [to] win the war in Viet Nam, to support those military advisers who recommend the bombing of airfields in North Viet Nam, [and] to enable American fighting men in Viet Nam to carry out the necessary missions to defeat the Communist aggressors."[38] YAF's objective was to incorporate its demands for change in administration policy into the main thrust of the parade; specifically, they tried to associate support for the troops with endorsement of removing the military restrictions on Americans fighting in Vietnam.

The hawks were certainly the winners on this occasion, in that many who appeared in the parade carried signs urging the use of greater force. Indeed, several of the signs carried by marchers urged the administration to "Bomb Hanoi."[39] The *New York Times* reported that the "usual atmosphere" of the parade was "belligerent; It showed clearly in such signs as: 'Down with the Reds,' 'My country right or wrong,' 'Hey, hey, what do you say; let's support the USA,' 'Give the boys moral ammo,' . . . 'God bless us patriots, may we never go out of style,' and 'Escalate, don't capitulate.'" According to the *New York Times*, although the parade was mainly orderly, "a dozen times paraders or their sympathizers attacked individuals displaying signs urging the end of the war or expressing such sentiments. A man who was said to be a bystander was smeared with tar and feathers." The overall image projected by the event was one of patriotic backing of the war and of the president rather than a lack of faith in administration policy. The mood created, particularly the violent ejection of a group of anti-war protestors who claimed they were expressing support for the troops by demanding their immediate return home, was ultimately one of faith in the cause for which the United States was engaged in Vietnam.[40]

Conservatives were already active in the effort to equate patriotic duty with advocacy of a victory strategy in Vietnam. Intellectuals decried the aid that protests gave to the enemy and argued that the administration had failed to make the public aware of the vital nature of the war vis-à-vis U.S. security and strategic interests. Politicians were more inclined to directly associate dissent with a lack of patriotism. Goldwater asserted in 1966 that he was "ashamed to . . . see [Democrats] telling the American people that our power has made America arrogant and self-righteous and expansionist and immoral." "No American," he declared, "has the right to or the justification to level such charges against his country. And that goes double for doing it in a time of war and in a fashion that lends comfort to our enemies."[41] Goldwater continued to maintain that the war was just and necessary, but he also conveyed the message that patriotism demanded that the sacrifice of American life and resources be balanced by full national support for the war. This view was reiterated by his criticism of Secretary McNamara, in which he claimed that so much had been sacrificed by 1967 that "no honorable man can walk away from a war to which he has sent hundreds of thousands of men."[42] Goldwater and his fellow conservatives were not alone in this view, especially in their association of anti-war protest with un-Americanism. While recognizing that many Americans were frustrated with the war by 1967, conservatives understood that broad antipathy toward the anti-war movement could prevent the growth of mainstream opposition to the war.[43] Conservatives promoted this process and actively welcomed the cultural and political polarization that the war appeared to be contributing to by 1967.

The origins of neoconservatism were related to Democrats' rejection of the trajectory of liberals' domestic and foreign policies during this period. But one must recognize the extent to which traditional conservatism reoriented its propaganda offensive in order to associate its agenda with that of groups who opposed the radicalism of the anti-war movement. David Levy notes that many liberal policy intellectuals drifted rightward in response to both the "lukewarm conduct of military operations" and the protest, which "seemed to represent profoundly troubling attacks upon the values, the institutions, the faiths that had made America the most successful country in history."[44] This shift to the right, symbolized by the development of such publications as *Public Interest* in 1965, signified a broader attack on the nature of liberalism, but it was also evidence of the increasing presentation of conservative goals in opposition to those of anti-war protestors and politicians.

For YAF, the founders of which had organized the Student Committee for the Loyalty Oath in 1958, teach-ins on the Vietnam War were not only unpatriotic but also bordered on treason.[45] Conservatives, including popular figures like the actor John Wayne, attempted to use the issue of protest to enhance support for the war. By utterly discrediting anti-war protestors and by extension the cause they advocated, proponents of the necessity of the war attempted to move popular support away from issues relating to initial engagement toward the association of patriotic duty with support for the Vietnam conflict. Reagan attacked anti-war protestors throughout his gubernatorial campaign in 1966 and also subtly opposed Johnson's policies by passively claiming that the military was "being denied the right to try for victory." Wayne was more forthright and stated in December 1967, "I think they oughta shoot 'em if they're carrying the Vietcong flag." Rick Perlstein writes that the "culture within which Ronald Reagan thrived was enveloping the nation."[46] While many of those who participated in the "We Support Our Boys in Vietnam" parade would have decried conservatives' social and economic policies, such events were nonetheless influencing the evolution of the conservative movement. As the war became more broadly unpopular, conservatives could not long ignore the power of harnessing popular rejections of the anti-war movement to serve their political fortunes.

YOUTHFUL ACTIVISM

Parades designed to honor the war effort and those who served in Vietnam were commonplace across the United States at this time. They tended to be small-scale events, often associated with local annual events such as Veterans' Day commemorations. Such initiatives were invariably short-lived campaigns or single events. Indeed, a demonstration on the scale of the mass We Support Our Boys parade of 1967 was not repeated until 1969. By 1968 it was obvious that young conservatives were the vanguard of public activism in favor of the war, echoing the role of students in early anti-war endeavors. YAF was responsible for both national and local campus demonstrations, which included the organization's picketing of the White House in 1965. YAF echoed hawks' focus on urging Johnson to "allow the military the freedom to secure victory" in Vietnam.[47] Gregory Schneider has argued that Tom Charles Huston, the national chairman of YAF in 1965, who subsequently worked as a Nixon presidential aide, "was obsessed about the Vietnam issue," having worked on behalf of the Asian People's Anti-Communist League and the World Youth Crusade for Freedom.[48] Huston's commitment to victory in Vietnam gave momentum to the students' activism, but it need not be seen as a defining force. Activism in the name of Vietnam was an extension of YAF's anticommunist efforts, which were without doubt the most vociferously implemented aspect of the group's credo.

Having succeeded in pressuring Firestone Tire and Rubber

Company to withdraw from a planned plant development in Romania, YAF launched similar campaigns of publicity, lobbying, and propaganda against American Motors Corporation and against IBM's trade with the Soviet Union.[49] The Firestone and IBM campaigns were designed to be emblematic of YAF's dominant objectives: highlighting the continued threat of international communism and undermining the acceptability of trade and cooperation with states supplying the North Vietnamese and, by extension, the southern insurgents with the means to attack Americans and their Vietnamese allies. In an attempt to demonstrate the absurdity of trading with those "captive nations" aiding North Vietnam, YAF campus chapters organized the shipment of medical supplies and reading material to Vietnam.[50] YAF disseminated a series of issues papers in 1968, the fourth of which was titled "East–West Trade: Committing National Suicide." Arguing that "it should have been self-evident that aid to the USSR is inimical to U.S. interests," YAF's national board charged that even the selling of wheat to the Soviet Union increased its war potential and its ability to aid North Vietnam: "Since 1963 the U.S. has built 15 fertilizer plants in the USSR, and now Soviet fertilizer is a major item of war aid to North Vietnam," while "Poland is levying a 10 percent surtax on all salaries to finance its aid to North Vietnam."[51] YAF explained that the government's "illogical" behavior could be explained by the fact that it viewed communist initiatives as "unrelated and uncoordinated." This assumption, they charged, was absurd.[52] In all its activities, not simply those directly related to anticommunism, YAF attempted to promote the cause and necessity of victory in Vietnam and to associate this issue with existing patriotic campaigns of support for the troops.

Between 1964 and 1968 these efforts were largely based around countering the anti-war opinions propagated by their left-wing counterpart, Students for a Democratic Society (SDS). At a national level YAF campaigned for a change in administration policy but urged its constituent members to concentrate on undermining the message of SDS on campus. One such figure, Harvey Hukari of San Francisco State University, began organizing the early pro-war events to counter anti-war teach-ins in 1964 and then founded the

YAF chapter at Stanford, which became one of YAF's most powerful, in 1966. In her study of young political activists of the 1960s the sociologist Rebecca Klatch found that the main catalyst for conservative student activism was anticommunism, while some stated "they were initially drawn to YAF because of its support for the war."[53] YAF's activism was divided between its twin goals of opposing the Left on campus and contributing to high-level discussions of government policy. Partly because of the ambitions of its leaders, the national board of YAF was often preoccupied with policy debates. In the long term this preoccupation would impact YAF's ability to effectively challenge anti-war activism on campus. YAF's policy prescriptions mirrored those expressed by conservative leaders, above all because of the group's close links to the ACU and *National Review*.

The Evolution of Conservative Policy

With the exception of the JBS's demonstrative rejection of the Vietnam War in 1965, the conservative position on the war changed little between 1965 and 1968. If conservatives had not been at the vanguard in pushing the United States into Southeast Asia in 1964, they undoubtedly became the primary advocates of winning the war once the Johnson administration publicly introduced the large-scale deployment of troops in 1965. Those who had advocated that the United States intervene to sustain its commitment to South Vietnam continued to argue in this vein, even as the American effort offered only mixed results. They also continued to use the war to lambaste Democrats' foreign policy priorities and military strategies. In January 1967, Burnham, echoing conservatives' attacks on the administration's failure to clarify the real significance of the war, declared the Vietnam War a "major historical turning point, comparable to, but probably more critical than, the Greek civil war and the combined Hungary–Suez affair." "Victory in Vietnam," he determined, "would vindicate those at home, as well as globally, who believe it better to confront threats standing up than crawling."[54] Meyer reiterated this point in October; he warned that "the true weakness of the Johnson Administration lies not in its continuation of the Vietnam war, but in its abysmal failure to comprehend the relationship of this war to the general struggle against Communism." He restated the conservatives' pre-war arguments that wars of national liberation would have to be fought by the United States, "if we are not to lose the overarching cold war to the Siamese twins of Soviet and Chinese Communism." Such wars, he concluded, were the "primary offensive resource in their drive to dominate the world under the conditions of a balance of nuclear terror."[55]

New pro-war voices emerged during 1967 to challenge conservatives' prescription of the necessary measures for victory in Vietnam and reflected the White House's efforts to shift political attention away from a focus on military victory. In an effort to thwart opposition to the administration's strategy, the Johnson White House created the Citizens Committee for Peace with Freedom in Vietnam (CCPFV). Ostensibly a nonpartisan educational committee, the CCPFV was organized when Johnson aides invited Paul H. Douglas, a former Democratic senator, to form a pro-Vietnam, pro-administration citizens' committee. It received vital funding from the administration, belying Douglas's claim that "we aren't part of any [administration] attack or counterattack and we have no ties to anyone or anything except our own consciences." With administration backing Douglas secured the active support of prominent individuals who had long supported the war. These included former government officials, including Presidents Truman and Eisenhower and Secretaries Dean Acheson and Arthur Byrnes. Gen. Omar Bradley was the most prominent of the military figures who joined the committee.

The White House was keen to ensure that the CCPFV represented diverse social and political interests and was not simply an organization made up of former government officials. Archbishop Robert Lucey of San Antonio, who was well known for his activism in improving the working conditions of laborers in Texas, accepted an invitation to join the CCPFV. His pro-war stance reflected that of the Catholic hierarchy in the United States. The nation's most renowned labor leader, George Meaney, the president of the American Federation of Labor/Congress of Industrial Organizations

(AFL-CIO), had long voiced his support of the American effort in Vietnam. His participation in the CCPFV was a function of the long-standing efforts made by Meaney and Jay Lovestone, the director of the AFL-CIO's International Affairs Department, to promote international anticommunist initiatives. The AFL-CIO formed close contacts with labor unions in Saigon and provided financial aid to sustain these unions throughout much of the war. Meaney's role in the CCPFV demonstrated his commitment to anticommunist efforts in South Vietnam as well as his public support of the Johnson administration's handling of the conflict. His high-profile backing of Johnson enhanced the image of organized labor's association with the Vietnam War. The administration attempted to promote this association and to portray support for the war as a position typical of mainstream values. In launching the CCPFV, Douglas decried partisan divisions and claimed that the group's "aim is to become the voice of those who support the bi-partisan fundamentals of American foreign policy." He said that the CCPFV would explicitly "speak for the 'Silent Center.'" The CCPFV was, he argued, "making the common sense presentation of the alternative to the extremes known as dove and hawk—the extremists who want to either pull out on the one hand or start dropping nuclear bombs all over the place and very possibly start World War III on the other."[56]

Douglas's attack on intellectual conservatives and their demands for greater use of military force was made without reservation, yet the CCPFV espoused many principles shared by conservatives as it sought to educate the American people about the vital importance of America's commitment to South Vietnam. The CCPFV denied the hawks' arguments that the war could be won by relying solely on bombing of the North, which was in reality a simplified view of the conservative argument, but they did not disagree with conservatives' concept of victory. Certainly the pro-administration group's understanding of victory differed from that of the conservative movement, most notably in the former's acceptance that limited war did not in itself constitute the triumph of the weaker side. Neither would conservatives in 1967 have been so sure of the CCPFV statement that "there is no purely military solution to the limited conflict in which we are engaged." They utterly rejected, furthermore, the claim that the "determination [of the United States] to succeed is no less strong because our resistance to aggression is limited." The tone of the CCPFV was markedly different from that of the ACU and YAF, but its overall thesis rested on the same foundations on which conservatives based the meaning of the war. Echoing conservative hawks, the CCPFV declared, "Hanoi cannot always take and never give; always demand everything and never concede anything. A sequence of unilateral concessions by us, not reciprocated by Hanoi, would be the road to surrender. It might take a little bit longer than a unilateral withdrawal, but it would be surrender all the same."[57] If the CCPFV's members did not necessarily demand escalation, they were not willing to countenance any kind of surrender or withdrawal from Vietnam. As such, they reflected the diversity of opinion among those who claimed to be supporters of the war. The CCPFV challenged dovish dissent against the administration's policies while demonstrating that calls for escalation were fruitless. It may have added legitimacy to the president's policies, but it could not overcome the ever-greater divisions between hawks and doves.

By 1967 some conservative leaders were beginning to attack the Republican Party for its apparent failure to more fully challenge the administration on Vietnam and to assume a more principled stand on major international issues. In part such reluctance was a sign of Republicans' concerns over appearing to be unpatriotic by openly challenging the administration's handling of the war. More significant, it was also a sign of the growing divisions over Vietnam within the party. Influential Republicans such as Sen. Mark Hatfield of Oregon and Sen. John Sherman Cooper of Kentucky articulated opposition to the war on the basis of religious and moral as well as strategic grounds.[58] Conservatives worried that the party was overly concerned with, at best, adopting the role of the loyal opposition or, at worst, openly questioning the purpose of the war. Meyer claimed that "a new form of opportunism threatens the integrity of the Republican Party." Rather than hold a firm anticommunist line, moderates in the party were truckling to the left-liberal and radical ideologues who questioned the necessity of fighting in Vietnam. Meyer recognized the political gains to be made by attacking the Democratic president's polices in Southeast Asia, particularly given public confusion over the war's purpose. But he argued that Republicans should instead emphasize Johnson's "failures—political, psychological, strategical—as commander-in-chief in the worldwide cold war against Communism." Simply accentuating the limits of his Vietnam policies was insufficient. He concluded, "To pander to popular confusion by attacking the waging of the Vietnam war instead, would be, both for the Republican Party and the country, an act of destructive cynicism."[59] Meyer's prescription for Republican Party policy was not necessarily indicative of his faith in the party, which by 1967 was minimal compared to that of many of his fellow conservatives, but it was indicative of growing divisions among those who labeled themselves hawks on the Vietnam War.

Burnham, while still convinced of the imperative of winning the war and committed to the Republican Party, privately accepted that victory was impossible because the present strategy, especially negotiations, was ineffective and unlikely to be dramatically altered.[60] Yet throughout the period from 1964 to 1968 conservatives not only acted to promote the war effort in Vietnam and persisted in the view that it was necessary to "save freedom *everywhere*" but also insisted that military victory and a relatively quick and easy conclusion to the war were both possible and essential.[61]

They were not immune to the domestic impacts of the war. A majority of Americans may have continued to support the war effort by late 1967, but public anxiety over what appeared to be a stalemate in Vietnam was growing. It is doubtful that conservative leaders placed much faith in the possibility of an unequivocal victory following the Tet offensive of January and February 1968 and Johnson's dramatic peace overtures of March 31, 1968. David Schmitz has convincingly argued that the significance of the Tet offensive was not related to its impact on public opinion. "Rather," he claims, "the Tet Offensive was the decisive moment in the Vietnam War due to its impact on senior officials in the Johnson administration and elite opinion that brought about Johnson's dramatic decisions and change in policy."[62] Public opinion had already been turning against the war, and public discontent rose dramatically during 1967 as a result of higher casualties in what appeared to be a deadlocked war, negative economic fallout from the war, and the growing legitimacy of dissent as a result of the Fulbright hearings. In October 1967 a plurality of Americans polled stated, by a margin of 46 percent to 44 percent, that the war had been a mistake. This shift in opinion was not brought about by the Tet offensive, but the trend toward believing that intervention had been a mistake took on new momentum for the rest of the year. An ever greater number of Americans came to believe that the United States was losing the war.[63]

Conservatives may also have believed that the United States was on its back foot in Vietnam during 1968, but they did not conclude that the cause was lost. Intellectual conservatives and the Republican right continued to argue that escalation was the only legitimate response to the dire military situation. They were aware by mid-1968, however, that the Johnson administration was unlikely to reverse its moves toward negotiation and a winding down of the war effort. Conservatives also had reduced expectations regarding the Republican Party, which resulted from the potential volatility of Vietnam as an issue in the presidential campaign. As the race for the White House intensified, conservatives stood as the most active pro-war lobby and were encouraged by their newfound political clout going into the Republican primaries. Richard Nixon, the formidable cold warrior who had built his early career on exposing communist sympathizers at home and who had forcefully challenged the Johnson administration's handling of the war since 1964, became the standard-bearer in the campaign to find a successful, victorious solution to the Vietnam morass. Nixon had built his return to politics on challenging Johnson's handling of the Vietnam War, and had by 1968 succeeded in making himself the president's debating partner on Vietnam.[64] He enjoyed the luxury of not being tied by the obligations of office at this time, and, as Johns notes, he was therefore "free to state his objections to policy without having to account to Congress or the electorate."[65] Nixon was better able to alter his policy as the winds of public opinion and military progress changed course. He proposed several alternatives to the president's policies between 1965 and 1968, and his preferred policy for ending the war remained unclear as his momentum toward the presidential nomination increased. The extent to which he viewed Vietnam in the same terms as his conservative allies remained to be seen.

CHAPTER 3
Conservatives for Nixon

The Domestic Politics of Vietnam, 1968–1969

> For four years this Administration has had at its disposal the greatest military and economic advantage that one nation has ever had over another in any war in history. . . . Never has so much military and economic and diplomatic power been used so ineffectively.
>
> Richard Nixon, speech on accepting the Republican presidential nomination, August 8, 1968

Richard Nixon's rhetoric on the centrality of the Vietnam War to America's credibility differed little from that of pro-war conservatives during the early to mid-1960s. Building on his reputation as an arch-anticommunist and determined to augment the political leverage of the Republican Party, Nixon used the Vietnam issue as he had anticommunism and the House Un-American Activities Committee during his early career. A vocal hawk, Nixon urged military escalation and railed against the administration's intermittent bombing halts. He began advocating a limit on the deployment of American troops in Vietnam while echoing hawkish demands for expanded and intensified air and naval campaigns. His vocal criticism of Johnson was based not on opposition to the administration's escalation of the war but on its failure to do so more rapidly and comprehensively. His position in this regard was wholly harmonious with that of pro-war conservatives.

Nixon's expectations, but not his understanding of the importance of concluding the war favorably, underwent subtle but marked alteration as popular support wavered and U.S. strategy in Vietnam reaffirmed rather than challenged the military and political stalemate. During the presidential primaries in March 1968 Nixon reportedly confided to his aides Richard Whalen, Patrick Buchanan, and Ray Price that he believed "there's no way to win the war." No president, he argued, could win a popular and congressional mandate for the military measures needed to accomplish that task. Whalen later reported that Nixon stated that although he no longer believed military victory possible, "we have to seem to say the opposite, just to keep some degree of bargaining leverage."[1] Nixon may have been alluding to the American negotiating strategy with the North Vietnamese, but he was also resolved to shore up his political support among people still pushing for victory. He was determined, furthermore, to appear as the candidate of national unity, the candidate who would defy the divisiveness caused by anti-war protest.

In conversation with Eisenhower in 1967 Nixon agreed with the former president that Johnson should have used greater force at the outset of the war, when popular support was firmly on his side. By 1968 Nixon was confident that such measures would no longer be allowed by public opinion.[2] He moved toward acceptance of ending the war by negotiated settlement but continued to assert the overriding relevance of Vietnam to the global position of the United States and starkly refused to accept the diminution of South Vietnamese freedom. America's objectives would be achieved by exerting military and diplomatic pressure on its enemies in Southeast Asia, including the Soviet Union. The means by which such leverage was to be levied upon the enemy altered depending on government policy, public opinion, and Nixon's personal political objectives. Primarily, the presidential hopeful relied on traditional hawkish demands: the bombing of North Vietnam, Laos, and Cambodia coupled with an ultimatum threatening greater material damage if a negotiated settlement was not accepted on American terms.

This gradual move toward acceptance of a negotiated settlement, albeit one with minimal American compromise, characterized the positions of conservatives as well, who had by then fundamentally altered their expectations of military victory. This did not indicate a diminished faith in the efficacy of full-scale military efforts to destroy the North Vietnamese capacity to wage war. Neither did it suggest acceptance that the war's outcome would not crucially affect the credibility of the United States and other foreign policy objectives. Indeed, in June 1968 Buckley outlined conservatives' expectations of the Republican Party, and topping the list was the demand that the party continue to recognize the value of the American effort in Vietnam and work to ensure that any agreement would prevent communists from gaining control of the South.³ The conservatives' altered position was impacted by rapidly changing public and governmental assumptions regarding the longevity of the war and the requirements for total victory. The gradual move toward acceptance of a negotiated settlement relied on demands that North Vietnam be given an ultimatum, the presumed rejection of which would lead to military strikes until the enemy capitulated and agreed to American terms for settlement. It was rooted in the conviction that communists could not be expected to uphold international agreements, must be forced into compliance, and be subject to heavy penalties for any transgressions. The *means* of ending the war remained as critical as the final settlement. And Nixon's determination and ability to deliver on these goals was unclear during 1968.

Nixon and the Hawks

By 1966 Nixon was actively courting the Right; his efforts to secure the support of the conservative wing of the Republican Party began as soon as Goldwater won the party's presidential nomination in 1964. He had not been a strong supporter of Goldwater before this time, however. Only days after Goldwater's success in the California primary, Nixon attempted to organize a Stop Goldwater campaign at the Republican governors' convention in Cleveland, sitting up "until 3 a.m. trying to convince [George] *Romney* to enter the race."⁴ Fearing that Goldwater's campaign and his image as an extremist might damage and divide the Republican Party, Nixon publicly stated, "Looking to the future of the party, it would be a tragedy if Senator Goldwater's views as previously stated were not challenged—and repudiated."⁵ Nixon was concerned about

Goldwater's image as an extremist in foreign affairs, particularly his outspoken opposition to all measures leading toward détente. The two did not sharply disagree over the conflict in Vietnam. But Nixon was preoccupied about Goldwater's domestic programs and correctly presumed that a Goldwater candidacy would divide the Republican Party and receive only minimal electoral support.

Nixon's position changed dramatically as soon as Goldwater won the nomination. Party loyalty may have been in his blood, but he was aware of the personal political leverage to be gained by appearing as a solid supporter of the party. *Human Events* declared with some irony that "Nixon campaigned harder for Goldwater than Goldwater did," having traveled over 35,000 miles in 35 states and given over 150 speeches promoting Goldwater's presidential bid.[6]

Most liberals and moderates in the Republican Party argued that Goldwater's electoral defeat signified the reduced influence of the conservative wing of the party. Nixon seemed to think otherwise. At a press conference the day after Goldwater conceded the election, Nixon declared that the "strong conservative wing of the Republican party deserves a major voice in party councils."[7] His efforts on behalf of the Goldwater campaign paid off. From 1964 he was consistently praised by Goldwater and won the approbation of other leading conservatives, including John Tower, Thurmond, Buckley, John Ashbrook, and the political strategist Peter O'Donnell.[8] Nixon's stance on foreign policy served to reinforce this support. Conservatives' championing of Nixon in the Republican primaries of 1968 was crucial in ensuring his success both in securing the nomination and winning the national election. By emphasizing law and order he convinced southern conservatives he would stem the tide of civil rights advances and thereby won Thurmond's decisive support. His broader appeal among conservatives was conditioned by his position on foreign policy, however. Nixon fostered a centrist political philosophy but judiciously cultivated an image of determined opposition to communism at home and abroad.

Nixon had in fact built his return to politics after his defeat in the California gubernatorial election in 1962 on opposition to Johnson's handling of the Vietnam War and thus capitalized on his anticommunist credentials.⁹ By the summer of 1964 Nixon had charged that Democrats such as Fulbright were advocating policies that were causing "our Asian allies" to lose "faith in us." Rejecting Fulbright's "more flexible, less firm policy toward communism" and his suggestion that U.S. policy toward China be reexamined, Nixon charged that such calls "have had a massive impact in increasing the fear that the United States will weaken its resolve, and that Red China is riding the wave of the future." The contrary was in fact true, Nixon declared, as communism had lost its popular appeal, could now be spread only by force, and was at its weakest point since the Second World War because of divisions between the Soviet Union and China. What was needed was recognition of American resolve in Asia, and, according to Nixon, the timing was fortuitous: "There are those who say that this is the wrong war at the wrong place at the wrong time. The contrary is true. If we are ever to stop the communist advance in Asia the time is now. The place is Vietnam. . . . If this country really wants to turn back the communist advance in Asia, this, then, is the time and place to do it."¹⁰

Nixon denied that the war might escalate to nuclear conflict, citing the Sino-Soviet split as evidence that the United States could look forward to holding a dominant position in Southeast Asia. This contrasted with conservatives' long-held argument that liberals had overestimated the tensions and rivalry between the Soviet Union and the PRC. That certain tensions existed between the two communist powers was largely undisputed, but the severity of the feud was attenuated, according to conservatives, by their common expansionist goals. Nixon did, however, articulate the conservative understanding of Vietnam as an opportunity for the United States to resurrect a strong foreign policy and concurred with many on the Right who denied that the Vietminh and the NLF had originated among the Vietnamese people. Their nationalist aspirations had been usurped by international "Communist colonialism," while the current insurgency was no more than "externally supported guerrilla action."¹¹ Nixon also subscribed to conservatives' push for the use of air and naval operations to cut off supply routes before the Johnson administration initiated Rolling Thunder in February 1965. Speaking to the Sales Executive Club of New York on January 26, 1965, Nixon stated that unless there was a change in strategy "we will be thrown out in a matter of months—certainly within the year." Nixon declared his opposition to the neutralization of Vietnam, stating, "Neutrality where the Communists are concerned means three things: we get out; they stay in; they take over."[12]

Writing to Goldwater following Johnson's initiation of the bombing campaign in February 1965, Nixon advocated a harder line. He feared that the Democratic administration would not follow through on its initiated policy. It was essential, he maintained, to push the government "to use whatever air and sea power is necessary to cut off the flow of all arms and men from North Vietnam into South Vietnam."[13] Nixon's public position was no less formidable, arguing that American military commanders were denied permission to bomb legitimate military targets around Hanoi and that Haiphong harbor should be mined immediately. His reference in May 1966, while in Birmingham, Alabama, to the "fact" that "thousands of American boys wouldn't be dead today" if Johnson had bombed North Vietnam earlier was representative of his consistent position.[14] That viewpoint helped cement his image among conservatives as the principal advocate of the hawkish position on Vietnam, an image no doubt aided by Johnson's attacks on Nixon's line of thought.[15]

Nixon's globalist perspective on the war in Vietnam appeared to preclude the possibility of an American withdrawal, which would lead to a collapse of the Saigon regime. He not only agreed with Eisenhower's maxim that such a move would lead to the PRC's assuming domination of 60 percent of the world's population, but also charged that in that event the United States would be unable to achieve any of its other foreign policy goals. By 1967 Nixon referred only to the immense importance of maintaining American prestige and credibility and gave little indication that his foreign policies might contradict basic conservative goals or ideology. This stance did not preclude some conservatives from questioning

Nixon, particularly given his failure to take a public stand on the question of China. Nixon's conservative defenders were quick to point out that any ambiguity rested on appearance, not substance.

Writing to Marvin Liebman, the conservative public relations guru, in June 1968, Tom Charles Huston, the former chair of YAF who was working on the Nixon campaign, questioned the extent to which conservatives could hope to convince Nixon to make a hard-line stand regarding China during the campaign. His concern was not with Nixon's position on China. "I have heard him say in private," Huston wrote, "that he believes China will be the most serious problem with which the next President will have to deal." Huston claimed that Nixon "is particularly concerned with Red China as a potential nuclear power." He concluded that the "members of his Foreign Policy working staff are nearly uniform in their commitment to a hard line," while he believed that with the help of Walter Judd it might be possible to push Nixon to make a firmer public commitment in opposition to concessions toward China.[16] In any case, Nixon's aim of "pulling China back into the world community . . . as a great and progressing nation, not as the epicenter of world revolution" was ameliorated by his focus on restraining "China's Asian ambitions" by strengthening Asian nations.[17] Conservatives had little problem accepting Nixon's China policy in the context of his overall hard line in relations with the communist world.

By 1968 Nixon's message to the conservative pro-war lobby was somewhat ambiguous; he did not publicly articulate a specific means of ending the war, but he was able to foster the impression that he would act with resolve against communist expansion. Dan Carter argues that by 1967 "Nixon's efforts were long on rhetorical warnings, short on specifics . . . and only marginally indicative of the kind of bold departures in foreign policy that would mark his presidency." Carter sees Nixon's image as a vociferous anticommunist as fundamental to his winning the support of key conservatives in the South who believed there was communist influence in the civil rights and anti-war movements, issues that greatly influenced the southern electorate in 1968.[18] Conservative leaders, whether primarily motivated by domestic or international policies, unmistakably based much of their understanding of Nixon's policies on preconceived ideas regarding the former vice president's arch-anticommunism.

Nixon's perception that he needed the support of conservatives to win the nomination and election was complemented by conservatives' resolve to undermine the influence of the southern populist George Wallace, the candidate of the Independent Party. The barriers between conservative political thought and political activity were breaking down at the same time the movement was threatened with further debilitating divisions because of grassroots and financial support for Wallace's populist conservatism.[19] Wallace's presidential bid was backed by many in the JBS, including such key figures as John Wayne, the Texas millionaire H. L. Hunt, and Dean Clarence Manion, whose *Manion Forum* radio show was a primary venue for the dissemination of conservative ideals. Goldwater and others such as Rusher had been very reluctant to disavow the JBS precisely because of the association of Manion and other popular conservatives with the group.[20] The choice of Gen. Curtis LeMay as his running mate bolstered Wallace's appearance of being strong on foreign policy, although the move soon proved contentious when LeMay asserted, "If I found it necessary, I would use anything we could dream up" to end the Vietnam War. Wallace was forced to interject that LeMay had not "*advocated* the use of nuclear weapons" and eventually decided to send LeMay on a fact-finding mission to Southeast Asia, largely in an effort to blunt the impact of the vice presidential candidate's image of extremism.[21]

While foreign affairs took a back seat to issues of domestic discord in rallying people to Wallace's cause, his supporters welcomed his pledge to delegate management of the war to the military and either end the conflict forthwith or withdraw U.S. forces. His position in many respects echoed the private preferences of many conservative Democrats, whose commitment to the standoff in Vietnam was ebbing at this time. Wallace's populist conservatism served only to exacerbate the Republican Right's objection to his unsophisticated foreign policy objectives. Conservative political support for Nixon, as opposed to the more obviously conservative ideologue Reagan, must be understood in light of this danger from Wallace's brand of conservatism. Writing in August 1968, the conservative columnist and political activist John Chamberlain declared that Wallace's persistence in running "can only result in making it easier for his worst enemies." Chamberlain proclaimed that Nixon might "save the day for the Republicans in some of the states that would otherwise go to [Vice President Hubert] Humphrey or to Wallace himself," particularly if he chose Reagan as his running mate. Nonetheless, conservatives could hardly afford the risk, and Chamberlain remained convinced that "Wallace will help the Humphrey or the McCarthy Democrats to some degree as long as he insists on running."[22]

If conservative leaders could broadly agree that Wallace's campaign was not a welcome development, there was less consensus about the choice between Nixon and Reagan. In no small part conservative leaders were increasingly aware of the need for practicality over ideology in the interim period if political power was to be increased. Thurmond's political aide Harry Dent, who later became an adviser to Nixon, played a prominent role in convincing the senator not to support Reagan. Support for Reagan, Dent argued, would simply divide the conservative vote, giving the nomination to Rockefeller and the southern conservative vote in 1968 to Wallace. Thurmond's support of Nixon was based on assurances that he would not be disappointed by the Nixon administration and that Nixon's vice presidential choice would be acceptable to the South. Declaring in June 1968 that Nixon "offers America the best hope of recovering from domestic lawlessness; a bloody no-win war in Southeast Asia; . . . strategic military inferiority; [and] loss of influence in world affairs," Thurmond made clear that a sizable and influential element of the conservative pro-war lobby was relying on Nixon to achieve its aims.[23] Thurmond's backing of Nixon was unflinching at the Republican National Convention, and he immediately withdrew his nomination in favor of Nixon as soon as his name was put forward on the first night of nominations.

Not all conservatives were as confident of Nixon. Rusher, supported by Meyer, vociferously urged his colleagues at *National Review* to endorse Reagan's belated effort to win the Republican nomination and sent bimonthly memoranda to the editorial board on the dangers of siding with Nixon.[24] He later lamented that "Goldwater's own ringing endorsement of Nixon . . . way back in early 1965, was one of the most important boosts that Nixon's candidacy" received; he thought the move resulted in Goldwater's feeling "an acute necessity to minimize the obvious threat that Reagan posed to the Nixon candidacy."[25] Goldwater had actually met with Nixon in June 1966 in order to discuss the presidential race of 1968. He wrote of the meeting, "There is no question in my mind that Dick wants to run," but the "Party and the people are clamoring for a new face," which left Reagan, George Romney, and Sen. Charles Percy. He noted that Reagan "has told me that if he wins [the gubernatorial campaign in California], he does not want to be pushed into a Presidential race as early as '68" but maintained that Reagan "certainly will be a bright new face and one for whom the great bulk of conservatives, . . . if you want to call them Goldwater people, will cry." Goldwater's assumption that "if Reagan emerges as a candidate Dick would not run" proved less prescient.[26]

Despite his hopes for Reagan, Goldwater consistently heralded Nixon's candidacy during 1967 and 1968, often urging Reagan to openly disavow the effort being made to draft him and to release his delegates to Nixon.[27] Goldwater's position reflected that of many within the conservative leadership, especially those within the Republican Party. His early support for Nixon impacted his later attachment to Nixon's presidency and helped determine his reluctance to openly challenge the president's Vietnam policies. In 1968 Goldwater admired Reagan's domestic and foreign policies, regarding him as a more committed conservative ideologue than Nixon. But Goldwater did not believe Reagan could win sufficient support at the Republican National Convention and feared a campaign by him would simply allow a liberal Republican to reap the benefit of a conservative split. In June 1968 Goldwater attempted to make the case more emphatically to Reagan. He predicted that Nixon could win on the first ballot, above all if he gained the support of large states like Texas and California. He reminded Reagan of the political benefits of not standing in the likely nominee's way: "California, which means you, could become the leading power in the Republican Party if Nixon were assured of victory because of a decision on your part to release your delegates together with a statement that your vote would go to Dick." "If we want to make sure that Rockefeller does not go to the convention with any possible chance of being nominated," Goldwater went on, "then a decision on your part along the lines I am suggesting would certainly do the trick."[28] The Reagan campaign was a means of publicizing conservative power and pushing Nixon to the right, but Goldwater was correct that it could not achieve the conservative goal of achieving more immediate political power.

While much of the conservative grassroots preferred a Reagan nomination, conservative leaders had good reason to expect much from a Nixon victory. Nixon's courting of the Right was complemented by the development of a team of conservative policy analysts, including Buchanan and William Gavin as speechwriters, Richard Kleindienst, who had worked on Goldwater's campaign, the economists Paul McCracken, Arthur Burns, Martin Anderson, and Alan Greenspan, and Richard Allen, who was responsible for foreign policy research. Nixon was also understood to have the support of a military advisory council that included the former chairs of the JCS Adm. Arthur Radford and Gen. Nathan Twining.[29]

Both Radford and Twining were forceful advocates of Eisenhower's "New Look" defense policies and publicly emphasized the necessity of relying more heavily on air and naval forces over the use of ground troops. Radford is credited with having first articulated the domino analogy of the probable spread of communism in Southeast Asia, in which each defeated country would cause its neighbor to topple also. As early as 1954 he advocated the employment of air strikes to thwart the Vietnamese advance during the siege of Dien Bien Phu and later recommended that the United States initiate a preemptive strike against the PRC in order to forestall an attack against Quemoy and Matsu, islands in the Taiwan Strait claimed by Taiwan. In 1958 Twining advised that the United States use any and all means to prevent the loss of the islands.[30]

Buchanan became highly active in reassuring those who suspected Nixon was a liberal masked by conservative rhetoric. He publicly declared his admiration for Buckley, one of many acts that both placated the Right and encouraged the association of Nixon with *National Review*.[31] In late 1967 the magazine ran a profile of Nixon, and Buckley invited him to appear on his television show, *Firing Line*. Rusher's continuing efforts on behalf of Reagan prevented the board of *National Review* from formally endorsing Nixon before the convention in Miami in August, but the association between Nixon and the leaders of the conservative movement was becoming increasingly obvious. Rusher described, with some lament, the scene at Miami: "On the convention floor ... Nixon buttons were sported by many another hero" of the Goldwater battle of 1964, including "incontestable conservatives like John Tower and Peter O'Donnell of Texas, Strom Thurmond and Roger Milliken of South Carolina, 'Bo' Calloway of Georgia, Everett Dirksen of Illinois, ... Carl Curtis of Nebraska, Charlton Lyons of Louisiana and a score of others."[32] Chamberlain declared shortly after the convention that Clif White's effort to rally conservative delegates in support of Reagan failed largely because Thurmond and Lyons refused to renounce their support of Nixon, so that "the linchpins in the Nixon pre-balloting strategic construction held."[33]

At the convention Nixon made every effort to dispel conservatives' fears that his foreign policy would not accord with their aims. He remained ambiguous about his specific policies for Vietnam, speaking in terms of "peace with honor" rather than articulating concrete means for achieving U.S. victory. Commentators reported that Nixon had a secret plan for ending the war, a plan he did not want to reveal for fear of undermining the Johnson administration's efforts to secure peace during 1968. Nixon never personally mentioned a secret plan, and in fact he had no such plan but did nothing to dispel the myth that he did.[34] Nixon's vagueness about future policy notwithstanding, he was praised by conservatives. His statement to the Committee on Resolutions of the Republican National Committee, in which he declared that the Johnson administration had wasted the "massive military superiority" of the United States in Vietnam, was interpreted by *Human Events* as an indication of his favored course of action.[35] Referring to the management of the war, Nixon stated simply, "The fact is that our men have not been out-fought; the Administration has been out-thought."³⁶ Nixon was somewhat less equivocating in describing his proposed foreign policy strategy to southern conservatives on August 6. His meeting with the southern Republicans came shortly after Reagan attempted to stake his claim to the hard line in foreign policy during his address to the Republican Platform Committee. In protecting the "national best interest," Reagan declared, it "is vital that we prevent the expansion of communist power in Southeast Asia." "Abandonment of our allies in Vietnam," he warned, "would open the way to greater aggression."

Critically, Reagan accepted the possibility of a settlement in Vietnam that might be less than total military victory: "Only when we increase the effectiveness of our allies' forces in Vietnam, only when political and economic pressures are brought to bear in the world arena, can we have productive peace talks. Our goal must never be less than an honorable peace—one which refuses to hand over South Vietnam—and Southeast Asia—to the Communists."³⁷ Nixon needed to stand firm on Vietnam if he was to retain conservative support, a factor that no doubt influenced the content of his presentation to southern conservatives.

Jeffrey Kimball attests that Nixon's "closed-door, off-the-record remarks" hinted at a policy tactic that has since been described as the "madman theory," the idea that excessive or irrational force *might* be used if the enemy did not comply with American demands within a reasonable period of time. Nixon, reflecting the dominant view within the party, believed that Eisenhower's "subtle diplomatic threat in May 1953 to use atomic bombs against the Chinese and North Koreans so intimidated the Communists that they subsequently compromised some of their demands at the Panmunjom talks," thus bringing an end to the war on terms more favorable to the United States.³⁸ While it can be disputed that Nixon intended to base his policy for ending the Vietnam War or for dealing with the communist threat on the madman theory, he certainly hinted at the likely use of force to coerce the enemy into negotiating during his meeting with conservative Republicans. Regarding Vietnam, he stated that he would follow Eisenhower's means for ending the Korean War: "We'll be militarily strong and diplomatically strong."³⁹ Nixon knew that conservatives would respond positively to his allusion to Eisenhower's alleged threats to the Chinese and North Koreans in 1953. Although many conservatives had opposed the nature of the settlement in Korea, there was widespread accord with regard to the means by which Eisenhower was believed to have compelled the enemy to negotiate. Writing in December 1968, Paul Scott of *Human Events* declared that President Eisenhower's warning to Beijing that the United States would "use all military force necessary to end the conflict . . . caused the Chinese and the North Koreans to agree to a cease-fire in Korea."[40]

Nixon reiterated his recent attack on the administration's "failure to train and equip the South Vietnamese, both for fighting their own war now and for the task of defending their own country after the war is settled."[41] In doing so he hinted at a policy of handing the war over to the South Vietnamese, a course that would become the cornerstone of his plans to extricate the United States from fighting in Southeast Asia. But conservatives were more focused on his suggestion that he would follow Eisenhower's example and use the threat of overwhelming force to bring about acceptable negotiations. Strength in diplomacy, Nixon made clear, was to be founded on military and economic power: "What we've got to do is walk softly and carry a big stick and we can have peace in this world. And that is what we are going to do." Hinting at the potential use of U.S. power, he declared, "I'll tell you one thing. I played a little poker when I was in the Navy. . . . I learned something. . . . When a guy didn't have the cards, he talked awfully big. But when he had the cards, he just sat there—had that cold look in his eyes. Now we've got the cards."[42]

By August 1968 Nixon appeared to have moved more firmly toward accepting a possible U.S. withdrawal from Vietnam.[43] In March he continued to reject withdrawal and urged Johnson to maintain pressure on the enemy, but he increasingly relied on the use of nonmilitary measures to bring the war to a successful conclusion.[44] To his conservative supporters, however, he maintained assurances that where Vietnam was concerned, "I certainly do not intend to change my position in the hope of gaining their [his critics'] approval."[45] Nixon acquiesced in accepting the need for a reduction in troops, but he promoted the use of airpower to force the North Vietnamese to comply with American terms for ending the war. The war could easily be shortened, he claimed, if the American people gave their full support to the effort, thereby denying the enemy the encouragement of domestic division.[46] Recognizing the limits of continued public support of the war, conservative leaders were satisfied to endorse this position.

Certainly many pro-victory analysts concluded that Nixon's position on Vietnam was equivocal. Soon after Nixon's nomination victory, Rusher argued that the "Republican Party, including Mr. Nixon, is purposely ambiguous in its Vietnam platform in order to get votes." Rusher was, at the time, implicitly supporting Nixon's campaign in opposition to Wallace and asserted during the debate that both Humphrey and Wallace were employing similar tactics of ambiguity in order to maximize voter support.[47] Others seemed more convinced that Nixon was the candidate "pledged to the early and victorious conclusion of the war in Vietnam."[48] Nixon's peace with honor was adopted almost at face value, without a great deal of analysis of its actual meaning or the methods by which it was to be achieved. Rather, pro-war supporters of Nixon relied on his foreign policy experience, his reputation as an arch-anticommunist, and his guarantee that there would be peace in Vietnam but no surrender. Conservatives realized that Nixon had shifted toward acceptance of a negotiated settlement and understood that his public position on how to end the war was ambiguous. Nixon's attempts to win over conservative leaders, coupled with his continued public commitment to anticommunism, allowed conservatives to overcome their potential anxieties about Nixon's handling of the war.

Both YAF and the ACU endorsed Nixon's candidacy once he had won the nomination. On September 24, 1968, Arnold Steinberg of YAF wrote to Buckley that the "Liberty Lobby [a far-right organization that opposed Nixon] and the Wallace people are disturbed that YAF ranks are solid for Nixon, so they have circulated stories about national YAF firing pro-Wallace leaders. Fact: one resignation, no firings."[49] In October 1968 the ACU issued a statement unanimously adopted by the board of directors, which included Rusher and Meyer of *National Review* and Rep. John Ashbrook.

Nixon, the ACU declared, "can not only unify this increasingly divided nation, but redirect it toward the ideals of true conservatism." In the "field of foreign affairs," furthermore, "he will hold a firm line against the forces of totalitarianism and international Communism which continue to threaten the peace of the world."[50] Public displays of support for Nixon were matched by private demonstrations of gratitude from the Nixon team. In October 1968 John Mitchell, Nixon's campaign manager, wrote to Buckley, "Your fidelity is a trust which both Dick and I gratefully hold at home or abroad."[51] Rusher maintained, as did many conservative leaders, that the Republican "convention was not only largely composed of but firmly dominated by conservatives from beginning to end, and when Richard Nixon was nominated it was because, and only because, a majority of the conservatives present had decided to support him."[52]

Vietnam and Electoral Politics

The Vietnam War impacted all aspects of politics during 1968, not least the presidential election. While the Democrats divided, publicly and acrimoniously, over the war, radical anti-war protest reached a climax at the Democratic National Convention in Chicago. Since 1967 increasing numbers of Americans had turned against the war and believed that military progress was unlikely. The complexities of public responses to the war, however, ensured that most Americans did not direct their support to anti-war Democrats. Certainly they showed only limited acceptance of the violent protests that engulfed Chicago. In most cases the protests invoked widespread public anger at the anti-war movement. Vietnam therefore became associated with disorder at home, and Nixon's rhetoric on restoring law and order appealed to those frustrated with anti-war demonstrations, much as it did to those who opposed the civil rights movement. As Colin Dueck rightly comments, Vietnam's association with social unrest at home "redounded against the Democrats, since this disorder had occurred on their watch, and was widely resented even by millions of their core constituents." It ultimately weakened Humphrey's electoral chances.[53]

Despite his failure to delineate his plans for ending the conflict, Nixon succeeded in capitalizing on public frustrations with the war. Nixon's refusal to commit himself on Vietnam during the campaign was explained by claims that he did not wish to jeopardize the chances of peace as steps were made toward negotiation during the autumn of 1968.[54] Nixon had come to believe that a military solution to the war was improbable, but he continued to privately oppose Johnson's handling of the war. While he stated that he would not comment on the war because of his hopes for the Paris peace talks, Nixon's failure to fully endorse the talks implied his preference for a militaristic solution. He also wished to keep his adversaries in the international arena guessing as to his possible actions and was, from a purely political point of view, reluctant to challenge policies that might prove successful or popular with the public before the election in November.

Although reflecting frustration with the candidate's decision to operate "under a self-imposed moratorium on discussion of the war in order . . . to give the peace talks a chance to succeed," *Human Events* echoed the dominant conservative belief that Nixon did not suffer from an overly zealous commitment to the Paris talks or to the policies of the past.[55] Nixon's image as a hawk and the suggestion that he had a secret plan to swiftly end the war sufficed to win over both committed pro-victory hawks and a public increasingly tired of the seemingly endless war. As Rowland Evans and Robert Novak stated in 1971, Nixon's policy was "Delphic, susceptible to favorable interpretation by dove and hawk alike."[56] Nixon had never in fact mentioned a secret plan, but he allowed this misrepresentation of his position to serve his political goals. By carefully refusing to be drawn out on the issue, he avoided having to disabuse his varied supporters of their interpretations of his Vietnam strategies.[57]

While avoiding public commentary, Nixon took private steps to ensure that the peace negotiations, slowly being organized at Paris, did not advance. Through the medium of a Republican activist, Anna Chennault, he urged President Nguyen Van Thieu not to endorse the negotiations until after the November election.[58] Henry Kissinger, Rockefeller's former foreign policy adviser, also put out a back channel of information on the Paris talks through his contacts with Richard Allan and John Mitchell.[59] The competing voices coming from the Nixon camp might have alerted those committed to victory in Vietnam to the probability that peace with honor would yield no such clear-cut objective. Indeed, in 1968 Rep. Melvin Laird, a Republican from Wisconsin who had long been a staunch supporter of the war, began calling for a withdrawal of American forces. Laird was closely associated with the Nixon camp during the campaign, and his calls for withdrawal might have worried his fellow conservatives. Yet Laird focused on reducing the American role rather than ending the war, and he gave no hint of a unilateral withdrawal or any form of American bugout or surrender. Ultimately, Laird, who had publicly criticized Johnson's handling of the war since September 1966, proved effective in reinforcing the hawkishness of possible withdrawal and negotiation. Conservatives were still convinced of the necessity of employing forceful measures to successfully conclude the war, but they moved ever closer to a more flexible interpretation of victory in Vietnam. Their faith in Nixon was reinforced by the policy options promoted by the Democratic candidate.

Humphrey's announced support for a bombing halt was made on September 30, 1968, apparently without the backing or prior knowledge of Johnson. During a telephone conversation with Nixon that evening, the president stated, "I have not read it [Humphrey's speech]. I just had the press secretary call me with the flash that he [Humphrey] says ... he'll stop the bombing—if elected. And then it indicates that he has to have direct or indirect, or deed or act, assurance that they will respect the DMZ [demilitarized zone]. I don't know really what he is saying."[60] Humphrey's position distanced him greatly from the policy of the Johnson administration and served only to enhance pro-war activism in favor of Nixon. Although Humphrey continued to demand North Vietnam's restoration of the DMZ as a prerequisite for any halt in the U.S. bombing of North Vietnam, his statement enhanced his credibility among the peace movement. But Humphrey's position permanently alienated conservative Democrats such as Sen. John Stennis, who were already bothered by his domestic policy preferences, and divided the Democratic Party even more. Not surprisingly, Nixon, to show his resolve to disrupt the enemy's confidence and surety, took the opportunity to lambaste his opponent for risking the lives of American troops. Sen. Everett Dirksen organized a debate in the Senate and concluded that the vice president's position had effectively lost the war. Nixon's running mate, Gov. Spiro Agnew, added that Humphrey's position amounted to sending additional enemy divisions into the field.[61] Nixon was reluctant to overtly accuse his rival of political maneuvering and instead tried to appear to be above the political fray by stating that he would go to Saigon to achieve peace, much as Eisenhower had promised to go to Korea for the same reason in 1950. But many of Nixon's fellow Republicans showed no such restraint. Reagan, for instance, said he thought it "tragic that American lives are being played with this way," while Tower noted that the "the whole thing smacks of politics."[62]

Humphrey's campaign chances lost little from the opposition of such figures; his position on domestic affairs, particularly his successful legislative record on behalf of the Great Society, made him abhorrent to most conservatives in his own party. His effort on behalf of international disarmament and his role in securing the Test Ban Treaty of 1963 assured the opposition of conservative anticommunists both within and outside the Democratic Party fold. His position on Vietnam, however, did much to weaken the resolve of pro-war groups traditionally affiliated with the Democratic Party. Nixon had courted the pro-war labor vote during the campaign, and Humphrey's newfound backing from the peace movement threatened to further erode his credibility among increasingly resentful antiprotest labor voters. The AFL-CIO platform proposals, released on July 29, 1968, declared that "every reasonable step consistent with our national interest should be taken to secure in the Paris negotiations an honorable and just settlement of the conflict in Viet Nam." This position was not wholly inconsistent with Humphrey's efforts to encourage the North Vietnamese propensity to negotiate.[63] The fierce anticommunism of the AFL-CIO leaders George Meaney and Jay Lovestone was reflected, however, in their preference for a policy that would force the Hanoi government to positively advance negotiations. They asserted that "our government should continue to take all measures necessary for safeguarding the independence and freedom of South Vietnam."⁶⁴ Like their conservative allies in the pro-war movement, the labor leadership was not convinced that Humphrey's apparent concession to the enemy was the most effective means of achieving this overarching goal. The major source of opposition to Humphrey's position came, however, from conservatives within his own party. Johnson, meanwhile, remained as fearful as ever that conservative Democrats would abandon him on his Vietnam strategies.

While reluctant to be seen to be following Humphrey's lead, the administration did decide to initiate a bombing halt shortly before the election. President Johnson announced that the administration had agreed to a halt of all air, naval, and artillery bombardment of North Vietnam on October 31. The cessation was predicated on enemy assurances regarding the reestablishment of the DMZ, a pledge that cities in the south would not be attacked, and an agreement to enter productive negotiations with the government of South Vietnam. Deciding on whether or not to pursue the halt in order to stimulate negotiations at Paris had not been easy for the administration. Now, the Johnson White House faced the additional quandary of attempting to ensure that the move was not construed as merely a "political stratagem."⁶⁵ Secretary of Defense Clark Clifford described the fear of Sen. Richard Russell of Georgia, an old guard southern conservative, that neither friend nor foe would interpret the bombing halt as a genuine effort to end the war. Russell was afraid it would be interpreted as a political move by the administration. Clifford, disagreeing that Russell's misgivings were well grounded, maintained that the halt would be publicly recognized as a sound attempt to negotiate a settlement ending the war. As Johnson rightly feared, the administration's conservative opponents were unlikely to allow the administration to push this message without opposition. Keeping his conservative friends on board thus became an imperative.

Johnson's telephone conversation with his longtime friend Russell on October 23, 1968, highlights the means by which the administration attempted to associate a bombing halt with a hard-line strategy in Vietnam. Russell, like many southern Democrats, did not possess the same ideological commitment to the war as intellectual and Republican conservatives, but he was loath to accept what could be interpreted as unilateral American concessions and fearful of playing politics with Vietnam in light of American losses. Johnson began by informing Russell that Gen. Creighton Abrams, commander of Military Assistance Command, Vietnam, "thinks it [the bombing halt] is desirable." Despite North Vietnamese demands for a seven-day lapse between the cessation of bombing and their termination of certain military measures, Johnson said, "We've told them that in no case would we go any longer than two or three days. . . . [W]e're not going to sit there on our fanny and let you tear down the Saigon government by waiting seven days and letting the people think that we've sold them out." Crucially, Johnson assured Russell that Abrams had been given "authority to act on his own to respond to violations of the DMZ." Gen. Earle Wheeler, Johnson assured Russell, had also stated that the enemy "can never do anything in that country [South Vietnam] unless they do hit the cities. So if they do agree not to hit the cities, it is a great military concession." Johnson's emphasis on the administration's unwillingness to compromise too much in order to advance the negotiations at Paris, and his continued insistence that U.S. military leaders in both Vietnam and Washington backed the measure, served as a necessary means of carrying the pro-war element in the Democratic Party.

Johnson was overly positive in assessing the extent of enemy concessions, especially in his claim that even if Hanoi refused to agree to refrain from hitting the cities, "but just don't do it," that could count as a meaningful compromise. Johnson's stress on the approbation of the military leaders proved to be a powerful way of convincing Russell of the merit of the proposition, but he also claimed that "our diplomats think that [North Vietnam's willingness to enter negotiations with the government of South Vietnam] . . . says to all the NLF and the Communists that [Hanoi has] finally come around to doing something they said they'd never do—they really recognize them," which "really strengthens" Saigon.

Such assurances, coupled with the military's endorsement of the measure, strengthened the administration's case. It was, however, the necessity of responding to enemy moves toward compromise and the possibility that Johnson's failure to do so would make him "look bad in history" that strengthened conservative Democrats' support for the halt. The president made clear his and the military's resolve, asserting that enemy violations of the agreements would result in all bets being off and might result in the bombing of Hanoi. Russell's response showed his unvarying insistence on taking a strong line with the North Vietnamese—"I don't think you have any other option but to do that. . . . Otherwise, it would make us look bad"—a position that revealed his ongoing preference for a military solution as a means of ensuring American credibility.[66] Russell's position also reflected hawkish skepticism that the communist enemy would comply with the conditions for the bombing halt. Still arguing for a military solution, hawks who agreed to refrain from renouncing the bombing halt did so not only for political reasons but also because they realized that Hanoi's continued belligerence might lead U.S. fighter planes back to North Vietnam. Party loyalty, far more than faith in the efficacy of a bombing halt, determined the position of conservative Democrats like Russell.

Johnson's efforts to keep leading conservatives in his camp and the acquiescence of the three presidential candidates did much to blunt the potential backlash of hawks. Yet while the Nixon camp remained coy about the potential consequences of the halt and maintained a public image of standing with the commander in chief, many of Nixon's supporters were less cooperative. In mid-October *Human Events* alleged that Johnson had rejected the military's advice to bomb the recently reconstructed base at Thanh Hoa, "the largest military supply depot in North Viet Nam," because he did not want to "blow up" the peace talks "before the November election." The ACU activist and journalist Ralph de Toledano averred that "not one of President Johnson's military advisers takes [the position that military victory is impossible]. . . . [I]n fact, just the contrary is true. The Joint Chiefs of Staff have pleaded with the White House to allow them to win the war in Viet Nam as a prelude to diplomatic negotiations."[67] *Human Events* reported on General Wheeler's meeting with a group of senators, led by Russell. Wheeler was said to have stated that since the bombing pause of March 1968 the "North Vietnamese have been able to repair the bridges and railroads as far south as Thanh Hoa, which is just below the 20th parallel." As a result, "Hanoi has now been able to move supplies night and day as far south as the 20th parallel 'for free,' and ... Thanh Hoa itself today is nothing but one tremendous military depot which is putting U.S. forces in South Viet Nam at a terrible disadvantage." Wheeler was also reported to have stated that North Vietnam had completely rebuilt its airfields since March. *Human Events* contended that Russell's group of senators had urged the president to resume and intensify the bombing of North Vietnam.[68] Following the halt, a *Human Events* column remarked, "It is as though LBJ were calling Ho Chi Minh on the phone and begging him, oh please, to start real negotiations or pretend to do so, before November 5."[69]

Republicans took up this line in order to further discredit the Democrats' position on Vietnam. Senator Thurmond issued a press release delineating the possible political motivations behind the move. "[M]any will view this unilateral cessation of bombing with suspicion," he declared, "and question why the Administration waited until five days before the election to announce this action."[70] One southern newspaper urged its readers to recognize the sole political reaction to the latest administration move regarding Vietnam: "Election of Nixon, Defeat of HHH Vital after Bombing Halt." The enemy could have made this move toward peace at any time, according to the editors of the *Shreveport Times*. They "know full well that they would have a lot easier time favorable to them for ending the war dealing with Humphrey than with Richard Nixon. . . . Nixon IS the one the nation must have in the White House if there is to be hope for peace with honor."[71] More hard-line conservatives were aware, as de Toledano charged in October, that the presidential candidates had "done little to confront the Johnson administration" regarding the possibility of military victory.[72] But Nixon's ambiguous talk of peace with honor had, by late 1968, become synonymous with much of the pro-war movement's understanding of victory in Vietnam. Nixon avoided the image of extreme hawk by standing behind the president's moves toward peace and thereby did not alienate support among a public increasingly frustrated by the long war. But his strong opposition to Humphrey's policies emboldened the Republican candidate's image as an advocate of victory in Vietnam among the pro-war movement.

Conservatives' belief that they had played a prominent, even decisive, role in Nixon's success in 1968 led to no less than euphoria at his presidential victory, a victory they believed offered a mandate for bold action.[73] Senator Tower's appointment as chair of the Nixon-Agnew Key Issues Committee buoyed such hopes. With reference to Vietnam, Tower, commenting on a confidential Johnson administration report in early December 1968, immediately demonstrated little faith in the efficacy of the administration's policy. The report, *Vietnam: The Situation and Alternative Strategies*, largely accepted the view of the intelligence community that much of the bombing of North Vietnam had been ineffective in either destroying war material or reducing the rate of infiltration into the South. Claiming that the more limited bombing campaign of March 31 to November 1, 1968, proved more effective in disrupting the enemy, the report's authors tried to debunk the hawkish view that the situation in Vietnam could be resolved simply by relying on more airpower. They argued that if any generalization could be made about the bombing it was that "the more we bombed the more he has infiltrated and the more he has been aggressive in the South." A resumption of the bombing would probably lead to a breakdown in the Paris talks and also reap significant "domestic political costs."[74]

Tower sharply disagreed with the report's findings, accusing the Johnson administration of not being wholly forthcoming about the situation in Vietnam. The administration was "keeping [a] lid on [the] seriousness of enemy buildup in Cambodia and just north of [the] DMZ." The "transfer of goods down the DMZ by road, rail and ship is at an all-time record pace," he claimed, while the "sizable enemy force just inside Cambodia can threaten Saigon at will"; a "terrorist campaign has been ordered for December and started 5–6 December."[75] The North Vietnamese, according to Tower, had fundamentally violated all of the conditions on which the administration had agreed to a cessation of bombing. He surmised that the "enemy is becoming convinced we will capitulate under conditions he finds agreeable," a circumstance that required the new Nixon administration to "give the enemy more uncertainty and lesser expectations." In order to avoid a collapse of public confidence once it became obvious that "we face another year of hard fighting and talking," the new administration must make clear that there was, in reality, no existing peace to be lost.

Charging that for "RN's sake and options we must put the facts on the record for the American people and we must shake up the enemy's confidence," Tower argued that the new administration should "take a page from the 1952 book when Ike remained silent, but [Sen. William] Knowland, [Sen. Robert] Taft, [Secretary of State John Foster] Dulles and others conducted a carefully orchestrated campaign of public comment in effect threatening the Chinese that dire things were ahead for them unless Korea fighting stopped." Tower urged the Republican Party to use foreign policy experts to point out to the public that the lame-duck president tolerated an enemy buildup and allowed Hanoi to violate the agreement reached in October. Johnson thereby bequeathed a dire military situation to Nixon. The North Vietnamese, Tower concluded, "are moving to present the new President with a position of such strength that he must capitulate at Paris. So far they hear nothing to discourage them."[76]

Tower may have wondered if his message was being heard, but conservatives in general appeared confident that Nixon's key advisers echoed the conservative senator's position. *Human Events* commented in late December that "President-elect Nixon is convinced he must wind up the Viet Nam war in from six to eight months either through negotiations or new military action." Laird, Nixon's appointee as secretary of defense, was reported to have recommended a "win the war or get out" strategy, while Eisenhower was alleged to have told Nixon that "the threat of a bombing resumption is a powerful weapon that he could use to force Hanoi to agree to a cease-fire." *Human Events* reported that several of the president-elect's advisers "want Nixon to send a secret warning to Hanoi that if a ceasefire is not agreed on by February 1 he will be forced to use all military force necessary to end the conflict."[77]

This line reflected conservatives' efforts to promote their understanding of peace with honor, which was based on the expectation that the new administration would respond with force to the enemy's transgressions and conclusively secure the freedom of South Vietnam. While people like Tower did not disregard intelligence analyses of the limited value of strategic bombing of North Vietnam, they continued to profess that pressuring the enemy, even by threatening the use of immense force, could compel the North Vietnamese to abandon their campaign in South Vietnam. Continued conservative faith in Nixon was not absolute, however; it was dependent on administration action and the formulation of policy by his White House.

The Development of Nixon's Vietnam Strategy

Conservatives' jubilation at Nixon's victory was more short-lived than even his conservative critics predicted. The president's hardline stance in early 1969, attributed by Evans and Novak to his fear of alienating conservatives, seemed to waver by the end of his six-month grace period.[78] His appointments record left most conservatives aghast, particularly in regard to his apparent failure to overhaul the State Department and his selection of liberals such as Daniel Patrick Moynihan and Robert Finch for key domestic policy positions.[79] In January the ACU called on conservatives to assert their political influence on the new administration, paying special attention to avoidance of a "coalition government."[80] The ACU was angered by Nixon's failure to select most of its recommended appointees; it said the first six weeks of the administration were "disappointing."[81]

The ACU's attack was not entirely effective, however. Dent, a Nixon aide, withdrew from the organization in protest, while Goldwater charged that responsible conservatives were applauding, not criticizing, the president.[82] The next month the ACU undermined its position by stating that the organization did not regret its endorsement of Nixon but lamented the fact that "the foreign policy of America is being administered by many faceless and some notorious liberals who have been in control since the

New Deal."[83] Buckley remained behind the administration, but he commented on its "strange hiring policies."[84] In April 1969 Buckley wrote, "The ACU has come out and said bluntly what is on the minds of those Americans who made possible the election of Richard Nixon. That Mr. Nixon's performance, so far, is not altogether reassuring. These are complaints that are not altogether fair. It is much too early to know whether Mr. Nixon will freeze under the pressure of Communist salients, in Vietnam, at the negotiating table in Paris, in Berlin."[85]

Goldwater frequently attempted to advise the president and his aides on the need to overhaul government departments with great speed. His conclusion was grave: "While I have no indication that Dick is losing any control of the Party or the government, I am afraid of what is going on." Nixon had retained "those civilians in the Defense Department and State Department who have contributed most to our dilemma around the world ... those people whose only interest is the disarmament of our country." Goldwater wrote also of "growing dissatisfaction among the members of Congress" because of the failure of Nixon's staff to inform them of the status of their recommendations for appointments.[86] Despite his personal distress over the rate of personnel change, Goldwater urged the public and his fellow conservatives to "be patient and give our new President a chance."[87] By April he became convinced that Nixon was perhaps doomed to suffer the fate of the Eisenhower administration, which, he warned Nixon's congressional liaison Bryce Harlow, "lost control of the government."[88] Although he conceded in June that he had "batted just a marginal few points above zero at the White House this year," he assured Dent he would "not quit defending the administration."[89] This expression of loyalty would become a hallmark of Goldwater's position on Nixon's Vietnam strategies.

Kissinger's appointment as assistant to the president for national security affairs came as a surprise to many, both hawk and dove, conservative and liberal. He was definitely an unusual choice, having had little to do with the Nixon team publicly, been most recently associated with Rockefeller, and having acted as a consultant to the Johnson administration. He was also, however, a staunch cold warrior and an expert in foreign affairs.[90] Kissinger's appointment was welcomed by many liberals, including Arthur Schlesinger Jr., the historian who had been a special assistant to President Kennedy,[91] while his national security team included a number of individuals committed to "some kind of rapid withdrawal from Vietnam."[92] Nixon's determination to dominate foreign policy has been well considered and acknowledged by scholars, and his appointment of Kissinger was a way of doing so.[93] Kissinger's views corresponded with many of Nixon's own, and his appointment was supported by many within the pro-war movement. *National Review* endorsed Kissinger and often cited his commitment to the war. In May Kissinger was reported as having said, "The commitment of 500,000 Americans had settled the issue of the importance of Vietnam. For what is involved now is confidence in American promises. However fashionable it is to ridicule 'credibility' or 'prestige', they are not empty phrases; other nations can gear their actions to ours only if they can count on our steadfastness."[94]

Kissinger differed from most hawks in acknowledging the civil war characteristics of the war, at least in South Vietnam, but maintained the position that for the sake of American credibility the Saigon government had to be buttressed and sustained.[95] Already committed to the disengagement of troops and denying that the war could be won on the ground, Kissinger favored a plan to combine broad diplomatic strategies with "irresistible military pressures."[96] His incline toward the "tough" option won the favor not only of Nixon but also of pro-war individuals, most notably Buckley. Buckley was sure that Kissinger would push for the initiation of a broad bombing campaign against North Vietnam in order to force negotiations.

The ACU meanwhile charged that the composition of Kissinger's staff, which included fourteen former Kennedy and Johnson advisors, ensured that "whatever policies in foreign affairs President Nixon may choose to follow, the apparatus he has established to execute those policies is controlled by the very liberals who have weakened American power and prestige for two decades."[97] The ACU's primary worry was Nixon's failure to overhaul the State Department and his appointment of liberal Republicans and

Democrats to White House positions. The group's criticisms were widely condemned by Goldwater and Tower. *National Review* was less hostile toward the new national security adviser, commenting that he would "render great service."[98] The disparate opinions of Kissinger in the early days of Nixon's presidency became more pronounced as the administration's foreign policy was revealed. To a certain extent the differences were a function of divergent foreign policy priorities, but, far more important, they related to differing perspectives on the relationship between the Nixon White House and the conservative movement. While the ACU wanted to highlight the weaknesses in Nixon's policies in order to signify the limitations of a bipartisan approach to foreign policy, the Republican Right was more interested in building effective political alliances. Personal political relations as well as the dictates of party politics therefore informed conservatives' diverse responses to the administration's foreign policies.

Buckley was a close friend of Kissinger and later took credit for having introduced him to the Nixon team through Mitchell.[99] Writing in December 1968, Allan Ryskind, the Capitol Hill editor of *Human Events,* sought Buckley's advice on Kissinger's position regarding Vietnam. The editors of *Human Events* had recently published a favorable article on Kissinger, which resulted in the editorial board "catching some flack." Ryskind, having read Kissinger's work and consulted such exalted figures within the conservative movement as Robert Strausz-Hupé and Fritz Kramer, concluded that "Kissinger is fairly hard-line on the subject of Communism," but he complained that the "[Adam] Yarmolinsky-Schlesinger-[John Kenneth] Galbraith laurels for Kissinger have scared off a number of conservatives." Ryskind's problem lay primarily with Kissinger's preferred policies for Vietnam. He stated that both "Fritz Kramer and David Martin (Dodd's office) believe Kissinger to be something of a hawk, but the newspaper accounts suggest he was opposed to the northern bombings and would generally like us to get out on almost any terms."[100] Buckley showed little distress that the charges of Kissinger's supposed dovishness might be accurate, stating to a conservative opponent of the new national security adviser, "I am at this moment especially convinced that

Henry Kissinger is a great patriot, and that you will one day come to agree about that."[101]

On the day Ryskind conveyed conservatives' doubts about Kissinger to Buckley, Kissinger also communicated with Buckley: "I . . . appreciate the support and confidence that you have shown. Please remember that you will always have an open line to my office."[102] Buckley was not, however, the only source of Kissinger's support among conservatives. James Burnham had views similar to Kissinger's regarding the intention of the Soviet Union and its potential role in ending the war.[103] Buckley and Burnham were convinced that Kissinger's role in the administration would be positive and that the new national security adviser was committed to adopting a hard-line policy toward the North Vietnamese.

Nixon's choice of secretary of defense proved less controversial within the pro-war community. Although during the campaign Laird indicated his support for conditional withdrawal, he too was seen as a hard-line cold warrior. Like many conservatives, he questioned the wisdom of a land war in Asia in 1964, yet also criticized the administration's emphasis on limited war following engagement.[104] De Toledano described Laird as having "mostly been part of what can almost be called the 'conservative caucus'" in the House of Representatives, while Rusher praised Laird's appointment.[105] Laird was, however, shrewdly aware of the potential for greater domestic opposition to the war and to the administration and the Republican Party if the conflict dragged on indefinitely. He understood that many Americans had been attracted to Nixon because of their opposition to the anti-war movement and his focus on law and order. They might defect from the president if the war was not ended and peace with honor not achieved. Laird therefore came to office determined to deflect such negative political consequences by dramatically and rapidly reducing the level of direct U.S. involvement in the war, particularly with regard to American troop and casualty levels. Laird's hope that such measures would signal America's good intentions to Hanoi and induce the enemy to negotiate was more fully accepted by his cabinet colleague in the State Department, William Rogers. Rogers's more dovish position troubled those who were committed to victory in Vietnam, yet their qualms were diminished by Nixon's distinct influence on the formation of foreign policy.

Much in the first months of the Nixon administration warranted conservative questioning of Nixon's foreign policy but little caused outright anxiety. The announcement in March of plans for the development of an anti-ballistic missile (ABM) system was an opportunity to gain some "mileage" with the "conservative element," according to Bob Haldeman, Nixon's chief of staff.[106] While in the early sixties many conservatives had denied the efficacy of a defense policy based on deterrence, by 1969 the ABM was welcomed as a demonstration of American commitment to make its deterrent threat more real. Nixon's assurances to Republican leaders that plans for the international Non-Proliferation of Nuclear Weapons Treaty, which had opened for signatories in 1968, were too advanced to be abandoned met with some resistance, including that of Sen. Gordon Allott. Senator Dirksen, however, argued that Republicans must support the measure for political reasons, while Senator Tower opined that the ninety-day escape clause made the treaty relatively meaningless. Disconcerted by the euphoria attached to the treaty, however, Tower begged leave of the president to vote against it.[107] Each of these events highlighted the conservatives' apprehensions about U.S. military strength vis-à-vis the Soviet Union, an issue that remained the dominant focus of conservative efforts throughout the Nixon administration. The events also underscored the extent to which domestic politics would affect how conservative Republicans interpreted the president's foreign policies.

Administration policy regarding Vietnam emerged incrementally over the course of Nixon's first six months in office. Nixon took office with the expectation and intention of ending the war and ending it successfully in his first year in office. The strategy of Vietnamization, a phrase coined by Laird to avert the characteristics of abandonment associated with de-Americanization, ultimately emerged at the heart of administration policy. Its principal aim was to transfer combat and support duties from American to newly trained and equipped South Vietnamese forces. It depended heavily on strengthening the Saigon government and its armed forces to withstand possible North Vietnamese and domestic communist attack. Yet, as originally conceived in early 1969, Vietnamization was coupled with plans for decisive military and diplomatic campaigns designed to end the war on terms commensurate with the primary aims of the United States. Steering a course between the alternative strategies advocated by his main advisers, Nixon did not rule out a sensational military attack intended to leave North Vietnam no choice but to capitulate, and he was not willing to undermine public support by hastily resuming bombing of North Vietnam. Laird's touting of Vietnamization can be seen in precisely these terms. It was a purely political move on his part, one designed to pacify the anti-war movement while preparing the American people for a protracted U.S. air and naval presence in Vietnam.[108]

Laird's rationale impacted administration policy, but Nixon remained averse to any form of unilateral withdrawal. Kissinger argued that a strong military measure would most likely jump-start negotiations. Nixon was adamant about the need to put military pressure on Hanoi in order to force the government to accept a compromise peace. They would do so, he contended, only when they had no other choice, an opinion reiterated by Kissinger.[109] As plans were being developed for the phased, conditional withdrawal of American troops, the administration was devising strategies for a knockout blow to the enemy in North Vietnam and along the infiltration routes to South Vietnam, an operation known as Duck Hook. The operation was never implemented, but it remained a policy option until at least October 1969 even though in its stead the United States had begun a secret bombing campaign against Cambodia in February 1969. Although Nixon had ruled out a purely military solution, military options steadily played a fundamental role in the administration's plans for ending the war on American terms. The extent to which this was made known to the public and to key individuals within the pro-war movement helped sustain support for administration policy among such figures.

A number of pro-war congressmen had been informed of the secret bombing of Cambodia, including Senators Stennis, Russell, and Dirksen and Representatives Mendel Rivers, Leslie Arends, and Gerald Ford.[110] Nixon tried to make his position public and reiterated this appearance of strength when meeting with representatives of *Time* magazine in March 1969. "There is a *very* fine line—far finer than most people realize," he contended, "between 'bombing them back into the Stone Age' (as some people put it) and just sitting there 'letting them hit us.'" "Negotiations," the president went on, "must be done softly [and] calmly." Hinting again at his infamous, but empty, secret plan, he assured his audience that "we should let them know that we definitely have something up our sleeve if they don't come around."[111] Nixon was indeed attempting to define the "fine line" between the phased withdrawal advocated by his secretaries of state and defense and the tougher positions demanded by the JCS and Kissinger. Buchanan, one of Nixon's most ardent conservative aides, concluded that "no reasonable person on the Vietnam issue can ask for more" than Nixon proposed, a factor indicative of the association of American success with Nixon's still vague policy regarding Vietnam.[112]

Nixon's hard-line position was somewhat compromised by his address of May 14, 1969, in which he delivered what he later described as his "first comprehensive peace plan."[113] Less than two weeks before the address *National Review* fired a warning shot over Nixon's bow. Counseling that the nation's "minimum objective" was to "guarantee South Vietnam against Communist takeover for the next period," the editors warned that "if the American forces withdraw from Vietnam as part of a pseudo-agreement that is only a cover for failure and sellout, then Richard Nixon will in due course be remembered, not for this false peace, but as the weakling who opened the gate to Communist engulfment of South Asia and the South Pacific, as the bringer of defeat and its cumulative train of disastrous consequences." *National Review*'s warning, rather than being indicative of the editors' views of Nixon's personal commitment to the war, was intended to forestall his succumbing to antiwar pressure. Nixon "may be sure," they summed up, "that those who now call on him most loudly for unilateral withdrawal are the ones who would most fiercely damn him for the disastrous consequences that unilateral withdrawal would bring."[114] To those who advocated victory in Vietnam and asserted that communists could not be relied on to uphold international agreements, the proposals seemed excessively generous.

In September 1966 Johnson and Thieu had issued a joint communiqué establishing the basis for negotiation with the North Vietnamese. The United States offered to withdraw its forces from South Vietnam within six months of an agreement being reached, on condition that: Hanoi withdraw its forces from the South; Hanoi agree to cease aiding the NLF military forces; and the overall levels of violence in the South decrease. A residual force of U.S. troops was to remain in Vietnam after complete North Vietnamese withdrawal. These terms became known as the Manila formula. Nixon's speech on May 14 was a quite dramatic departure from the Manila formula in that he said the United States offered to withdraw all of its forces concurrently with those of North Vietnam. Nixon also signaled his willingness to accept "neutrality for South Vietnam if that is what the South Vietnamese people freely choose," a departure from his vocal opposition to such a policy during the Johnson administration.[115] While the joint statement insisted that the United States "resolve to reject any attempt to impose upon the Republic of Vietnam any system or program or any particular form of government, such as coalition, without regard to the will of the people of South Vietnam," the principle of a coalition government was not rejected, as conservatives demanded.[116] Nixon's failure to disavow a coalition government resulted in significant unrest among conservatives. Their alarm would only grow with each successive peace offering.

Nixon was determined to minimize the fallout from conservatives' disquiet. The day before the speech he told congressional leaders that "if the North Vietnamese think that combining the military offensive [expected in June] with a peace offensive is the way to negotiate with him, they would be sadly mistaken." Nixon asserted that Republicans who equated his actions with those of Johnson "were making a serious mistake" and warned that individuals "who have been critical" of administration policy "may look very bad a few months from now."[117] Following the speech,

Nixon and Kissinger, conveying an impression of "buoyant confidence," according to Buchanan, assured the assembled congressional leaders that "despite what you might read in the public press, the South Vietnamese were pleased with the speech and are solidly behind us." "One of the great effects of the speech," the president and his adviser declared, "was to dramatize to Hanoi the failure of its effort to affect us psychologically."[118] To the high praise of pro-war advocates, Nixon publicly stated, "I must make clear, in all candor, that if the needless suffering continues, this will affect other decisions."[119] Although Nixon failed to articulate the nature of these "other decisions," his position hinted at the possibility of a military response designed to force North Vietnamese compliance.

Still, the mixed media reports of Nixon's policies in respect of Vietnam soon began to stimulate hawkish opposition and questioning, particularly after the May peace proposals and the announcement of troop withdrawals.[120] The *National Review* for May 6 featured an editorial in which the authors claimed there was "no objective reason why this final phase of the present struggle should be conceived as excluding re-escalations or novel forms of escalation from current combat levels." Such actions "could only serve," according to *National Review,* "to impress Hanoi with the firmness of American intentions."[121] Judd, commenting on the above statements, noted that "subjectively," it was "almost impossible" to expect military escalation, an indication that among certain elements of the pro-war movement there was little hope for a military solution to the war. Judd did, however, concur with the view expressed in *National Review* that it would be "shocking and shameful" if the United States could not outlast North Vietnam, asserting, "If U.S. cannot and does not outlast North Vietnam, then U.S. cannot last—period."[122] The relationship between the outcome of the Vietnam War and overall U.S. foreign policy continued to preoccupy political activists within the pro-war movement, therefore, much as it did the president. By mid-1969 it had become less clear that Nixon's views on ending the war were harmonious with those of conservatives demanding a successful end to the war, one that would send a resounding message to the communist world. Nixon's May peace proposals and his embryonic policy of

Vietnamization did not provide the unambiguous policy conservatives favored, but neither did it seem that a militaristic solution to the war had been fully precluded.

The response in Congress indicated that pro-war leaders were still determined to reconcile peace with their own objectives. Minority Leader Ford acknowledged that the "Nixon administration has ruled out any idea of seeking a military solution in Vietnam" but tempered this avowal of a negotiated settlement by saying, "The other side cannot possibly succeed in imposing a military solution." "The United States," Ford assured his pro-war audience, "will not sell out South Vietnam."[123] Majority Leader Carl Albert, who consistently promoted a pro-war position, praised the president's policy, insisting that "peace does not mean surrender . . . peace without honor is no peace at all."[124] Still others, including Rep. Edward Derwinski, emphasized the international origins and consequences of the Vietnam War, warning against being "lulled into a false sense of security or hope by the President's great address." Derwinski further remarked that as "practical and sound as [the president's proposal] was, the real menace to world peace remains the diabolical plans of the tyrants in the Kremlin and Peking."[125]

Although Nixon signaled America's willingness to accept simultaneous withdrawal of American and North Vietnamese troops from South Vietnam, the initiation of U.S. troop withdrawals was not announced until Nixon's meeting with President Thieu at Midway Island in June. Nixon and Thieu confirmed that the American presence in Vietnam would be reduced by twenty-five thousand troops beginning in July, an announcement that came as a "complete surprise to the press corps, as to timing and amount."[126] It was not a surprise to the JCS, who had privately argued against phased withdrawal since January 1969.[127] Kissinger was also to be disappointed within weeks of the Midway conference when Nixon gave "rather startling answers on some Vietnam questions." According to Haldeman, the president "said he hoped to beat *(LBJ Secretary of Defense)* Clark Clifford's goal on withdrawals (all out by end of next year); there would be more withdrawals this summer, decision in August; he wasn't 'wedded' to Thieu regime; he was not opposed to a cease-fire etc."[128] Haldeman's notation and Kissinger's exclamation that Nixon's statements "will probably mean collapse of South Vietnam government" and would be "interpreted as unilateral withdrawal" were both exaggerated. In response to questions about being "wedded" to the Thieu regime, Nixon made clear his government's unwavering commitment to the Saigon government.[129] Kissinger's concern that Nixon had decided to "reverse the Vietnam plan," assuming a more dovish approach, was largely unfounded but it was a sign of rising anxiety over the nature of administration policy.[130]

The precise meaning of Vietnamization and its function as an indicator of overall administration foreign policy remained undefined. The policy has engendered a plethora of alternative interpretations since its inception, not least among historians. Some argue that the policy was either a hopeful fantasy to which the administration succumbed or a charade designed to disguise a precipitate withdrawal and win popular backing.[131] Kimball considers Vietnamization within the context of Nixon's madman theory and argues that it was initially developed in cooperation with the possibility of escalating air and naval force.[132] Larry Berman agrees with Kimball's assessment in many respects, referring to Nixon's secret bombing of Cambodia as evidence of the president's plans to negotiate while fighting, although Berman emphasizes the extent to which Nixon and Kissinger planned to continue the war by alternative means once the United States had withdrawn its troops under the auspices of a supposed settlement to end the war.[133] Still others have assessed the development and significance of Vietnamization as part of the Nixon Doctrine, the principle of helping other nations to defend themselves against aggression in situations where nuclear weapons were not a factor, rather than the application of direct U.S. military force.[134]

Kimball has, however, shown that the Nixon Doctrine was to a large extent a consequence of Vietnamization rather than its progenitor. The policy had been developed by Nixon "in virtual solitude and delivered without careful preparation by the NSC [the National Security Council]" and was an attempt to devise a global framework to permit the continuation of U.S. internationalism in the face of domestic attacks.[135] This view is substantiated by

Haldeman's brief reference to a press backgrounder at Guam. The president was returning from his meeting with the astronauts of Apollo XI and held a short press conference in which he mentioned what became known, following a public relations campaign by the White House, as the Nixon Doctrine. Haldeman described the day as being "pretty historic and fascinating," but he acknowledged later that his reference had little to do with the announcement of Nixon's so-called doctrine.[136] The policy's development and application to the situation in Vietnam and the rest of Southeast Asia were based primarily on its popularity and its implication that the administration might use military force, such as bombing, to ensure the security of its allies. This augured, in some respects, a return to the Eisenhower years, when the U.S. had avoided long-term military commitments abroad. Focusing on the use of air and sea power, the United States would avoid setting itself against an apparently unlimited reserve of Asian manpower.[137] Nixon said that "his plan did involve a retreat from overextended American military commitments, but that was not the same . . . as writing off the world to chance." At the same time he was urging his staff to promote the doctrine, he was stressing that a loss in Vietnam (an "elegant bug-out") would result in a retreat from the world by the United States and would destroy the confidence of the American people in themselves.[138]

The use of the Nixon Doctrine served as a means of adding lucidity and profundity to what might otherwise be viewed as a unilateral withdrawal of American forces from Vietnam. Nixon was determined to publicly reaffirm his commitment to conveying military strength to the communist enemy. He showed this in a speech he gave at the Air Force Academy in June in which he affirmed the need for the United States to remain militarily strong and active in the world. Nixon's promotion of his commitment to the ABM program was also a part of this public relations initiative. He stated in his address at the academy that he held a "totally different world view" from that of people who "assert that the United States is blocking the road to peace by maintaining its military strength at home and defenses abroad." He flatly denied the liberal argument that the United States was responsible for tensions in the world and contended that withdrawal from "assuming the responsibility for defending peace and freedom in the world" would result in the world living "in terror." Echoing conservative charges against the spending and development programs of the McNamara Defense Department, Nixon asserted, "We must rule out unilateral disarmament, because in the real world it wouldn't work." "The adversaries in the world," he declared, "are not in conflict because they are armed," but are rather "armed because they are in conflict."[139]

Wishing to advance this image, Nixon ordered his aides to disseminate positive news stories about his Vietnam policies. He favored headlines like those in the *Charlotte Observer* ("If Reds Escalate, Hanoi in Danger") and the *Miami Herald* ("Nixon to Bomb Again if Reds Step Up War"). The president pointed to a column of June 26 that was carried in most of the Knight chain of newspapers. It stated that Nixon was prepared to resume bombing of North Vietnam, "with no strings attached," if the communists escalated the fighting in response to U.S. troop withdrawals. The column concluded that this was the "ace in the hole" Nixon was keeping in case his main strategy did not work and that the administration would "take the gloves off" to protect remaining U.S. troops in Vietnam.[140] The administration's effort to disseminate this material was not simply designed to disturb the leadership in Hanoi but also served its attempts to assuage the growing demands of hawks regarding the implications of withdrawal and peace in Vietnam.

By early July the Republican Right was beginning to voice its uneasiness with administration policy in Vietnam, as noted by Haldeman: "Problem of right wing Republican unhappiness, because we're not adequately cutting spending, welfare etc., and they feel we're softening in Vietnam." Haldeman noted that Kissinger was becoming "discouraged, because his plans for ending the war aren't working fast enough and Rogers and Laird are pushing for faster and faster withdrawal." Kissinger was indeed fearful of Laird's focus on the importance of decreasing the number of American troops on the ground in Vietnam. Haldeman commented that Kissinger thought this represented a "'cop out' by next summer, and that, if we follow that line, we should 'cop out' now. He wants to push for some escalation, enough to get us a reasonable settlement within six months."[141] Nixon's public "doctrine" may not have been developed specifically to meet this challenge, but it was widely applauded within the pro-war community once it was expressed in combination with a firm commitment to the continued freedom of South Vietnam and America's other allies. Conservatives, unaware of the differences of opinion between Laird and Kissinger, saw important opportunities in the president's new approach.

Conservative leaders had been calling for the use of air and naval power to end the war ever since its beginning, but they had also consistently derided the need for high levels of American troops. In this regard they differed from many military officials, especially General Westmoreland, whom they so regularly championed. Conservatives emphasized the importance of bringing the war to the North and recommended that troops other than Americans assume a greater share of the burden in combating the insurgency in South Vietnam. Thurmond subscribed to the use of Chinese nationalist anticommunist forces, which, he argued, would be well suited to the anti-guerrilla style of warfare required in South Vietnam. Nixon's policy seemed to afford the possibility that the ideas of Sir Robert Thompson might also be implemented. Conservatives agreed with Thompson's stipulation that the military should have greater control of war planning. They also welcomed his claim that the "future of Western civilization is at stake" in regard to how the United States handled itself in Vietnam.[142] Nixon's meetings with Thompson enhanced the standing of administration policy among advocates of victory in Vietnam. Thompson explicitly endorsed the president's Vietnamization policy, so long as it was undertaken with due care and withdrawal was commensurate with the conditions outlined by the president. He did not, in fact, share conservatives' preference for a bold strike to force negotiations. In a meeting with Nixon and Kissinger on October 17, 1969, he rejected Nixon's suggestion of an "option to the Right," by which the president meant escalation.[143] Indeed, Thompson's earlier assessment that Vietnamization would take two years to succeed helped legitimize Laird's and Rogers' opposition to the implementation of a bold strike during November.[144] Thompson was hired by Nixon as a consultant, traveled to Vietnam in November 1969, and, upon his return, offered his assessment that the Saigon government held the "winning position."[145]

The conservative lobby's focus remained concentrated on the use of airpower to end the war, however, a view that by no means conflicted with the dictates of Vietnamization. The extent to which the Nixon administration would implement the policy was less definite, leading to increasing debate and division within the conservative and wider pro-war movement regarding the nature of Nixon's policies in Vietnam and the wider international arena. One critic, Gen. Thomas Lane, posed the basic question in June 1969: "Does he really know how to end the fighting?" Lane displayed little faith in administration policy: the "reduction of U.S. troops in Vietnam came as no surprise" and "few observers believed administration statements that our forces would withdraw only as North Vietnamese forces withdrew." He concluded that the withdrawal "operates as a delaying action to arrest leftwing pressures in the United States," which gained "time for Mr. Nixon." The administration's next move remained unclear, Lane argued, and time was "running out."[146] Lane had consistently railed against the restrictions placed on military action in Southeast Asia, charging in 1967 that "never before in history has any army been so hobbled and sacrificed as are our forces in South Vietnam today."[147] Lane not only referred to the decreased likelihood of military success as allied strength in Vietnam was reduced but also questioned the extent to which the American people would be willing to go along with a policy of limited military action that was likely to require several years to fully secure the Saigon government. This was a key issue for many supporters of the war; the problem with public opinion was not, in their estimation, that people were disillusioned with the war itself, but that they were frustrated by the American government's insistence on restricting targets and not going all out to force Hanoi's capitulation. Support, they contended, would improve once decisive action was taken.

Of perhaps greatest interest in Lane's assessment of administration policy was not his emphasis on the need for bold military measures, but his assertion that the United States did not need "all that strength," that is, upward of half a million troops, "to win."[148] This was a common theme among pro-war supporters of the administration. Stennis and Russell concluded that the withdrawal of twenty-five thousand troops was not very significant in military terms, a view promulgated by administration and military officials.[149] Thurmond argued that "from the standpoint of American forces levels, the action will be a reduction; but from the standpoint of the fighting generally, it will be a replacement."[150] Goldwater reiterated this position, assuring his constituents that his meetings with Laird and Nixon had persuaded him that "the troop removal will not advance the communist cause."[151]

Such assumptions regarding troop withdrawal were not, however, without reservation. Before Nixon's May peace proposal, Goldwater stated that he believed the administration may have "issued some ultimatums to the North Vietnamese which had not been made public."[152] By July he asserted that troop withdrawals would not be allowed to hinder American objectives in Vietnam. Nixon was "not going to tolerate any soft peddling" with the North Vietnamese and would do what was "necessary militarily to bring this war to an end."[153] Such was Goldwater's public position. Although he remained somewhat uninformed about the administration's intentions, his private position varied little during this period. "I think [Nixon's] movements in Vietnam," he wrote, "have been wise in that his troop withdrawal has been based upon a formula whereby the South Vietnamese divisions, as they come into proficiency and can take over, will do just that, relieving an equivalent number of American boys."[154] While praising Nixon's policies, claiming that "for the first time we have an administration that has the courage to look at the situation in Vietnam realistically," Thurmond reiterated the need to acknowledge that Vietnam was but one element of a global struggle and that disengagement would depend on the international environment. "The first condition for achieving peace," he said, "is to recognize that the Soviets bear the chief responsibility for the continuation of this war." The "real roadblock to peace," he warned, "is not in Paris, or even in Hanoi, but Moscow."[155] Pro-war advocates thought the wisdom of administration policy depended heavily on adherence to the criteria for withdrawal outlined by Nixon in June, particularly the readiness of the armed forces of South Vietnam to assume a greater military burden. Within the conservative community, support for Vietnamization was based on the fundamental assumption that it would be coupled with more forceful military measures if the generous overtures of the United States were not met by North Vietnamese reciprocity.

The Militarization of Vietnamization

Conservatives' questioning of the president was becoming more common by the fall of 1969. Lane, writing in *Human Events*, claimed that when he was a candidate Nixon's policies for Vietnam had been acceptable, but he had since fallen victim to presidential advisers who urged unnecessary restraint. He named Kissinger as the individual most responsible for Nixon's assumption of a liberal foreign policy and proclaimed that the national security adviser's strategy for ending the Vietnam War was much in evidence in recent months. As a result, the Saigon political base had been broadened, a charge that once again reflected conservatives' fears of a coalition government being imposed on South Vietnam. The president's rejection of a military solution only played into the hands of the enemy, according to Lane: "The gambits," having been "made and rejected" by the enemy, left the United States in a weaker position. "Time," Lane lamented, "is on the side of the enemy." Until Nixon initiated such military measures as ending the enemy's use of sanctuaries in Laos and Cambodia, an honorable conclusion to the war was impossible, according to Lane, a position that reflected the military's preferred policies.[156]

Lane's assessment of Vietnamization was not, however, dominant in pro-war circles. This reflected a division between a minority who demanded total war and the destruction of the Hanoi government and a majority who believed that Vietnamization did not preclude certain military options from being implemented which could lead Hanoi to accept American terms for peace. Rather than reject the president's policy, conservative leaders offered an alternative, more positive assessment of Vietnamization. Their support was based on the administration's maintaining of its outlined criteria for withdrawal. Greater control of military aspects of the war, furthermore, would need to be handed over to the South Vietnamese leadership. Continuing faith in Vietnamization was encouraged by strenuous efforts on the part of administration officials, most notably Kissinger.

On the whole, moderate and conservative Republicans, coupled with pro-war figures in the Democratic Party, the majority of labor leaders, commanders of the veterans' organizations, and conservative activists interpreted Nixon's policies to de-Americanize the war favorably. Even those like Representative Ashbrook who questioned the implications of Vietnamization agreed to withhold judgment. Having counseled against appeasement of communism with "full confidence that President Nixon will reject such dangerous advice," the ACU's board of directors sanctioned administration policy after the troop withdrawal was announced in June. The ACU called on the president to "reaffirm American support for victory over Communism in Vietnam" and stated its approval of the "present duly elected government of South Vietnam which has been the most stable and unifying regime since the fall of Diem." Reiterating conservatives' opposition to a coalition government, the ACU charged that "if South Vietnam is abandoned, drastic political repercussions can be expected in the United States but far worse, the Free World will lose not only Vietnam to Communism but eventually all of Asia." During the lead-up to Nixon's meeting with Thieu at Midway the ACU kept up the pressure on the administration to vociferously oppose a coalition government, but they did not renounce the Thieu government's willingness to allow the NLF to participate in free elections. Rather, they recalled Nixon's statements of March 1968, in which he had said he opposed a coalition government for Vietnam, claiming that a "coalition with the Communists is like putting a cobra and a mongoose together—they try to eat each other." Nixon, according to the ACU, had figured that the "North Vietnamese realize that once they have a coalition government they have the first installment on victory."[157]

This position was reflected by the policy statements of the Citizens Committee for Peace with Freedom in Vietnam (CCPFV). Founded by the Johnson administration, the CCPFV nevertheless acted as a mouthpiece for the Nixon White House line. It also continued to display a strong commitment to victory in Vietnam. While acknowledging that an honorable solution could still be reached, the organization cautioned against "wishful thinking," arguing that "a continuing series of unilateral concessions, unreciprocated by the enemy, is the road to defeat." This road, CCPFV officials declared, was "marked by precipitous or premature withdrawal of American forces from Vietnam—withdrawal before the South Vietnamese are prepared to take over the job of protecting themselves from the Vietcong and the invaders from the North." The committee's warnings voiced worry about the possibility of too-rapid withdrawal and about the ambiguity of the criteria prescribed by Nixon in June. Arguing that it was imprudent to rely on "lulls" in the level of enemy fighting, the CCPFV had little faith in the possibility of reaching a settlement at Paris. The talks, they lamented, demonstrated that "the enemy is unwilling to face the challenge of free elections, wants the United States to throw the Thieu government out, and then wants the United States itself to get out unconditionally after having installed a peace-at-any-price coalition government for the future convenience of Hanoi."[158] Such caveats were intended to inform and influence administration policy; they also betrayed the fact that many organizations created at the behest of the White House demonstrated an independent commitment to the war. In large measure the CCPFV's arguments were aimed at dissuading anti-war calls for more rapid de-escalation. "Look before cutting," the CCPFV advised the administration in a challenge to those who were accused of pushing a policy of "cut and run."

The CCPFV's overall assessment of Vietnamization was positive, however. It publicly claimed that the progress achieved in such a brief period was remarkable and "clear testimony of the feasibility of 'Vietnamizing' the struggle." Commenting on a recent fact-finding trip, the CCPFV proclaimed its surprise at the fact that the policy of Vietnamization was only a year old, a statement that negated the Johnson administration's role in devising the concept. The CCPFV's assessments of the situation on the ground in South Vietnam suggested that a turning point had been reached in the war. The eighteen-month-old People's Self-Defense Force was heralded as an agent of change, an indigenous South Vietnamese armed force that had rapidly secured rural areas and was securing vast numbers of South Vietnamese.[159] General Wheeler echoed this sentiment upon leaving Vietnam on October 6. Asserting that "progress in Vietnamization is being steadily and realistically achieved," he concluded that U.S. troops would continue to support the South Vietnamese "for some time to come."[160] The future of the American operation in Southeast Asia and the survival of South Vietnam continued to trouble CCPFV officials, but they viewed the anti-war effort, not government policy, as the primary source of danger. While it became evident that Vietnamization was not the panacea that would bring immediate security to South Vietnam, the CCPFV unwaveringly championed the president's policy.

Conservatives' backing of the president's peace proposals and of Vietnamization was based largely on the supposition that such measures might be coupled with more forceful military action in the event the North Vietnamese refused to cooperate with the liberal overtures of the administration. Thurmond wrote in October that if "the president is to choose wisely, he must ignore those advisers who believe that diplomacy can secure a political settlement that has eluded us upon the battlefield." But the president's Vietnamization program, he thought, did not forestall more militaristic strategies. He called on Nixon to follow the policies outlined in his article on Vietnam from 1964 and stated his belief that Vietnamization would allow such policies as the destruction of sanctuaries and interdiction of supply routes to take place. Perhaps ignoring the realities of the continued bombing halt, Thurmond argued that the administration could now interdict supply routes in order to support the policy of replacing American troops with those from South Vietnam. By using these and "other Asian troops," the Nixon administration was demonstrating its commitment to opening up the war and ending the "inadequate missions" orchestrated "by incompetent civilian advisers." Nixon, Thurmond concluded, "could win the war in 1969 by using his plan of 1964."[161]

Leading figures in the conservative movement accepted Nixon's assurances that the transfer of combat operations from American to Vietnamese hands formed part of a wider initiative in foreign policy. This was understood not as a knee-jerk reaction to a stalemated war but as the logical next step in the process of reducing the Americans' burden in Southeast Asia. Conservatives viewed U.S. troop withdrawal as affording an opportunity for a new phase of the war to begin, one in which South Vietnamese forces might be freed from the political constraints hindering U.S. military action. They had little faith in the likelihood of North Vietnamese compliance and wished to challenge the possibility that the Hanoi government would simply await withdrawal before relaunching attacks against Saigon. Conservatives thus promoted the use of greater military action by both the United States and South Vietnam even as they lauded the policy of Vietnamization. Indeed, their support of the new policy was based on the realization that it afforded the only hope of auguring a new chapter in the militarization of the war.

This is not to suggest that pro-war lobbies did not question the administration's policy on Vietnam during this period. Rather than disavow such policies, hawkish supporters of Nixon charged that the door to a military solution to the war remained open. In this respect many of Nixon's allies on the right did not fully accept the idea that the president had disavowed a military option to end the war. Writing to a disillusioned citizen who had accused him of abandoning principle out of party loyalty, Goldwater reiterated his conviction that the Nixon and Laird approach was a good one. He said that the peace talks in Paris had to be pursued for a "reasonable time." After it became clear that no substantive gains could be made at the talks, Goldwater surmised that the administration "will be ready to take what military action is necessary to bring this conflict to a conclusion."[162] Goldwater's position was not simply political posturing. He wrote privately in his political journal that the return of twenty-five thousand U.S. military personnel was based on the readiness of South Vietnamese forces, and he expected that an additional fifteen thousand returnees would be announced in August.[163] Troop withdrawals, or replacements, did not loom large in Goldwater's thinking or that of most hawks simply because they did not preclude the initiation of policies that would force North Vietnamese compliance and surrender. "I do feel," he wrote, "that the President must, in the very near future, take a definitive and strong stand relative to the Paris Peace Talks by saying in effect, 'Either do it or get off the pot.' In other words, if we can't begin to see some achievement at Paris, we're going to resume bombing and by resuming bombing, I would suggest a complete bombing of Haiphong and the opening of the Red River dikes."[164]

Goldwater did not suggest that he believed the administration was about to pursue such policies, yet he continued to hold that they were still on the table, and he displayed no sign that Vietnamization or indeed the president's peace proposals of May ruled out an intensified bombing campaign. During his meeting with the president in September, Goldwater continued to urge military action but reassured wary citizens that Nixon was on the "right track" and would "soon reach some conclusion regarding the war."[165] He had, in fact, acknowledged in early September that "it would appear" that the bombing halt "will continue to be the case."[166] The senator was, therefore, disillusioned with the pace of American policy, continuing to believe that a swift blow directed at North Vietnam would quickly end the conflict. His stance was indicative of pro-war Republicans who acknowledged the political pressures facing the administration, but it demonstrated a continued faith in Vietnamization and a supposition that the policy allowed for military measures to be invoked to successfully conclude the war. Such faith in Vietnamization was determined, ultimately, by a particular conception of the policy's meaning, one that relied as much on its failure as on its potential success.

The prevailing political atmosphere may certainly have impacted hawks' favorable interpretations of Vietnamization. The fissures within the Democratic Party continued to grow, but partisan loyalty was no longer a factor in keeping war-weary Democrats tied to support for Vietnam. As a result of their newfound political freedom, many Democrats were more comfortable openly questioning a war that was increasingly unpopular. Most members of Congress remained behind the administration's policy, a factor that reflects the legislature's general inactivity on stemming the president's war powers at this time.[167] Still, the evidence of increased Democratic and liberal opposition to Nixon's war strategies served only to increase vocal hawkish support for Vietnamization. The administration also did a great deal to further this process, continually prompting its hawkish allies to pressure Congress. As congressional hawks challenged dovish support of the anti-war Moratorium of October 15, the administration focused on developing the "Massacre Enabling Act" line in reference to the Goodell Resolution.[168]

The Goodell Resolution, introduced on September 25, 1969, referred to legislation proposed by Sen. Charles Goodell, a Republican from New York who had a liberal record in recent years. The resolution required U.S. troops to withdraw from Vietnam by the end of 1970 and prohibited the use of congressionally appropriated funds after December 1, 1970. Although the resolution was defeated in the Senate, Senators Mark Hatfield, Jacob Javits, and George McGovern proposed similar legislation over the next three weeks. Nixon urged that the claim that the resolution "sentences to death 500,000 Catholics" be promulgated. De Toledano surmised that those promoting such legislation had "wildly miscalculated." "Many who looked askance at what they considered the President's 'soft' policy on Vietnam," he accurately predicted, "will now rally 'round, shocked at the notion of surrender. Others who quietly supported Mr. Nixon's 'gradualist' policies in Viet Nam will become more vocal."[169] Such actions, coupled with the administration's hints that it had set a deadline of November 1 for the North Vietnamese to cooperate before unleashing extensive military attacks, undermined the volubility and legitimacy of calls for immediate military action or a more definite policy for bringing the North Vietnamese to submission. Anti-war challenges to Vietnamization thereby helped keep conservatives in Nixon's camp, despite their misgivings about the direction of his policies. Nixon's speech of November 3, 1969, reduced opposition and tied the pro-war movement ever closer to peace with honor and Vietnamization.

In early October 1969 the Nixon foreign policy team effectively abandoned the possibility of a massive escalation of military measures when the president rejected the Duck Hook operation. During July and August the administration notified Moscow and Hanoi that it would escalate the conflict after November 1 if Hanoi failed to meet American demands for negotiation. Such escalation would include extensive bombing of North Vietnam and mining operations off coastal ports to prevent the delivery of Soviet supplies to their ally. These acts were designed to psychologically impact the society and political leaders of North Vietnam and were not intended to be simply an escalation of the Johnson administration's attacks on military targets. The operation therefore afforded the opportunity to implement conservatives' long-held interpretation of how to secure military victory. It was rejected by the president for several reasons, not least of which were the questionable military effectiveness of such an operation and the potential international risks of escalation. Public opinion also played a role in Nixon's decision making. As Kimball notes, "Nixon was as sensitive as Laird to political winds." Vietnamization had been part of the effort to win public backing for his Vietnam initiatives.[170] Unleashing a devastating attack on North Vietnam not only might have infuriated the reenergized anti-war movement, which had announced a series of national rallies for October and November, but also might have alienated the public at large. By September only 35 percent of Americans polled favored the president's handling of the war. Recent trends indicated, furthermore, that a majority of Americans identified more readily with the arguments for withdrawal advocated by doves. Indeed, by November less than one-third of those polled identified themselves as hawks.[171] Laird's fixation on Vietnamization further weakened the president's commitment to the highly risky option of extensive military escalation. Nixon's rejection of Duck Hook did not, however, mean he would never again entertain the possibility of military escalation, but it was a private admission that Vietnamization and negotiation were the primary tools in the administration's strategy for ending America's military role in Vietnam while securing the South's independence.

Nixon knew he had to make a dramatic announcement, both to undermine Soviet and North Vietnamese conclusions that he had simply backed down in the face of their intransigence about the November 1 deadline and to rally the public behind his new strategy for de-Americanizing the war. Nixon ordered a series of secret military measures that heightened the readiness of U.S. nuclear forces and dramatically enhanced the activity of conventional forces across the globe. The historians William Burr and Jeffrey Kimball argue that the purpose of these maneuvers, known as the Joint Chiefs of Staff Readiness Test, was to send a signal to the Soviets that Nixon was still committed to the possible use of force.[172]

Domestically, Nixon employed perhaps his most effective strategy at keeping the public onboard as he slowly tried to end the Vietnam War. On November 3, Nixon took the CCPFV's theme of the silent center a step farther, asserting his claim to the "great silent majority of my fellow Americans." The "Silent Majority" speech firmly established Vietnamization as the basis of U.S. policy in Southeast Asia, reducing the likelihood that a large-scale, decisive military operation would be employed. Nixon firmly tied Vietnamization to the "major shift in U.S. foreign policy," the so-called Nixon Doctrine. The "primary mission of our troops," Nixon announced, "is to enable the South Vietnamese forces to assume the full responsibility for the security of South Vietnam." Nixon spoke less of ending the war than of winning "America's peace." Affirming that the U.S. withdrawal would be "made from strength and not from weakness," Nixon spoke of reduced air operations as well, a factor that contradicted the hawkish emphasis on increasing bombing in all theaters of the war. The overwhelming support Nixon received from pro-war lobbies was thus determined by a number of factors not directly related to the policy as outlined by Nixon on November 3. Certainly Nixon's appeal for united American support, his call for citizens to be "united against defeat," his claim that "only Americans" could humiliate the United States, and his emphasis on achieving a "just and lasting peace" did much to engender hawkish and conservative support. Where pro-war backing of Nixon's policy existed, however, it was based on the supposition that his firmness toward domestic opposition to the war would be matched by equal strength in dealing with the North Vietnamese. It was also determined by a somewhat novel interpretation of the authority that would be assumed by the South Vietnamese government and forces.

Vietnamization, pro-war supporters of Nixon proclaimed, would alter and possibly revoke the restrictions on military policy in Vietnam that had plagued earlier attempts at a military victory.

Conservative support for the policy rested on the understanding that a phased withdrawal by the United States would complement, indeed enable, a more aggressive military campaign by the armed forces of South Vietnam. Indeed, this was the principal theme of the documentary film *No Substitute for Victory*, produced by John Wayne in 1970. The liberal argument that China would intervene if its North Vietnamese buffer zone were invaded by U.S. troops could hardly apply, conservatives argued, if the operation were conducted by and for the defense of South Vietnam. Neither would world public opinion, an unnecessarily debilitating force in the eyes of conservatives, be outraged by measures undertaken by South Vietnam to provide for its own security in light of its neighbor's invasion and fostering of domestic insurrection. Such an interpretation of Vietnamization appeared to be corroborated by Nixon's public statement that, following changes in General Abrams's orders, "the primary mission of our troops is to enable the South Vietnamese forces to assume the full responsibility for the security of South Vietnam."[173] *Human Events* questioned whether the United States had the right to "dictate the ground rules under which the South Vietnamese must defend themselves as we shift the major burden of the fighting to Saigon." Nixon's willingness to grant such authority to Saigon, *Human Events* noted, "will determine whether his Vietnamization policy is designed to help them defend their country or is only a cover for the planned withdrawal of U.S. forces."[174]

A White House press release of November 5 avowed that the "predominant view" among the public "at this point is that the President is pursuing the only course open to him." Vietnamization, officials accurately proclaimed, "has particular appeal to the public."[175] The popularity of Nixon's policy was not lost on pro war activists. While the primary attention was paid to Nixon's attacks on anti-war protest and divisiveness in the domestic arena, pro-war conservatives argued that Nixon's willingness to negotiate was predicated on the possibility of greater force being used to compel the enemy to negotiate. Meyer wrote that Nixon's speech had failed to communicate "the meaning of the war in terms of our national interest and security in the century-long struggle with Communism."[176] As the speech promoted popular support for the war, it reaped ardent pro-war praise. Such positive tributes were forthcoming not only from the veterans' and patriotic groups that most unquestioningly endorsed government policy. They also featured in conservative commentary. Continuing to emphasize the use of airpower to secure Vietnamization, conservatives converged as much on the *means* of achieving "a just and lasting peace" as they did on the nature of such a peace.

Conservatives' commitment to the war had changed little since Nixon's campaign began in earnest in 1968. Goldwater, Thurmond, Buckley, and ultimately Reagan believed conservatives had played a vital role in securing Nixon's election, and also saw his understanding of the war's significance as according with their own. Although the administration had failed to grant the conservative movement and its leaders either the respect or the policies they had initially desired, the administration did not fail in its objective of securing conservative endorsement of its Vietnam strategy. Nixon's greatest success in this regard was perhaps his ability to convince conservatives that the policy of Vietnamization had been formulated as part of the Nixon Doctrine, that it was a means of transferring control of the war to the South Vietnamese, rather than an ad hoc strategy designed to facilitate American withdrawal even as the administration attempted to secure a negotiated settlement. Although the ACU and *Human Events* had begun to question the administration's willingness or ability to withstand the political pressures for withdrawal, *National Review* remained firmly committed to the administration's line. Few conservatives were willing to reject Nixon's policy, particularly given its newfound popular appeal, and all remained convinced that Vietnamization did not preclude the implementation of more forceful and unrestricted military measures against North Vietnam. Faith in Nixon's arch-anticommunism proved sufficient to secure conservative support during 1968. Nixon's ability to rally public opinion to his side in late 1969 played no small part in ensuring that this faith had only marginally diminished among conservative leaders. Without a knockout blow against North Vietnam, however, it was unclear how long conservatives would continue to follow the public's line on Vietnamization.

CHAPTER 4

From Victory to Honor

Making Peace with Withdrawal, 1969–1972

> As we withdraw our control and manpower support of the South Vietnamese, it seems likely and not unwise that they would no longer follow ground rules for prosecuting a war for their survival set down by John F. Kennedy.
>
> Patrick Buchanan to the president, December 18, 1969

> If we pass along our political repression to South Vietnam, the strategic outcome is clear. Victory for the enemy.
>
> William F. Buckley Jr., December 18, 1969

Nixon's "Silent Majority" speech engendered a patriotic campaign that rivaled the anti-war effort in its breadth and lasting impact. Patriotic groups and veterans' organizations rallied in support of the president's call for national unity, exemplified by full endorsement of his policies of Vietnamization and negotiation. Labor leaders who continued to back the war, particularly Meaney and Lovestone, urged their memberships to rally behind the president's agenda for solving the Vietnam problem.[1] The speech helped galvanize grassroots support for Nixon's Vietnam agenda and steepened a trend whereby the push for military victory was no longer the basis of activism in favor of the war. Rather, activists focused on challenging anti-war arguments and emphasized the need to support those serving honorably in Vietnam. To build on this momentum the White House unleashed Vice President Agnew to attack anti-war protestors. Agnew was becoming increasingly popular among conservatives, who endorsed his hard-line approach

[125]

to student protest and anti-war activism. He evoked a staunch populist anticommunism that had been more common during the 1950s and that many conservatives believed was necessary to shore up public support for a strong foreign policy. As one editorial surmised, Agnew's appearance might also "provide an explanation for the President's all-out effort to achieve a show of national unity for his Vietnam policy," in light of emerging conservative questioning on this new supposed consensus on Vietnam.²

Indeed, shortly after Nixon's speech in November the ACU expressed its dissatisfaction with government policy in Vietnam and with Nixon's plans for improving relations with the communist world. Commenting on a poll of conservatives and Republican leaders conducted in September, the ACU pronounced that a clear majority favored a "win the war" strategy for Vietnam, a factor that had encouraged the ACU to issue a scathing criticism of Vietnamization in October. "The only real difference," the ACU board declared, "between President Nixon's decision to seek a slow withdrawal of American troops from Vietnam and the screaming demands to 'get out now' from Hanoi and their fellow-traveling dupes in the United States is the matter of timing." Acknowledging that victory could be achieved "even without a large commitment of U.S. ground troops," the ACU questioned whether Nixon would pursue the necessary military steps, such as "blockading Haiphong, bombing supply routes, destroying North Vietnamese bases and power sources." They queried, furthermore, the administration's willingness to allow the South Vietnamese "to carry the war into North Vietnam, as we have so far forbidden them to do." Reiterating a consistent theme of both the Right and other pro-war advocates, the ACU questioned the proposition that the "Communists, [who are bent on] world conquest of which Vietnam is only one step ... will suddenly reverse forty years of history and change overnight." The ACU statement ended by affirming the meaning of the war to U.S. national security interests: "Make no mistake, if America loses this war, there will surely be other Vietnams far more difficult than our present involvement."³

The ACU was remarkable in its failure to accept the political constraints impacting administration policy and in its reluctance to embrace a redefinition of American victory in Vietnam. Differences among conservatives over the meaning of Vietnam were therefore becoming increasingly clear. While the ACU continued to push for a clear military solution to the war, other conservatives realized that public opinion had to be taken into consideration. In an attempt to popularize conservative support for Vietnamization, Buckley therefore charged that Washington had simply failed to convey the new policy's true meaning.[4] He determined to confront the charges made by people such as Burnham that Vietnamization represented an attempt to thwart the enemy from achieving his objective without actually defeating him.[5] Vietnamization, Buckley claimed, enhanced the probability that escalated military measures would be implemented to compel Hanoi to negotiate. For Vietnamization to be successful, the United States must not "pass along our political repressions to South Vietnam." Saigon could not be pressured into succumbing to the unwarranted fear that South Vietnamese action, such as an "amphibious landing north of Haiphong cutting a swathe across central North Vietnam and dividing the country," would result in Chinese intervention. He again argued that "any military authority capable of neutralizing a peashooter" would immediately block the harbors at Haiphong and Sihanoukville, introduce troops to North Vietnam, and cut the Ho Chi Minh Trail from the east. In essence, Buckley argued, "true Vietnamization would set up equilibrium."[6] "True Vietnamization" would result in a situation whereby the United States would provide aid to Saigon similar to that provided by the communist powers to Hanoi and would release South Vietnam from unnecessary political and military constraints. Hanoi's rejection of Vietnamization, based on the expectation that the policy would stiffen the Saigon government and reduce the possibility of reunification, served only to legitimize this interpretation of Vietnamization.

Following his visit to Southeast Asia in December 1969, Goldwater concluded that Vietnamization was a "fine plan to bring our soldiers home without giving up Vietnam to the Communists." He continued to affirm the view that "unless we resume the bombing in the North, there is no way that we can win this war" and asserted his "hope that the President will take this action in conjunction" with phased withdrawal.⁷ Remaining consistent with regard to how to end the war, Goldwater held that the withdrawal of troops, accomplished without undue haste, did not weaken America's position in Vietnam. "Our strength lies," he said, "in our air power, and we can still take advantage of this if we have to and not expose our ground troops to ... danger."⁸ Goldwater may have been somewhat disingenuous when he averred that the administration was "beginning to think as I do," but he genuinely harbored hopes that a military solution could be introduced as troop withdrawals began and accelerated.⁹ As American casualties decreased and the much-anticipated draft reform was introduced, bombing and other necessary military measures would, according to conservatives, surely become more acceptable to the American people.

Buchanan pushed the conservatives' agenda from the White House. His efforts were important for two reasons: they made the administration aware of the causes of conservatives' frustrations; and they helped the administration keep conservatives in line. Despite Buchanan's unrelenting pressure on the administration, he was unable to secure acceptance of the conservative agenda. He succeeded, rather, in helping the White House respond rhetorically to conservative criticisms. In late 1969 conservatives' limited influence on Nixon's Vietnam policies was not clear. Buchanan argued that this was the point at which the president should make plain to the American people the North Vietnamese violations of Laotian neutrality and the terms of the 1968 bombing halt agreement. Recognizing that the American people would not long sustain the large-scale introduction of U.S. troops into Laos, Cambodia, or across the DMZ, Buchanan asked, "Who—besides our political enemies anyhow—is going to get outraged if the South Vietnamese should make a foray into the jungles of Laos in strength and engage the Communists on their supposedly safe grounds?" Buchanan urged that the vice president be instructed to make a speech outlining the communist record of duplicity. He believed this would negate many of the arguments put forward by anti-war critics of the administration. Agnew "can state that in his view the agreements are no longer binding upon us; that it is now not any agreement, but only American restraint, the Presidential desire for peace, that prevents a resumption of bombing; he could argue that no American combat troops are going into Laos or Cambodia, but that as far as our allies fighting for their own survival, we no longer intend to impose upon them arbitrary and artificial conditions in a fight for their life."[10] Despite acknowledging the need to keep conservatives satisfied, Kissinger rejected Buchanan's suggestion, arguing that such a course would likely give the impression that the administration was encouraging President Thieu to "broaden the area of combat."[11] The administration's failure to publicly endorse conservatives' interpretation of Vietnamization led to increased division among conservatives.

In March 1970 some conservatively oriented organizations that were primarily concerned with foreign policy allied to form the American Council for World Freedom (ACWF). This loose federation of approximately twenty groups espoused the principles of the World Anti-Communist League and included among its founding members John Fischer of the ASC, who became president, Walter Judd, who became the founding vice president and then president in 1971, Stefan Possony, William Rusher, Fred Schlafly, David Keene and Michael Thompson of YAF, Adm. Thomas Lane, and Lee Edwards.[12] The ACWF was intended to unify the efforts of anticommunist groups working in the United States and hinder the erosion of support for the anticommunist crusade. Despite the breadth of its support base and perhaps because of its federal nature, the ACWF failed to organize a sustained campaign of education and lobbying. What it represented, however, was the growing collaboration of conservative-oriented groups and their growing doubts about Nixonian foreign policy.

Such disillusionment, particularly with the administration's failure to embark on a policy of military superiority vis-à-vis the Soviet Union, threatened to undermine conservative endorsement of Nixon's policy of Vietnamization. Allan Ryskind of *Human Events*, articulating conservatives' anger with administration policy in both the domestic and international spheres, counseled Nixon's conservative aide Harry Dent that the White House "can't be zigging and zagging all over the ideological spectrum and expect to retain any loyalty and respect."[13] The disillusionment of conservatives with the administration in early 1970 was, however, based primarily on concern about overall conceptions of foreign policy rather than a specific rejection of Vietnamization, and as was true of the groups associated with the ACWF, they remained largely quiet. Such was the case to an even greater extent among conservatives in the Republican Party.

Cambodia

The front page of *Human Events* for May 2, 1969, made available during the last week of April, displayed the headline, "Will Administration End Vacillation? Cambodia Needs U.S. Military Aid." Having originally assessed Vietnamization in positive, if measured, terms, the editors of *Human Events* now argued that Nixon's recent withdrawal announcement "flies in the face of advice" offered by the JCS. On April 20 the president had addressed the nation in a live televised broadcast and had announced that 150,000 American troops would be withdrawn from Vietnam within the year. This was the third and by far the largest troop withdrawal announced by the administration since taking office. Nixon's administration, "hit by an acute case of paralysis," was, *Human Events* stated, withdrawing troops at a time that it should have been sending military aid to the beleaguered Cambodian government in Phnom Penh. Claiming that the situation was reminiscent of Hungary in 1956, *Human Events* charged that there was "far more at stake" in Cambodia and avowed that a "friendly Cambodia out of Communist hands" offered the "magnificent opportunity of winning the Viet Nam war militarily." According to the editorial, "There is general agreement in the Administration that the total collapse of the new Lon Nol government would pose a sizable threat to allied operations in South Viet Nam and have far-reaching consequences for the security of the entire Indochina peninsula." The article maintained that "the President's Guam Doctrine announced last November" required America's material aid to the "plucky Cambodian regime."

The editors thus understood the Nixon Doctrine and Vietnamization to be synonymous and to dictate the extensive provision of aid to the states of Southeast Asia. The editors charged that every "logical reason dictates" that aid be sent to the Cambodian government. Such aid clearly fell within the terms of the Nixon Doctrine, given that the "plucky Cambodian regime" was created specifically to oppose a North Vietnamese invasion of Cambodia.[14] Division within the administration over whether or not to close the port of Sihanoukville was potentially as explosive as the debate over Haiphong harbor, *Human Events* alleged, such that the outcome of the Cambodia question could determine the entire future course of the war.[15]

On April 30 Nixon once again addressed the nation about Vietnam. He dramatically announced that his administration had taken a bold new initiative in its effort to end the Vietnam War: it had decided to send troops into Cambodia. Nixon's decision to launch an allied incursion into the border regions of Cambodia, ostensibly to cut supply routes from North Vietnam, to capture the port of Sihanoukville, to thwart communists' use of sanctuaries, and to destroy the enemy's supposed command base for South Vietnam, exceeded even conservatives' expectations. Finally, the pro-war campaign seemed to be having an impact on administration policy. Nixon's perspective on Cambodia did correlate with that of conservatives, but he was certainly not acting simply to maintain their support. As the hasty U.S. withdrawal would demonstrate, conservatives at this point were not overly influential in determining policy in Vietnam.

From the standpoint of pro-war activists the immediate factors affecting administration policy were less relevant than the symbolic significance and fundamental righteousness of the allied campaign. The operation may indeed have been determined because the secret bombing of Cambodia was proving ineffective, while the power of the country's former prime minister, now perceived to be allied with Hanoi and Beijing, was rapidly developing. In his address to the public Nixon said the operation was undertaken in response to increased enemy activity and had, at its heart, a singularly important goal. "To protect our men who are in Vietnam and to guarantee the continued success of our withdrawal and Vietnamization programs," the president stated, "I have concluded that the time has come for action."[16] Nixon's heroic rhetoric was an attempt, according to Evans and Novak, "to clothe the Cambodian intervention in apocalyptic terms that would persuade the American people that this was no mere military operation but an act of national courage, with high political significance directed not just at the enemy sanctuaries in Cambodia, not just at Hanoi, but at Moscow itself."[17]

By outlining communist disregard for the neutrality of Cambodia and the enemy's privileged use of the sanctuaries along the Cambodia–South Vietnam border, Nixon directly appealed to the demands of his pro-war critics for a presidential explanation of the situation in Vietnam. Echoing advocates of stepped up military responses to enemy activity, Nixon said, "We will not react to this threat to American lives merely by plaintive diplomatic protests. If we did, the credibility of the United States would be destroyed in every area of the world where only the power of the United States deters aggression." Threatening the enemy and in the process offering renewed hope to pro-war lobbies, he again put forward an ambiguous warning to the North Vietnamese: "Tonight, I again warn the North Vietnamese that if they continue to escalate the fighting when the United States is withdrawing its forces, I shall meet my responsibility as Commander in Chief of our Armed Forces to take the action I consider necessary to defend the security of our American men."[18] Vietnamization seemed to once again offer the hope of military escalation.

This is not to suggest that advocates of military escalation were entirely satisfied with the specifics of the Cambodian incursion. During a briefing shortly before the incursion began, Agnew urged the president to authorize a more extensive military campaign than that ultimately conducted during the initial phase of the planned operations. He proposed that the United States and South Vietnam attack all known and presumed enemy sanctuaries rather than only those within the area covered by Phase I (the Fish Hook offensive). Phase II was intended to encompass a broader American invasion of Cambodia but was never fully implemented. The JCS expressed limited faith that South Vietnamese forces were capable of undertaking the invasion, while military and intelligence services doubted the feasibility of capturing the elusive enemy headquarters.¹⁹ As a means of undermining the Khmer Rouge, the Cambodian communist party, and sending a clear message to the North Vietnamese regarding the possibility of intensified military action, the Cambodian operation had somewhat greater merit. Despite the limited scope of the incursion, its presentation, coupled with its implications for future U.S. policy, determined much of the pro-war, particularly conservative, reactions.

Many pro-war and patriotic organizations were informed in advance of the contents of the president's speech and offered unanimous praise for the operation.²⁰ Perhaps because of his organization's growing skepticism of Vietnamization, YAF's executive director Randal Teague was invited to a White House briefing on April 28 and delivered the youth group's subsequent endorsement of presidential policy regarding Cambodia and Vietnam. An aide to Nixon, Charles Colson, stated that YAF was placing full-page advertisements in Sunday's and Monday's *Washington Star* backing the president and requesting that telegrams of support be sent to all congressmen and the White House; it was also sending petitions to Congress and the Paris peace talks.²¹ Such efforts by the White House catalyzed, rather than determined, the responses to Cambodia of organizations such as YAF, the services leagues, and veterans' organizations.

Despite genuine support for the incursion among a majority of Americans, however, the White House public relations campaign was unable to dent the passion of anti-war protest. Among supporters of the operation, anti-war violence and the perception of dovish extremism in Congress served only to enhance support for the embattled president and to augment the hawkishness of the allies' limited engagement in Cambodia. The operation became a symbol of Nixon's willingness to take forceful measures when necessary and signified the attainment of one of the pro-war lobby's long-standing goals. Goldwater claimed that this was the action from which Nixon would achieve "his greatness." He expressed pro-war hopes and passions when he declared the operation "decisive" and its architect "courageous." The operation, he later said, "should be sufficient evidence to prove that President Nixon is not giving up the fight for freedom in Southeast Asia."²²

Thurmond was no less effusive in his praise of Nixon, exulting that the "operation against North Vietnamese sanctuaries . . . is the most courageous action taken by a President since the war in Vietnam began." Reiterating the White House line, Thurmond highlighted the president's role as commander in chief and his obligation to protect the lives of Americans serving in Southeast Asia. He demonstrated as well that he understood the need to help shape public opinion. Leaving an Arms Services Committee briefing at the White House, Thurmond ventured that "the public will also back any stronger moves that he [the president] might take that are designed to bring this war to an earlier end."[23] The allied attack on enemy sanctuaries was, among pro-war lobbies, to be the beginning of a new process for ending the war. While rejecting the antiwar definition that this represented an expansion of the war, advocates of victory in Vietnam charged that the incursion initiated the expansion of militaristic solutions to achieve America's goals. The operation further convinced supporters of the war that congressional liberals, not Nixon, threatened the success of the American campaign in Southeast Asia. This was an important distinction, one that would serve the administration well throughout the war. In May and June 1970 it precluded developing conservative fears regarding the efficacy of administration policy from transforming into open hostility.

Nixon took comfort from the approbation of patriotic groups and veterans' organizations, many of which organized campaigns to demonstrate popular support for the president and his efforts in Cambodia. The American Legion and VFW united to issue a statement endorsing the administration's steps to protect Americans in Southeast Asia. Labor leaders were also vociferous in their praise, especially after pro-Nixon demonstrations organized by labor leaders in New York City in late May (see chapter 5). Backing from the AFL-CIO leadership was unsurprising but more and more unreliable as labor unions began to divide over the Vietnam issue. Determined to sustain the vital labor vote, administration officials were charged with convincing figures such as Meaney to maintain the image of labor's commitment to the cause in Vietnam. Unlike pro-war critics who claimed that the president had failed to clarify the stakes in Cambodia, on May 1 Meaney declared that the "president has clearly outlined the problem to the American people." It was "unmistakably clear," he said, "that he made his decision on the basis of his clear obligation as commander-in-chief to protect American servicemen." Given that military victory was no longer the goal in Vietnam, longtime champions of the war began to advance the theme of supporting the troops. This was not only understood as a way of highlighting the negative consequences of an abrupt withdrawal, but also promoted the continued morality attaching to support for the president's policies. Declaring that Nixon acted "with courage and conviction," Meaney called on the American people to give the president their "full support" during this "crucial hour." Meaney concluded, Nixon "certainly has ours."[24]

The administration recognized the significance of securing the support of Meaney and Lovestone, but despite the promise of Meaney's statement, the constancy of labor was no longer absolute. In describing Meaney's influence, Colson stated that the AFL-CIO president "still runs a one-man show" with regard to the executive council. Colson declared that Lovestone was still "very hard line on foreign policy." Nixon's meeting with Meaney and Lovestone on May 12 was intended not simply to satisfy their queries regarding policy in Vietnam but also to achieve a stronger, more broad-based statement than that originally issued by Meaney. Recognizing the limitations on Meaney, Colson warned that a "stronger statement will be somewhat controversial with the Council" of the AFL-CIO—"certain international presidents will dissent." While the president conveyed the success of the operation to Meaney during their meeting, Colson urged that he make clear to Meaney that "basic U.S. policy in Vietnam is unchanged." Vietnamization and American withdrawal remained the foundation of Nixon's policy for ending the war. Appealing to the arch-anticommunists' concerns about credibility, the president was also advised to assure Meaney and Lovestone that the Cambodian operation "delivers the message that the U.S. will not play the role of the helpless giant," yet again confirming the possibility that similar operations might be undertaken to force an end to communist intransigence.[25] Meaney and Lovestone, along with a majority of labor leaders across the country, continued to defend and praise the Cambodian incursion. No additional statement from the executive council was forthcoming, however, exacerbating the sense of war-weariness that increasingly challenged the administration's room for maneuver regarding policy and action in Southeast Asia.

Press coverage of the incursion also weighed on the minds of administration officials. The Washington Special Actions Group (WSAG), an interdepartmental group within the NSC, issued a memorandum on June 15 that reiterated the need for all group members to "take a confident line with the press and in backgrounders." Stated simply: "The line that 'Cambodia is doomed' must be stopped."[26] Perhaps like no other single event during the war, the invasion of Cambodia provoked a decidedly robust negative response. It reawakened the recently quiet anti-war movement and sparked a campaign of activist opposition within Congress. In the short term the Cambodian incursion produced increasingly well-supported end-the-war amendments—the Cooper–Church amendment called for the withdrawal of U.S. forces from Cambodia by June 30 and ultimately succeeded in influencing, possibly determining, administration policy regarding the incursion.

The Cooper–Church amendment was the first legislation passed in the Senate to limit presidential war powers during a time of war. It was attached to the foreign military sales portion of the Defense Department appropriations bill, and its passage would bar funds for future military operations in Cambodia. Although the administration had already stated its intention to withdraw U.S. troops from Cambodia by June 30, the amendment was passed in the Senate on that date by 58–37. It was defeated in the House of Representatives, but this was not the only threat to the administration's policy. The McGovern–Hatfield amendment called on Congress to terminate all funding for the war in Southeast Asia by the end of 1970 and demanded that all U.S. troops be withdrawn by the end of 1971. This amendment did not pass the Senate, but a major gain for the anti-war faction in Congress had already been achieved. Shortly before the Cambodia operation began, the Senate Foreign Relations Committee voted to repeal the Gulf of Tonkin Resolution, a factor that further inhibited the administration's room for maneuver. The increased likelihood that the resolution would be repealed motivated the administration to act. In order to combat the potential threat that such a measure could have on his credibility regarding Vietnam, Nixon attempted to usurp the repeal issue. Sen. Robert Dole thus attached a repeal amendment to the Foreign Military Sales Act, and on June 24, 1970, the Senate voted 81–10 in favor of repealing the resolution. Dole, on behalf of Nixon, wished to convey the message that the executive did not require such a resolution in order to engage in military efforts such as that in Southeast Asia. But as Lien-Hang Nguyen properly notes, "Time was running out for the war in Vietnam."[27]

Congressional dissent took its toll on administration officials. Colson recalled that a "siege mentality" developed within the White House during this period, an impression enhanced by the belief of advisers such as John Ehrlichman, Bob Haldeman, Daniel Patrick Moynihan, and Ron Ziegler that the nation was embroiled in a "civil war."[28] The White House became increasingly centered on opposing the anti-war movement in both its radical and mainstream, congressional forms. This resulted in a series of ill-fated initiatives designed to uncover international communist and other radical influences on the movement. These efforts may have satiated White House officials' frustration with the anti-war movement in 1970, but they did little to muster widespread support for the war and the president's policies. In fact, they may have detracted from the important goal of keeping political figures in line on Vietnam. Colin Dueck comments that Nixon "almost seemed to welcome" the bitter polarization within American society that was revealed by responses to the Cambodian operation. As he correctly notes, many in the White House, including Haldeman, Agnew, and Buchanan relied on this "positive polarization" to create a new political majority by appealing to social and cultural conservatives.[29] Others in the White House, Colson in particular, were certainly not averse to this kind of political opportunism, but they recognized that the divisions within American society over the war were complex. Many, Colson realized, who were angered by the anti-war movement and who vocally proclaimed their support of the president also wanted the war to end and end quickly. Nixon's failure to achieve this goal might easily result in their becoming frustrated with the president. Such concerns added weight to the arguments against escalation offered by Laird and William Rogers, who had opposed the Cambodian operation. Domestic policy advisers like Donald Rumsfeld also questioned why Vietnamization could not be implemented more quickly.[30]

Congressional opposition to the operation certainly limited the president's policy options in Cambodia, but it also threatened to undermine his whole strategic conception for ending the war. It was still unlikely that a blatantly anti-war amendment would succeed in passing both houses of Congress. Yet the impact of such efforts jeopardized the legitimacy and efficacy of Vietnamization by augmenting the possibility that the rate of withdrawal would depend on factors beyond the control of the president. Of the Cooper–Church amendment Thurmond warned in June, "While it is my belief that the House of Representatives will never accept the amendment, the psychological effect [of its passage by the Senate] will be a repudiation of the Nixon Doctrine which called upon our Asian allies to stand together in their own defense.... The Senate would in effect be casting Cambodia into the jaws of the Communist expansion and if engulfed South Vietnam and Thailand could follow."[31] Despite Thurmond's backing of the president, his warning hinted at questioning of the administration's implementation of its own doctrinal contribution to U.S. foreign policy. With regard to Vietnam, however, such fears were undermined by the drama unfolding in America with regard to the Cambodian operation. The congressional challenge to presidential war powers produced an equivalent siege mentality among advocates of the war. Rather than further challenge the Nixon policy of limited war and negotiation, pro-war lobbies ever more vociferously demanded and provided support for Vietnamization, now linked to the president's alleged Cambodian triumph.

The conservative community responded with an almost unanimous endorsement of the Cambodian operation. *Human Events* declared passage of the Cooper–Church amendment shameful and Nixon's policy of extrication from Vietnam successful.[32] Supporters of the president claimed that passage of the Cooper–Church amendment jeopardized the safety of American troops and prisoners of war (POWs) in Southeast Asia, wrecked any chance for a negotiated settlement, and amounted, in the words of Thurmond, to "the waving of a white flag to the forces of tyranny and oppression."[33] The conservative activist James Jackson Kilpatrick described his reaction as one of pride and elation on hearing of Nixon's "courageous, necessary and wise" decision to launch an attack against enemy sanctuaries. Nixon had not simply revealed his understanding "that the enemy retreats from a positive show of force" but also had answered "the question in Hanoi, in Moscow, in Peking" as to whether he was bluffing in his promise to respond to intensified enemy activity.[34] Under a headline reading, "America Stands with Nixon," the ACU's *Battle Line* retracted its earlier questioning of Vietnamization: "Last December in these pages we questioned what would happen at that fateful point at which the withdrawal of American troops produced the inevitable Communist military offensive aimed at taking advantage of reduced U.S. strength in Vietnam. Now we have an answer. The President of the United States has determined that he will act, and act decisively, even if it supposedly means the diminution of his own and his party's political fortunes." "Common logic," *Battle Line*'s editors argued, dictated endorsement of the president's chosen course in Vietnam and Cambodia.[35]

The ACU's board was also quick in its positive response to the allied operation. On May 1 John Ashbrook urged the commander in chief to ignore voices of dissent and opposition and declared that the president's act "is a courageous recognition that the surest way to win an honorable peace in Southeast Asia is the swift and complete destruction of Communist forces and facilities on the ground."[36] The Cambodian incursion cemented the heretofore nascent pro-war interpretation of Vietnamization as a U.S. troop withdrawal coupled with extraordinary militaristic efforts to force effective enemy surrender.

While praising the Cambodian incursion, Goldwater exhorted the administration to take greater measures to explain to the American people the critical nature of the incursion and the "extreme value of that part of the world."[37] Overall, Goldwater remained positive about the incursion. He attended a White House briefing on the operation and wrote privately afterward that carrying the war into Cambodia put the "monkey" on the "back of the North Vietnamese who if they loose (sic) in Cambodia and are forced back into Laos, will probably sue for peace." He acknowledged that the incursion was "a gamble and a very serious one, but I think the decision he made was one of those that Presidents occasionally are faced with such as Harry Truman in the use of the Atomic Bomb and eventually into Korea."[38] But Goldwater displayed a semblance of mistrust regarding the policy of Vietnamization when he wrote to the president on May 6, "Unless you have given up achieving a victory by our forces and are going to put that monkey on the backs of the South Vietnamese with our withdrawal, I think that bombing of the north must be resumed." The conservative obsession with bombing North Vietnam indicated that they expected an element of victory to be achieved by forcing the enemy to comply with Americans' terms for ending the war. Goldwater summed up as follows: "The enemy will not quit until he is hurt and this enemy has not been hurt where hurting must be done, namely, close to home. I again urge you to proceed with the destruction of the stockpile of material north of the DMZ and progressively go far north to convince Hanoi that we want to win."[39] The Cambodian incursion coupled with limited bombing of North Vietnam did not, therefore, satisfy conservatives' demands for military escalation. It did, however, add sufficient credibility to Vietnamization to warrant committed, public conservative backing.

Burnham, who had earlier despaired of Nixon's withdrawal policy, was given hope by the incursion, the bombing of North Vietnam, and the occasional success of the South Vietnamese armed forces.[40] *National Review,* in fact, published consistently positive analyses of the president's policies regarding Vietnam in the months following the incursion, including a legal defense of the operation and a repudiation of the Cooper–Church amendment.[41] Buckley reasoned that despite Americans' actions in "bombing the hell out of the Ho Chi Minh Trail" and their success "in intercepting a great deal of the enemy's traffic," enough material always got through to sustain the enemy's effort in Cambodia and South

Vietnam. Buckley thus argued that the "logistical responsibilities" of Vietnamization clearly demanded American action to support and supply its ally and thwart the effort of the enemy, just "as the Soviet Union accepts the logistical responsibilities of supplying the North Vietnamese communists who are pouring into Cambodia." The stakes were so high, Buckley declared, that by caviling "over the technicality of Cambodia, we are throwing away everything we have fought for during the past six costly, bloody, tragic years."[42]

Buckley's brother James, who successfully ran as a senatorial candidate for New York on the Conservative Party ticket in 1970, also praised the president, although he took a somewhat softer line. He declared that Nixon "made it clear his sole objective is to protect American lives and to achieve an early but honorable end to the Vietnam war, and that the strike against a major North Vietnamese base in enemy occupied Cambodia is essential to the attainment of these ends."[43] While the conservative response was one of praise for the president's course of action, it was more diverse in its implications than it originally appeared. Support for the admittedly limited incursion into Cambodia and restrained bombing of North Vietnam encouraged conservatives' belief that Vietnamization would result in additional militaristic measures and would allow the South Vietnamese to pursue an attack against North Vietnam. The extent to which such support would be maintained in the light of continued withdrawal was unclear, however.

The Cambodian operation and its aftermath in the domestic arena did have its downside within the conservative movement. The killing of four students by Ohio National Guardsmen during a protest at Kent State University, for example, prompted many Americans to question the toll the war was taking on their society. Whereas many may have been willing to simply blame the anti-war movement for sparking divisions during the early years of the war, the emergence of mainstream dissent and a credibility gap relating to the administration's assertions regarding Vietnam reduced any possibility that radicals could be branded as the sole cause of social division. The operation resulted, most notably, in the complete defection of Garry Wills from the pro-war cause. Wills, a Buckley protégé and well-known conservative political commentator, opposed the war as early as 1968, but the Cambodian incursion was the point at which he chose to join the ranks of the heterogeneous anti-war campaign. Wills's defection greatly unsettled the conservative ranks, not least because it coincided with growing opposition to the continuation of the war among conservative Democrats in Congress. Writing to Buckley shortly after the Cambodian incursion began, Wills declared that he had begun his own column and had "signed on for the duration of the war." Warning Buckley, "You won't like them" but appealing to his mentor to "stay 'soft' on their author," Wills divulged his position on the war: "I decided the day after Kent State—Nixon has to be stopped. The war has to be."[44] Buckley lamented Wills's loss of influence through his hasty retreat into the ranks of the anti-war side.[45] It was difficult to deny, however, that the war's longevity and Nixon's policies of phased withdrawal were likely to draw greater conservative opposition, above all among grassroots activists angered by the war's contribution to the growing extremism and divisions within American society.

Rusher, writing to Buchanan shortly afterward, assumed a more resolute stance. "I hope it may console you," he wrote, "to know that Frank Meyer, in his column in . . . *National Review* . . . sorrowfully but firmly reads Garry out of the conservative movement altogether."[46] Meyer's position symbolized the continued conservative commitment to the Vietnam War, despite its potentially negative effect on U.S. maneuverability in the international arena. Describing his position on the war, Wills hardly exemplified the typical advocate of immediate withdrawal: "A friend, indignant on the phone, said, 'You don't want instant withdrawal, do you?' I said yes. 'You mean you want the Russians to take over Vietnam?' I said that did not seem likely. But by his standards I *should* want it to happen: if Vietnam could cause Russia even half the trouble it has caused us, surrendering that country would be our best coup of the Cold War."[47] Wills's stance resonated with conservatives who were disillusioned with the administration's policy of limited war. But most conservatives continued to believe that success in Vietnam was vital to American credibility. The symbolic boldness of the Cambodian incursion, coupled with the onslaught of anti-war rhetoric, prompted the conservative leadership to ever more vociferously defend the administration's position on Vietnam. The defense of the administration was visible in a series of grassroots displays of support for the Nixon administration, events that culminated in the pro-Nixon Honor America Day Rally on the National Mall (see chapter 5).

Human Events used the Cambodian operation to highlight the intransigence and political posturing of anti-war congressmen. In reference to the Democratic doves' failure to extol Nixon's announcement that because of the Cambodian operation an additional fifty thousand troops could be withdrawn, Morrie Ryskind, the scriptwriter and director turned political activist who was the father of Allan Ryskind, surmised that the doves would have preferred it if Nixon had announced defeat in Cambodia.[48] Agnew's prognosis was music to conservatives' seemingly ignored ears: "Why should the aggressors make the ground rules for the conflict; why should the Communists determine the time and the place of the battle; why should we circumscribe our operations when they do not constrict theirs? . . . We do not need gratuitous advice from those who could neither end the war nor win it on how to conduct this quest for peace successfully—from those who stay up days and nights justifying their blunders and dreaming up new concessions to the enemy who takes concessions as signs of weakness—whose goal is not a negotiated settlement—but a Carthaginian peace. We are going to deny the enemy that victory."[49] The operation quickly became a symbol of the administration's steadfast refusal to accept the arguments of the anti-war movement regarding the morality of America's cause and the efficacy of military escalation.

According to Nixon's admirers the operation had been decisive in capturing enemy supplies and the vital port of Sihanoukville, which prevented an enemy offensive during the dry season in 1970 and would severely disrupt any future assaults against South Vietnam. Such assessments of the operation were overly positive. They echoed the administration's rhetoric and assurances and were based on ideological and theoretical assessments of the operation's effectiveness rather than on independent evaluations of its strategic value. Kissinger claimed that the operation served a vital function in weakening North Vietnamese capabilities regarding attacks on South Vietnam for the duration of the war.[50] A secret WSAG report described the president's desire to continue some air activities to reduce enemy interdiction, a policy that took precedence over avoiding risks with regard to public opinion. Echoing hawkish sentiment, Nixon expressed the view that South Vietnamese forces should be let loose to react to enemy activities after the deadline of June 30 established by Congress. "Possible South Vietnamese actions," the WSAG report declared, "are one of the main deterrents to North Vietnam; this deterrent effect must be maintained," while "South Vietnamese forces should undertake offensive spoiling actions."[51]

Nixon could hardly ignore the clamorous calls for withdrawal from Cambodia that emanated from Congress and echoed across the country. Opponents continued to challenge the Cooper–Church amendment, but its passage in the Senate on June 30 by a vote of 58 to 37 hardly came as a surprise to the administration. The White House had already made the decision to withdraw American ground forces from Cambodia and would continue to denounce measures such as the Cooper–Church amendment for the duration of the war. Nonetheless, Congress was thereafter seen as a formidable foe, one that could affect the course of the war. On June 30, 1970, Nixon delivered another address to the nation on the subject of the incursion. Reiterating the significance of the Cambodian sanctuaries to enemy activity, Nixon presented the allied withdrawal from Cambodia as a logical, intended aspect of the operation. Nixon's private position was similar to that of his pro-war supporters, a fact that was emphasized to such figures. Speaking in July, Nixon questioned whether the Cambodian incursion would be as decisive as Stalingrad or D-Day, stating "Only history will tell," but he certainly conveyed the decisiveness of the operation in terms of forestalling the enemy's plans and allowing the continuation of Vietnamization. The operation demonstrated, Nixon declared, "that the South Vietnamese now, for the first time tested in battle by themselves against the North Vietnamese, can handle themselves, that Vietnamization can work and will work, and that we can get out, and they can stay in and hold their own." Of greater import to hawks, however, were Nixon's contention that the operation had changed the military balance and his assertion that while U.S. troops would not be reintroduced to Cambodia he would "use, as I should, the airpower of the United States to interdict all flows of men and supplies which I consider are directed toward South Vietnam." "In fact," Nixon continued, "at the time we embarked on the April 30 operation, I ordered some attacks on some sites in North Viet-Nam which had been shooting our planes," an action much applauded within hawkish ranks. Appealing to hawks' preferred policies, he continued, "If those attacks should now develop again, I will, of course, use our American airpower against North Viet-Nam sites that attack our planes."[52]

The bombing campaign and the incursion may not have been implemented to hawkish tastes, but they supported the thesis of pro-administration conservatives that Vietnamization would enable a more conventional conduct of the war to be brought to bear. Nixon's "non-intellectual way of dealing with the foe . . . seems effective," Morrie Ryskind wrote, while opposition to the operation was simply evidence of the doves' attempt to "snatch defeat from the jaws of victory."[53] Still, there could be no denying the strength of anti-war opinion in Congress and the clear evidence of war-weariness among the wider public. If Vietnamization was to succeed, it would have to do so sooner rather than later.

Pushing Nixon to the Right

Throughout his tenure as commander of the American war in Vietnam, Nixon considered what was referred to as the "option to the right," which effectively amounted to large-scale U.S. troop withdrawal coupled with massive bombing of North Vietnam in order to destroy the enemy's ability to wage war and force its surrender. Kissinger consistently cautioned against the idea. The strategy was usually considered when negotiations were stalemated or the military situation in Vietnam seemed to deteriorate. It was also considered as Congress moved closer to setting a deadline for withdrawal but was undermined as a viable option by this same process. Yet there was only limited public evidence of the president's support for escalated bombing. By late 1970 the kudos earned by the Cambodian incursion began to recede within certain circles of the pro-war community.

In August 1970 Ralph de Toledano charged that *National Review* had become a "house organ" of the Nixon administration. De Toledano's claim reflected his personal animosity toward Rusher, the ACU, and *National Review*.[54] This broadside, while inaccurate, originated in Buckley's close association with the administration and was evidence of a perceived failure on the part of the *National Review* circle to fully criticize the long list of Nixon policies that were anathema to conservative goals.[55] Buchanan later warned that Nixon was no longer perceived as a credible custodian of the conservative political tradition of the Republican Party.[56] Although it challenged certain of the administration's domestic measures, during late 1970 *National Review* regularly backed Nixon's Vietnam policies, a factor that enhanced claims that the journal was pursuing an insider, accommodationist policy as far as the administration was concerned. According to Buckley's biographer, most conservatives believed that Kissinger in particular was doing a PR job on Buckley.[57] David Keene later remarked that he thought Buckley had been taken in by Kissinger: "Bill was very con-able, partly because he did want to be in, and Kissinger gave everybody that he talked to in those days the sense that they were indeed 'in.'"[58] In interview with *Playboy* in 1970 Buckley reacted by turning humorous about his closeness to the administration, saying he had "discovered a new sensual treat. . . . It is to have the President of the United States take notes while you are speaking to him, even though you run the risk that he is scribbling, 'Get this bore out of here.'"[59] Buckley undoubtedly valued his relationship with the administration very highly. He was appointed to serve on the five-member advisory commission on information of the United States Information Agency in 1969 and did so until he declined reappointment in late 1972. He was then appointed by President Nixon as a public member of the United States Delegation to the 28th General Assembly of the United Nations. Like Burnham, he understood that future conservative power rested solidly within the ranks of the Republican Party and was, for the moment, dependent on Nixon's patronage.

Nonetheless, some within the White House were evidently uneasy about the political fallout from a potential conservative defection. Buchanan, writing to the president in January 1971, in a memorandum titled, "Trouble on the Right," cautioned that, "while Buckley's influence nationally is enormous, his influence among the hard-core right politicos is being diminished, and we cannot count on his bringing them over [in the 1972 election]." He concluded, "Buckley gets a bit of the same constant criticism that conservatives in the White House do—that they've 'sold out.'"[60] Such debate and division regarding Vietnam and the Nixon administration began to take a toll on the conservative political movement. Libertarians had, by the late 1960s, abandoned the conservative consensus regarding the Vietnam War, a development that caused a controversial and debilitating split at the YAF national convention in August 1969.[61] At *National Review,* stalwarts of the pro-war campaign such as Meyer and Rusher turned up the volume as they coaxed their fellow conservatives to break with Nixon. Meyer deplored the negative effect the protracted Vietnam conflict was having on the conservative consensus, believing that its longevity was blunting popular approval of the struggle against communism. While acknowledging that Nixon had done much to withstand anti-war protest, especially congressional pressure, Meyer and others increasingly bemoaned the association of conservatives with the administration's limited policy in Vietnam.

The tensions among conservatives were evident at the tenth anniversary celebrations honoring the founding of YAF, held at Buckley's estate in Sharon, Connecticut, in September 1970. YAF was rapidly becoming a vocal critic of the Nixon administration, which reflected the ACU's increasingly public challenges to the White House's domestic and foreign policy agendas. The aim of the gathering was to underscore the continued unity of the "responsible Right." Providing a forum for a collective response to the prevailing policy considerations of the day, foreign policy issues dominated the agenda and the writings of Goldwater, Reagan, Thurmond, and John Tower, who joined Buckley in contributing to the special edition of the *New Guard.* Tower, a resolute enthusiast of the administration's policy in Vietnam, used his position as a member of the national board of YAF to promote the hard-line nature of the president's foreign policies at this event. Tower asserted that if the United States relaxed its national defense posture, "there will be no turning back and there may be no hope for our own future." With regard to Vietnam, he lamented the difficulty the United States encountered fighting a guerrilla enemy but felt that "measured success" had been achieved. Stating that the "Nixon administration is determined to see the issue to a successful and honorable conclusion," he assured conservatives that the administration was "not prepared to accept a camouflaged surrender to the demands of Hanoi." Tower did more than simply reaffirm the administration's standard line: he also stated that there was "no doubt that a substantial residual American force will have to be maintained there for some time." Referring no doubt to conservative expectations and hopes regarding the implementation and implications of Vietnamization, he asserted that "we will have to continue to provide logistical, air and naval support to the South Vietnamese," while also looking "to the sanitization of Laos and Cambodia."[62] Tower was determined to prevent conservative questioning of administration policy from turning into outright opposition, but his rosy depiction of the administration's strategies could serve to stem this tide only momentarily.

Conservatives, indeed, found themselves defending administration policy in light of the growing strength of anti-war efforts in Congress. Writing after the war, Kissinger acknowledged that during the debate over the Cooper–Church amendment, conservatives had become "demoralized by a war that had turned into a retreat." In August 1970 Senators Harry Byrd Jr. and Gordon Allott had urged the president to end the war as quickly as possible, an episode that apparently prompted Nixon to remark, "When the Right starts wanting to get out, for whatever reason, that's *our* problem."[63] Byrd, who had represented Virginia in the senate since his father's death in 1966, demonstrated his independent streak in 1970 when he officially broke with the Democratic Party over his refusal to sign a loyalty oath to the party. Byrd was not alone among southern Democrats in doubting the utility of continuing the slow withdrawal from Vietnam. Many of the original "heavier bomber boys" from the South were now privately expressing their limited commitment to the continuation of the war. Allott, a Republican from Colorado, had been an early and strong advocate of military escalation. His admonitions to Nixon mirrored Laird's preoccupation about the political fallout from a long-term continuation of the war under a Republican administration. Nixon faced the additional pressure to end the conflict stemming from hawkish Republicans' anxieties about the midterm elections of 1970. In October Nixon dropped his earlier demand for a mutual withdrawal of troops. This did not particularly bother the broad swathe of his supporters, but it did result in stringent opposition from activists in the conservative movement.

Conceding the likelihood of pro-war dissent, the administration attempted to persuade hawks that the president's military advisers supported the measure and that unilateral withdrawal was possible because of the newfound strength of the South Vietnamese armed forces, which were then preparing for an offensive against North Vietnamese troops in Cambodia that began on October 24. During a cabinet meeting on the day the peace initiative was announced, Nixon stated that the proposal "goes very far—frankly as far as we can go" in terms of concessions.[64] Days later Colson advised the president to stress General Westmoreland's favorable opinion of the proposal during his forthcoming meeting with Meaney and Lovestone. "In view of Meaney's 'hawkishness,'" Colson wrote, "it is important to point out that in Westmoreland's opinion, we will gain a military advantage from the cease fire." The president was also advised to convey the inevitability of withdrawal from Vietnam, either through a negotiated settlement or Vietnamization, "on a basis that protects both our fighting men and our objectives in Southeast Asia."[65]

Secretary Laird's testimony before the Senate Foreign Relations Committee on October 24 reinforced the ambiguous nature of the president's policies. Laird continued his now-standard line of referring to the limited bombing of North Vietnam as "protective reaction." The Americans' reaction was simply based on the enemy's violations of the agreements of 1968, that is, North Vietnamese attacks on reconnaissance planes and their shelling of Hué and Saigon. He also hinted at the possibility that the United States might renounce its "understandings" with Hanoi and resume extensive bombing of North Vietnam. "The situation is such that I would recommend calling off that cessation of bombing," Laird stated, "should there be major violations of these understandings. I have always said that if a major force comes across the DMZ, I would be strong in my recommendation . . . that we commence bombing."[66] While quick to point out to the committee that U.S. policy had not changed, Laird noted in his testimony the administration's recent frustration with enemy activity and the need to at least appear to be responding to conservatives' latent anxieties.

Buckley, writing days after Laird's testimony, demonstrated his alarm at the administration's failure to resume large-scale bombing of North Vietnam. He was also frustrated by Laird's stated rationale for the recent attacks, namely, that they were simply a response to attacks on U.S. reconnaissance planes. He acknowledged that the president had to wait some time after his election before resuming the bombing in order to avoid dashing the "hopes of the free world," thereby confirming the "suspicions of those Americans who warned against the election of a Dr. Strangelove." But Buckley was puzzled by the continuation of the bombing halt in light of the enemy's demonstrated aggressiveness. Citing the evidence that the bombing of North Vietnam between 1965 and 1968 had caused major damage to the enemy, he second-guessed the Defense Department's stated rationale for initiating the recent bombings. He demanded to know why the administration had not stated that "a reason for resuming the bombing and indeed stepping up the bombing on a steady basis, [was] the enemy's principal default on its agreement." The "shooting down of an airplane with two American pilots in it" was obviously just such a violation. But of far greater significance was the enemy's "prolongation of a war which, although it is costing less and less, still accounts for the death of more Americans per week than all the North Vietnamese negotiators who sit in Paris, doing nothing, and doing nothing on purpose."[67] Buckley was concerned less with administration policy in this instance than with the ways in which such policies were being explained and sold to the American people. Rationalizing the bombing on the basis of specific transgressions of the 1968 agreement failed to convey the larger, international, and moral impetuses defining the American purpose in Vietnam.

Pro-war frustrations with administration policy were muted, however, by the now-extreme demands of the anti-war campaign and the rising popular appeal of withdrawal options. Opposition to the setting of a deadline or specific timetable for withdrawal preoccupied pro-war energies and limited genuine dissent against the administration. Furthermore, after Hanoi rejected Nixon's proposals in October and declared on December 5 that it would continue to attack reconnaissance planes it seemed likely the administration would heed Buckley's demands. Conservatives were also responding to the administration's largely symbolic acts, the most significant of which was the American raid on the POW camp at Son Tay, near Hanoi, on November 30. U.S. Special Forces entered the prison camp, but the raid failed to secure the release of any prisoners, who had been moved from the prison in July. While the limited availability of up-to-date intelligence suggested that this might be the case, the administration was determined to initiate a bold gesture to rescue American POWS. Writing in the *New York Times,* Barbara Ondrasik of the National League of Families of American Prisoners and Missing in Southeast Asia, commented that "the daring commando raid . . . could be termed a failure militarily," but "in terms of morale, the raid was outstanding."[68] The focus on symbolic gestures was never highly appealing to conservative supporters of the war, but at this time it signified the administration's willingness to openly defy the anti-war movement and to directly strike into North Vietnam.

In December *Newsweek* reported that the president seemed poised to resume intense bombing of North Vietnam, "to the dismay of doves in the U.S. Congress, the anger of the enemy in Hanoi and the puzzlement of many Americans." Nixon, while continuing to refer largely to retaliatory attacks for the shooting of reconnaissance planes, posited ambiguous criteria for a return to greater bombing. "Now," he said, "if as a result of my conclusion that the North Vietnamese, by their infiltrations, threaten our remaining forces, if they thereby develop a capacity, and they proceed possibly to use that capacity to increase the level of fighting in South Vietnam, then I will order the bombing of military sites in North Vietnam."⁶⁹ The continued possibility that Nixon might escalate the bombing attenuated conservatives' willingness to publicly oppose the administration. Yet their misgivings could not be fully allayed by such reports. Rather than affirm administration policy, conservatives began a process of pushing Nixon to the right.

In January 1971 Buchanan had cautioned, "We have a serious political problem developing on the Right." He said that the "originally localized . . . infection is spreading and now being broadcast, through the press, to the party structure nationally." Detailing conservative opposition to Nixon's "liberal Democratic domestic program" and his apparent lack of sensitivity to conservative interests beyond election times, Buchanan's dire summation was that "the situation on the Right is as bad as I have known it, since joining RN."⁷⁰ He supplemented his analysis with a more damning report on attitudes toward the government: "Left and right, most now argue aloud that the President, and his Administration, do not take decisions on the basis of political principle—but on the basis of expediency; that ours is an 'ad hoc government,' which responds only as pressures mount from left or right." Reflecting conservative fears with regard to the strategic defense capability of the United States, Buchanan warned against the administration's policy of underscoring "how much more rapidly we are bringing Americans home from Vietnam and the rest of the world" and the tendency to "congratulate ourselves on each new cut in the defense budget."⁷¹

Publicly, Meyer lambasted Nixon's failure to pay adequate attention to defense spending and charged that "our national existence depends upon the credibility of our deterrent, and the maintenance of an unquestionable deterrent power must be the first charge on our revenues."⁷² In January the ACU issued a broad attack, born of frustration and anger, on Nixon's foreign policies: "Appease Red China. Encourage Red trade. SALT [Strategic Arms Limitation Talks] talks forever. Cut defense costs to the bone. Get out of Vietnam, with only the pace of withdrawals the issue. Victory? Barry Goldwater's beloved blockading of Haiphong? No, sir."⁷³ Despite their evident displeasure with the administration's foreign policies, neither the ACU nor *National Review* was willing to openly challenge Vietnamization. In part, their reluctance stemmed from conservatives' focus on defense spending as the greatest weakness of the administration's foreign policy record; and in part, it was conditioned by the widespread popularity of Vietnamization among grassroots supporters of the war. Recognition, in fact, that Nixon was at least attempting to salvage some measure of American credibility in Vietnam earned conservatives' grudging appreciation.

Conservative leaders in the Republican Party, attuned to the program's popular appeal, were loath to disavow Vietnamization. Goldwater wrote of his meeting with the president in mid-December 1970, "I told him I thought his Vietnamization plan was going along as well as could be expected, but I still had reservations about the South Vietnamese infantry being able to come up to battle standards in any number sufficient to offset the skill and equipment of the North Vietnamese and the remaining Viet Cong." He praised Nixon's decision to bomb North Vietnam, describing it as "absolutely correct," but conveyed an overall tone of pessimism regarding Vietnam policy.[74] Writing a month later in a confidential memorandum, Goldwater said, "Looking back over the past several months I continue to be amazed at the ineptitude that President Nixon has shown in the operation of the government."[75]

Publicly, however, Goldwater offered a resounding endorsement of the administration, a position in large part replicated by the leadership of the conservative movement at the annual Conservative Awards Dinner in February. Meeting days before the awards dinner, Buchanan pressed his colleagues to emphasize the president's commitment to conservative values regarding the economy and his dedication to a strong foreign policy. With regard to Vietnam, Buchanan dwelled on one of the administration's greatest strengths: the president's refusal to assuage the demands of the anti-war faction in Congress. "Despite national opposition," Buchanan commented, "*he has hung in there in Vietnam.*" Averring that Nixon possessed "the courage to do what Rusk and Johnson would not do," Buchanan again stressed Nixon's invasion of Cambodia "*to wipe out the sanctuaries.*" Referring to the Son Tay raid, the administration's unwavering attention to the POW issue, and the favorable military situation in the northeast of South Vietnam, senior officials solicited promotion of the view that "RN has stayed the course for an anti-Communist Vietnam against massive media pressure, and against continuing public disillusionment with the war."[76] While domestic issues preoccupied conservatives' energies during this period, conservative supporters of the administration, citing its foreign policy record, demanded overall buttressing of the president's policy agenda. Both Representative Crane and Senator Buckley "urged conservatives to back this Administration."[77] Although many were beginning to question such issues as lessening trade and travel restrictions with communist China and the continuation of SALT, the dominant position of the conservative leadership was one of support for Nixon's foreign policy.

Lam Son 719

Lam Son 719, the Republic of Vietnam's incursion against enemy sanctuaries and supply routes in Laos, began on February 8, 1971. The United States supplied air and logistical support, but forces of the Army of the Republic of Vietnam (ARVN) met ferocious enemy opposition and largely failed in their objectives. On a popular level in the United States, the operation was perceived as evidence of the limited success of the Vietnamization program. It not only increased congressional pressure for a withdrawal deadline but also acted, according to the political commentators Evans and Novak, as "the unexpected catalyst that brought into the open this politically pre-eminent fact: public opinion had sustained nearly all it would or could in Vietnam."[78] Nixon, always mindful of the impact of Vietnam on the elections of 1972, could ill afford to ignore popular frustrations. Furthermore, Nixon's and Kissinger's disappointment with President Thieu's handling of the invasion forced them to reconsider the trajectory of the administration's policies, which resulted in continued air sorties by the United States over Laos and North Vietnam. Determined to boost the credibility of Vietnamization, Nixon emphasized America's commitment to supplying South Vietnam with adequate materials for its own defense and reiterated the possibility that the air force might well be employed against North Vietnam following troop withdrawal. Privately, Nixon continued to consider playing the massive bombing card to force North Vietnamese compliance with American peace proposals.[79]

Conservatives had high hopes for the Laotian campaign. Writing to Ambassador Ellsworth Bunker shortly after the commencement of the operation, Judd asserted his faith that Hanoi would have to "throw everything she has into defeating the effort to cut off the Laotian supply routes." "If Hanoi fails," he concluded, "then it seems fairly clear that it will simply have to call off its aggression and return its forces to North Vietnam with real hope for a good future for Southeast Asia."[80] Bunker's assurances that despite early pessimistic reporting the Laos campaign had gone "exceedingly well" and his focus on the vital importance of American air support echoed the administration's guarantees to the pro-war community. The provision of logistical and air support to the ARVN during the campaign, coupled with American sorties against North Vietnam, engendered a high degree of pro-war support. The Laos campaign was not only hailed as a final justification of pro-war calls for cutting the Ho Chi Minh Trail and attacking the Laotian sanctuaries, but also understood as a vindication of the pro-war interpretation of Vietnamization. Speaking shortly after the Laos campaign began, Thurmond defended the use of U.S. airpower in Laos, describing it as a "legitimate function of our presence in Southeast Asia" and "necessary to protect our troops during the period of withdrawal." Thurmond believed the operation allowed Saigon to assume further control of the war, such that the "United States would not interfere if South Vietnam decided that the time had come to march into enemy territory." This option was made possible, he claimed, by withdrawal and the transfer of adequate aid to the South Vietnamese over the course of the Vietnamization program. "Vietnamization," Thurmond declared, "is the answer to the Communist plan of terrorism and violence."[81]

Thurmond did not greatly reassess his public position on Vietnamization once the outcome of the operation became clearer. In April he declared that the president's policy "is working," stating that the "fighting is no longer significant within South Vietnam."[82]

Battle Line said the operation was "long-overdue" but also claimed it was a "potentially significant step." Admiral Lane wrote in *Human Events*, "By 1972, it will be clear that the war was ended not by talks in Paris, not by the withdrawal of U.S. forces . . . but by support of our allies in Southeast Asia. They will defeat North Viet Nam, doing under President Nixon what Presidents Kennedy and Johnson would not allow them to do." Hanoi had now been put on the defensive, so that the regime "faces not an assured victory, but an assured defeat." Lane challenged anti-war opposition to the operation: "Why shouldn't South Viet Nam and Thailand, *which can defeat North Viet Nam*, defend Laos and Cambodia, which cannot? . . . How can the Nixon Doctrine ever succeed in keeping the peace if we cripple our allies with restraints on their rights of self-defense?"[83]

Arguing that the invasion could severely disrupt Hanoi's ability to supply its troops in Cambodia and South Vietnam, the ACU claimed that the operation's real value rested with its implications for South Vietnamese control of the war. This was not simply political posturing; as Sarah Katherine Mergel notes, "Conservative intellectuals believed that the results of the operation in Laos showed that once the negotiations reached a settlement, the South would be able to resist pressure from the North."[84] Clearly hinting at a possible invasion of North Vietnam, the ACU surmised that the operation "establishes a precedent that will be extremely valuable to Saigon as the Vietnamization program continues: a border-crossing operation both conceived and executed (at least on the ground) by South Vietnamese soldiers." Despite its earlier criticism of administration policy, the ACU now confirmed Sir Robert Thompson's view of Vietnamization as being unassailable. The administration's policy, *Battle Line* remarked, had made "remarkable gains," ensuring that "an honorable conclusion" looked more and more probable.[85]

Much of the conservative response to the Laotian operation was based on assumptions about the efficacy of military measures, such as air attacks, in thwarting the North Vietnamese and NLF campaigns. Having promoted the implementation of such measures since the initial American engagement in Southeast Asia, hawks were predisposed to issue positive assessments of the operation's military and strategic value. The administration, however, played a prominent role in disseminating positive assessments of the incursion and bombings. The backgrounder, "attributed only to military sources," that Goldwater received in late March boasted that the military operations conducted by the South Vietnamese "succeeded in disrupting vital portions of the enemy's logistical system, capturing or destroying significant quantities of supplies and inflicting considerable damage on the enemy units within the area of operation."[86] The State Department, while stressing that the action would be a "limited one both as to time and area," reaffirmed the conservatives' position. The department stressed the effectiveness of the operation in protecting American and South Vietnamese lives, the necessity of responding to North Vietnamese violations of Laotian neutrality, and the Lao government's request for U.S. aid. The operation, in short, was intended to "aid in the Vietnamization program."[87] As in the case of the Cambodian operation, conservative backing of the Laos campaign was determined primarily by its function as an example of coupling diplomacy with overwhelming military superiority.

Conservatives were not, however, blind to the obvious military limitations of the operation. While conservatives praised the administration's use of airpower, they emphasized with greater consistency the need to enable the South Vietnamese to take the war directly to North Vietnam. In a congratulatory message to Nixon, Judd praised his decision to "fight the war intelligently and successfully." But he offered a veiled reference as well to the need to extend further aid to South Vietnam: "Surely Vandenberg dictum applies here that no use to throw 16 foot rope to a man drowning 20 foot off shore."[88] At the same time, Reagan was relieved of his disquiet over the rate of withdrawal with optimistic reports of the operation, which continuously emphasized the overall success of Vietnamization and the effective steps, such as increased bombing, taken to reduce the enemy's battlefield effectiveness.[89] Kissinger assured Reagan that such reports were made "available to you exclusively for your eyes so that you will be aware of the significance of what has been done."[90] By such means the administration was remarkably successful in promoting and tempering pro-war sentiment among conservatives within the Republican Party. The glaring weaknesses of the Laos campaign notwithstanding, conservatives were unable to offer a unified response or challenge to administration policy.

Division within Conservative Ranks

By March 1971 YAF's active enthusiasm for its pro-war campaigns had diminished, as had its support for the administration's Vietnamization campaign. YAF's defection from the Nixon camp was brought on in part by its disillusionment with administration strategy but was primarily determined by the failure of the White House to aid the youth group in its efforts to promote the war. Speaking shortly after YAF's national board declared its opposition to Nixon's policy of "gradual surrender," Executive Director Teague described the White House role in subverting YAF's proposed fact-finding mission to Southeast Asia. While Teague declared that YAF had not attempted to secure the official help of the U.S. government, "what happened is that the White House did, in fact, scuttle the trip." Teague made little effort to disguise his indignation with the Nixon White House: "Roadblock after roadblock, delay after delay, promise after promise, failure after failure. The White House made the trip impossible." Teague bitterly judged that Nixon wanted to aid the promotion of anti-war sentiment in order to facilitate faster U.S. withdrawal, despite the encouragement that American withdrawal gave to the enemy in Hanoi. His official statement proclaimed, "We've had it. Nixon can sink by himself. His actions show us that he doesn't need any help in doing it."[91]

Teague's statements brimmed with youthful anger, but they were indicative of conservative activists' ever-growing exasperation over their lack of influence in the White House. Indeed, despite their public support for Nixon's Vietnam strategies, conservatives did not appear to have any real role in determining the administration's policies. The administration's lip service to conservatives' issues was increasingly less effective, and this lack of influence forced conservatives to reevaluate the efficacy of Nixon's

Vietnam policies. Beyond YAF's tantrum-like opposition, however, conservative leaders remained very reluctant to publicly oppose Vietnamization for fear of being associated with extremist hawks. Buckley seemed unlikely to advocate a repudiation of the administration, thereby ensuring that *National Review* remained unopposed to Nixon's Vietnam strategy, a factor that enormously undercut potential conservative dissent. Reagan, too, refused to publicly challenge Nixon's Vietnam policies. So much was Reagan convinced of the need to uphold the president that he wrote to YAF in May 1971 to recommend that the national board reconsider its opposition to Nixon. Having received "in-depth briefings on the war and the international situation," he warranted that he was privy to inside information and was fully behind the Vietnamization policy.[92] Reagan's plea fell on deaf ears, but the issue was of little consequence. YAF's skepticism, like that of the ACU, about the rate of withdrawal and the failure to implement more forceful military measures to compel the enemy to negotiate did not result in a resolute effort to broaden dissent over the war. Rather, it led only to increased division within the conservative movement.

The ACU obliquely attacked Vietnamization, questioning Secretary Laird's suitability to execute the program and charging that budgetary constraints ensured that "the gap between policy and execution could hardly be wider." Addressing the practical and moral implications of Vietnamization, the ACU stated, "There is no justification for the Administration's policy of gradual and responsible withdrawal unless every possible effort is made to improve the fighting ability of the South Vietnamese." The next month the ACU said that Nixon "personally and professionally, has staked too much on an acceptable conclusion to the war to get away with setting a date for full unilateral withdrawal, solely in exchange for the release of prisoners." The ACU's timidity was the result of its reluctance to disavow its alliance with such exalted and powerful figures as Goldwater, Reagan, Tower, and Buckley, an almost inevitable consequence of any repudiation of Nixon's Vietnam strategy. Tower had already withdrawn from the national board of YAF following its public opposition to Nixon's reelection, while Reagan had threatened to do so unless YAF ceased its promotion of a Reagan-for-president campaign. Rusher, too, attempted to mitigate the negativity of conservative opposition, writing to Buckley, "I don't believe in merely becoming shrill about Mr. Nixon; but I do think the ACU serves a useful function—and even, perhaps, one that Mr. Nixon wants served—when it keeps the pressure on him from the right."[93] Rusher's intimation that the ACU and YAF campaigns were part of the more general conservative effort to push Nixon to the right was intended to secure the increasingly fragile conservative alliance.

In addition, positive assessments of Vietnamization served the goal of unifying conservative leaders. Much of conservatives' support for Vietnamization was based on the assumption that it would be coupled with continued U.S. air support and a return to the bombing of North Vietnam and that a residual force of U.S. troops would remain in South Vietnam even if a negotiated settlement was reached. Thompson's authoritative assessment of Vietnamization speculated that U.S. troops would have to remain in South Vietnam into 1972 "partly for military reasons . . . but also partly for psychological reasons to show that you still support them."[94] Conservatives applied Thompson's reading to oppose the viability of setting a withdrawal date for the end of 1971 and to highlight the continued primacy of military measures as a means of successfully concluding the war. Nixon's vagueness regarding the issue of a residual force thus threatened to enhance divisions among conservatives over his Vietnam strategies.

After Nixon's announcement that an additional one hundred thousand troops were to be withdrawn by December 1971, *Human Events* wrote, "If the public rallies around the President, he may even be able to keep a good-sized residual force in [Vietnam] for some time to come." "Indeed," the editors declared, "it is imperative that such a force be retained." *Human Events*' praise for Nixon's defiance in the face of congressional opposition to his Vietnam strategy was unrestrained, indicating the role of anti-war pressures in maintaining conservative support for Vietnamization. With regard to the residual force, the editors noted that there was "ample precedent for such a position," referring to the U.S. forces in Korea and Germany. They concluded, "The President, we believe, would very much like to leave a healthy American presence in South Viet Nam—not to fight wars, but to prevent them. He is not going to be able to do so, however, unless the American people rally behind his efforts."[95] Buchanan warned his White House colleagues not to underestimate the potential of this issue among pro-war conservatives. Despite Republicans' awareness of the limitations imposed by public weariness with the war, they were not yet prepared to accept any semblance of an impulsive withdrawal that seemed dictated by domestic political concerns.

Maintaining the ACU's attack on the administration's continuous focus on the pace of withdrawals, Jeff Bell of the ACU conveyed his unease to Buchanan in April 1971.[96] Bell objected to the administration's recent association of withdrawals and a residual force in Vietnam to the POW matter. According to Buchanan, conservative "feeling is that the prisoners issue alone is a weak intellectual and political reed on which to hang the 'residual force.'" The "case for a residual force, and for gradual as opposed to immediate withdrawal," he maintained, "needs justification . . . in terms of the United States overall objective in Southeast Asia." Nixon must, according to Bell, vindicate America's commitment to South Vietnam by leaving enough material to ensure the country's security, including air and logistical support. Conservatives were, at this time, deeply worried by widening public support for end-the-war resolutions that focused on the return of POWs as the sole requirement for complete withdrawal from Vietnam. The POW issue rallied popular support for Nixon's policies of phased withdrawal and negotiation (see chapter 5). It did little, however, to enhance cooperation among pro-war groups, as veterans' and patriotic organizations, student groups and labor unions moved toward promotion of the POW issue as a means of justifying both withdrawal and the American experience in Vietnam. Conservatives were right to believe that their former allies in the pro-war cause were more and more willing to define victory in terms that had little to do with the defeat of North Vietnam or even the continued freedom of South Vietnam. Rather than push the POW campaign or related efforts to foster national unity, the ACU demanded what Buchanan described as polarization, which would serve to at least "shore up the eroding support for overall Administration policy."⁹⁷ Nixon was more than willing to use the technique of polarizing the nation in order to create a viable majority of supporters, but he comprehended that further polarization could aid the anti-war cause in Congress.

Republicans were not willing either to adopt the strategies of polarization the ACU proposed. Nixon worked hard to maintain eroding conservative support during early to mid-1971 and enjoyed definite gains from doing so. Meeting with Senate Republican loyalists in April, he said that if "the world begins to think that the United States is content to be a second rate power (and even if that seems to fit well within the United States) it will not be conducive to peace in the world." He restated the necessity of ending the Vietnam War in such a way that South Vietnam would be able to survive. But on this occasion there was no discussion of the need to ensure South Vietnamese freedom perpetually. Rather, the South Vietnamese were to be given a "chance" of survival. The distinction was highly important and pointed to a change in the meaning of peace with honor. If Republicans, including Goldwater, objected to the administration's altered objective in Vietnam, there is no record of dissent in the chronicle of the Oval Office meeting; neither is there evidence that they were so concerned with the issue as to publicly voice anxiety.⁹⁸ They continued to project faith in Nixon's peace with honor but largely failed to acknowledge that its meaning and implications had fundamentally been modified. Even in the face of the furor on the right, conservative Republican politicians stayed on board with the administration and acquiesced in the subtle, yet potentially meaningful, change in policy.

NATIONAL REVIEW STRIKES BACK

National Review was a fixed source of strength for the administration on Vietnam. Buchanan urged the president to call Buckley, "thanking him and the staff of National Review" for their continued lauding of the president. The journal's support "on foreign policy and economic policy . . . remains a continuing source of strength for the President on the Right."⁹⁹ *National Review* demonstrated special support for the administration during its legal battle to prevent publication of the leaked classified documents known as the Pentagon Papers by the *New York Times*. The collection of classified government documents relating to early options for Vietnam was compiled under the direction of Secretary McNamara in 1967. Daniel Ellsberg of the RAND Corporation, which held the volumes of documents, copied and distributed the papers to the Senate Foreign Relations Committee in 1970 and then leaked them to the *New York Times*, the *Washington Post,* and seventeen other newspapers in June 1971. The first report on the documents was written by Neil Sheehan and published in the *Times* on June 13. The White House instructed the Justice Department to seek injunctions against further publication of the documents and on June 15 succeeded in winning a temporary restraining order against further publication in the federal district court in New York City. The government failed to secure a preliminary injunction against the *Post* and requested that the Supreme Court review the case. The *Times* also requested that the Supreme Court review the appellate decision in New York in favor of the government. On June 30 the Supreme Court voted 6–3 to allow publication of the documents.

Although their publication provoked a rally-'round-the-president phenomenon within pro-war ranks, *National Review* was somewhat ambiguous in its response to the documents' publication. The editors supported freedom of the press on ideological grounds. But they condemned the anti-war position they associated with the *New York Times* and offered support, tantamount to endorsement, to the administration's effort to prevent further publication, based on Nixon's argument that publication damaged national security. But *National Review* went farther; rather than simply condemn the publication of the papers, *National Review* conservatives emphasized the documents' function in justifying American action and the pro-war case for managing the war. Once it became clear that the documents were to come into the public domain, *National Review* determined to use them to advance conservatives' interpretation of the Vietnam War. Declaring that the papers "do not appear, so far, seriously to disturb the thesis that we did what had to be done," Buckley attempted to counteract anti-war arguments that the papers proved the illogic of early U.S. policy in Vietnam.[100]

The Republican Party's *First Monday* declared that the publication of the "McNamara papers" resulted in a "steady stream of correspondence" to Senator Goldwater's office, the theme of which was "pretty much the same: You were right in 1964, we were wrong and we're sorry we voted for Lyndon Johnson for President." Goldwater seized the opportunity to urge the electorate to "throw the radical-liberals out of Congress."[101] *National Review*'s effort corresponded with that of the administration, particularly that of Agnew, the new conservative hero. Agnew had not originally been a favorite of traditionalist conservatives, but his outspoken opposition to communism and liberalism strengthened his position, with the result that he became a useful tool for the administration in garnering conservative praise. Agnew became the White House mouthpiece for a campaign to make "obvious that President Nixon's earlier criticisms of U.S. policy in Vietnam have been justified by the recent disclosures."[102]

National Review went a step farther and embarked on an effort to more vigorously promote the view that conflicting opinions had coexisted in policymaking circles during the early years of the war and that the policies advocated by conservatives since 1962 had been erroneously dismissed. In late July the front cover of *National Review* purported that additional secret documents had been made available to the journal's editors. Inside the magazine thirteen pages were dedicated to publication of and commentary on these secret documents. In a press release *National Review*'s managers stated that the articles were "fragments from more extensive files . . . made available to National Review in protest against . . . the impressions conveyed by the documents published by the New York Times."[103] They suggested, therefore, that the *Times* had selected only those documents that supported its position on the war. According to *National Review*, these documents proved that "from 1950 on, the nature and significance of U.S. interest in Southeast Asia have been repeatedly stated, without essential dispute."

Some of the most controversial of the documents published by *National Review* related to the possible use of nuclear weapons and other military measures in Vietnam. One document from 1962 argued that, while a "major American military presence" was not required to ensure South Vietnam's freedom, "the internal conflict cannot be resolved without knocking NVN [North Viet Nam] out of the war, since it is NVN (with the backing and support of the USSR [Union of Soviet Socialist Republics] and the Chicoms [Chinese Communists]) that commands and controls the internal SVN [South Viet Nam] struggle, and it is the primary source of arms, supplies, training, regroupment, and, to an increasing extent, personnel." This document detailed the need to undertake such measures as closing the ports at Haiphong and Sihanoukville, blockading the North Vietnamese and Cambodian coasts, and destroying rail links to China and the Red River dikes.[104]

Most of the documents published by *National Review* dealt with the role of the Soviet Union and China in Southeast Asia and the paramount importance of discouraging, through U.S. victory in Vietnam, further communist waging of wars of national liberation. While focusing on the military measures essential to achieving the American aim in Southeast Asia, the documents opposed a policy of protracted or limited warfare. "Long Term Warfare (LTW)," a document dated December 1963 asserted, "will yield a no-win posture, thousands of deaths, and will have serious effects on our, as well as Saigon's, political institutions.... Gradual, slow escalation of the war over a period of years does not create in the Vietnamese people a sense of purpose or destiny. It will only create horror and depression.... The Administration should not start the Vietnamese operations if they see the war as an LTW affair." This document stated that a protracted war would likely result in an anti-war movement reaching a "broad and developed level," allowing the communists to "be in a position of psycho-political leverage from which they could exercise a considerable degree of control over the U.S. political process, at least with respect to Indochina."[105] The final document in the series discussed a high-level State Department meeting of February 10, 1965, during which the positive and negative arguments for seeking a declaration of war were discussed. The document's tenor indicated that a declaration of war was unnecessary because of precedents in which U.S. troops were committed without such a declaration.[106]

Without exception the *National Review* documents promoted

some aspect of the conservatives' pro-war position. Their release produced a temporary furor among the news media and within political circles. Shortly after the magazine's publication, the *Washington Star* reported a Justice Department spokesman as saying that the assistant general for internal security, Robert Mardian, had conferred with the general counsel for the Defense Department, J. Fred Buzhardt, to determine whether *National Review*'s publication of the papers jeopardized national security.[107] Both the president's daily news briefing and the United States Information Agency's Voice of America reported that the documents were accurate. Senior officials alleged to have composed memoranda and briefings contained in *National Review*'s collection were unable to deny their authenticity.[108] The publication of the documents achieved one of the editors' goals: the promotion of the view that military solutions to the conflict were plausible, while a policy of limited warfare had been rejected by senior military and intelligence officials. *National Review*'s documents were, however, composed in the Manhattan offices of the journal's editors. *National Review*'s most activist effort in favor of the war in Vietnam was a hoax.

The ruse did not last long. At a press conference on July 21 Buckley announced that the documents had been faked in order to make three key points: (1) that the Pentagon and the Central Intelligence Agency were not staffed by incompetents, as many were led to believe by the "fragmentary revelations" of the *Times* and the *Post*; (2) that such forged documents were plausible, a fact "demonstrated far beyond our own expectations," because alternative military options were proposed between 1962 and 1967; and (3) that "the U.S. military and intelligence did not fail us during the crucial years." "The failure," Buckley concluded, "was a failure of will: a political failure."[109] The inability of all of official Washington to disavow the papers proved, according to Buckley, that such papers in fact existed.[110] Rusher defended the editors' actions by proclaiming that for about twenty-four hours Americans "were treated to an account of U.S. policy deliberations on Vietnam which, while technically false in the sense that the documents were fabricated, were actually closer in spirit to what really went on than the lopsided and tendentious version stitched together with obvious hostility by the Times and other liberal media from their miscellaneous collection of real documents."[111]

While declaring that the editors had acted in something of an "ethical vacuum," Buckley said they had not expected the forged documents to remain unchallenged for more than an hour or two. He informed only a few key conservative backers that *National Review* intended to perpetrate the hoax, which he deemed "warranted ... because those who come on these documents under this dramatic dispensation will read them in a particular way." He surmised that it would not be long before the fraudulent nature of the documents was discovered, but even so, he contended, "the documents' intelligence, their inherent plausibility, the sure hold they exhibit on the nature of the world crisis, on the provenance of the Vietnam crisis, on the character of the American people, are best appreciated seeing them on stage, written back in the sixties."[112]

Buckley's colleagues in the news media for the most part sharply disagreed with this logic. Walter Cronkite of CBS News focused on Buckley's use of the term "ethical vacuum," declaring that the phrase betrayed "at least some self-doubt" amidst Buckley's supreme confidence in "the rightness of whatever he does."[113] Eric Sevareid, also of CBS News, was less restrained in his analysis of the affair: "Mr. Buckley, the official jester of the conservative intellectual court, revealed that he had concocted [the documents] to make a point. The point was clear to him, but lost on most everybody else."[114] The so-called prank resulted in a severe loss of credibility for those at *National Review* and mixed responses within the pro-war community. Buckley's column was canceled by several leading newspapers, the editor of one proclaiming that despite his faith in Buckley's brilliance, he was unwilling to "harbor someone who at this crucial hour plays games with the public's faith in print journalism."[115]

Despite the considerable harm the incident caused to *National Review*'s reputation as a serious journal of current affairs, Buckley and his fellow editors defended the reasoning behind their decision to produce the false documents. The crucial hour required extraordinary measures beyond the normal boundaries of journalistic integrity, a reasoning that mirrored pro-war suppositions regarding the liberal, anti-war agenda of the *New York Times* and the *Washington Post*. A biographer of Buckley comments that the "papers incident is characteristic of its perpetrator's stance toward Vietnam—he believed the cause so inherently noble as to sanction more aggressive and devious policies than were then being pursued."[116] Yet the timing of *National Review*'s activist policy corresponded with a particular low point for the pro-war cause. While challenging liberals' use of the leaked documents, the hoax also highlighted the need for the pro-war lobby and the administration to assume more forceful and pejorative responses to anti-war activities, particularly those in Congress. The effort sprang from powerlessness in the face of growing public and political hostility to administration policy and the continuation of the war.

National Review's creation of the false documents followed the passage of the Mansfield amendment in the Senate in June. The amendment was introduced by Senate Majority Leader Mike Mansfield and stated that U.S. troops must be withdrawn within nine months of the enactment of the bill subject only to the release of POWs. It was passed in the Senate on June 22 by 55–42. Although defeated in the House of Representatives, the amendment's limited success was sufficient to warrant anti-war jubilation. The divisiveness of the issue contributed to the increasing war-weariness within the Congress and the nation as a whole. Throughout this period conservative Democrats moved closer to the dominant position of the party with regard to Vietnam, a factor that not only contributed to the success of the Mansfield amendment but also presaged the collapse of the already fragmented pro-war alliance. Through its effort to discredit Democratic handling of the Vietnam War and to promote the justification of alternative military measures, *National Review* asserted its claim to honesty and success with regard to the Vietnam War. Because its documents had been faked, however, anti-war campaigners and many wavering in their commitment to the war questioned the credibility of pro-war arguments. With its overall credibility undermined, the activist *National Review* campaign was severely dampened and never recovered. Very soon, however, conservatives would have bigger problems that would also threaten their commitment to the Vietnam War.

CHINA CHANGES EVERYTHING

Since assuming office Nixon had faced challenges to détente from throughout the pro-war movement. His administration consistently argued that it was committed to ensuring that the United States was sufficiently strong vis-à-vis the Soviet Union in strategic and political terms. But by early to mid-1971 such assurances increasingly fell on deaf ears. In June, Stefan Possony charged that the administration was "playing an extremely dangerous game of Russian roulette which could cost the United States dearly." Possony wrote, "For the past three years ... the Soviets have been striving for global military superiority while simultaneously inducing the United States to emasculate its own military might."[117] *Human Events* argued that if immediate measures to increase U.S. military strength were not enacted, the Soviets would achieve military superiority by the mid-1970s.[118] Goldwater charged that the United States had entered a phase of unilateral disarmament. Conservatives were also anxious about American overtures to the government of the People's Republic of China (PRC), which had begun during the Johnson administration. Thurmond opposed any form of trade with the PRC and asserted that there was "little to be gained and much lost in the long run ... from so-called 'normal' relations with our self-declared enemies."[119]

While recognizing the political limitations on the president with regard to escalatory actions in Vietnam, pro-war leaders demanded that the administration revise its rhetoric and overall policies regarding the communist world. Buckley warned that if Soviet concessions were not forthcoming at SALT, Nixon "won't win again," an implicit threat about conservative intentions in the election of 1972.[120] Kissinger was asked by Haldeman to talk with Buckley and other conservative columnists. Haldeman said that the president "feels you should lay it on the line with no quarter given as to why they should be strongly defending the President on foreign policy instead of nit-picking here and there on every little thing."[121] Conservative leaders seemed unresponsive and arranged a series of summit meetings of their own to discuss administration policies. While these meetings featured talk about the growth of conservative opposition to Nixon's policies, such figures as Buckley and Burnham refused to countenance a break with the administration. Stressing the need to push for increases in defense expenditure, the leaders of the conservative movement again determined to push Nixon from the inside.

On July 15, 1971, Nixon announced his intention to visit the PRC before May 1972. Having orchestrated an effective campaign to solicit the support of key Republicans, the conservative congressional caucus remained silent. Such was not the case among the majority of conservative political activists. On July 26 representatives of the leading conservative bodies, including *National Review, Human Events*, the ACU, YAF, and the New York Conservative Party, met at Buckley's Manhattan townhouse. Although the meeting had been planned for some time, its intended agenda was set aside and now took up the China issue, which resulted in the release of a suspension of support of the administration. The draft resolution was written by the journalist and ACU chair M. Stanton Evans, who refused to sign the final version because of its failure to fully repudiate Nixon. The final version was signed by Buckley, Meyer, Rusher, and Burnham of *National Review*; Allan Ryskind and Tom Winter of *Human Events*; John Jones and Jeff Bell of the ACU; Randal Teague of YAF; Neil McCaffrey of the Conservative Book Club; Anthony Harrigan of the Southern States Industrial Council; and J. Daniel Mahoney, the chair of the New York Conservative Party. Representative Ashbrook, until recently the chair of the ACU, did not sign the statement, as no public officials were invited to join in the effort, no doubt because key conservative Republicans in Congress were unlikely to join the assault on Nixon. Shortly after the document's release, the group was being called the Manhattan Twelve, a name that did little to convey its agenda or to dignify its endeavors with mass backing. Nixon's China initiative pushed Buckley and Burnham into the opposition camp, and yet they continued to reject a complete repudiation of Nixon, including in the group's statement a resolution that read, "We consider that our defection is an act of loyalty to the Nixon we supported in 1968."[122] For much of the conservative movement, however, the China initiative was confirmation of the ACU's oft-repeated suspicions about the trajectory of Nixon's foreign policies. To conservative leaders it offered both an obstacle and an opportunity and ultimately divided the conservative leadership and redefined the struggles against international communist expansion.

Asked in 1970 to describe the event or development of the previous decade that had been most influential, Buckley said, "The philosophical acceptance of coexistence by the West."[123] The United States had, in Buckley's view, lost a measure of moral legitimacy through its reliance on containment. Referring to Nikita Khrushchev's visit in 1959, Buckley said it "signified the end of an era during which, while we continued formal relations with the Soviet Union, we built into them the kind of official chill which signified the moral isolation to which we consigned the Soviet Union." Since that visit the United States was "never quite so convincing ... in [its] anti-Communist posture." Recognition of the PRC would serve only to foster the weakening moral position of the United States.[124]

The China initiative afforded those opposed to Nixon's move toward détente the opportunity to effect more concerted opposition to his overall foreign policies. The president's policies were enormously popular, however. This again revealed distinctions between conservatives such as Goldwater and Reagan who were greatly attentive to public opinion and those who were more focused on taking a strong ideological position on foreign policy matters. Limited by the popular appeal of the president's moves, the Manhattan Twelve concentrated on using their political might to force the administration to move to the right, especially with regard to defense spending. While this effort was not new, it received newfound impetus from the rallying effect of the opening to China, an organizational momentum the Vietnam War had failed to provide. Rather than simply oppose the China initiative, the Manhattan Twelve charged that without substantial increases in defense expenditure détente with the communist powers was an impossible goal. Now relying on deterrence, the conservatives stated that above all their opposition to Nixon was based on "his failure to call public attention to the deteriorated American military position . . .

which ... in the absence of immediate and heroic countermeasures, can lead to the loss of our deterrent capability, the satellization of friendly governments near and far, and all that this implies."[125] Nixon's dramatic turnaround on China opened the opportunity to mount a challenge to disarmament that incorporated critiques of the strategic and philosophical bases of his foreign policy. Motivated by philosophical factors, the Manhattan Twelve tried to use political means to achieve their ends.

Shortly after the declaration of opposition, Bell assured his allies that the "statement was an unprecedented source of worry for the Administration" because "for the first time doubts were raised as to the political loyalty of conservatives." He cautioned, however, that the "odds are in fact very good that the Administration will offer no more than token concessions, on the familiar assumption that 'They have no place else to go.'"[126] Mahoney concurred with Bell's emphasis on the need to use conservative political leverage to debunk the idea that conservatives had no option but to endorse the Republican candidate. "If we are correct," he said, "that President Nixon cannot win the general election without the active support of the conservative movement ... it seems to me that we should undertake a campaign to spread our disaffection with the current performance of the Nixon Administration and increase the pressure to make conservative accommodations." Mahoney's position was not, however, a rejection of Nixon. He ended by saying, "We have it quite recently, on very high authority, that the Nixon Administration would welcome increased conservative pressure." "Patriots," Mahoney wryly stated, "do not trifle lightly with such presidential mandates."[127]

Although the conservatives were aware of the financial and practical limitations on their abilities to mount an effective oppositional campaign to Nixon's nomination, they were confident of the righteousness of their position and certainly overconfident about their political leverage with the administration. Unable to agree on the efficacy of mounting a challenge to Nixon in the Republican primaries, they agreed on the benefit of presenting a series of suggestions, or rather demands, to the administration. Warning against allowing a situation whereby "the President can make some minor improvements in the defense posture and put us in the position of seeming to be answered," Meyer stressed the priority that must be assigned to defense expenditure. He demanded that several measures be undertaken to avoid an irreparable deterioration of U.S. strategic strength: substantial increases in Minutemen and Poseidon submarines; expansion of the anti-ballistic missile system to cover all Minutemen sites; and intensive development of the Underwater Launched Missile System.[128] McCaffrey thought the rearmament plank was uniquely important: "If Nixon gives us *real* rearmament but nothing else, I think we would be foolhardy not to support him."[129] After a lackluster endeavor to receive guarantees of change from administration officials, the Manhattan Twelve composed a list of demands that they submitted to Colson in early November. Allan Ryskind remarked that Colson "was cordial and indicated that the Administration was not at all intolerant of our recommendations and would respond to them sometime between November 15 and November 21."[130] Galvanized by the vote in the United Nations in October to expel the Republic of China, the conservatives attempted to demonstrate the priority that must be given to vastly superior defense capabilities if détente was to allow any form of international credibility for the United States.

Overall, the demands indicated a wariness of the trajectory of administration foreign policy and were designed to augur symbolic gestures that would undermine the recent emphasis on détente. The conservatives not only opposed a SALT agreement that would allow the Soviet Union to retain a strategic advantage in any area, but also enjoined the administration to convey its criticism of Ostpolitik (the Federal Republic of Germany's normalization of relations with states in the Eastern bloc), cooperate with efforts to obstruct communist inroads in Latin America, retain its embargo of Cuba, and ensure that NATO guarantee the security of the Persian Gulf states. They recommended that a number of these positions be made clear in the president's State of the World address.[131] With regard to Asia the conservatives expressed their continued belief in the significance of preventing the expansion of communist influence. They asked the administration to reply to their points, proposing a deadline of November 25, 1971. In asking Gen. Alexander Haig of the NSC to comment on the points, Colson remarked, "For obvious reasons, we would like to respond agreeably on all the points possible, and try to indicate common ground on most of the remaining points."[132]

Conservatives remained divided in their views of the administration. Buckley and Ryskind, for instance, tried to use the rearmament issue to salvage a measure of conservative support for the administration. Faced with increasing calls for a complete repudiation of Nixon's policies, the two men were involved in drafting the list of demands that were designed to enable the president to attest to his conservative credentials. Reporting on the meeting of the "Twelve Apostles" in New York on October 21, Buchanan asserted that Buckley, Ryskind, and Evans made up the subcommittee formed to formulate the list. According to Buchanan, "Ryskind is strongly pro-Nixon, anxious to find ground to re-support the Administration; Bill is of course under the greatest pressure to split finally; and Stanton Evans, as I understand is, perhaps, the most anti-Nixon of the three."[133] Many of the demands related to specific requirements for the defense budget of 1973. Conservatives had been arguing for increased defense spending throughout the administration and had been largely dissatisfied with the Defense Department's handling of what they perceived to be one of the most pressing matters facing the government: the failure to finance programs of research and development. The Manhattan Twelve underscored the need for both research, development, and procurement of long-range missiles and the extension of the existing Minutemen III and Poseidon forces.[134]

Vietnam did not figure prominently among the conservatives' demands. Indeed, the original statement applauded the president for his "steadfastness in resisting the great pressures upon him to desert Southeast Asia."[135] Within the context of preventing an expanded communist influence in Asia, the subtext of the conservatives' position demanded a successful conclusion to the war, a conclusion that would demonstrate the American commitment to this region and its willingness to implement the use of force if necessary. The first of the conservatives' six points relating to Asia stated that "U.S. air support for Laos, Cambodia and South Vietnam" be offered, "regardless of prisoner release or any other factor, short of war's end." By "war's end," the conservatives made clear that such a situation was possible only if the United States provided a "level of military and economic assistance necessary to maintain the anti-Communist character of the governments of Laos, Cambodia and South Vietnam." The Vietnam War thus became the means by which the United States could demonstrate that its foreign policy was not "controlled by the illusion of détente."[136]

Vietnam remained ideologically important to conservatives, but in the face of wider challenges to their anticommunist philosophy it increasingly assumed symbolic value. Burnham concurred that Nixon's grand strategic turn undermined the rationale on which the Vietnam War was being fought. "In a world of SALT and kowtowing to Peking," he argued in 1972, "the Indochina campaign makes no sense."[137] The China initiative thus challenged the original pro-war interpretations of Vietnamization and the Nixon Doctrine. Rather than attack the president's Vietnam policies, the Manhattan Twelve, most of whom had resolutely affirmed the programs for withdrawal, concentrated on admonishing détente, using the Vietnam issue as a way of enfeebling the communist commitment to genuine accord.

In the midst of détente with both communist powers, Vietnamization represented not a new means of fighting the Cold War but a failure to do so at all. Implicitly threatening the administration, Buckley wondered to what extent the conservative community, in the wake of moves toward détente, could be rallied "to bring considerable pressure to insist on salvaging the Southeast Asia enterprise." Buckley highlighted the paradox of U.S. involvement in Vietnam. "Either South Vietnam," he wrote to Kissinger, "was (is?) the salient of the whole of the enemy, viewed globally; or it is a local infection."[138] The immensity of American involvement in Southeast Asia over the previous decade nullified the alternative that it was a local conflict. Using the Vietnam issue to dispute Nixon's new policy, Meyer wrote that the trip to China "puts into question the lives of tens of thousands of Americans who died in Vietnam." The proposed trip, which Meyer claimed amounted to de facto recognition of the communist government, not only symbolized the "liquidation of the anti-Communist stance of the

American government" but also called into doubt "any meaning" to the Vietnam War. Rather than consider the possibility of withdrawal, Meyer labeled the whole Nixon foreign policy a tragedy.[139] Nixon's new foreign policy, Burnham claimed, revealed the administration's failure to view the Vietnam War as it should have been considered all along: as a "campaign or subwar in the global conflict." In Burnham's view the administration's blindness to this singularly critical factor could lead to only one outcome: failure in Vietnam.[140] Despite growing disillusionment with Vietnamization and growing dissatisfaction with the administration's failure to initiate more extensive bombing, conservative leaders did little more than use the Vietnam issue to highlight the ambiguity of administration foreign policy toward the communist world.

In spite of the vociferousness of the opposition from such sources as the Manhattan Twelve and the old China lobby, the administration was able to sustain the support, however reluctant and cautious, of the Republican Right. Other typical supporters of the *National Review* circle refused to join their effort for fear it might weaken the sway of conservatives and bring about little change in administration policy. Ernest van den Haag, who acted as a representative of *National Review* during a fact-finding trip to Vietnam, voiced his fear that "on the China issue conservatives will paint themselves into a corner."[141] His position echoed that of the anticommunist campaign heroes Goldwater, Reagan, Tower, Thurmond, and James Buckley. Each not only agreed to withhold judgment on Nixon's China initiative until after the visit was completed but also condemned the public position of the Manhattan Twelve. Rather than present a forum for a renewed debate on administration foreign policy, the China issue divided the conservative movement more than ever before.

Reacting to the Manhattan Twelve's statement, Senator Buckley stipulated the political import of the conservatives' position, saying, "Their opinions reach tens of millions of Americans and their final verdict on Richard Nixon can kindle or extinguish the kind of enthusiasm and willingness to work on which elections depend." His primary stance, however, was one of support for the president. He disagreed with some of the conservatives' specific analyses, "perhaps," he remarked, "because during these past six months I have occupied a position from which I have been able to gain a better appreciation of the political constraints within which the President is required to operate."[142] Goldwater and Reagan cited their understanding of the inner workings of the Nixon administration as convincing them that Nixon's efforts to increase defense expenditure were genuine and, more significant, that the president's policies with regard to China would not weaken the international position of the United States. Rather than join his fellow conservatives in lambasting the administration's defense record, Goldwater charged that McNamara was "the man to blame for any deficiency that exists in our military system." Reiterating the position of pro-war adherents of the president's military options in Vietnam, Goldwater protested that the Democratic Congress had prevented the president from implementing necessary and desired defense spending.[143]

The administration attempted to convince hawks that the trip to China, coupled with Nixon's triangular diplomacy, might hasten an end to the Vietnam War by enervating the support of the communist powers for the North Vietnamese effort. Although Kissinger was marginally successful in his efforts to thwart Buckley's opposition to the administration, he was unable to blunt the animosity of ACU officials, including Rusher and Meyer. Having been outraged, according to Buchanan, by the administration's response to their list of demands, the conservatives moved closer to a complete break with the administration and the sponsoring of an alternative candidate for the Republican nomination. Agnew and his aide David Keene were dispatched to pacify conservative anger. Meeting with Buckley and Rusher on December 15, they sought to offset the possibility of a nomination challenge to Nixon. Rusher conveyed his complete unwillingness to even consider backing Nixon. He told Agnew that, in the wake of the conservatives' withdrawal of support, the administration could not have done a better job of "devis[ing] the most offensive possible series of gestures toward conservatives."[144]

While conservatives had in fact been broadly in favor of the administration's Vietnam policies since 1969, their repeated public hints at their dissatisfaction with aspects of Vietnamization prompted the White House to try to discredit the importance of their support. This marked a shift in White House policy vis-à-vis conservatives and Vietnam. In light of conservatives' potential to openly dispute the administration's withdrawal strategy, the White House concentrated on discrediting their interpretation of Vietnam. Colson worked on ensuring that the veterans' organizations and leading Republicans remained in the Nixon camp. By early September the American Legion and VFW had publicly endorsed the president's foreign policy. The American Legion recommended, however, that before making any agreements the United States should oblige the Chinese government to "agree to stop all further aid and assistance to North Vietnam and the Viet Cong."[145] Meeting with the national commander of the American Legion, Alfred Chamie, in the weeks after his China announcement, Nixon received a firm commitment of personal and organizational support. Much of Chamie's favor was based on what he termed Nixon's "credibility in this area," that is, the president's record of taking a hard line in matters of foreign policy. Nixon's assurance that he was not going to be a "patsy" or let anyone "blow smoke in my eyes" was indicative of his position when dealing with wavering supporters.[146]

Similarly, Nixon told Goldwater in late August, "You know me, I am not going to sell out," referring not only to his upcoming meeting with the Chinese leaders, but also to the disarmament negotiations with the Soviets and the peace talks regarding Vietnam. Speaking of the Beijing trip, Kissinger satisfied Goldwater that "Hanoi was complaining bitterly."[147] Thurmond agreed with this position. Telling his audience of radio listeners that the president understood the "slim" possibility of achieving "solid accomplishments from summit diplomacy," he argued that the North Vietnamese campaign, "sustained and prolonged primarily because of the aid and assistance given by the two major Communist powers," might be debilitated by an "understanding between Mao's government and our government."[148]

Two events in late December served the administration's attempt to prove that its China policy might hasten an end to the war. First, the Soviet Union publicly accused the PRC of backing U.S. policy in Vietnam because of the Chinese government's endorsement of a peace plan that would prevent Hanoi from controlling the South. This division between the communist powers allowed the Nixon administration to claim that its policy of triangular diplomacy was working. More important, the United States initiated the most acute intensification of bombing since Rolling Thunder. For five days North Vietnam was subject to intense bombing of airfields, missile and anti-aircraft sites, and supply facilities. Nixon authorized the campaign following the breakdown of the Paris talks on December 9, which occurred because Hanoi refused to countenance the demand that Thieu remain in government. Nixon's decision was also influenced by the worsening military situation in Cambodia. On December 27 Laird said that the bombing resulted from North Vietnam's violations of the agreements of 1968.

These two events helped win over hawks in Congress, pro-war activists like Meaney, and the heads of the veterans' organizations. The bombing campaign won conservatives' praise as well, but it did little to alter their attitude toward the efficacy of relying on China to aid the Americans' exertions to bring the war to a satisfactory end. Denying that Beijing's posture as a protagonist in the Vietnam War would be softened by closer ties with the United States, Ashbrook argued that it was not in China's interest to help the United States extricate itself from the domestic predicament arising out of the Vietnam conflict.[149] *National Review* dismissed the administration's reliance on linkage or carrot-and-stick diplomacy. Referring to claims that Nixon hoped "to persuade Mao Tse-tung to play the *deus ex machina* in rescuing the Vietnamization policy," the journal simply concluded that "in politics, as in most else, you never get something for nothing."[150]

Division within the conservative community explains in part the muted nature of the conservative position on Vietnam. Preoccupied with the effort to move Nixon to the right, conservative leaders were unwilling to further endanger their weakened political position by rejecting Nixon's popular program of phased withdrawal. As Congress moved ever closer toward limiting the time frame in which Nixon could achieve peace with honor or "our minimum way in Vietnam," as Buckley described it, pro-war activists were left with little option but to again push for increased bombing of North Vietnam and post-war aid to South Vietnam.[151] With regard to Vietnam, therefore, the oppositional conservatives often mirrored the public positions of supportive figures such as Goldwater and Reagan, despite both groups' deep misgivings about the efficacy of administration policy in Southeast Asia.

Goldwater's private anxiety in January 1972 was indicative of that of Republican conservatives who increasingly queried the ambiguity of the administration's Vietnam policies. Writing to Kissinger, Goldwater called on him to explain why the campaign of bombing North Vietnam, as outlined to Goldwater in November 1971, had not been carried out. Referring to "certain targets that we intended to bomb in the north," Goldwater charged that nothing had been accomplished because "the targets we talked about remain untouched.'"[152] He expressed his bewilderment at the limited nature of the campaign as summarized by Adm. John McCain during Goldwater's journey to Vietnam over the Christmas period. Writing privately, he stated, "The briefing by Admiral McCain was . . . somewhat disturbing. . . . I'll have to say the results [of the bombing] were not what I thought they were going to be or were from the press accounts, and I was very disappointed that the general target that Mr. Kissinger had told me about had not been approached and remains a target, and now I have my doubts as to whether or not the President and the Joint Chiefs will be willing to risk it."[153] Goldwater recognized that the administration was worried about the negative public reaction to additional bombing of North Vietnam, while he understood that the military was reluctant to undertake large-scale operations without full freedom of maneuver and congressional support. Perhaps because of his awareness of such limiting factors, but also because of his reluctance to put forth an unrealistic and unpopular prescription for policy in Vietnam, Goldwater's anxieties remained undeclared.

This pattern had been clear since 1969, but in the final year of the war it reflected two characteristics of conservatives' positions on Vietnam. First, the Republican Right was acutely aware of the political importance of remaining supportive of the administration regarding Vietnam. While people like Goldwater and Reagan might publicly question the utility of Nixon's visit to China, the public would not tolerate a policy that aimed at prolonging the war in order to achieve military victory. Indeed, Ashbrook's challenge to the White House was meaningful largely because he was an anomaly among conservative Republicans. Second, conservatives as a whole increasingly stressed the symbolic importance of Vietnam, pointing out the need to reach a settlement through the demonstration of force. This was important not simply because conservatives believed this would help ensure that the North Vietnamese might uphold the agreement, but also because it would vindicate their preferred policies and at least hint at American willingness to respond to communist expansion.

Nixon denied that the peace terms represented an abandonment of America's ally, but the proposal allowed for the South Vietnamese presidential elections to include representatives of the NLF, thus opening the possibility of a coalition government. On the occasion of Nixon's meeting on January 26 with the Republican leadership, which, unusually, included Goldwater, Nixon said that "what we have done if as far as we can go" in terms of concessions.[154] Such reassurances helped relieve growing fears among conservatives that Nixon might accept other anti-war demands, namely, that a coalition government be imposed on South Vietnam, that the United States agree to the removal of President Thieu, or that the United States assent to a deadline for withdrawal. The president's hard-line stance, particularly his public assertion that he would act to protect American troops if the enemy stepped up military action, won over Goldwater. He was reported to have responded in blunt terms that the administration should take this proposal and "shove it down [the Democratic doves'] throats."[155]

Goldwater's comment betrays his disgust with the anti-war movement, particularly in response to Kissinger's emphasis during the meeting on the negative impact of the Mansfield amendment on negotiations. It reflected the sense of justification among supporters of the president's Vietnam policies who had continuously stressed the enemy's intransigence. But it also revealed conservatives' frustration with the war. Goldwater wrote privately the next day that Nixon had declared he would not abandon the government of South Vietnam and concluded that Nixon "feels, as I have often said, that if we do this it will end the United States as a world power as it would destroy the confidence of the world."[156] Despite his reservations about the specifics of Vietnam strategy, Goldwater endorsed the president's peace proposals, urging his fellow conservatives and the nation as a whole to follow suit.

Battle Line's issue of January 1972 charged that Nixon's peace proposals came dangerously close to betrayal of America's ally.[157] *Human Events* remarked that the peace proposal had been a "political masterstroke," had cut congressional doves "off at the legs," and had built up the case for Vietnamization. The editors surmised, however, that Kissinger and his aides were "spending far too much time devising peace formulas designed to accommodate Communist demands" and concluded that the "Nixon–Kissinger plan . . . would seem to have moved a good distance toward conciliating the enemy." The editors were especially put off by the potential limit on aid to South Vietnam and the failure to propose that a residual force remain in Vietnam following the ceasefire.[158]

The *National Review Bulletin* similarly questioned the future of Vietnamization, charging that it was at a "perilous juncture," primarily because of the apparent primacy given to U.S. domestic political considerations: "The rate of troop withdrawal is a function, primarily, of domestic U.S. considerations, which dictate: the faster, the better. The rate of consolidating a viable South Vietnamese regime depends on domestic South Vietnamese considerations—and on the actions of the enemy. It is, a priori, very unlikely that these two time curves should converge at the point most convenient and desirable for the U.S. President. The recent heavy bombing by U.S. aircraft and the start of the U.S. election year are proof that they are still far from converging."[159] The basis of Vietnamization had therefore fundamentally altered, for it too was to be determined by domestic, rather than purely Vietnamese, considerations. Such had been the case, to a large extent, since the inception of the policy. But now the momentum of détente undercut the remaining credibility of U.S. withdrawal. Vietnamization and the extent to which it merited support had become intrinsically linked to Nixon's overall polices of détente toward the communist world.

By February Goldwater was using the term "reasonable chance" to describe his expectations for South Vietnam's future freedom from communism, a change in tone that reflected his weakening faith in the potential success of the Vietnamization program.[160] While he often echoed the administration's position that Vietnamization was succeeding, his perspective was in fact closer to that of the *National Review* conservatives, who argued against the administration in demanding unrestricted U.S. aid to South Vietnam. Nixon's withdrawal announcement at the end of January made clear that the United States was, in all practical terms, completing a unilateral withdrawal.[161] Buckley claimed that the United States had "lost, irretrievably, any sense of moral mission in the world" because of Nixon's "capitulation in Peking."[162] Conservative leaders identified the president's Vietnam policies with potential failure and a further weakening of the anticommunist spirit in the United States. Having contributed to the legitimization of Nixon's withdrawal policy, conservative disaffection might have posed a considerable challenge to the administration's credibility. The continued support of key figures of the Republican Right, coupled with the divisiveness within conservative ranks, undermined this threat. The pro-war movement had changed by the beginning of 1972. At a popular level, backers of the war focused less on the national security considerations that had prompted early support for Johnson's war and now rallied around Nixon's withdrawal strategies. Conservatives could no longer hope to hold the political cards when it came to endorsing the president's Vietnam policies. Of perhaps greatest significance in sustaining popular support for Vietnamization, therefore, were factors extraneous to the conservative movement, not least of which were the association of patriotism with Nixon's peace with honor, the surge to challenge the anti-war movement, and heightened awareness and symbolism of America's POWs in Vietnam.

CHAPTER 5

THE SEARCH FOR A NEW MAJORITY

Popular Support for the War

I flew over the Ho Chi Minh Trail and nothing was moving. (Pause) There was such a traffic jam that nobody *could* move.

    Bob Hope, United Service Organizations (USO)
    Christmas show in Vietnam, 1968

Patriotism is considered by some to be a backward fetish of the uneducated and the unsophisticated.

    President Richard Nixon, address to the
    Air Force Academy, June 4, 1969

Each president who dealt with Vietnam understood that military intervention would have far-reaching political ramifications. Both Kennedy and Johnson sought to avoid a debate on Americanization of the conflict precisely because they realized that the complexities involved in whatever strategy was pursued would invite both opportunistic political challenges and sincere questioning of policy. Johnson attempted to rally public opinion behind his policies by deflecting political challenges and by openly insisting on the need for bipartisan support of American war aims. He also presented U.S. strategy within the widely understood contours of the Cold War consensus. The administration's explanations of U.S. policy remained vague, however. Johnson's conservative critics continually harangued him for not fully explaining to the American people the goals of the United States and the importance of the war to national security. Their challenges ignored the extensive endeavors of the Johnson White House to limit debate and to maintain a popular consensus behind the president's limited war strategies. The war's longevity precluded the success of these tactics. Popular support for the president's handling of the war had plummeted by 1968, but the extent to which many people in the United States remained committed to achieving success in Vietnam was more difficult to measure. Traditional conceptions of how to express patriotism and a commitment to legitimizing the service of those Americans who had died in the war limited many Americans' acceptance of anti-war arguments. A majority of Americans did not endorse conservatives' interpretation of the purpose of Vietnam or the significance of the war. Many people, however, did take to the streets in support of the war effort and so helped redefine the meaning of success in America's struggle in Southeast Asia. They served a powerful function in helping President Nixon continue the Vietnam War.

The role of public opinion in determining the administration's room for maneuver in Vietnam had been abundantly clear to the White House since January 1969. Indeed, Nixon had always understood its function, better perhaps than his predecessor. It is difficult, perhaps impossible, to measure public opinion regarding Vietnam—polling questions, the nature of victory, the "sunken cost" of engagement, government policy, and pro- and anti-war activism changed dramatically over time. Nixon, like many contemporaries, saw public opinion as something more fixed and tangible than was warranted. But he understood, perhaps better than many of his contemporaries, the vital importance of harnessing the forces of pro-war sentiment in support of whatever policy he pursued. The period of the Nixon administration witnessed a newfound emphasis on appealing to the middle Americans who had yet to voice their position on Vietnam. It was also the period in which independent grassroots efforts to back the war effort appeared to find new voice through an intensified association of patriotism with support for the war.

Questioning of the war by powerful elites, most notably the Fulbright hearings that began in 1966, undermined the direct association between patriotic duty and support for the president's warfare policies, allowing dissent to burgeon. This was particularly the case within academic circles and among the news media after 1968.

Among other sectors—national and local veterans, patriotic and civic groups—such opposition to government policy engendered vociferous proclamations and demonstrations of support for the administration. These campaigns often relied on existing patriotic symbols to sustain backing for the war in Vietnam without engaging in in-depth analysis of government policy. Pro-war efforts to co-opt traditional symbols and qualities associated with American patriotism were made simpler and more profound by large-scale popular opposition to the anti-war movement. For many Americans not committed to the war per se, its function as a symbol of duty and loyalty to one's country proved compelling. But this also reflected the ambiguities and contradictions inherent in support of the war at this time. The wife of an American POW held in North Vietnam described her reasons for endorsing the war: "We should be there, but we shouldn't keep going like we are. We can't just pull out though. There are too many who have given too much for that to happen."[1] By the time Nixon assumed office the war's cost served a critical function as warranting, perhaps demanding, the support of those who ascribed to a traditional interpretation of American patriotism.

Demonstrations of support for the president often acted as a means of signifying approval of the war. For those not challenging a national policy, "simply declaring that they 'stood for the president' or 'backed our fighting men' was sufficient to locate them with respect to the Vietnam question, to make clear to their neighbors just where they stood on this thing."[2] The campaigns waged against the anti-war movement by individuals and organizations across America can be interpreted as demonstrations of support for the American effort against communism and an implicit sanction of the war in Vietnam. While this stance was riddled with ambiguity and contradiction and was by no means unified, it too indicated support for the war, if perhaps a more emotional than philosophical attachment stimulated by the war's costs and ties to patriotism. Certainly the so-called silent majority could not simply be equated with a pro-war position; but its utilization by the Nixon administration did serve to widen the scope of pro-Vietnam activism. It served to distract from pro-war demonstrations that focused on national security. The motivation behind many of the pro-war campaigns undertaken during this period, therefore, was quite distinct from that which influenced conservatives' attitudes toward Nixon's policies. Popular engagement with Nixon's silent majority was not an indication of overwhelming support for the war. Indeed, public questioning of the Cambodian incursion suggested that Nixon enjoyed support for his policies precisely because he was winding down the war through Vietnamization. Yet the self-identifying silent majority was loath to accept that America's effort in Vietnam was without purpose and entirely unnecessary.

These campaigns changed the nature of pro-war activism, moving it away from an emphasis on national security, which characterized early activism in favor of the war, to a focus on American sacrifice and the values of duty and honor associated with military service. The conservative community attempted to use popular support for the war, however, and was heartened by the widespread rejection of the anti-war movement. Conservative leaders learned of the power of harnessing public opinion only late in the war and sometimes vied with the Nixon administration to influence grassroots attitudes. The power of patriotism was something both groups identified, yet neither was able to control its meaning for their own ends.

The varied ways in which patriotism was harnessed by supporters of the war to advance their goals shaped popular understandings of the meaning of the conflict. An analysis of the activities of veterans' organizations and patriotic groups offers evidence of how supporting the troops was used to gain backing for continuing the war and for Nixon's policy of Vietnamization. Organized labor harnessed working class resentments and energies to yield a vocal, if misunderstood, source of support for the war. Although large-scale pro-war demonstrations were orchestrated by labor union leaders, they served the purpose of creating the appearance that many in the working class favored the war. More significant, these demonstrations were part of a process that helped weaken the ties between the working class and the Democratic Party. Unsurprisingly, the Nixon White House developed a propaganda campaign that played on popular desires to succeed in Vietnam.

These initiatives met with limited success, but one such campaign captured the popular imagination: the foregrounding of the plight of American POWs in North Vietnam. Its roots, outside of the White House propaganda machine, originated in both humanitarian and political concerns. Its effect was to enable vast swathes of middle America to engage in positively redefining the meaning of the Vietnam War. Each of these forces promoted endorsements of the administration's policies and helped legitimize the pro-war argument that anti-war activities contributed to the failure of the president's peace initiatives by reducing morale in the field and offering false hope to the enemy.

Standing Up for the Home Team

The large-scale anti-war demonstrations that took place in October and November 1969, collectively known as the Moratoria, engendered disparate but ideologically cohesive counterattacks across the United States. The "home team" was the slogan that a loose coalition of groups demonstrating in support of Nixon's Vietnam policies during November 1969 ascribed to their activities.[3] Throughout Nixon's time in office veterans' organizations concentrated less on the substance of administration policy in Vietnam than on the symbolism attached to the war. This motif also characterized civic and patriotic organizations. Adopting the war to put forward a specific vision of American patriotism, such groups pinpointed the contrast between those dutifully serving their country in Vietnam (and by extension those loyally applauding their service) and those actively opposing the war. The motto of the American Legion regarding Vietnam, "For God and Country Support Our Boys in Vietnam," not only allied morality with patriotism, but also provided a context for supporting the war that had little relation to reasoned arguments justifying foreign military engagements. The organization's national office, like those of smaller veterans' groups, offered a plentiful supply of resolutions that endorsed administration policy and advocated the greater use of military force in Vietnam. Such resolutions were consistently used by the administration to shore up positive views of its policies.

In terms of influence, however, the American Legion's alliance of supporting both the troops and the president must serve as its most lasting. Through a series of welcome home parades for returning Vietnam veterans, campaigns that sent personal letters and standard gift packages to soldiers, pro-administration petitions, and "Support Our Boys" rallies in towns across America, the American Legion and the VFW demonstrated a proactive, positive means of seeing the conflict. The issue of supporting the troops proved effective in limiting dissent toward government policy among many Americans. Pro-war activists urged their fellow citizens to take such actions as leaving porch lights and headlights on during the Moratoria as a demonstration of opposition to anti-war radicalism. These quiet acts of protest, invariably relating to the domestic, served as a direct retort to the open, public demonstrations against the war taking place on city streets.

Vocal backers of the war cited the unholy alliance between the North Vietnamese and the anti-war movement. Vice President Agnew and Governor Reagan were among the many public figures who called attention to the public support of the Moratorium expressed by the premier of North Vietnam, Pham Van Dong. Hanoi's depiction of the protests as "a timely rebuff" to the Nixon administration, the description of American deaths in Vietnam as useless, and the praise lavished on Students for a Democratic Society in North Vietnam's official publication, *Nhan Dan*, heightened antipathy toward the dissenters. In early October an article that appeared in *Nhan Dan* described American protestors as "our heroic comrades-in-arms."[4] Reagan was explicit in articulating the negative impact of anti-war protest. Because of domestic protest, he lamented, "some young Americans living today will die tomorrow." Many of those marching in the name of peace, he declared, "carry the flag of a nation which has killed almost 40,000 of our young men." He demanded that all loyal Americans support the president: "Those entrusted with the immense responsibility for the leadership of our nation deserve not only our support but our rejection of those in our streets who arrogantly kibitz in a game where they haven't even seen the cards with which the game is played."[5] Such attacks would continue for the remainder of the war and become a rationale for American military failure after the war. Late 1969 marked the high point of popular activism against the anti-war movement, activism that had been steadily growing since 1967. The week of Veterans Day, November 11, 1969, saw many Americans respond to Reagan's call to arms.

One of the more extensive and well publicized of these initiatives was a weeklong campaign that originated with two organizations, one entirely ad hoc, the other more established in the field of interpreting and promoting patriotism. National Unity Week was conceived by Edmund Dombrowski, an orthopedic surgeon from Redlands, California. Dombrowski decided to organize a pro-America rally in order to contest the divisiveness in American society he attributed to anti-war protest. Dombrowski's agenda called for a petition drive to enhance the public's involvement in localized patriotic events. Having asked a local heiress, Mary Shirk, who had inherited the Kimberly-Clark Paper Company, for a financial donation of five thousand dollars, Dombrowski contributed an equal sum from his personal capital. He used the money to establish a Committee for a Week of National Unity, which was composed mainly of local businesspeople and patriotic activists.

Dombrowski claimed he had not been a political activist before, having never organized anything bigger than a Fourth of July parade, which enhanced the campaign's image as an entirely grassroots effort. Angered by campus and peace activists, he was also influenced by his discussions with high school students about the Moratorium activities. According to Dombrowski's assessment of their views, they believed that the president was doing all he could to end the war but did not want to have to parade in the streets to show their support. This attitude prompted Dombrowski to organize more modest displays of unity and backing for the president. Within two weeks of the committee's founding in mid-October, the publicity drive received its greatest asset, when Bob Hope enthusiastically agreed to become its honorary chairman and urged Americans to participate fully.[6] The offices of the committee, opened on both coasts, distributed promotional leaflets and over two hundred thousand National Unity bumper stickers on a daily basis for several weeks. Hope was joined by a fellow celebrity, Art

Linkletter, and sent telegrams on behalf of the committee to most of the country's mayors and governors, urging them to promote National Unity Week. The committee recommended that citizens be encouraged to fly the American flag, wear red, white, and blue armbands, turn on car headlights during the day, leave houselights on over the weekend, pray for POWs, and sign petitions.[7]

The committee's primary theme presaged and was further encouraged by Nixon's emphasis on the silent majority during his speech in October 1969. Its petition was simple and deliberately ambiguous so as to avoid political feeling around the war: "We are proud to be Americans. We support the integrity of our elected leaders." Dombrowski held that everyone could endorse the unity campaign and asserted that people who favored the initiative "merely want all Americans to stand up and be counted for justice, honor and integrity." Hope was more explicit about the need to demonstrate support for the Vietnam War: "If we ever let the Communists win this war, we are in great danger of fighting for the rest of our lives and losing a million kids, not just the 40,000 we've already lost."[8] Indeed, the *Chicago Tribune* commented that the committee had been created specifically in response to President Nixon's "televised appeal to the 'silent majority' to back his handling of the war in Viet Nam."[9] The committee therefore questioned the prevailing contestation of patriotism and used Vietnam as a means of situating individuals on a particular side of debates relating not only to the nature and prosecution of the Cold War but also to social, cultural, and moral norms.

During the same period Charles Wiley of the National Committee for Responsible Patriotism (NCRP) developed a similar patriotic campaign. Wiley's New York–based committee was founded in the wake of the original "We Support Our Boys in Vietnam" parade of May 1967. The NCRP had a permanent board of directors, of which Wiley was executive director. Although it had a permanent office at the Commodore Hotel, its staff of volunteers was assembled for specific campaigns during periods of intense activity. Wiley, a freelance journalist, had been involved in anticommunist ventures since the late 1950s. In 1960, while reporting on Cuba, he was held by Cuban army intelligence for eight days without charges. Also in 1960 he testified before the House Committee on Un-American Activities about the U.S. delegation to the World Youth Festival in Vienna in 1959, which he claimed had been run by communists.[10] By 1969 Wiley had managed to rally around him an ad hoc group of volunteers who were assembled for specific campaigns.

Having denied that his group was merely reactive when questioned about the committee's plans to counter the October Moratorium, Wiley told a *New York Times* reporter that his organization planned to develop a counter-demonstration "at some later date."[11] He was moved to action, however, by the projected scale of the anti-war events. Encouraged by popular discontent arising from Moratorium events, the NCRP developed its Honor America Week campaign. Wiley asserted that Honor America Week was not simply an "antimoratorium venture" but a way of overcoming the debilitating divisiveness in American society. Explaining the position of the NCRP, Wiley averred that during a war nothing should be done that could be construed as aiding the enemy or damaging morale at home. He thought responsible critics might disagree with the administration's policy or short-term aims. Disagreement would not "suggest bad motives on the part of the United States" or "question the greatness of our country's heritage, the motivation of our servicemen or the basic honorable intentions of our leaders."[12] Fierce anticommunism may have shaped his viewpoint, but Wiley's perspective was by no means unique.

Wiley petitioned the White House for support and publicly said he had received endorsements from Nixon and the cooperation of the major labor unions and veterans', fraternal, police, and firefighters' organizations.[13] Adopting familiar patriotic tropes, the NCRP's posters showed images of the Liberty Bell and a moon-walking astronaut. Honor America Week urged patriotic Americans to display the flag as a symbol of loyalty to the president's Vietnam policies. While its posters called on Americans to "pray for our gallant men in Viet-Nam and an honorable peace as quickly as possible," the NCRP made clear its association of "honorable peace" with a measure of victory in Vietnam. Future wars, which would bring "the enemy closer and closer to *our* shores," were, according to Wiley, the inevitable result of leaving Vietnam prematurely. America's commitment to its Vietnamese ally was tied to its moral integrity as well as its national security. Americans could not abandon their commitment to their allies or, indeed, to their dead. "When you think about conscience," Wiley stated to CBS, "how do you explain to the loved ones of the nearly 40,000 Americans who thought they were dying to defend their honor—that their cause was immoral?"[14]

The National Unity and Honor America campaigns did not formally unite but cooperated in order to promote the adoption of their similar programs by local veterans' and civic groups. The *New York Times* reported that the two organizations "have offices three doors apart in downtown Washington" and were both involved in "suggesting ways to organizations around the country to generate and demonstrate support of 'the President's search for peace.'"[15] The two campaigns asked little of their projected audiences: flying the flag at full staff, driving with headlights on, and attending veterans' parades were the staples of projecting confidence in the president and the war. The *Chicago Tribune* noted that National Unity Week was sponsoring seven activities: "Prayers for prisoners of war, letters to service men, displaying the flag, wearing red-white-and-blue armbands, turning on headlights, volunteering in hospitals and educational programs, and displaying national unity posters and bumper stickers." Describing the response to their activities as fantastic, a representative of the committee declared that they had run out of buttons after the first day and that the supply of red, white, and blue ribbon in stores in Redlands was exhausted.[16] Tens of thousands of bumper stickers and buttons were in fact distributed, but it was often unclear what organization was promoting these activities. The *New York Times* reported simply that a "coalition of veterans groups, educators and conservatives are sponsoring an 'Honor America Week,'" while in New York the VFW, American Legion, Uniformed Firefighters Association, and Patrolmen's Benevolent Society endorsed similar demonstrations of support for the president.[17]

Many people who participated in the Honor America Week activities were more intent on creating national unity than on winning the war. Nonetheless, they explicitly challenged the messages of the anti-war movement and demonstrated faith in the president's need to continue the war. Each organization relied on the traditional Veterans Day parade as a focal point for community activism, a measure that was highly successful in terms of providing a forum for explicit expressions of patriotic fervor. As the *Times* commented, from the Los Angeles Coliseum, where Gen. Omar N. Bradley urged America to "keep the faith," to the colonial streets of Manchester, New Hampshire, where housewives in a Silent Majority Division marched beside veterans, the war dead of the past were linked to the war effort of the present.[18]

The war dead of the past certainly aroused popular activism in favor of the war. While parades were not billed as pro-war events, the co-optation of such activities by the Honor America and National Unity committees heightened their association with implicit support for the president's policies in Vietnam. Whether because of the publicity campaigns of the committees, Nixon's rallying call to the "great Silent Majority," or simple frustration with anti-war activism, the Veterans Day parades of 1969 had turnouts of unprecedented proportions throughout much of the United States.[19]

Perhaps the most explicitly pro-war of the Veterans Day rallies was that organized as the climax of Honor America Week. The "Rally for Freedom in Vietnam and All the World" took place at the Washington Monument and was originally conceived by Charles Moser, a lecturer of Russian at George Washington University and faculty adviser to YAF. Lee Edwards, a prolific conservative public relations activist, was responsible for organizing the Washington gathering, which was further publicized by YAF and *National Review*. Edwards said he hoped more than ten thousand people would come to the monument to hear speakers and listen to country music singers.[20] The association of country music with patriotism and approval of the war was furthered by a number of famous country songs lambasting anti-war dissenters, the most successful of which was "Okie from Muskogee" by Merle Haggard, which stayed at No. 1 in the *Billboard* country singles charts from November 15 until December 13, 1969. Haggard, who had been jailed for robbery in California in 1963, was later given a full pardon by Governor Reagan. Up to fifteen thousand people listened as the stars of the Grand Old Opry performed, but having hoped that the rally would rival that of the anti-war protests on the National Mall, the organizers may have been disappointed with this turnout.[21] As noted by *Time* several weeks afterward, however, the demonstrators "represent a fresh force in the national controversy over the war."[22] Billed as part of Unity Week, the rally's emphasis on achieving success in Vietnam, rather than simply supporting the troops, highlighted the implicit priorities of the Committee for a Week of National Unity and the NCRP relative to the war. The *Chicago Tribune* reported that many of the signs carried by participants explicitly challenged the anti-war movement—"Dr. Spock has Colic," "Judas William Fulbright," "November 15 Marchers Tell it to Hanoi," and "Nixon Stands for America."[23] Many of those who attended such rallies did not endorse an explicitly conservative interpretation of the war's meaning, but they signified a new way of defying the anti-war perspective and helped legitimize conservative activism.

Human Events reached a similar conclusion, writing that the "silent, undemonstrative presence of thousands of persons who probably would have rather been home by the fireside on that chill fall day but whose principles and patriotism caused them to turn out as evidence of dissent from the dissenters" revealed the power of the silent majority.[24] Among those in attendance were several members of Congress, including Thurmond; Rep. John Buchanan, a Republican from Alabama; Rep. John Marsh, a Democrat from Virginia; Rep. Olin Teague, a Democrat from Texas; and Rep. Donald Lukens, a Republican from Ohio. Rep. Mendel Rivers heartened the crowd by declaring, "There are more of us patriotic Americans than those pro-Hanoi-crats."[25] The rally's keynote speaker was John Tower, who emphasized the theme of "peace with freedom for South Viet Nam" throughout an address in which he stated, "I want this war to end as much as anyone. But I want this war to be the *last* one we have to fight."[26] Patriotism, particularly respect for those who had died, was exploited to reinforce existing support for the president's policies. It was a trend repeated in parades nationwide. Commenting on the rally's success, Colson suggested to Alexander Butterfield that the White House attempt to "use this as a grass roots asset" and promoted Moser's and Edwards's planned marches in February.[27]

In Atlanta, Gov. Lester Maddox rallied supporters by claiming that the purpose of dissenters was to "betray our boys in battle." Gen. William Westmoreland, who participated in a parade in Pittsburgh that drew a reported crowd of one hundred thousand people, remarked that war protests "tend to confuse Hanoi as to our national will."[28] Nixon's official representative at the ceremonies at Arlington National Cemetery accused protestors of doing "an injustice to America's 40 million veterans living and dead." Speaking at a parade on Fifth Avenue, the commander of the New York County American Legion urged support of Nixon: "He tells us he has a solution—and the solution requires our unity behind him. We must now give him the chance to do the job we elected him to do." Signs reading "Don't Reason with Treason," "Bomb Hanoi," and "Support Our Men in Vietnam" were common in many of the parades. The themes of national unity and the relevance of success in Vietnam to the national consciousness were, however, dominant. General Bradley associated the Vietnam mission with national vigor: "If we, as a nation . . . lack the courage to stand firm in our beliefs, then we are unworthy of the sacrifices our veterans have made and are making for us."[29]

The Veterans Day rallies of 1969 marked the climax of national demonstrations in support of the Vietnam War. But activists attempted to keep up the momentum. The NCRP tried to build on its earlier activism regarding Vietnam and to catch the favorable tide of public opinion. To demonstrate its commitment to those in the armed forces, the NCRP had developed Operation Gratitude, which was effectively a publicity drive to encourage patriots to engage in such activities as volunteering at Veterans Hospitals and writing letters to American personnel in Southeast Asia. As a means of associating the organization's programs with support for the administration, the committee organized what it billed as the "largest motorcade in our nation's history," which traveled from New York City to the White House on December 5, 1969.[30] Allowed a meeting with presidential aides at the White House, the motorcade represented a high point of the committee's activist agenda at a national level. The NCRP, like many patriotic and veterans' groups, continued to encourage localized campaigns but increasingly focused its attention on the POW issue.

Those organizations which attached support for the war to mainstream patriotism proved most successful in garnering widespread acceptance of their efforts, a factor that encouraged activists and administration officials to organize an Honor America rally on the National Mall on July 4, 1970. The rally was not officially associated with the NCRP, but, at the behest of Nixon, the Honor America Day Committee borrowed many of the themes of the November campaign. The committee was chaired by J. Willard Marriott, a friend of Nixon and the chair of his inaugural committee, Hobart Lewis of *Reader's Digest*, Bob Hope, and the Reverend Billy Graham. Marriott financed much of the operation and was the organizational impetus behind the determinedly pro-Nixon rally. While the organizers did not make extensive arrangements for travel to the event, H. Ross Perot, the Texan multimillionaire who became a POW advocate, chartered a plane that brought two hundred high school students to Washington for the rally.[31] In July 1970 the Honor America Day Committee made arrangements with CBS and NBC to show a thirty-minute film, *Proudly They Came*, narrated by the actor Jimmy Stewart.[32]

Graham focused on the importance of national unity, but his speech explicitly emphasized the dangers of the permissive social culture that was popularly associated with the anti-war movement. While he and other rally organizers explicitly denounced any agenda other than to unite the country, anti-war advocates tried to convince war opponents to stay away from the event. An anti-war activist and former Presbyterian minister, Steward Meacham, advised boycotting the event: "Any attempt to get into it makes it more interesting and builds it," he declared.[33] In line with the White House's role in privately sponsoring the rally, the event focused quite explicitly on supporting Nixon's agenda. This rally harked back to early demonstrations in favor of Vietnam in that it focused explicitly on backing the president, despite Marriott's claim that the "program would in no way support the war."[34] Its speakers did not engage in lengthy analyses of the meaning of the war or the importance of securing military victory. Instead, they subscribed to a traditional interpretation of American patriotism, which demanded unity in the face of external threats and bolstering of the president during wartime.

Human Events claimed that between 350,000 and 400,000 people attended the rally, for which Hope was the emcee and Graham provided the keynote speech. While acknowledging that the rally "was billed as non-political by its sponsors," *Human Events* argued that a "top-heavy majority of the . . . participants reflected hearty support of the President and faith in the country's institutions through personal comments, flag-waving, applause—and by just showing up.'"[35] The *Chicago Tribune* touted the theme of attacking the anti-war movement. It emphasized and praised the restraint of the police force, which was forced to combat violent attacks by 4,000 anti-war activists, "mostly bearded and unwashed," who protested against the rally.[36] Conservatives recognized that overt acts of patriotism such as Honor America Day did not necessarily equate with full support for the Vietnam War, but they recognized the value of using such events to combat anti-war activism. Indeed, by 1970 it was proving difficult to promote backing of the war on any other terms. The political nature of the rally, furthermore, could hardly have been lost on those who attended.

In part, the theme of national unity was designed to also combat the extreme right. Conservatives were concerned that the demands of extreme hawks would confuse the public regarding the implications of their continued support of the war. One such hawk was the Reverend Carl McIntire, a fundamentalist Presbyterian pastor who came to public prominence via his syndicated radio show. McIntire offered conservative commentary on issues ranging from international relations to sex education. In 1941 he had helped found the American Council of Christian Churches as a challenge to the increasingly liberal Federal Council of Christian Churches, and he became a vocal critic of the World Council of Christian Churches, in large part because of his view that it failed to take a sufficiently anticommunist line. His anticommunist activism was on display in 1970; his Victory in Vietnam March of April 4, 1970, was the first large-scale pro-war demonstration to take place in Washington that year. While less well attended than the later Honor America Day rally, McIntire's event was no less successful in terms of garnering media coverage.

The White House and its adherents saw the need to challenge

pro-war advocates such as McIntire, whose commitment to military victory challenged their focus on national unity and peace with honor. Some fifty thousand people, many of whom carried signs declaring, "No Substitute for Victory," marched along Pennsylvania Avenue toward the Washington Monument.[37] McIntire's far right political views, his insistence on attaching religious programs to the parade, his fiery denunciation of negotiating with communists, and his bombastic criticism of the administration ruled out any endorsement of the march by the White House. Although McIntire was the face of the march, he had been prompted to begin organizing the demonstration by a Vietnam veteran named Richard Barrett, a segregationist who worked for Wallace's presidential campaign in 1968 and founded the white supremacist Nationalist Movement. Barrett had been organizing pro-Vietnam marches in the South since 1967. McIntire often opposed aspects of the civil rights movement and legislation and had publicly and resoundingly attacked such popular figures as Graham. Convinced that the administration was attempting to thwart his efforts, McIntire was not disposed to yield in his attacks on Nixon. The organizers were obliged to change the date of the rally by one week because the original date clashed with an annual flower display on the National Mall. Days before the rally was to take place, a White House aide mistakenly reported that the march had been canceled owing to the conflicting events on the Mall. This prompted McIntire to charge that there were "Communists in the White House and to call for an investigation by the Federal Bureau of Investigation."[38] The march lost the support of those advocates of the war opposed to McIntire's far right position—namely, traditionalist conservatives—and those unwilling to countenance such opposition to the president

While Maddox, Rep. John Rarick, and Rep. Mendel Rivers agreed to join McIntire, pro-war stalwarts such as Thurmond and Goldwater praised the concept of a victory demonstration but were unwilling to attend McIntire's picketing of the White House. Thurmond, who publicly professed to endorse the Victory March, said he was unable to attend because of a prior engagement, a measure designed to avoid alienating the White House.[39] Goldwater wrote to a constituent who questioned the senator's failure to attend that a "commitment of long standing prevented my physical participation in the March. However, I did publicly indicate my support for this effort."[40] He subsequently wrote to a person who was upset by the president's failure to endorse or praise the march that he was "surprised that the President did not recognize this group, as least by a telegram, because they basically are his people." Such assertions can be understood more as an attempt to co-opt the activism of those who participated in the march than a genuine statement of support for the march's principal organizers. Goldwater ended his letter by stressing his attempt to arrange a march in promotion of the POW issue in May, the activist issue he recognized as being less contentious than a march for victory and likely to secure presidential favor.[41]

McIntire's actions threatened to derail conservatives' efforts to control the pro-war agenda on Vietnam. He provoked additional controversy in September when he announced, following a meeting with South Vietnam's vice president Nguyen Cao Ky in Saigon, that he expected Ky to speak at the Victory March scheduled for October. He boasted that Ky would "out-Agnew Agnew" in his speech.[42] It seemed probable that Ky would attend the march, but Kissinger rounded-off the administration's efforts to prevent him from doing so by meeting with him in Paris. Anti-war demonstrators had threatened to counter McIntire's march and subject Ky to intense public attack.[43] While the White House was angered by McIntire's open opposition to its Vietnam policies, Nixon's team was primarily motivated to act by fears that the rally might provoke further anti-war demonstrations in Washington.[44]

Notwithstanding the lack of mainstream pro-war support for his endeavors, McIntire persisted in his organization of Victory Marches, announcing in October that a series of "patriots' marches for victory in Vietnam" would take place monthly and culminate in a rally at the Washington Monument on May 8, 1971.[45] McIntire's last march on Washington was attended by approximately fifteen thousand people, a "mixture of Bible classes . . . and men who identified themselves as labor union members," according to the *New York Times*. Having predicted that the march would attract greater numbers than the anti-war demonstration of April 24, attended by an estimated two hundred thousand protestors, McIntire was disappointed with the comparatively meager turnout.[46] Considering the vocal denunciation of McIntire's marches coming from the White House, the limited tradition of pro-war activists' participation in demonstrations, and the reality that the war was effectively winding down, it is not surprising that the number of marchers was scant. The march itself attested, however, to the continued volatility of the Vietnam issue and the increasing challenges to the administration emanating from the pro-war sector.

Partisans of the administration paid greater attention to popular demonizing of the enemy, while veterans' organizations and patriotic groups consistently held that protest and dissent offered aid and comfort to the enemy, factors that further diminished the likelihood of those who considered themselves patriots opposing the war. The American Legion fostered this theme, asserting that American efforts to implement the justified policy of containment, as exemplified by U.S. engagement in Vietnam, were "dangerously diluted by acts and activities of a misguided segment of American opinion." The group directed its rancor at Congress, stating its abhorrence at "those legislative maneuvers . . . that have created division and confusion and have precluded the realization of that National Unity which alone will serve notice to North Vietnam of our determination and persistence to prevail."[47] Colson, who assumed much of the responsibility for dealing with veterans' organizations and managing the administration's public relations on Vietnam, commented to Nixon that the VFW "has probably been the most valuable organization we deal with."[48] Colson masterminded the White House's endeavor to emphasize the theme of national unity in opposition to the anti-war movement rather than the overt focus on victory preferred by conservatives.

Continuing a theme of constant support for the administration, the commander in chief of the VFW, Joseph Vicites, charged that those senators failing to condemn the North Vietnamese invasion of South Vietnam in 1972 "want South Vietnam to fail and the enemy to win" and that they were "seeking political profit at the expense of their country."[49] Reiterating his administration's refusal to accept weakness in foreign policy and defense matters,

Nixon appealed to his audience at the American Legion by denigrating those who failed to serve and praising the veterans of Vietnam and, by extension, those who supported them. In ending the war, the president declared, "we will not make a mockery of their sacrifice and devotion by talking of amnesty for deserters and shirkers while some of their comrades lie chained in brutal North Vietnamese prisons."[50] Nixon's rhetoric served to accelerate the process whereby pro-war activism was focused on demonizing the Vietnamese enemy and their supposed allies in the American anti-war movement. While helping to sustain popular hostility toward anti-war dissent, it undermined the international and security imperatives inherent in America's engagement in Southeast Asia. This signified the evolution of the pro-war message during the Nixon administration: victory was no longer tied to outright military success in Southeast Asia. This message was adopted by conservative Republicans and leading activists such as those at *National Review*. This is not to suggest that conservatives entirely welcomed the shift in emphasis; rather, it signified recognition on their part that the war was rapidly becoming politically untenable. The new unity campaigns, furthermore, offered an opportunity to divide the Democratic Party's political base even more and opened avenues to political gain by the conservative movement. Popular hostility toward the anti-war movement, however, could sustain backing of phased withdrawal only for so long.

The Hard Hat Riots

As it did in all sectors of American society, the Vietnam War caused division and controversy among labor leaders and within the rank and file of unions. The powerful head of the United Automobile Workers (UAW), Walter Reuther, questioned the necessity of military escalation of the war as early as 1965 and openly opposed it by 1968. He was strongly critical of President Nixon. Reuther's position differed markedly from that of Meaney, a division that was a microcosm of broader divergences in the labor movement. This discord was extensive and complex at the rank-and-file level: more extensive because it incorporated issues of class resentment and disaffection with traditional political elites, and more complex because working-class attitudes toward the war were affected by traditional expressions of patriotism and the preponderance of war casualties among the working class.[51] The working-class had changed in terms of race, gender, age, and work in the postwar period to such an extent that the image of unionized white men in hard hats does little to illuminate the attitudes of ordinary working people regarding Vietnam. But, as David Levy comments, the stereotype of workers as "having less education, less interest in politics," preferring "easy answers," and espousing a "more frequent resort to force" did much to cement the perception of working-class support for the war.[52] The power of this image outlasted the decline of activism in favor of the war and indeed outlasted the war, serving a powerful function as a means of allowing conservatives to associate themselves with ordinary Americans' values and foreign policy goals.

Frank Koscielski's study of workers in Dearborn, Michigan, reveals the contentious nature of the Vietnam War among unionized workers. Union opposition to the war grew in line with public questioning of the government's credibility regarding Vietnam, and thus the stereotype of labor's support for the war ignores the nuances of working-class sentiment. Koscielski writes that the working people he analyzed "were no more supportive of the war than the general population as a whole."[53] Christian Appy cites public opinion surveys that indicated little difference between the opinions of workers and those of middle-class and of wealthy Americans.[54] This does not mean that most union members opposed the war but implies that they shared the national ambivalence and confusion that dominated opinion of the war.

One must distinguish between the stance adopted by unions and the opinions of union members. In real terms, the majority of unions remained supportive of the war or at least remained committed to the president's policy of phased withdrawal of troops. Meaney's role in perpetuating the image of union support for the war accentuated the pro-war stereotype of the working class. The pro-war attitude among prominent American figures of the Roman Catholic Church also cemented the image of ethnic working-class support for the anticommunist crusade in general and for the Vietnam War in particular. Despite the inaccuracy of this stereotype of the working class as a whole and despite the failure of the public, media, and government to acknowledge the nuances of working-class attitudes toward the war, the image of patriotic middle Americans in favor of the war was a compelling contrast to the supposed elitism of anti-war campaigners. Nevertheless, the stereotype had an element of truth regarding popular support for the president's policies in Vietnam and a popular desire for a successful conclusion to the war.

Much of the historiography dealing with working-class responses to the Vietnam War has emphasized the role of class resentments in determining the character of labor activities having to do with Vietnam. Class animosity, as the historians Appy, David Farber, and others argue, is especially relevant in understanding such outbreaks of working-class anger as the hard hat demonstrations of May 1970.[55] The contemporary image of working-class backing for the war was in part a result of the media's failure to recognize and address such issues as a growing class divide and a developing anti–"Rights Revolution" attitude within American society. Rather than expressions of support for the war, therefore, apparently pro-war sentiments and pro-war demonstrations were, according to Appy and Farber, manifestations of class resentment.[56]

Referring to workers' opposition to student protesters, Farber explains that many working-class Americans agreed with the students' opinions but "could not stomach the idea of a nation not only being run by corporate elites but also listening so seriously to the clamorous claims of the corporate elites' privileged children."[57] The image of student radicals embodying an affront to the values of the working and middle classes was reinforced by such groups as YAF as a way of cementing the connection between endorsement of the war and traditional American principles of equality of opportunity and social mobility. In promoting its campaign of asking people to wear blue buttons as a sign of opposition to protestors, YAF declared that, unlike the majority of taxpayers, "most student radicals come from well to do homes." Such "rich student militants," the group proclaimed, "act as if they have a claim on the hard earned money of the poor." They behaved, according to YAF (which was a predominantly middle-class organization), like "an Aristocratic elite above the laws."[58] Such nascent use of class division was fueled by stereotypes of working-class support for the war but was also promulgated as an effective means of achieving pro-war aims because of the evident hostility of ordinary Americans toward anti-war protesters.

YAF was not the only pro-war organization to recognize the power of harnessing social anxieties to prompt support of the war. Writing in early May 1970, the presidential aide Tom Charles Huston (as noted, a former chair of YAF) advised White House officials to be aware of the class resentment and anger of the blue-collar workers. "Fed up with more, of course, than rampaging students," Huston wrote, "construction laborers, clerks, store-keepers, taxi drivers or factory workers" were frightened by the rapid pace of change in American society. Such people, he continued, were "confused and frustrated and getting angry."[59] The White House was determined to exploit such sentiments. Ostensibly geared toward creating a new Republican majority, the White House's effort ultimately focused on maximizing support for Nixon rather than for the party. Huston saw the potential of using popular distress over social change to stoke anger toward the anti-war movement and, indeed, to question the Democratic Party's vision for America. By harnessing the public's antagonism toward the anti-war movement, the White House may indeed have succeeded in creating the appearance that substantially more people were deeply committed to the war than was in fact the case. However exaggerated the level of popular support for Nixon and his continuation of the war, it allowed the president to impede the growth of anti-war activism, particularly in Congress.

Huston was prompted to compose his memorandum to his colleagues by the events of May 8, events that became known as Bloody Friday. As the most widely publicized "pro-war" demonstration of the Vietnam War, the so-called hard hat demonstrations quickly became synonymous with pro-war activism. The major demonstrations began when New York City construction workers attacked a group of students who were protesting the recent killing of four students by Ohio National Guardsmen during an anti-war protest at Kent State University. Construction workers interrupted the anti-war protest in lower Manhattan and marched to nearby City Hall, where they forcibly hoisted the American flag to full staff. They were reported to have believed that the flag was flying at half-staff at the behest of Mayor John Lindsay in honor of those who had died at Kent State. Lindsay, a prominent liberal Republican, had been condemned by conservatives for his anti-war stance. The violent attacks on protestors became headline news across the nation. Recognized by Huston as "the first manifestation of a willingness to fight for the America the blue collar American loves," the hard hat action became a symbol of the working class's belief in a traditional interpretation of American patriotism. While it was understood at the time that such demonstrations did not necessarily equate to full support for the war, they helped the administration equate anti-war activism with elitist, un-American opinion.

The historian Joshua Freeman attests that the "explosive character" of the hard hat demonstrations resulted from a "combination of class resentment and perceived threat to patriarchal notions of manliness."[60] This view reflects recent scholarship dealing with the societal change of the 1960s, but it was understood at the time. The *New York Times* argued that the violence was a "tragic reflection of the polarization brought about by the Vietnam war, campus turbulence, racial tensions and an Administration-fostered mood of political repression." The editors concluded that the "hardhats, long scornful of excesses by privileged longhairs on campus, were obviously delighted to pour out their hatred on the students."[61] As Huston's memorandum indicates and as was explored to some degree by Kevin Phillips in his book of 1969, *The Emerging Republican Majority*, a new middle America had emerged. Rather than being read simply in the context outlined by the *Times*, the hard hat demonstrations made Nixon's silent majority seem plausible.[62] They also encouraged the administration and pro-war activists to fervently pursue the theme of a great body of silent Americans supporting the war.

Nixon was keen to make use of the issue, despite its ambiguous but clearly divisive connotations. The president arranged to meet with representatives of the New York unions at the White House, dismissing the advice of aides who warned that a direct connection with those held responsible for the riots might alienate many Americans angered by yet more violence on the streets. Both at the time and in more recent scholarship, evidence that the workers' acts were less than spontaneous has shed light on the role of union leaders in prompting and endorsing vocal pro-administration and pro-war events. Anthony Summers writes that the White House aides Richard Howard and John Ehrlichman later hinted that the White House had laid on the hard hat demonstrations. Philip Foner argues that workers were paid for their involvement and cites news sources of the time which queried the impulsiveness of the marches.[63] The White House encouraged Peter Brennan of the New York Building and Constructions Trades Union to organize the pro-Nixon demonstration on May 20, 1970. But there is little to indicate that the White House was directly involved in organizing the initial march of May 8 on Wall Street.

A series of often violent confrontations between anti- and pro-Vietnam demonstrators took place in south Manhattan almost daily following the first outbreak on May 8. Chanting "Lindsay is a bum," hard-hat demonstrators besieged City Hall and hung Lindsay in effigy for his alleged un-American attitude toward the war. Many of the marchers expressed their concern over the depth of the divisions in society and professed anger at Lindsay for supposedly perpetuating them. A number of signs proclaimed, "Lindsay for Mayor of Hanoi."[64] This march evoked the theme that anti-war protestors were the source of national division, a concept originally promoted by the We Support Our Boys in Vietnam rallies in 1967. Designed to counter the negative image of rampaging, violent workers, the march of May 20 played on a love-of-country theme, reinforcing the link between patriotism and support for the war.

The peaceful parade, in which as many as 150,000 people were thought to have taken part, included labor union members and their families, police and fire department officers, and thousands of individuals who wished to express their endorsement of the president.[65] In the midst of tumultuous opposition to Nixon's Cambodian incursion, a strong element of enmity toward the anti-war movement pervaded the march, which culminated in a ticker-tape parade on Wall Street. Koscielski remarks that the march was billed as an opportunity to express one's love of country rather than as a pro-war demonstration.⁶⁶ The parade's organizers and many of those interviewed emphasized their desire to show their patriotism and to counter the supposed anti-Americanism of the radical protesters. There was evidence, however, that many participants were ardent cheerleaders for the president's Vietnam policies and often repeated the arguments of pro-war advocates such as administration officials and conservative activists about the need to contain communism.

Although the Cold War consensus was foundering and was severely challenged by the longevity of the Vietnam War, it retained sufficient sway among the middle America to which Nixon appealed to warrant their backing of the president's Vietnam policies. It may have been that union members were encouraged to attend the parade, but participation was also a genuine expression of support for the president and was echoed by thousands of comparable small-scale events. The week before the march on May 20 *Time* declared, "Nixon's Silent Majority may be bewildered and unenthusiastic about Cambodia, but the demonstrations are moving its members to rally behind the President."⁶⁷ While accurate in pointing out the silent majority's irritation with protesters, *Time*'s analysis failed to understand the extent to which support for the president's stand in Vietnam had become synonymous with patriotic duty. As was the case among conservative pro-war activists, Nixon's Cambodian operation and the anti-war fallout did much to resurrect support for Nixon and for the war itself. The successful and justified waging of the Vietnam War was an affront not just to the communist enemy, but to the domestic enemies of American traditions, everything for which hardworking Americans claimed to have striven.

Nixon's meeting with labor leaders, all of whom promoted the rally of May 20, at the Oval Office on May 26, enhanced the stereotype of labor's allegiance to the war. Having presented Nixon with a hard hat inscribed with the words *Commander-in-Chief*, Brennan declared, "The hard hat will stand as a symbol, along with our great flag, for freedom and patriotism to our beloved country." Brennan went on to emphasize the necessity of permitting the president to achieve success in Vietnam and the importance of unity in "building a greater America, morally and physically for all Americans."[68] The hard hat, he said, was also a "symbol of our support for our fighting men and for your efforts in trying to bring the war to a proper conclusion." Brennan lauded the boost in morale that the Cambodia incursion had given to troops in South Vietnam and called on all Americans to give Nixon's plan a chance.[69] Many, including administration officials and conservative pro-war activists, had deplored the resort to violence demonstrated on May 8, but the hard hat marches not only added credibility to Nixon's "great Silent Majority," they also rallied dispirited Americans to the pro-war cause.

Seen at the time as displays of faith in the war, the nationwide pro-Nixon and pro-America demonstrations that took place after the Cambodian operation dulled the impact of anti-war demonstrations. While it was not possible to rally Americans to accept the possibility of the war continuing indefinitely, the pro-war demonstrations gave Nixon much-needed political capital as he prolonged the increasingly unpopular war. They also constituted substance for the administration's own pro-war campaign and ultimately allowed Nixon to continue the slow withdrawal from Vietnam. Although the labor leaders who met with Nixon in May promised to continue the marches in support of the president, the rally on May 20 was the last great parade in the vein of the We Support Our Boys in Vietnam parade of May 1967. As Nixon intensified the winding down of the war, so fervent supporters and patriots reduced their activism. Few anticipated that the war would last almost another three full years. In time an ever-greater exigency arose for the White House to take control of the pro-war message and actively create demonstrations in support of the war.

Propaganda and Persuasion

Nixon's aides developed an extensive network of patriotic programs and pro-war organizations designed to blunt the effectiveness of the mainstream anti-war campaign. The White House was encouraged by independent pro-war demonstrations, and it lent direct support to particular initiatives, including Honor America Day and union-managed events. But Nixon's aides showed a remarkable unwillingness to really back and utilize existing pro-war campaigns. To ensure that all pro-war activism was synonymous with support of the president's policies, the White House created its own nominally independent organizations. By failing to engage conservative organizations, however, the administration divided the pro-war movement. The White House undertaking celebrated hostility to anti-war sentiment largely via the populist appeal of Agnew's attacks on student radicals, television networks, and congressional doves. This campaign was designed to trumpet traditional values and displays of patriotism, for which Nixon appeared a more natural representative than his more liberal Democratic opponents. It was also aimed at winning the political backing of disaffected middle Americans for the presidential election in 1972.

The White House made little distinction between the goals of sustaining an image of popular defense of the war, which would serve to limit congressional anti-war efforts, and maximizing overall presidential popularity. Both were vital to Nixon's foreign policy agenda, which relied heavily on the appearance of strong presidential authority. Nixon, for instance, vigorously promoted a flag-waving drive, for which he drafted the American Legion, the VFW, and the conservative-leaning *Readers' Digest*. He saw this initiative as part of the administration's broader pro-war drive. Other White House energies were spent on appealing to elite audiences and were fashioned to limit dissent among media, academic, and political circles. This plan, while preoccupying White House energies, did not prove as successful as the patriotic drive, particularly as it related to associating the POW issue with support for the president's policies in Vietnam.

In his passion to win what Herbert Parmet described as the war for the "soul of America," Nixon established a secret Middle America Group in the White House in October 1969.[70] The committee included Martin Anderson, Buchanan, Dent, Huston, Bud Krogh, Clark Mollenhoff, and Lyn Nofziger. The committee's existence, like its activities and recommendations, remained largely secret from the general White House system. Buchanan, who believed that domestic politics were fundamental to victory in Vietnam, warned Nixon that "the war in Vietnam will now be won or lost on the American front." The administration, Buchanan continued, needed to appeal to those who were "beginning to feel themselves the moral inferiors of the candle-carrying peaceniks who want to get out now." The Middle America Group was tasked with attracting the support of "the large and politically powerful white middle class," which was "deeply troubled," and from early 1970 was engaged in reaching "the blue collar worker."[71]

This committee was part of Nixon's counterattack against the anti-war movement, much of which was directed from Colson's office. After careful consideration, the White House decided to ignore the Moratoria of October and November rather than directly use the veterans and patriotic organizations to mount a campaign of opposition. Instead, the newly created Middle America Group launched a clandestine counteroffensive. It intensified the covert and heretofore largely futile investigations and infiltrations of anti-war organizations and began its war for what the CCPFV had recently called the silent center. The means by which the administration attacked anti-war protestors helped to shore up support for Nixon's Vietnam policies. By contributing to the intensifying polarization of American society, the administration's public relations campaign limited the legitimate framework for dissent regarding Vietnam. The success of the "Silent Majority" speech, after which only 21 percent of those surveyed in a Gallup Poll favored an immediate withdrawal, added fuel to this campaign.[72]

Nixon's appeal to the silent majority was part of his attempt to associate patriotism with support for his policies, which culminated in the POW campaign. These campaigns did not focus on defining the reasons for America's involvement in Southeast Asia. Influenced by the potential need to accept a so-called decent interval solution, the administration reduced its emphasis on the significance of the war to national security. Instead, it concentrated on publicizing reasons for backing the war that related primarily to domestic issues. A central facet of the White House program was to equate anti-war activists with the provision of aid to the enemy. Nixon was determined to uncover communist influence in the anti-war campaign and augmented the existing programs of harassment and infiltration undertaken by the CIA, FBI, and IRS. Despite the consistency of intelligence reports denying the role of foreign communists in orchestrating anti-war activities, the president approved such programs as that developed by Huston during the summer of 1970. The Huston Plan recommended a series of surveillance operations designed to disrupt New Left activism, including "(1) increased domestic electronic surveillance, (2) monitoring of international communications by Americans, (3) relaxation of restrictions on opening mail, (4) planting informants on campuses, (5) lifting restrictions on 'surreptitious entry,' and (6) creation of a new Interagency Group on Domestic Intelligence and Internal Security, to be controlled from the White House."[73] In discussing the legality of "covert mail cover," Huston commented, "Covert [mail] coverage is illegal, and there are serious risks involved. However, the advantages to be derived from its use outweigh the risks." Surreptitious entry, he noted, "is clearly illegal: it amounts to burglary. It is also highly risky and could result in great embarrassment if exposed. However, it is also the most fruitful tool and can produce the type of intelligence which cannot be obtained in any other fashion."[74] Nixon approved the plan but it was abandoned when Director J. Edgar Hoover of the FBI opposed it, largely because he thought it would be ineffective and would undermine the bureau's independence.

Still, Nixon found willing advocates of the plan's interpretation of anti-war dissent, including Ashbrook, Goldwater, and Reagan. Acting as the frontline man in this new campaign, Vice President Agnew personified the aims of the Middle America Group and effectively was a figurehead and medium for those fed up with the messages of the anti-war campaign and with the Johnson administration's apparent failure to take on the protestors. Agnew was chosen by Nixon in 1968 as a concession to southern conservatives because of his strong stand while governor of Maryland against anarchic outbreaks during recent race riots in Baltimore. Agnew became increasingly popular in the broader conservative movement following his public attacks on anti-war protestors and his effective use of rhetoric that emphasized the elitism of student protestors. He played the role of the White House attack dog and from mid-1969 was unrestrained in his assaults on anti-war protestors and those who were in league with them. Agnew's utility to conservatives was determined largely by his delegitimizing of any form of anti-war protest by characterizing protestors as subverters of mainstream American values. His increased relevance among conservatives demonstrated Agnew's suitability for the role of the administration's outspoken hawk, while his function as the mouthpiece of the silent majority gave clarity to an ambiguous cause.

Agnew's increasingly extreme attacks on protestors and the media troubled even his colleagues in the White House, but his displays of vitriol, often written by Nixon's speechwriters Buchanan and William Safire, furthered the image of anti-war advocates as "sunshine patriots." The cover of *Life,* published the week of the hard hat demonstrations, heralded Agnew's role as the "stern voice of the Silent Majority."[75] Agnew's association of anti-war critics with weakness and isolationism in international affairs, equivocation and softness in matters of law and order, social depravity, and intellectual elitism directly appealed to the anxieties of middle America. During 1970 his increasingly hard-line stance helped cement a popular association between patriotism and support for the war. By alienating the silent majority not only from the anti-war protest movement but also from dissent over Nixon's policies, the Agnew program helped alter the context of popular responses to the Vietnam War. Buckley may have derided Agnew's use of language and his seemingly impetuous attacks on opponents of the administration, but the vice president's popular appeal encouraged the pro-war movement to assume a similar line of attack. Indeed, Buckley and the *National Review* circle eventually came to view Agnew as a hero.

Agnew was central to controlling the pro-war message of the White House. Conservatives' early questioning of administration policy caused anxiety among White House officials, leading to fears that hawks' lack of dependability could later undermine the president's push for a negotiated settlement. Rather than use the groups and individuals that were most vociferous in advocating victory in Vietnam, which were predominantly part of the conservative movement, the Nixon White House sought the active support of moderate Republicans and the existing Vietnam lobbies, the CCPFV and the AFV. The CCPFV reportedly stated that it "attempts to speak for what it calls for majority, silent center or United States public opinion." The organization blamed a lack of public understanding of Vietnam on the apparent rise in public questioning of the war. Anticipating Nixon's "Silent Majority" speech, which was delivered two days after the CCPFV issued its statement, the organization publicly declared that if the president continued the "road to peace with freedom—and we have every reason to believe that he will—and if he speaks out frankly, simply and fully on the consequences of defeat, a substantial majority of the American people will rally behind him."

Nixon's team used the CCPFV, furthermore, to supply the independent, positive analysis of Vietnamization that was necessary to prevent any semblance of a credibility gap. The CCPFV not only offered an optimistic assessment of administration strategy in October 1969 but also emphasized the administration's restraint through its continuation of the bombing halt. Regarding calls for an immediate withdrawal, the CCPFV warned that such a policy would destroy the progress being made toward an honorable peace, and would "nullify negotiations, represent an American sellout, and encourage the victors to try for one, two, three more Viet Nams."[76] Again in April 1970 the CCPFV recommended "civil and military Vietnamization" and a "prudent, flexible program of U.S. troop withdrawals" as the most effective ways of achieving America's aims. Yet again the committee affirmed the principle that "the struggle in Southeast Asia is of great significance for American and world security."

Speaking with an authority garnered from a visit to Southeast Asia and meetings with President Thieu and Vice President Ky, CCPFV officials added legitimacy to the administration's claims of success in Vietnam.[77] To a large extent, however, the CCPFV spoke only to those still behind the war. Recognized by Colson as a group of crucial importance to the administration, the CCPFV functioned in the administration's interest to the extent that it could persuade pro-war advocates that Vietnamization did not represent an elegant surrender. While avoiding Agnew's vitriolic posture, the CCPFV reiterated the administration's claims that the news media had neglected to report the improving situation in South Vietnam. The "unfolding of one of the most sweeping land reform programs in modern history" was virtually ignored, the CCPFV claimed, by a national news media preoccupied with such domestic crises as an air traffic controllers' "sick-out."[78] For its role in advancing the cause in Vietnam (and that of the administration) the CCPFV was rewarded by White House attention and high-level briefings and was a crucial element of the Colson-led propaganda machine.

During this period the AFV continued to produce educational tracts on the need to maintain America's pledge to South Vietnam. The group's publication rate and its ascendancy were dwindling, however, as financial constraints and public apathy about Vietnam curtailed its activities and its appeal. Much of the AFV's activity was now predicated on defense of the administration's position. In January 1970 an AFV spokesman, William Ward, presented the group's response to a CBS editorial that had described Nixon's withdrawal program as inadequate because "the plan will fall short of thoroughly disengaging the country [i.e., the United States] from the unsound position we have taken up in Vietnam and Southeast Asia."[79] Ward, in a vein characteristic of the AFV, denied the premise that "our whole interest and involvement in Southeast Asia has been a mistake" and that the United States should now "cut our losses and run." The AFV relied on the initial rationale for American engagement in Vietnam while arguing that every Southeast Asian country except North Vietnam "supports the American presence in the region, with varied degrees of open commitment."[80] Shortly afterward Frank Barnett, the president of the National Strategy Information Center (NSIC), a council for international security affairs based in New York, wrote to Colson about the AFV.[81] Barnett described the AFV as a "Pro-Nixon 'liberal' group" with "enough 'credibility' to influence CBS." The diversity, or "unlikely mix," as Barnett described it, of the AFV suggested bipartisan and liberal support for the president.[82] By 1970, however, the AFV's sway among liberals opposing the war was minimal and its ability to affect the media questionable. The AFV represented the liberal anticommunism that so impacted the development of neoconservative principles, but its organizational clout in the early 1970s was limited.

Having lost the financial wherewithal to employ a full-time staff, the organization by mid-1969 let its administrative affairs rest with one of its long-term members, William Henderson.⁸³ Henderson attempted to revive the AFV's contacts with administration officials, which had added prestige and proved financially useful to the group during the Johnson years. After a request Colson made to Henderson by telephone on March 6, 1970, Ward issued a statement of support for Nixon's announcement of the bombing of Laos. Referencing "Hanoi's massive invasion of Laos" and the free world's responsibilities to Laos under the Geneva Agreement of 1962, Ward asserted that "the President's statement . . . is a clear and appropriate warning to the Hanoi regime that the U.S. is determined to resist this latest episode of Communist aggression."⁸⁴ Colson rewarded the AFV's approbation by meeting with Ward and offering to arrange briefings for AFV officials by State Department and NSC staff.⁸⁵

The AFV's endorsement of Nixon's policies and its affirmation that they corresponded with the attainment of the original American goals in Southeast Asia were useful, but Colson expressed reservations about investing in the AFV. Henderson acknowledged, as early as April 1970, that AFV directors had considered "liquidating the organization" because of financial constraints and had decided against doing so only because "such a step might be interpreted as a vote of non-confidence in United States policy, and even in the concept of a free and independent Vietnam."⁸⁶ Although the White House, in the person of George Bell, requested that Bill Baroody of the American Enterprise Institute call Henderson and "at least talk about their problems," it offered no direct aid.⁸⁷

Seeing a resurgence in the AFV over the summer of 1970, demonstrated by its plans to organize a seminar on Southeast Asia under the chairmanship of Frank Trager and the resumption of publication of its journal, *Perspectives,* the White House was wary of possible "anti-Administration viewpoints" among the group's adherents. Bell warned there were indications that AFV officials felt the administration was too preoccupied with military aspects of Vietnamization and was not giving sufficient attention to pacification and economic problems in South Vietnam. There were also signs that AFV devotees endorsed the "superhawk opinion."[88] Although Colson remarked on its "good record of support," he noted that the AFV had "prestige as a hawk outfit." Colson also observed that the group, which was "looking for funds," had "spent unwisely" the money given at the instigation of the Johnson administration.[89] As support for Nixon among hawks was not without reservation in 1970, Colson's worries about the AFV divulged the administration's endeavor to undermine the opposition of pro-war bodies. They were also evidence of a determination in the Nixon White House to control the pro-war argument and to retrospectively change the whole meaning of the war.

Colson's team set about establishing a number of ostensibly independent organizations that would promote the administration's line on Vietnam and other foreign policy matters. Gene Bradley of the International Management and Development Institute, who was also Washington vice president of NSIC, responded positively to Colson's suggestions that a focus group aimed at promoting a strong peace be established. The result was Americans for Winning the Peace (AWP), which resembled the CCPFV, although its relationship to the Nixon administration and its operational remit were more extensive. The AWP said its interests lay in "the total spectrum of 'priorities for peace in the 1970s,"' yet it was formed to oppose the McGovern–Hatfield amendment in the wake of the Cambodian incursion. The AWP's claim that it was "an evolutionary development" was accurate in the sense that many of its leading members and directors promoted similar policies prior to joining the organization in the summer of 1970, but it was also an association assuredly oriented and managed by Nixon. By November 1970 the AWP committees, which were based in twenty-eight cities, included such figures as former treasury secretary Henry Fowler, former defense secretary Neil McElroy, Mary Lord of the CCPFV, George Meaney, and Eugene Rostow. The AWP's executive committee included former ambassadors Theodore C. Achilles and Livingston T. Merchant and Gen. Alfred M. Gruenther, while the astronaut Frank Borman, Edward Bursk of the *Harvard Business Review*, Peter Clark, the publisher of the *Detroit News*, H. Ross Perot, Abbott Washburn, the public relations director of Citizens for Nixon in 1968, Charlton Heston, Clare Booth Luce, and Paul Nitze were members.

Although promoted as a bipartisan organization, the AWP, Colson assured the White House aide Dwight Chapin, had as its purpose "the active support of the President's peace plans through the private sector."[90] Colson's team publicly denied that the AWP was a "Republican Party attempt to further advance the image of a partisan Silent Majority" or that it was "a front for the President in his attempt to push his Southeast Asia policy through the Congress without a real debate." Colson categorically denied that the AWP's activities and positions were cleared with the White House.[91] All such statements contained false information.

The AWP directly responded to anti-war activism in Congress, publicizing its position paper on the McGovern–Hatfield amendment, which was released in August 1970. This paper mirrored the administration's position on all issues, stating that the president's plan to end the war was "in operation" and succeeding. It also attempted to disprove anti-war claims that more rapid withdrawal would save American lives, that a withdrawal deadline would help the Paris negotiations, and that U.S. national security was not at stake in Vietnam. The AWP reiterated the pro-war position that "surrender in Vietnam" would project the image of a "new American isolation," from which it would be impossible to tell "where the aggression and intimidation might stop." Such a "retreat to isolationism," the AWP declared, "would be fatal," whereas Nixon's policies in the nuclear age were directed toward "peace with security." Enacting the White House emphasis on retaking the moral high ground, the AWP declared that "instant withdrawal by the United States would bring a bloodbath of unprecedented proportions" and "could destroy all we have fought for" in Southeast Asia. The AWP hinted that the so-called surrender amendment "might well 'enliven' the Communist negotiations in Paris just as the Munich negotiations 'enlivened' Hitler."[92] Although the AWP presented its positions in the form of legitimate analyses of national security concerns, its methodology belied its political goals and its aim of enlivening popular, unconditional support for the Nixon administration.

After opposing the McGovern–Hatfield amendment, a campaign that relied on newspaper advertisements, editorials, and letters to the editor, to members of Congress, and to organizational leaders, the AWP concentrated on working for political candidates in the midterm elections of 1970. At Bell's suggestion, Bradley mobilized AWP regulars to "upgrade the issue of winning the peace" by boosting the candidacy of individuals who endorsed the president's foreign policy.[93] In order to enhance the profile of the group and promote nationwide activism, the White House contributed to the planning of a conference of AWP regional leaders in Washington in January 1971.

At the behest of Kissinger's staff, a series of briefings at the State and Defense Departments and meetings with Kissinger and his staff were arranged for the more than two hundred conference participants. In recommending that the president address the conference, Colson said that the group who had accepted invitations "reads like a 'Who's Who.'" Nixon had apparently wanted to create just such a committee for some time, that is, a committee modeled on the one led by William Allen White that advanced President Franklin Roosevelt's challenge to isolationist and noninterventionist foreign policies. Colson rejoiced in the creation of AWP. Although he acknowledged the president's concern that the group might lose credibility if it appeared to be dependent on the administration,[94] Colson warned of the danger of not giving AWP leaders the "treatment."[95] "Rightly or wrongly," he wrote, "these people consider themselves important; all of them have been recruited, as was the case with the 'William Allen White Committee' on the basis that the President needs them—they will wonder if he really needs them if there isn't some involvement, regardless however brief or limited."[96] Because of a continuing fear that appearing to be too closely tied to the administration would make the AWP "virtually useless to us," coupled with the president's proposal to be away from Washington during the conference, it was suggested that Agnew fulfill these duties. The AWP successfully called for policy papers and organized conferences in support of the president's line but could not elicit broader support. Despite Colson's promotion of the group and Kissinger's assessment that it "can provide useful help in the private sector and in our relations with the congress," the momentum created by its opposition to McGovern–Hatfield did not translate into populist programs that benefited Nixon.

In search of greater relevance to the pro-war cause, Bradley proposed in late December 1970 that the AWP become more involved in strengthening Nixon's position on the POW issue. Bradley had noted in October that the "POW issue promises to get hotter . . . and it's possible that 'Americans for Winning the Peace' could build sentiment for *our* cause."[97] But his proposals for mobilizing community action relied largely on endorsing the activities of existing POW campaigns, such as the letter-writing drive promoted by Jimmy Stewart.[98] The AWP's limited organizational scope thereby compounded its image as a pro-Nixon lobbying group. By January 1971 Colson insisted that the AWP assume greater financial independence, an indication of White House misgivings that its reliance on administration funding would undermine the credibility of Nixon's foreign policy message.[99] Within weeks Colson was again forced to assure a *Washington Post* reporter that the White House had not been responsible for creating or sponsoring the committee.

Bradley too denied the White House connection. The AWP incorporated "middle-of-the-road Democrats and Republicans," he said, and its aim was to "try to pull the center together to support the commander-in-chief, whoever he may be." Such statements did little to augment credibility that the AWP was independent. In particular, Bradley was linked to William J. Casey, an active member of NSIC who had been Republican national chairman and headed the pro-ABM group Citizens Committee for Peace with Security. He was also believed to have connections to the White House.[100] The AWP was able to highlight its opposition to end-the-war amendments and challenges to presidential powers and prerogatives, but it had only a limited effect in mobilizing public opinion in favor of the president's overall foreign policy. In providing a forum for the championing of Nixon's Vietnam policies among those unlikely to join demonstrative pro-war organizations, the AWP was more useful. The demise of the AWP in 1971, largely because of managerial failure, foreshortened the activism of such people, contributing to a growing perception of apathy with regard to the Vietnam War.

By March 1971 the administration was forced to deal with an additional source of division over Vietnam. Lt. William "Rusty" Calley was convicted by a military court on charges of homicide in Vietnam. In November 1969 the freelance journalist Seymour Hersh found a publisher for his account of the massacre of hundreds of Vietnamese civilians by U.S. forces. The massacre had occurred over several hours on March 16, 1968, in the village of My Lai(4). Hersh detailed not only the brutal massacre, but also the military's efforts to investigate and deter public scrutiny of the killings. The event provided the anti-war campaign with substance for its allegations of American war crimes. Initially the White House tried to downplay the event and distanced itself from the issue, relying on the argument that the investigation and prosecutions were military affairs and that White House intervention in this apolitical matter would breach military justice. This reasoning was valid, but Nixon's closest aides perceived the volatility of the issue and the limited scope for maneuver.

The army charged fourteen officers with having covered up information relevant to the investigation of the killings, but most of these charges were dropped. Only one individual, Lieutenant Calley, was convicted of responsibility for the murders and, in March 1971, was sentenced to life imprisonment. Popular responses to the murders and to Calley's conviction were problematic. The killings highlighted the brutality of the war in Vietnam, becoming for many what the *New York Times* would describe as "a kind of metaphor for the American way of war in South Vietnam."[101] But Calley's prosecution raised the doubts of many Americans, who believed he was being unfairly expected to live by rules that did not apply in warfare. Many who opposed the war supported his claims that he had been following orders; the war and the military hierarchy were responsible for Calley's brutality. During his defense testimony Calley stated, for instance, that he had never been taught about the Geneva Convention and that he had in fact been "given specific instructions that everyone in Viet Nam could be the enemy."[102] To many others the Calley trial signified the importance of supporting the cause for which the troops fought and were forced to kill in Vietnam. Vice President Agnew, speaking shortly before Calley's conviction, stressed the hypocrisy of those who called for Calley's prosecution, while honoring those who betrayed their country by avoiding service in Vietnam. Alluding to anti-war activists, he said "a masochism" had swept the country: "It seems to be a compulsiveness to find something wrong with the U.S. and something right with their enemies."[103] Calley was therefore broadly understood to be a scapegoat. As Rick Perlstein comments, "Superpatriots and peaceniks both thought Calley a martyr."[104]

The administration's room for maneuver was stymied by its need to uphold the integrity of the army's legal processes, while also appealing to popular desires for a presidential commuting of the guilty verdict. According to Evans and Novak, "To hawks, Calley was raised to heroic stature as the American warrior, tethered and restrained by politicians refusing to permit the military to seek victory."[105] This view ignores the opposition of conservatives to a change in the verdict, as shown by Buckley's position. Buckley argued that the popular outcry against Calley's conviction actually demonstrated faith in the armed services: "So, without exactly realizing why, many Americans view the conviction of Calley as an elaboration of the [anti-war] attack on the military. And they view the attack on the military as a vote of no confidence in the society the military is supposed to defend."[106] While Buckley disagreed with the public's desire for Calley's sentence to be reduced, he, too, used the issue to denigrate the anti-war position. This theme was becoming more and more noticeable in conservative critiques of the war and its meaning. The administration soft-pedaled conservatives' objection to its interference in the military's legal protocols, concentrating on their rejection of the anti-war movement's use of the issue. The White House's public position ultimately came to reflect what it deemed was popular sympathy for Calley.

Nixon supported the position recommended by his aide Jon Huntsman, who in mid-April 1971 recommended, "We should catch opinion as it shifts, get in front of it—not reaming Calley, but defending the Army, the process of law in this country, our belief that excesses in combat will not be tolerated—and giving a good scourging to the guilt-ridden, war-crime crowd that is on the other side of the fence, and of the national fence."[107] Attempting to "catch" public opinion proved difficult, as both hawks and doves exploited the Calley situation, and individuals like George Wallace used unambiguous support of Calley to win political backing. While the White House eventually responded by reducing Calley's sentence, Nixon's aides treated this episode as part of the wider anti-war campaign.

Colson invoked the aid of a superficially independent organization, Vietnam Veterans for a Just Peace (VVJP), that the White House had been largely responsible for founding in May 1971. Although VVJP included many veterans fully committed to its aim of promoting support for the war, its founders were sponsored by the Nixon White House and dedicated to furthering its line. Organized by two veterans, Sgt. Bruce Kesler, U.S. Marine Corps, and Lt. John O'Neill, U.S. Navy, the VVJP was quickly co-opted by the administration. Colson wrote to Nixon in mid-1971 that the group was "an organization specifically set up to counter [John] Kerry," the prominent spokesman for Vietnam Veterans Against the War (VVAW), while Haldeman remarked in June 1971 that Colson had "put this [VVJP] together."[108] Both the White House and the VVJP's leaders were keen to publicly show its independent character, and it was launched by a group of Vietnam veterans, including Kesler and O'Neill on June 1, 1971, at a press conference at the National Press Club in Washington. The statement of formation that accompanied the launch declared that the primary function of the group was to ensure that "our sacrifices not be in vain."[109]

VVJP's contention that most Americans did not understand the nature of conflict and the situation in Vietnam was designed to inspire acquiescence in Nixon's continuation of the war. The veterans' group endorsed Vietnamization as a means of "making withdrawal possible in a responsible manner by leaving behind a viable South Vietnam with the capability for self-defense." A VVJP flyer explicitly endorsed "President Nixon's withdrawal and Vietnamization program," which it claimed was the only policy that "provides for preserving the accomplishment of 6 years of American sacrifice and blood."[110] Immediately setting itself in opposition to the VVAW, Kerry's group, VVJP asked "patriotic Americans" to declare whose side they were on, positing stark alternatives: "The forces of 'righteous' indignation, revulsion and weariness? Or those who struggle to disengage from Vietnam responsibly, with orderly programs of reconstruction, and with proper respect for American blood?"[111]

In attempting to develop widespread popular backing of the war, the VVJP had two specific functions, namely, fostering the success of Vietnamization and foiling the message of Kerry and the VVAW. According to the VVJP, the enemy's main force units in Vietnam had been "defeated in bloody battle and his hard-core cadre severely decimated." Maintaining that the enemy "languishes in the jungles and mountains," the organization warranted that Nixon's bold actions had brought success. The Cambodian incursion, the pro-war veterans said, sealed off one of the enemy's two vital supply routes, while the operation in Laos and the bombing of the Ho Chi Minh Trail severely restricted the flow of war materials to the South. The favorable outcome of Vietnamization, furthermore, meant it was "possible for American troops to be withdrawn honorably from Vietnam."

Kesler challenged Kerry to "face us in debate" and charged that with the help of the biased news media, he "has monopolized the airwaves for too long." O'Neill had served in the same unit as Kerry but did not know him personally. He contended that Kerry's testimony before the Senate Foreign Relations Committee had been replete with misrepresentations, and he avowed that Kerry represented only the 10 percent of Americans who sympathized with the Viet Cong. This "radical minority" was in danger of governing the "complacent majority" because of their willingness to use violence and appear in mass demonstrations. "Shall Mr. Kerry and his little group of 1000 embittered men," O'Neill asked rhetorically, "be allowed to represent their views as that of all veterans because they can be mustered anywhere and appear on every news program? I hope not, for the country's sake."[112]

This message was reiterated by conservatives, who were also very much involved in the campaign to discredit Kerry. Buckley asserted that the "indictment" of Kerry was complete because of his statement that the U.S. government's hypocrisy was based on "the mythical war against communism."[113] Buckley said that the ignorant Kerry had offered a "total indictment of the practices, and motives of America and its leaders." He concluded, "Myself, I will listen patiently, decades hence, to those who argue that our commitment in Vietnam, and our attempt to redeem it, were tragically misconceived. I shall not listen, ever, to those who say that it was less than the highest tribute to the national motivation, to collective idealism, and to international rectitude."[114] Buckley's position betrayed the fact that conservatives were now trumpeting the morality of America's struggle to defend the free peoples of Southeast Asia and relying less on arguments that related to American security interests. Conservative leaders were impacted by the populist campaigns to promote championing of the war for reasons of patriotism. Popular war-weariness forced conservatives to pull on the heartstrings of a public largely unwilling to accept the anti-war view that U.S. policy was immoral.

O'Neill was invited to a much-publicized meeting with Nixon in the Oval Office on June 16 and fulfilled his role as a foil to Kerry during a debate on the *Dick Cavett Show* on June 30. He said that Kerry was "the type of person who lives and survives only on the war-weariness and fears of the American people" and proclaimed the anti-war activist's culpability in hyping a false image of American soldiers being routinely involved in war crimes. O'Neill attempted to portray himself as a typical Vietnam veteran and typical patriotic American. Fifty-five thousand Americans had died in Vietnam, O'Neill declared, "because they believed in this country." It proved much more difficult to portray Kerry and his fellow veterans as unpatriotic than it was to dismiss the petitions of radical student protestors. Neither the VVJP nor the broader pro-war movement ever found a way of doing so during the war. Indeed, O'Neill's focus on the war crimes issue heightened, rather than diminished, popular discontent with the war. Rather than address specific issues of policy, O'Neill and the VVJP concentrated on propagating the administration's line, a factor that enhanced the image of veterans' support for the war but did little to weaken widespread anxiety with the divisiveness of Vietnam.

The VVJP had greater fortune in buttressing its position through its emphasis on the association between the administration's policies and support for POWs. Speaking in defense of his organization's backing of Nixon, O'Neill said, "We all realize that if we come home from Vietnam leaving our POWs rotting in North Vietnamese jails, that we will leave the heart and soul of this country there also."[115] Although the VVJP, which remained a loose federation of veterans' groups, failed in trying to fully discredit Kerry and the VVAW, the group's leaders succeeded in exploiting popular disquiet over the protesting veterans. They allied their patriotic duty to support for Nixon's policies, successfully promoting the image of anti-war protestors attacking returning soldiers and focusing attention on the fate of the war's true victims, the American POWs.[116] In creating nominally independent organizations the White House enjoyed some success in boosting the president's standing but its fixation on controlling the pro-war message led it, as YAF had complained, to ignore and sideline many active pro-war groups. Rather than simplify the pro-war message being consumed by the public, such marginalization diversified and complicated the pro-war line, a phenomenon evident in war supporters' work to enhance the POW issue.

POW Campaigns and the Bloodbath Argument

Pro-war activists' use of the POW issue stemmed from long-held arguments about the cruelty and inhumanity of the Vietnamese Communists. Proponents of American involvement in Southeast Asia asserted, to varying degrees, that communist domination of the region would not only subvert the personal freedom of its inhabitants but also yield a repression sufficiently grotesque to warrant indictment as a bloodbath. Allegations of communist atrocities during the siege of Hué following the Tet Offensive in 1968 added fuel to the fire of recrimination. Rep. Roman Pucinski compared the killings to the murders of Polish soldiers by the Soviet army in 1940 and foresaw "mass graves and mass executions . . . [as] the business of the day in South Vietnam if the Communists were to emerge victorious." He demanded that those "who would today urge peace at any price" consider such "tragic consequences" of withdrawal by the United States.[117] In 1969 demonization of the enemy, an additional rationale for continuing the war, became prominent. Directly related to the pro-war movement's campaign and encouraged by the administration, this move was designed to appropriate the POW issue and thereby deploy an emotional stimulus to raise popular support for the war. The campaigns proved to be double-edged swords for the administration. First, they reduced faith in the efficacy of negotiating with the enemy and helped promote the conservative argument that the Paris talks were futile. Second, by directing too much public attention on the POW issue the president risked losing the support of his conservative base, which remained more committed to publicizing the national security rationale for U.S. policy in Southeast Asia. Finally, despite the White House's best efforts, it was not able to control POW organizations, many of which began to question Nixon's strategy for securing the return of prisoners as the war's ending proved a long, drawn-out process.

The Johnson administration had muted discussion and debate on POW issues for fear that highlighting American suffering would hasten popular opposition to the war and force the administration to start negotiating for prisoner releases. As Michael Allen discusses, concern for POWs was not an invention of any administration. Neither was this issue the sole preserve of conservatives and advocates of the war.[118] POW groups were created in 1965 and were predominately organized by prisoners' families. By 1969, when the POW issue became the focus of wider public attention, demonstrations of apprehension over POWs did not necessarily signal backing of the war. The anti-war movement was quite effectual in acquiring information on POWs from the North Vietnamese government. Furthermore, popular support for the POW cause helped change the meaning of the war in ways that fundamentally challenged conservatives' emphasis on the international implications of the conflict. For many Americans, victory came to be defined as the return of America's prisoners.

For many others, however, the POW campaign represented a means of expressing pro-war sentiments. Nixon's POW campaign proved an effective way of proposing a supposed national unity regarding Vietnam, a factor that enormously increased popular activism around the issue. Requiring less analysis than questions of America's involvement in Vietnam, active concern for POWs effectively resulted in a demonstrative campaign of propping up Nixon's policies of negotiation and withdrawal. In terms of convincing the public of the righteousness of their position, pro-war campaigners ultimately proved more effective in utilizing the issue than their anti-war counterparts. This involved marked redefinitions of the meaning of victory, however, and of the purpose of the war. While the POW cause thus gave the administration additional time for negotiations and Vietnamization, it may not have served the primary purposes of the pro-war advocates who attempted to wield it to gain public endorsement.

Secretary Laird voiced the administration's opening gambit of its attempt to use the POW issue on May 19, 1969, publicly signaling a campaign the White House had initiated earlier that year. Speaking at a press conference, he declared, "Hundreds of American wives, children, and parents continue to live in a tragic state of uncertainty caused by the lack of information concerning the fate of their loved ones. This needless anxiety is caused by the persistent refusal by North Vietnam to release the names of U.S. prisoners of war." Laird said the administration's goal was "the prompt release of all American prisoners."[119] Nixon's focus on the issue earned the public gratitude of POW campaigners, who at this time were mainly family members of prisoners and missing men. They had become frustrated by the Johnson administration's silencing of the issue and welcomed the Nixon administration's interest in their cause. The extent to which the organizational structure of the POW campaign was developed at the behest of the Nixon administration is contentious, however.

Local, family-oriented groups advocating for POWs and missing in action (MIA) had existed since the beginning of the war and had invariably formed part of the wider armed forces support structure. The National League of Families of Prisoners of War and Missing in Action in Southeast Asia, commonly referred to as the National League, was formally founded in April 1969 and chaired by Sybil Stockdale, the wife of the most senior officer known to be a POW in North Vietnam. Before the official founding of the national organization, Stockdale's San Diego–based family group met with

Assistant Secretary of Defense Dick Capen, who spent the early part of 1969 traveling to forty-five sites to meet with families and POW-oriented groups. Soon after, the National League expanded its campaign to popularize domestic concern for POWs. Stockdale stated in a solicitation letter of 1969 that her original San Diego group had invited representatives from the State and Defense Departments to meet with her and answer questions.[120]

Laird's speech and Capen's visits reveal the active role the administration played in promulgating the issue on a national level. This activism created a codependency between the White House and the National League and earned Nixon a certain loyalty among nonfamily POW activists that was initially very useful to the administration. Whatever the origins of the National League, its chair enunciated the goal of the organization: "Ours is an effort to supplement that which our government is doing to ensure humane treatment of our men and in no way reflects any discredit on the efforts made by our government."[121] Although the National League was a departure from localized groups, its loose organizational structure and its insistence that only family members of those held prisoner or missing be allowed to join signified a continuation of earlier practices.

The establishment of the National League was a turning point in that the POW issue transformed from one based on gaining private information on POWs and MIAs to one founded on educating the American people about the plight of American servicemen held by North Vietnamese captors. When the North Vietnamese responded to such demands by offering information, often through anti-war groups, POW campaigners changed their focus and began emphasizing the cruelty of the North Vietnamese in their treatment of prisoners. Once it had been established as a national nonprofit organization the National League received free use of a Wide Area Telephone Service line from the White House and was offered free office space by the Reserve Officers Association.[122]

The aid given by the administration to the National League formed part of its wider effort to make the POW issue a particularly pro-Nixon endeavor. The billionaire founder of Electronic Data Systems, H. Ross Perot, had created a pro-Nixon group, United We

Stand, in 1969 at the behest of the White House. Under Perot's directorship and financial sponsorship, the group's attention turned to the POW issue. Perot subsequently maintained that Kissinger had personally asked him to mount the private campaign on behalf of the administration, a claim that was certainly in line with White House objectives and activities during this period. When questioned in 1992 about his role in the development of United We Stand, Perot said he had been approached by Secretary of the Navy John Warner and asked to found a private citizens' group because of his recent outspokenness in support of POW families. When asked why the administration had thought the citizens' committee necessary Perot responded, "The POW project had to be a completely private project, otherwise it would have had no credibility with the Vietnamese, and these were the people we were trying to impact." He further stated that it had been the idea of either Kissinger or Haig to keep the administration's role private.[123] Perot's opinion that his actions were designed to create leverage with the North Vietnamese reflected popular understandings of the purpose of such activism and indeed garnered significant conservative support. In reality, the programs merely served the administration's domestic purposes. The POW issue was not utilized by Kissinger during his secret negotiations with the North Vietnamese, and it served only symbolic value at the Paris talks. The White House saw this not as a matter of foreign policy but as a means of reorienting the public's gaze away from the specifics of Vietnam policy and toward celebrating Americans' honorable service in the war.

The White House can only have been pleased by Perot's financing of an advertisement purporting the full support of United We Stand for the president's Vietnam policy. The advertisement was carried in 108 primary newspapers and on 22 television stations, at a cost of $1 million, according to Perot.[124] During the pro-Nixon demonstrations surrounding Honor America Week in 1969, Perot stated that Nixon's critics had developed effective ways to show their dissent, but that "the average American has no opportunity to speak out on the issues. We simply want to give the common man an entry point into the system that overwhelms him."[125] The White House was determined to provide the "common man" with a means of supporting Richard Nixon as much as a means of supporting the prisoners. But, as Colson warned in late 1969, there was a danger in relying too heavily on an independently managed organization to secure the administration's purposes regarding POWs.[126] While the POW issue helped secure popular backing for the administration's withdrawal strategies, Colson's doubts would ultimately prove highly relevant in defining public consumption of the POW issue.

The Nixon administration attempted to redefine the context in which individual Americans could project support for the war by emphasizing the priority attached to gaining information on and the eventual return of POWs. It was not difficult to link the POW issue to that of communist cruelty. Congressional pro-war members accused their anti-war counterparts of refusing to recognize the nature of the communist enemy, a position made more effective by reference to North Vietnam's supposed failure to adhere to the Geneva Convention relative to the treatment of POWs. Goldwater urged his colleagues to provide the "essentials" of "determination, unity and resolve" so that the administration could achieve its goal of securing better treatment for POWs. Indicating the pro-war lobby's determination to use the POW issue to present the malevolence of the enemy, Goldwater remarked on the need to carefully avoid hastening into "commitments in Paris or elsewhere with a government unwilling to honor even the humanitarian accords of the Geneva Convention."[127]

Such warnings usually referred to North Vietnam's failure to comply with the agreements of 1962 on Laos, but the POW issue gave an emotional weight that moderated the often bellicose, alarming messages of pro-war activists. The presentation of the enemy as merciless, reinforced by comparisons with supposedly more humane treatment of prisoners by the United States and South Vietnam, helped legitimize the president's more forceful military measures. Tower made a simple connection between support for the administration's conduct of the war and support for innocent Americans: "I call upon those who criticize American firmness in Vietnam to protest the inhumanity of the North Vietnamese as manifested in their callous refusal to end the needless suffering of American civilians. Perhaps the great force of world opinion with which this Nation often seems so preoccupied can provide an impetus to the North Vietnamese to demonstrate understanding of human decency."[128]

The POW campaign temporarily deflected attention from the specifics of Nixon's Vietnam policies, while also serving to present the commander in chief in a positive light as figurehead of the POW cause. That status was solidified by Nixon's declaration of a National Day of Prayer and Concern for POWs, held on November 9, 1969, and his appearance with representatives of the National League at the White House on December 12. During this meeting Nixon stated that the POW issue would be handled "on a humane basis apart from the political and military issues of the war." This was consistent with Nixon's line that all Americans, regardless of their political proclivities, should unite behind the POW issue. Nixon also was noted to have stated, however, that "there would be no precipitate withdrawal which could leave the prisoner issue unresolved, noting that such a withdrawal would also imperil the security of the remaining U.S. forces."[129]

At pains to project an image of national unity on the issue, the White House encouraged Sen. Bob Dole, chairman of the Republican National Committee, to organize a bipartisan gala honoring POWs and their families at Constitution Hall in Washington in May 1970. The rally was labeled an "Appeal for International Justice" and included speeches by Vice President Agnew, Senators Dole and Goldwater, Perot, the astronaut James Lovell, and returned POWs. Although the event was attended by members of both political parties, it was tinged with a decidedly pro-war air. Agnew was celebrated for his attacks on those protesting the war. The event marked a celebration of America designed to contrast with the supposed anti-Americanism of anti-war protestors, furthering the administration's contentions that protesting the war added to the suffering of POWs. The rally was the climax of a series of activities that included the testimony of Perot and five wives of POWs before the House Foreign Affairs Subcommittee on National Security Policy and the attendance of approximately one thousand POW/MIA relatives at a reception in the Rayburn Office Building. The reception included addresses by Laird, Adm. Thomas Moorer, the chairman of the JCS, and other members of the JCS.

This was a bandwagon no one wanted to be left off of. During 1969 and 1970 the U.S. Postal Service issued a POW stamp, Congress inaugurated a National Day of Prayer for POWs, and Nixon nominated Frank Borman as his personal representative on a twelve-nation fact-finding mission to determine the fate of American servicemen missing in Vietnam. Shortly after his return, Borman, in an address to Congress, said, "I strongly beg you not to forsake your countrymen who have given so much for you."[130] The reference to government abandonment was reinforced by the popular song "Don't Forget the Eagles," promoted by the NSC staff member Dolf Droge.[131] Each of these programs, designed to heighten awareness of the plight of POWs, pinpointed the need for national unity in order to induce Hanoi to offer more favorable treatment of prisoners. Statements like those of Borman validated the administration's implication that any semblance of surrender in Vietnam would undercut the possibility of securing the release of all POWs and would certainly prevent the possibility of fully accounting for MIAs.

More than any other lobbying effort having to do with Vietnam, the POW issue established a broad-based foundation of support. POW-related groups developed throughout the United States and in many cases were related to existing patriotic and armed forces organizations. Veterans' organizations and labor unions worked for POWs and exhorted their members to get involved in organized petition drives, letter-writing campaigns, and days of recognition and prayer. In most cases such groups equated being mindful of POWs with at least a moratorium on the questioning of the president's policies toward Vietnam. The Nixon administration exploited the POW issue, but the campaign's disparate grassroots base precluded White House control. Each POW group demanded that North Vietnam comply with the provisions of the Geneva Convention and proclaimed their campaign a humanitarian rather than a political one.

With the exception of the POW-related activities of the anti-war activists, all groups relied on castigating the barbarity of the enemy. The "government of North Vietnam and its lackeys, the Viet Cong and the Pathet Lao," the American Legion resolution declared, "have systematically violated each and every [one] of the ... rules of civilized warfare." The resolution referred specifically to the North Vietnamese failure to comply with the Geneva Convention.[132] Perot's United We Stand initiated its POW campaign by developing an exhibit displaying the cruel and unusual treatment experienced by POWs in North Vietnam. The New York–based Council for the Civilized Treatment of POWs urged Americans to "condemn the brutal and barbarian mistreatment to which Americans captured in Southeast Asia have been and are being subjected.... The flagrant violation of civilized behavior in the treatment of prisoners-of-war must be stopped." While conveying its desire to reach certain goals with regard to POWs' treatment, the council rejected the "concept of a built-in profit factor in the abuse of prisoners and their families," thereby affirming a notion held by many POW groups that prisoners were being used as hostages by the North Vietnamese.[133] This sentiment was aroused by Lt. Robert Frischman, who became a celebrity of the POW campaign after his release from a North Vietnamese prison in May 1970. Frischman, in his role as spokesman for Concern for Prisoners of War, wrote to members of Congress in April 1971 to announce that the communists would negotiate for the release of POWs "only when they feel that it is in their best interest to give up that asset."[134] Concern for Prisoners of War advised the administration to "put a stumbling block in the path of what the Communists want ... no more troop withdrawals without a proportional release or internment in a neutral country of POWs."[135]

Although the National League stressed the need to keep the POW issue out of politics, it too publicly upheld the president's policies and accused anti-war activists of sapping the administration's attempts to secure information on POWs. Far from welcoming congressional end-the-war amendments, which stipulated that U.S. troops would be withdrawn once all POWs had been released, the National League accused doves in the Congress of exploiting POWs for political gain. At least until 1972 success in Vietnam, defined in terms of reaching Nixon's ambiguous peace with honor, was presented by leading POW organizations as the only way the POW/MIA problem could be resolved. This view had much to do both with the desire of POW families to justify the sacrifices of their loved ones and with opposition to any semblance of surrender in Vietnam. It was determined also by the activist role of the Nixon administration and the pro-war political agenda of the most pioneering citizens' POW groups.

Nixon stepped up his public effort on behalf of POWs with two extraordinary acts in October and November 1970, each of which was designed to reinforce the idea that only his policies could reap rewards when it came to POWs. During his Vietnam speech in October, the president proposed "the immediate and unconditional release of all prisoners of war held by both sides," asserting that such a step "would be a simple act of humanity" and could also "serve to establish good faith, the intent to make progress, and thus improve the prospects for negotiation."[136] For the first time, the administration set as its stated goal the *immediate* release of American prisoners. While improving his public image, Nixon's proposal was unrealistic, and administration officials expected it to be ignored or rejected by the North Vietnamese.

The popularity of the measure prompted Nixon to authorize the second extraordinary step: a raid on the prison camp at Son Tay in North Vietnam. Although the mission failed—the camp had been abandoned and all its prisoners moved—it gave the White House an unparalleled boost by legitimizing the president's resolve to secure the rescue of the POWs. In an op-ed in the *New York Times*, the National League averred that although no prisoners were rescued "in terms of morale, the raid was outstanding."[137] Defending the foray on the grounds that the administration had recently learned of "increasing deaths" in North Vietnamese prison camps "because of mistreatment," the White House aide Herbert Klein insisted that the president had "used all diplomatic and political channels which are open to him in his efforts to gain their freedom."[138] The White House converged less on providing humanitarian, legal, or military justification for the raid than on its popularity among POW families and its symbolic value as an indication of the president's efforts on behalf of prisoners. Bell assured Haldeman that all of the major veterans' groups had been contacted in order to prompt maximum endorsement of the would-be rescue.[139] Having instructed that only volunteers carry out the raid, the White House portrayed the action as a symbol of the patriotic commitment to duty intrinsic to those concerned about the POW issue. Through its emphasis on this issue the Nixon administration cultivated by implication the impression that the continuation of the war was necessary simply to free American POWs. While this idea had limited value over time, it did afford the president additional time to continue the process of Vietnamization.

Pro-war activists like Reagan reinforced the notion that continuation of the war was necessary in order to secure the release of American prisoners. Speaking at a POW/MIA fundraiser in June 1971, Reagan remonstrated with a peace activist who had said the POW issue was a joke and had declared that there was no way to realize the return of all POWs without setting a firm date for withdrawal. "The issue of prisoners," Reagan declared, "is not a joke. It is the single most important issue involved in this long and savage war and we want them back *now*." Reagan was appealing to his audience, but his language directly reinforced the administration's projection of itself as the primary advocate of POW well-being. Continuing the campaign to divide the peace movement from the POW issue, Reagan lamented the "tragedy" experienced by POWs unable to "take comfort in the knowledge that whatever their hardships, America is united behind them." For the first time in the history of the country, Reagan claimed, American prisoners had to endure the "bitter awareness" that many of their fellow Americans were "more concerned about the enemy than about them" and were in effect abetting the enemy's use of psychological warfare.[140]

Reagan was on the defensive. Sympathy for POWs and their families, as demonstrated by consistent anti-war backing of POW-related resolutions in Congress and the use of the issue by opponents of the war to promote their end-the-war amendments, did not equate with support for American intervention in Southeast Asia. Indeed, anti-war activists, as noted, were able to gain information on POWs held in Vietnam and received released prisoners from Hanoi. In 1969 the Committee of Liaison with Families of Servicemen Detained in North Vietnam was formed in New York. Chaired by the New Left activists Dave Dellinger and Nora Weiss, the committee strongly opposed Nixon's policies and was involved in securing mail from American POWs in North Vietnam. In January 1971 Dellinger and Weiss argued that the renewed bombing of North Vietnam and the raid on Son Tay in November 1970 had made plain the administration's exploitation of the POW issue for political gain. They asserted that "the release of men . . . can be achieved only when the Administration sets a date for the total withdrawal of American troops from Vietnam."[141] In March 1971 Weiss said that receipt of mail had been delayed by the bombing of Laos.

By May 1971 families frustrated by the National League's failure to endorse end-the-war resolutions formed the POW/MIA Families for Immediate Release. This organization agreed with Weiss's claim that the Nixon administration was using the POW issue for political advantage. If the United States was intent on withdrawal, the group argued, it should simply adopt this strategy immediately, and concluded that the return of POWs should be the only criterion determining the rate of withdrawal. Despite the committee's activities and its securing of the receipt of mail from and delivery of Christmas packages to North Vietnam, the vast majority of POW family members continued to endorse the administration and support the war. Indeed, Stockdale asserted unequivocally that the "peace groups have done those things which will further Hanoi's propaganda about the prisoners."[142]

The argument that anti-war campaigners were making political use of the POWs and aiding the enemy assumed heightened potency in July 1971. After a similar declaration was made by the North Vietnamese in June, the delegation of the Provisional Revolutionary Government (PRG) at Paris included in its seven-point peace proposal a clause allowing for the possibility of an immediate release of POWs. Provided the U.S. government set a terminal date for withdrawal of "the totality" of its forces, "the parties will at the same time agree on the modalities . . . of the release of the totality of militarymen of all parties and of the civilians captured in the war (including American pilots captured in North Viet Nam) so that they may all rapidly return to their homes."[143] While many POW groups, including the National League, again accused the North Vietnamese and PRG of holding POWs to ransom, the enemy's apparent willingness to abide by the provisions outlined in successive end-the-war amendments endangered the Nixon administration's leverage over the POW cause. This development did not impact public opinion strongly in the short term, but it signaled to the White House that its use of the issue might actually prove a limiting factor in its continued prosecution of the war. Time, the White House recognized, was not entirely on its side. The threatening possibility that the National League and other campaigners would lose patience with the Nixon administration's slow ending of the war became more real with each passing year.

The administration therefore remained determined to control the message that the public consumed on the POW issue. In addition to Nixon's highly publicized meetings with representatives of POW organizations, beginning in mid-1971 Kissinger held bimonthly meetings with the National League's board of directors. The meetings were partly a response to the group's increasing willingness to openly question administration policy, a process that intensified during 1972. Nixon's promises of peace with honor were welcomed in 1969 and 1970, but the continuation of the war spurred doubts that Vietnamization was moving quickly enough. Many in the National League began to echo the anti-war line that if the war was ending anyway, it should simply be ended immediately. By 1972 the POW campaign was stimulating patriotic fervor and allowing for open championing of the president's Vietnam campaign, yet it was also engendering a movement liable to awaken skepticism of Nixon's understanding of the war.

Notwithstanding the involvement of anti-war activists in supporting POWS, the issue ultimately gave the pro-war campaign much-needed impetus. The largest POW organizations maintained full support for the administration. Pro-war activists, most notably students and young people associated with the National Coordinating Committee for Freedom in Vietnam and Southeast Asia, produced a series of POW "myths" (see chapter 6). These opinion pieces disputed claims made by the anti-war movement about the treatment of American POWs. They argued that a bloodbath would follow any impulsive American withdrawal, thereby denigrating the sacrifices for which so many Americans had died. The corresponding demonization of the enemy afforded the Nixon administration an emotional and political credibility that allowed it to stay the course in its programs for ending the war.

In his analysis of the factors influencing the persistence of the myth that live POWs were held in North Vietnam and Laos after March 1973, H. Bruce Franklin comments that the existence of live prisoners was used to prove "undeniably the cruelty and inhumanity of the Asian Communists, the fortitude and heroism of the American fighting men, and the noble cause for which the United States fought in Indochina."[144] The idea of live prisoners effectively abandoned by their government reinforced the argument that the military had been prevented from achieving even minimal success in Vietnam because of the constraints imposed by the civilian leadership in Washington. This interpretation did not derive simply from a post-Vietnam analysis of how America lost the war but was based on the wartime pronouncements of hawks who lambasted the government's failure to implement a more forceful bombing campaign. It was also based on the success of pro-war activists who used the POW issue to alter the context of success in Vietnam.

The Growing Significance of Patriotism

Nixon's Vietnamization program was subject to less scrutiny on a popular level than was certainly the case among conservative political organizations. Administration officials, not least the president and his foreign policy advisers, desired the legitimization by political and intellectual elites of their Vietnam strategies. The White House soon realized, however, that it could also achieve its goal of continuing the war by soliciting the support of more populist organizations and by creating an association between patriotic duty and endorsement of the president's Vietnam policies. Much of the White House campaign was influenced by the large-scale pro-war campaigns that took place in response to the Moratoria of 1969 and that climaxed in the rallies behind the Cambodian incursion. These supposedly apolitical patriotic drives provided the long-sought context in which ordinary people could project their support for the president and their wholesale rejection of the antiwar movement. Long after the majority of Americans had become war weary these events and campaigns helped sustain an image of popular backing of the war, based on the image of a silent middle America. Rather than require that citizens debate the issues of the Vietnam War, pro-war groups such as the veterans' organizations and pro-administration labor unions simply demanded that loyal Americans endorse the nobility of the cause for which American servicemen had fought and died. In so doing, they allowed Nixon to declare that peace with honor was commensurate with both American goals in the region and America's core values.

The administration was determined as well to sway public opinion by appealing to popular concern for American POWs. In attempting to control the pro-war argument, the White House relied primarily on its own nominally independent organizations, largely because administration officials feared the potential for dissent from those still ideologically committed to outright victory in Vietnam. Popular war-weariness and the perception of a credibility gap fundamentally weakened national support for the war, but the administration's endeavor to reorient public attention toward the patriotic, rather than national security, reasons for endorsing intervention only added to popular confusion. Thus while the pro-war campaigns succeeded in challenging the anti-war movement and evidenced widespread support for the basic cause in Vietnam, they could not sustain support for a continued war indefinitely. Nixon's articulation of a withdrawal strategy was vital to the success of these populist efforts, in large part because pro-war leaders were able to point to a clear exit strategy as they requested that the nation unite behind the president.

The populist campaigns in favor of Vietnam espoused markedly different ideals from those of conservatives in relation to the significance of the war. Although they supported such patriotic endeavors as the National Unity Week of November 1969 and the Honor America Rally of July 1970, the *National Review* circle remained preoccupied with promoting the anticommunist basis of American intervention in Southeast Asia and the continued meaning of the war vis-à-vis America's relations with the communist powers and its international credibility. Conservatives unmistakably engaged in efforts to demonize the enemy and welcomed the

POW campaign because of its focus on North Vietnamese cruelty and intransigence. Such demonization was counterproductive, conservatives recognized, if its only effect was to further reduce popular understanding of the rationale for U.S. engagement in Vietnam. By 1972, however, the administration was more worried about sustaining popular backing for its withdrawal policies than in assuaging conservatives' demands to focus on the international implications of the war. The conservatives' pro-war campaigns and the patriotic endeavors undertaken to shore up the president were symbiotic to a certain extent. But by helping to create a means of expressing patriotic support for the president's policies without necessarily demanding victory in the war, the populist drive fundamentally weakened conservatives' objectives around Vietnam. It also changed their approach to the war and to the administration and, furthermore, helped cement the divisions among conservatives (see chapter 7).

CHAPTER 6

TELL IT TO HANOI

Student Pro-War Campaigns

> Not So Loud. . . . The Enemy Is Listening
> National Student Committee for Peace with Freedom in
> Southeast Asia, brochure, summer 1971

> Communist massacres . . . are an integral part of Communist war policy rivaling the brutality and atrocities perpetrated by the Nazis during World War II.
> Young Americans for Freedom, April 1970

In 1961 the young conservative activist M. Stanton Evans published a book that, in its opening pages, described the Right's "revolt on the campus." Evans confidently envisaged historians recording "the decade of the 1960s as the era in which conservatism, as a viable political force, finally came into its own."[1] Conservative student activism was not diminished by the prevailing liberal political climate on many campuses, but it altered with the rise of the New Left. Student groups such as YAF increasingly challenged academic administrations only in regard to their failure to restrain New Left activity on campus and became involved primarily in campaigns opposing anti-war radicalism. Theirs was not simply a campaign against the anti-war movement, but the characteristics of their activities were often in a reactionary vein. YAF's most well publicized pro-war campaign was called Tell it to Hanoi. It explicitly associated opposition to the war with support for the enemy, a connection that was essential to promoting YAF's political and philosophical agendas.

[242]

Similarly, the campaigns undertaken by moderate political activists, such as those who founded the Victory in Vietnam Association (VIVA), relied heavily on denigrating student radicalism on campus, often to the point of charging such activists with implementing an anti-American agenda. The nature of student activism in favor of the war differed from that of the conservative political movement and patriotic groups and veterans' organizations. Most important, student pro-war activists were forced to respond directly to the anti-war movement long before their elder counterparts faced serious challenges to their support of the Vietnam War. These students were determined to counter the dominant image of widespread youthful opposition to the war. Their varied campaigns represent divergent means to a similar end: the proselytizing of pro-war sentiment on campus. While pro-war students initiated educational programs promoting the necessity and righteousness of American action throughout the war, the need for retaliation against the anti-war movement appeared to be the most salient course of action during the period before widespread disillusionment with government policy developed in 1967. Once put into practice, pro-war students' emphasis on attacking their anti-war counterparts assumed a vitality that was difficult to moderate. Although sometimes tenuous, the mutual connections developed by pro-war student groups and their efforts to forge links with one another were more extensive than those of any other pro-war sector. The student groups failed to form a cohesive pro-war lobby, but they succeeded in subsuming at least some of their differences in order to launch campaigns of mutual reinforcement with regard to Vietnam.

During the Nixon administration, David Keene, a former chair of YAF and aide to Vice President Agnew, attempted to influence YAF's public position regarding the administration. Buchanan and Huston, on the other hand, advocated that the White House appeal to students through moderate groups like the College Young Republicans and the Association of Student Governments (ASG), which was founded in opposition to the National Student Association (NSA) because of the supposed dominance of radical students in the NSA.[2] Despite its initiatives to raise awareness regarding support for the war, the Nixon administration did little to foster the allegiance of groups such as YAF and VIVA and offered only minor aid to more moderate student organizations such as the College Republican National Committee (CRNC), the Young Republicans, and the ASG. Nixon officials also fell victim to the tendency to cast aspersions on anti-war students rather than offer aid to their pro-war supporters. Speaking of the anti-war movement, Haldeman declared that, "a *lot* of people . . . especially the younger segments of it . . . were simply motivated by the desire to get out and raise hell." They had not the "slightest concern of what they were raising hell about," Haldeman continued, and their aim was certainly not "to stop the war." The Nixon speechwriter Ray Price concluded that many student activists were simply trying to be cool and were "unaware of even the most elementary facts about whatever issue they were inflamed about."[3]

Particularly after 1968, when student radicals became ever more extreme, the understanding of *all* student activists as negative forces that deepened the national divide over the war became more prominent. Those students who actively campaigned in favor of the war were a minority, much as those who opposed it comprised a minority. Many whose approval of the war was undemonstrative supported it from a sense of inertia or unquestioning faith in American leaders and the parameters of patriotic duty. James Hijiya notes, for instance, that "many young conservatives went to fight in Vietnam," but these young men were invariably not the most politically active. He cites John McCain as an example of a young conservative who served in Vietnam "primarily out of a family tradition of military service."[4] Several pro-war student groups did emerge, however, the most consequential of which were YAF, the National Student Coordinating Committee for Victory in Vietnam (NSCVV), VIVA, and the CRNC. Each group had a distinct philosophical identity, and each interpreted the war's meaning differently. That each group operated in an environment in which a majority of students responded negatively to all forms of protest determined the nature of their campaigns and resulted in a consistent, although uncoordinated, emphasis on patriotism rather than on victory.

Conservative Activists: Young Americans for Freedom

YAF's prominence as the vanguard of pro-war student activism owed much to its association with adult leaders of the pro-war conservative movement. Having evolved from the youth campaign of the heady Draft Goldwater drive of 1960 and come to national renown in 1964 as part of the Goldwater political machine, YAF's national reputation, financial wherewithal, and managerial competence relied on continuing its alliance with the ACU and the *National Review* circle. While the conservative youth movement was based on genuine foundations of philosophical idealism and political ambition, its reliance on traditional political alliances, compared with those of the New Left, reduced its share of national media attention and undermined its apparent authenticity as a student organization. Nevertheless, YAF did represent an important voice on college campuses. By promoting support for the war, by challenging the limited war policies of both the Johnson and Nixon administrations, and by demonizing the enemy, YAF contributed much to the debate over Vietnam and to the polarization of popular opinion. But, preoccupied with financial difficulties and committed to the practice of traditional political campaigns on campus, YAF's pro-war activism was less impassioned than that of its antiwar counterparts.

Throughout YAF's existence its national board assumed responsibility for articulating and presenting the organization's position on matters of foreign policy, exemplified by Alan McKay's testimony opposing IBM's trade with the Soviet Union and Keene's congressional testimony on the subject of East–West trade. Designed as a mass membership association, YAF adopted the widespread conservative practice of developing grassroots bases of politically active individuals.[5] Its weapons in the domestic Vietnam War were those of communication, according to Michael Thompson, who was appointed head of YAF's Vietnam campaign in 1967.[6] Albeit with prodding from the national office, YAF's means of communication were overwhelmingly individualistic, relying on the initiative of its chapters to organize and implement broadly defined national campaigns. YAF's Vietnam activities must be understood as a series of individual measures intended to promote a generally defined anticommunist foreign policy.

In terms of both aim and implementation, YAF's campus-based projects and its efforts to lobby government must be differentiated. Rather than seek a comprehensive endorsement of its policies, YAF's campus campaigns were designed to undermine the message of the New Left and to appropriate sentiments that opposed anti-war and anti-radical viewpoints. This, YAF activists believed, would engender an environment in which the group's conservative principles could prosper. In terms of its campus pro-war activism YAF was therefore more similar in many ways to the Republican Right than to its benefactors at *National Review* and the ACU. Describing students' responses to Students for a Democratic Society (SDS), Evans wrote that "on one campus after another, conservative-to-moderate student forces are being mobilized to counteract the pressure from the left." He described the creation of a Society for the Prevention of Asinine Student Movements at Wichita State University, the blood drives organized by students in the Reserve Officer Training Corps (ROTC) at Purdue University, and the antiradical groups that had sprung up at Stanford, Columbia, and the universities of Texas, Tennessee, and Wisconsin. Influenced by YAF, such groups, according to Evans, were an expression of the majority's opposition to the anti-war message of the New Left.[7] YAF certainly was the most active antiradical organization on the national level, and its influence was demonstrated by the proliferation of campus events it sponsored and organized. Despite its philosophical opposition to conscription, YAF supported ROTC recruitment on campus.[8] The organization's leaders recognized the possibility of channeling ROTC members into YAF.[9] As part of its pro-Vietnam initiatives the organization encouraged individual chapters to mount legal campaigns against school closures because of anti-war demonstrations and student violence.

YAF chapters replied to the anti-war message of the New Left through alternative teach-ins, debates, educational pamphlets, and reading lists. One of the largest and most active chapters, California YAF (CalYAF), launched a blue button campaign, in which students wore buttons provided by YAF as an expression of opposition to radical students. Wearers of the blue button included Governor Reagan and his entire staff.[10] Though YAF denounced the violence of the Left, several of the group's most celebrated episodes involved members of YAF directly engaging anti-war students in violent conflict. In April 1969 YAF members forcibly occupied the Boston headquarters of the anti-war group Resistance and subsequently repeated the violent endeavor in New York.[11] Charging that they had liberated the offices, they hung the flag of the Republic of Vietnam on the walls and distributed pamphlets illustrating communist atrocities in Vietnam.[12] Also in April 1969 YAF members became involved in a violent clash with anti-war demonstrators at St. John's University in New York. National Secretary Ron Docksai described YAF's blockade of the campus, set up to prevent SDS members from other universities from joining the St. John's Liberal Student Coalition in protest against the war, as "the greatest thing I have ever seen."[13] Buckley congratulated Docksai on his "victorious putsch."[14] Ad hoc actions of this nature, designed to counter the anti-war message on campus, were commonly carried out by YAF members.

By 1969, in fact, the national board believed it was essential for the organization to expand its operational remit in order to spread the conservative message on campus. Responses to anti-war protestors could help win over students who opposed campus radicalism, but such activities did little to educate students about conservative political goals. YAF's engagement in clashes with anti-war students also hindered the group's appeals to students disillusioned by violent protests. In January 1969 the national board launched a more comprehensive anticommunist campaign Titled "Young America's Freedom Offensive" and billed as "the all-encompassing, umbrella program approach" by which YAF's projects were to be implemented, the campaign was organized in order to overcome the heretofore official and practical divides between YAF's campus and noncampus programs. The offensive included six projects. The first was called Freedom v. Communism and was aimed at pushing state legislatures to enact laws requiring high school students to complete a course titled "Americanism v.

Communism" as a requisite for graduation. The YAF national office prepared and distributed, at a cost of two dollars each, a Freedom v. Communism "kit of information and materials." The kit contained model bills that state legislatures might introduce and copies of statutes already enacted in three states. It furnished students with a Report of the Committee on Cold War Education of the National Governors' Conference, which supported YAF's arguments, and proposed training courses for teachers. Given YAF's penchant for gaining media attention, the kit unsurprisingly included sample news releases.[15]

Several of the Freedom Offensive's other programs were also focused on impacting state and national policy, including its campaign for a volunteer military and its challenge to East–West Trade. This latter campaign was "predicated upon the introduction in the Congress of a comprehensive bill to totally revamp our East–West trade laws so as to tighten up the loop-holes and to amend the legislation which enables extensive trading by American corporations in strategic and border-line strategic goods with communist countries." In an effort to recruit "the uninitiated in politics and the uneducated in structured political thought into the ranks of the conservative movement," YAF promoted its Independent Sector campaign, whereby it promoted an "approach to problems which we feel can be done better through independent, volunteer service and action than through governmental intervention and welfare." Again focusing on the importance of recruitment, the Freedom Offensive included an emphasis on Youth in Politics, which was a means by which individual YAF members could become acquainted "with the successful techniques of political action."

Only one of the Freedom Offensive's programs, the Majority Coalition Campus Action Kit, dealt exclusively with the campus environment. This campaign provided "the background knowledge and materials to ensure that the New Left will not be left without opposition, that the responsible student majority will be able to effectively reflect the true student opinion on college demands and educational reform."[16] Designed to attract the uncommitted and the unlearned among American students and young adults, the Freedom Offensive represented a departure from YAF's recent preoccupation with "defensive measures" against the New Left. At the national level YAF had provided proactive measures and policies, particularly in the area of U.S. foreign policy. This "offensive" strategy had been somewhat lacking in its campus-based activities, as shown in the organization's failure to mount a consistent national program of support for the Vietnam War.

The absence of a Vietnam campaign from the freedom offensive is notable, but only because the organization's leaders wished to appeal to as many students as possible and only because the anticommunist freedom offensive was a means of implicitly promoting backing of the war. By early 1969 YAF leaders determined to mount a comprehensive conservative campaign that would achieve national exposure and create an "effective, assertive, and influential voice in American politics."[17] By inaugurating a thorough conservative political program and by formulating an activist agenda YAF's leadership revealed its desire to achieve long-term political and social influence. To a certain extent the national board's initiatives of 1969 betrayed the fact that it had failed to lead the way in challenging the anti-war message on campus. Students on the ground were compelled to act by the vigor and extent of anti-war activity, and so YAF campus chapters organized so-called majority campaigns that included exhibitions of the burning of Viet Cong flags and attacks on anti-war demonstrators. But YAF's local responses to anti-war demonstrations remained ad hoc and failed to take advantage of the group's national organizational power. The necessity for the national office to take a more activist role in guiding local campaigns had been made clear by YAF's failure to rival the anti-war movement in terms of publicity.

YAF became more engaged in creating a national campaign during 1969, but its methodology did not entirely change. Many of YAF's pro-war campaigns were actually predicated on one of the programs of the Freedom Offensive: the Majority Coalition. Students involved in campaigns to oppose leftist or radical campaigns on campus may not even have been aware of the organizational role played by YAF chapters or the national board.[18] In turn YAF often received little recognition or credit for its role in developing coalition groups and managing coalition campaigns. This was evident in one of its primary endeavors regarding Vietnam, its role in organizing, managing, and financing the NSCVV. Founded in 1967 as a means of coordinating the pro-Vietnam activities of diverse student groups, the NSCVV was not organized as a mass membership group. Subsequently described as the ad hoc committee of the YAF national board, the NSCVV was not originally envisaged as a disguised arm of YAF, but neither was it independent.

The NSCVV's leadership indicated a preference for the Vietnam strategy promoted by conservative political leaders. The basic issues, according to the NSCVV, were not related simply to whether or not the United States should maintain its current level of military activity, introduce a cessation of bombing, declare war, or impose economic sanctions against those states trading with North Vietnam. The primary question presupposed the answers to all such problems: "Do you accept as valid the concept of a limited war with limited objectives against an enemy which has vowed to settle for nothing less than unconditional surrender by the United States?"[19] In the autumn of 1968 Thompson appeared to answer this question when he urged NSCVV activists to "try to prove to President [elect] Nixon that VICTORY is the only acceptable way to end this conflict." The goal of the NSCVV, he said, was to "show this country that the students want victory in this war rather than a negotiated defeat."[20] Such declarations did little to alter the fact that NSCVV activity, particularly as it related to campus campaigns, expressed only a coherent opposition to the Left, not a lucid, unified, and independent movement in support of the Vietnam War. Support for the war, therefore, often appeared to be a reactive technique by conservative or moderate students to the excesses of the campaigns of anti-war and New Left students rather than an expression of genuine faith in the efficacy of achieving victory in Vietnam.

The group's principal functions were twofold. First, the NSCVV distributed pro-war educational material amounting to approximately eighty thousand pieces of literature through an estimated three hundred college representatives during its first year.[21] Robert F. Turner, a Vietnam veteran and student of international relations associated with the Hoover Institution, acted as the research director of the NSCVV and in 1968 began writing a series of "Vietnam clichés," or short essays. Turner completed a master's dissertation on the Vietnam War at Indiana University during the mid-1960s. A staunch supporter of the war, he volunteered for Army ROTC and was commissioned as a second lieutenant in the Armored Branch of the Intelligence Service. While awaiting orders in 1968 he undertook, at the behest of Stan Evans, his friend and the newspaper's editor, a number of research visits to Vietnam for the *Indianapolis News*. Having written on the psywar, or psychological warfare, vulnerabilities of the North Vietnamese, Turner was asked to join the North Vietnamese/Viet Cong Affairs Division of the Joint U.S. Public Affairs Office of the American Embassy in Saigon and was assigned to Military Assistance Command, Vietnam in January 1971. On his return to the United States he completed a doctoral degree in international relations.

Turner's short essays were presented as well-researched and well-informed assessments of the international situation, and each was advertised as "a devastating reply to one of the most commonly used empty arguments of the 'Left.'"[22] Turner contradicted many of the claims associated with the anti-war movement. These included arguments that Ho Chi Minh was the George Washington of Vietnam and that the United States should allow the United Nations to consider the Vietnam question. Turner wrote that between 1925 and 1954 "Ho and his Communist followers either murdered or betrayed to the French almost all of the effective Nationalist [noncommunist] Vietnamese leadership," a fact Turner claimed merited the "title 'Vietnam's Benedict Arnold.'" Without the communists, he concluded, "Vietnam might have gained independence earlier, without division or bloodshed." In this way Turner reiterated the pro-war theme that Ho Chi Minh's communism took precedence over his nationalism.[23] Turner asserted that the United States had tried to "turn the charges of [North Vietnamese] aggression over to the U.N." but that "the Communists won't let us!" He concluded, "It should be obvious that the barrier between the United Nations and consideration of Vietnam is not the United States or South Vietnam—it is the Soviet Union and North Vietnam. If the U.S.S.R. would refrain from using its veto, the Vietnam question could be considered by the United Nations."[24]

Printed in YAF's monthly publication the *New Guard*, which was distributed to its members and directly to campus students, the clichés were also circulated by the AFV and VIVA, and Turner wrote of these "myths" for *Human Events*. In September 1972 the AFV published his monograph *Myths of the Vietnam War: The Pentagon Papers Reconsidered*, which was originally serialized in the AFV's journal, *Southeast Asian Perspectives*. Turner used the published documents to dispute a number of the theses of the war put forth by critics of administration policy. He claimed that the myths were "a collection of historical and factual inaccuracies and half-truths which, in the aggregate, provide the foundation for almost all of the most widely used arguments against U.S. policy in Vietnam."[25] *Human Events* was eager to use Turner's ideas to undermine the anti-war argument that a bloodbath in Vietnam would not occur after the Americans' complete withdrawal.[26]

The NSCVV's second function was to create an appearance of unified majority student support for the war. Its activities were predicated on opposing those of the anti-war movement, which NSCVV directors termed the Campus Cong. Offering "some suggested pesticides" for the anti-war "worms" who had recently been in "hibernation," NSCVV directors promoted a number of proactive pro-war projects. While the memorandum of spring 1968 instructed constituent chapters on how to combat anti-war opinion on campus, it exposed the group's weakness in terms of managing specific projects. Unlike its anti-war counterpart, the NSCVV was disinclined to organize major demonstrations or dramatic events and left much of the implementation of its proposed measures to the caprice of localized chapters. The organization did eventually decide to organize a national event but still failed to recognize the power of collective action with centralized coordination. Writing of the proposed "Victory in Vietnam Week," due to take place during April 13–20, the national directors commented that participating chapters should "not in any way feel obligated to follow our April 13–20 suggestion."

Still, they encouraged the leaders of chapters to seek proclamations from mayors, city councils, and local government officials, holding that such "would be a big publicity boost" for the week of "campus victory activities." The NSCVV informed chapter leaders on how best to secure pro-war speakers and supplied sources of reading material. The NSCVV national office recommended that its chapters contact returning Vietnam veterans through Veterans Clubs that were being established on campuses. They instructed members to consult the edition of *Pace* magazine for April 1968, which analyzed veterans' attitudes toward the war and toward campus protestors. Noting the group's relationship with the conservative movement, the NSCVV urged its members to contact one of several groups associated with or run by conservative figures in order to attract pro-war speakers to their campuses. The recommended groups were Asian Speakers Bureau; American Conservative Union Speakers Bureau; World Youth Crusade for Freedom; Education About Communism Through Refugee Program; and the All American Conference to Combat Communism. The NSCVV recommended as well that its chapters put on showings of the pro-war documentary *Why Vietnam?*, which was available from the Armed Forces Film Libraries. The NSCVV did little, however, to coordinate student activity or encourage a unified program of events. They underestimated the potential stimulus, in terms of gaining publicity and catalyzing activity, of a single, dramatic display of support for the war.

Throughout 1968 the NSCVV programs were intent on challenging "the other side to a 'fight to the finish'" rather than on developing a wholly independent pro-war student movement. Forced by time and budgetary constraints to abandon plans for a poll of student opinion regarding Vietnam, the national office prodded its members to campaign against the anti-war options offered as part of *Time* magazine's "Choice '68" poll, which was conducted on campuses throughout the United States.[27] The NSCVV's stance on this issue is indicative of the pronounced sense of assault under which they felt they and their cause were operating. Attacks on the anti-war movement and on leftist sentiment were seen as the most effective means of encouraging endorsement of the war.

To maximize interest in the committee, NSCVV leaders proposed campaigns to raise funds for South Vietnamese orphans and to send Christmas cards to American servicemen in Vietnam. They recommended that members take part in such apparently nonpolitical measures as visiting local veterans' hospitals and encouraged sororities and girls' dorms to bake cookies for the men in Vietnam. The extent to which these local campaigns succeeded in channeling the energies of students into positive programs of support for the war is difficult to determine. Considering the national office's failure to manage single, dramatic campaigns, it is not unreasonable to venture that its members directed their attention toward such localized and uncontroversial endeavors. By late February 1969 YAF's national board acknowledged that the NSCVV "had not been as active as hoped," in part owing to Thompson's obligations as the chair of Missouri YAF. Having distributed "large volumes of materials" since the initiation of the bombing halt on October 31, 1968, the NSCVV promised that a spring campaign for Vietnam was being developed, one that would be launched from Columbia, Missouri.[28] YAF's prioritization of the Freedom Offensive, coupled with the national board's continuing emphasis on responding to government policy in Vietnam rather than building a grassroots network of backing for the war, ultimately undermined its implementation of this campaign.

By October YAF's and the NSCVV's Vietnam activities were almost wholly occupied in countering the anti-war Moratorium. Thompson reported on the good financial health of the NSCVV in October and promised a mailing of legal materials relating to the Moratorium, thus continuing YAF's theme of using legal measures to prevent the suspension of classes. The YAF board determined to distribute three hundred thousand tabloids lambasting the antiwar stance, but unanimous appreciation of the significance of the Moratorium did little to prompt YAF or the NSCVV to launch a unified national counterattack.[29] Acknowledging that YAF "must do something" to indicate student support for the war, the YAF executive director Randal Teague lamented in late October that interest in opposing the Moratoria had been too great for YAF or the NSCVV to handle. YAF requests for two-dollar contributions "to set up nationwide campaigns against the protestors" had met with marked success, according to Teague. He later exhibited contempt for the resources of the Moratorium Committee, which amounted to "an expenditure of $1.1 million with twenty-three paid employees," "more than we have for an entire year at YAF." Granting that such factors did not moderate the demands of anti-Moratorium students for action, Teague concluded that, because requests for materials, speakers, and activities had been so great, YAF "would have to abandon all programming to undertake a counterthrust" to the Moratoria.[30]

As early as September 1969 Phillip Abbott Luce, YAF's college director, had informed all chapter chairmen that, having sifted "through the myriad proposals" put forth for opposing the Moratoria, the national office "decided that it should be the individual initiative of campus YAF to take what action they deem appropriate on October 15." The decision to refrain from launching a countercampaign was determined by the national board's view that it would be difficult to mount an effective one on short notice or to ensure that "enough bodies" could be mobilized for a countermarch in Washington on November 15, when the second Moratorium event was to take place during a mass demonstration in Washington. Primarily, however, the national board was reluctant to continue what it described as "wind mill chasing." Rather than simply react to every left-wing initiative, YAF decided to "pick and choose our action," which in the fall of 1969 meant focusing on the Freedom Offensive programs. YAF's interest in building long-term political power overwhelmed its resolve to promoting support of the war. Luce stated that by calling "on our members to stress the Freedom Offensive over countering the moratorium demonstrations we are not denigrating the inherent dangers of these demonstrations. We feel, however, that unless we mount an offensive on our own terms that there is little chance of seeing that the future will not hold even more dangerous demonstrations." The Freedom Offensive, coupled with the nationwide legal attack "against those that would use the campuses as a launching pad for revolution," should, the national board declared, "provide members with all the action that they can handle in the coming months."[31]

The magnitude of the Moratoria and conservatives' opinion that the news media implied that all students opposed the war forced YAF to reevaluate its position regarding anti-war protest. Teague reiterated in early November that if YAF "attempted to stage a competing nationwide demonstration at this late date we may show up badly and the public would get the wrong impression" about the level of student support for the war. He publicly stated, however, that the group was launching a campaign based on Nixon's theme of a "great Silent Majority," a theme that Teague associated with victory in Vietnam.[32] "Unless YAF is able to mount a positive alternative," an urgent bulletin to the membership read, "public opinion will continue to move toward surrender and defeat, especially on the campuses."[33]

On these grounds YAF revitalized a campaign which had originated with the NSCVV. At first titled Sock it to Hanoi, the educational initiative and publicity drive formed the second aspect of YAF's Vietnam activity and its first truly national campaign: Tell it to Hanoi. The campaign consisted of three central projects: an Alternative Weekend (December 12–13, 1969), during which prowar demonstrations were to take place across the nation; a petition condemning North Vietnamese aggression and asserting support for President Nixon's policies; and a publicity drive consisting of newspaper advertisements, leaflet distribution, and campus exhibitions highlighting communist atrocities in Southeast Asia. The purpose of the weekend action was twofold, according to Keene: "(1) to promote on college and high school campuses an understanding of the realities of the conflict in Vietnam, and (2) to demonstrate to the American people and to Hanoi that the majority of American students do not favor U.S. defeat."[34] Despite misgivings within YAF about Nixon's commitment to victory in Vietnam, YAF's Tell it to Hanoi campaign consistently encouraged endorsement of the president. Its petition contrasted Nixon's efforts to achieve peace with the intransigence of the North Vietnamese, while its use of the silent majority theme implied an association with administration policy.

On November 13 Thompson launched YAF's series of proVietnam rallies in opposition to the November Moratorium with a march in St. Louis. The rally combined the themes of supporting American troops and pointing out communist atrocities and included expert speakers such as Nguyen Ngoc Bich, second secretary for information at the embassy of the Republic of Vietnam in Washington. The climax of the rally was a candlelight procession. The march in St. Louis provided the format that all YAF chapters were encouraged to emulate.[35] YAF leaders also fostered measures, such as leaving lights on and wearing red, white, and blue armbands, that had been used as part of the Honor America Week in October. Publicizing Vietnam: Alternative Weekend, Ron Dear, YAF's director of regional and state activities, declared that over one million copies of the Tell it to Hanoi tabloid would be distributed, while activities were planned on six hundred college campuses.[36]

One of the more prominent Tell it to Hanoi rallies took place the week before the Alternative Weekend in Boston. Designed to coincide with the anniversary of the Japanese attack on Pearl Harbor, the rally incorporated overtly patriotic symbols and included the singing of traditional patriotic songs. Beginning with a candlelight parade that started at the State House, the events culminated in a gathering at Boston Common, where an audience of some twenty-five hundred people heard Vietnamese officials praise Vietnamization and accuse American peace activists of impeding measures aimed at achieving peace and reunification in Vietnam. They watched as two Vietnam veterans burned a Vietcong flag and listened to Don Feder of YAF lambaste the media's coverage of the pro-war movement. Praising Agnew's attacks on the television networks, Feder asserted that the "press cannot continue to ignore us" and claimed that Boston newspapers had neglected YAF's press conference regarding the rally and had hidden stories about it.[37] In addressing himself to "an effete corps of impudent snobs," former YAF chair Alan McKay embraced the Agnew approach. He announced, "Patriotism isn't dead, it's alive and well on Boston Common."[38] YAF's attempt to usurp patriotism in support of its pro-war campaign was neither novel nor a radical departure from its earlier campaigns. Alternative Weekend rallies and Tell it to Hanoi literature differed somewhat from YAF's earlier policy in that they increasingly championed the administration, largely in response to the vehemence of anti-war opposition to Nixon's policies.

While the official YAF response to Nixon's policy of Vietnamization remained one of cautious support, the Tell it to Hanoi campaign prompted both moderate and conservative students to back the president. Speaking of YAF's Alternative Weekend message, Rep. Page Belcher, a Republican from Oklahoma, pinpointed YAF's emphasis on the administration's willingness to "negotiate everything except the right of the people of South Vietnam to determine their own future," while North Vietnam had done nothing to end the war. Belcher's call for all Americans to recall the administration's efforts, to consider Vietcong atrocities, and to reflect on Hanoi's failure to comply with the Geneva Convention echoed YAF's activist position.[39] It was a stance based as much on countering anti-war influence, especially that expressed during the Moratoria of 1969, when large numbers of Americans joined the anti-war campaign, as it was on a reasoned assessment of the best means of securing success in Vietnam. The Tell it to Hanoi program distorted the meaning of success in Vietnam and reduced the national security argument, the basis on which YAF had consistently supported the war, to secondary importance relative to the simple moral challenge to the North Vietnamese regime and their domestic supporters. While official policy did not change, the means by which YAF promoted widespread support for the war and the basis on which it demanded such support was fundamentally altered.

YAF continued its work by concentrating on its Tell it to Hanoi petition in early 1970 with the intention of presenting a catalogue of over one million names to the North Vietnamese delegation at the Paris talks in April.[40] Designed as a publicity stunt, the petition gave YAF the means of declaring itself to be the "only patriotic youth force capable of giving effective battle against the New Mobe [the New Mobilization Committee to End the War in Vietnam, one of the groups responsible for organizing the Moratoria]." YAF trumpeted its claim that it was "the 'silent majority's' young and vibrant voice." YAF's national board sent a form letter containing these messages to prominent supporters of its causes with the request that they sign the letter and forward copies to those whom they thought would donate to the youth organization to help finance its pro-Vietnam War agenda. On March 6, 1970, Teague forwarded the letter to Goldwater, who duly signed it and returned it to YAF.[41]

The national office enhanced the organization's apparent endorsement of Nixon's strategy by issuing an almost wholly uncritical report of the situation in Vietnam following a ten-day visit there by a YAF team in April 1970.[42] During this period the group's propagandist efforts, above all its focus on demonizing the enemy, ultimately amounted to unequivocal aid to the Nixon administration. Keene proclaimed that many responsible students were afraid to support Nixon's policies for fear "of what might happen to them if they openly disagree with the left," a position that echoed YAF's modus of denigrating the desire for peace and the sincerity of anti-war protesters.[43] The attitude reflected a new-found alliance, however ambiguous, between YAF activists on campus and the Nixon administration. This tenuous connection was cemented by YAF's role in acclaiming the Cambodian incursion in May.

The subtle distinction between the preferred policies of the national board and those of the administration was somewhat lost on its overall membership. Responding to the domestic chaos bequeathed by the Cambodian incursion, YAF's national board demanded that all Americans unite behind Nixon. Elaborating on a theme favored by pro-war groups, YAF issued a Support Our Fighting Men petition as a means of attracting support for the Cambodian incursion. Rather than analyze the incursion in terms of overall administration policy, the national board simply headlined its advertising campaign with the assertion that YAF "supports our fighting men in Cambodia: we stand behind you, as president and as commander-in-chief, in your affirmation, 'We will not be defeated.'"[44] The position of the national office reinforced a tendency of the regional chapters to engage in activities that increased support for Nixon. This tendency to garner generic support for the war rather than support for specific principles or strategies had been fundamental to the success of the Tell it to Hanoi drive.

While continuing to espouse victory in Vietnam, YAF campus activity was ever more directed at challenging the premises on which the anti-war movement based its growing popular opposition to the conflict. The organization's response to the killings of four unarmed students, some of whom had been participating in a peaceful protest against the war, by Ohio National Guardsmen at Kent State University highlighted YAF's public association with the administration. Having argued that the guardsmen "fired their guns in response to obvious physical danger," YAF's national secretary said, "The student majority on the campus . . . will not continue to allow the good name of peace to be monopolized and patented by those isolationist students who treat our nation's capitol as a foreign power." He exhorted "young Americans to ignore those fascist bums who would facilitate campus destruction and violence in the name of democracy. We urge you to truly work for peace; Nixon does every day."[45] Despite its ongoing campaign of building support for the president on campus, the Vietnam issue became more and more divisive within YAF ranks, not least because Nixon's policies accentuated the contradiction between YAF's official prescription for ending the war and the chapters' emphasis on applauding the administration. In late 1970 this situation came to a head.

YAF first divided over Vietnam at its national convention in September 1969. Resulting largely from the libertarian versus traditionalist struggle for power in YAF, which had become intense in CalYAF during 1969, the controversy brought to the fore the discord in YAF and culminated in the national office's effective purging of libertarian leaders from the organization. One libertarian argument regarding Vietnam charged that the war encouraged a fascist system in the United States, whereby individuals were stripped of freedom by the draft, taxes were used to fight the war, and law and order measures were imposed to limit dissent.[46] During the convention, David Lee Houffman, a self-declared libertarian, stood in the crowded auditorium and set fire to his draft card, resulting in a violent scuffle reminiscent of YAF–SDS confrontations. The anti-war resolutions emanating from the libertarian caucus were summarily rejected, while Houffman was subsequently expunged from membership in YAF.[47]

The rise of the so-called libertarian caucus in CalYAF preoccupied the national office during 1969 and detracted from its enacting of pro-war campaigns on the influential California campus battlegrounds, but libertarian questioning of the war did not result in an active anti-war campaign within YAF. The fact that popular and successful YAF activists such as Harvey Hukari, who had founded the YAF chapter at Stanford University, found themselves under suspicion in 1969 because of their libertarian leanings did little to further YAF's activist agenda. The alienation of thriving chapters, most notably that at Stanford, certainly did not benefit the pro-war campaign on such campuses, but libertarians did not join the ranks of the New Left in opposing the war and largely remained inactive in relation to Vietnam.[48] The crisis, however, marked the potential volatility of differences of opinion over the war. Nixon's less than clear commitment to victory seemed only to exacerbate the potential for division, contributing to the organization's increasing reliance on ambiguous campaigns designed to foster endorsement of the war without requiring a too-principled stand regarding the means for achieving victory.

While the debate in 1969 was contentious, it did not force a fundamental reconsideration of YAF's Vietnam position, mainly because the divide was blamed on the libertarian–traditionalist schism. The debate sparked by Jerry Norton, a Vietnam veteran and member of YAF's national board, in September and October 1970 was quite different: it was the first time the conventional position of the national board was challenged from within. Norton wholly condemned the organization's position on Vietnam. His memorandum to Teague, which opened with the avowal that "YAF's position on Vietnam has disturbed me for some time," set off a debate among YAF officials that revealed the gap between official policy and grassroots organizational activity. "At one point," Norton declared, "our position was a clarion call for rapid victory through escalation, and a condemnation of the Johnson technique of reliance on massive ground troops and halfhearted, spasmodic and ineffectual escalation." "With Nixon's election," he continued, "YAF's position has ostensibly remained the call for victory, but we're kidding ourselves if we don't admit that, whatever the resolutions at conventions or board meetings, for all practical purposes our position has shifted to support of the Nixon policy, a policy of gradual withdrawal."

Norton's call for a "quiet YAF withdrawal from Vietnam" was not, therefore, based on a dovish conception of foreign policy. Norton attempted to demonstrate how the war contributed to a weakening of preferred conservative foreign policy objectives. He said the war diverted resources from the development of a nuclear weapons shield and other modern systems, "directly contributed to the climate that gives liberals voting strength to slice ever deeper into that already barebones defense budget," and allowed liberals, "under the guise of preventing more Vietnams," to reduce military aid to U.S. allies. The war, Norton declared, also gave the foremost impetus to the New Left and was "the main obstacle to conservative success on campus." In sum, he charged that "Vietnam is seriously damaging our national defense, the security of other allies, and our economy, is alienating students and G.I.s from the right, and continues to kill Americans."

Norton's assessment of the debilitating impact of the war on defense expenditure and the priority he gave to overall American strength in strategic arms, echoed the position of leaders in the conservative political fold. He articulated a course of action that in many respects imitated that of formerly active pro-war groups, including the veterans' organizations, which turned to promotion of patriotic and pro-president campaigns rather than specifically pro-Vietnam endeavors. His recommendation called for the national board to "back quietly away from Vietnam." He did not call for an "official reversal or withdrawal from the field" but recommended that "no new National projects" be undertaken and that "a gradual de-emphasis on and cut in expenditures [be made] for present projects." This would leave "Vietnam up to local chapters" and allow the board to concentrate on "worthier things nationally."[49] Except for its Tell it to Hanoi drive, which was executed by local chapters, YAF's active strategy regarding Vietnam differed little from that outlined by Norton. Although unwilling to state so publicly, YAF's position echoed that of leading conservatives, who had also reduced the terms for victory and had engaged in a policy of supporting and promoting, with only limited public analysis of, Nixon's process of Vietnamization and withdrawal. Notwithstanding the accuracy of Norton's assessment of YAF's "practical

... position" vis-à-vis Nixon and the war and the fact that the local chapters were already engaged in individualized pro-war activities, Norton's memorandum ignited a firestorm of recrimination in the leadership ranks of YAF.

Norton's colleagues on the national board, while disagreeing over the relative merit of Nixon's policies and the significance of gaining a resolute victory in Vietnam, unanimously rejected his counsel that Vietnam be silently abandoned. Thompson described it as "Norton's quiet 'bug-out' memo."[50] The national board's position showed ongoing faith that YAF activity on campus was effective and vital in preventing the development of a single anti-war voice emanating from the universities. Docksai asked Norton whether he had considered the probability that YAF's "bug-off" of the Vietnam issue would be "unilateral on our part." "If YAF disposed of Vietnam as an issue," Docksai asked, "aside from the potential recruits to a pro-Vietnam position we could not attract, would the Left not be accurate to say that there is a national student consensus in favor of a total, immediate pull-out from Vietnam?" In reference to Norton's call for YAF to concentrate on boosting capitalism and other conservative programs, Docksai retorted, "When the Moratorium committee conducts their anti-America crusade via the Vietnam war, are we to counter it by a MINIMUM WAGE: HOW IT'S BAD FOR NEGROES or SOCIAL SECURITY: HOW IT'S UNECONOMICAL counteroffensive? Are we to leave the responsible, anti-communist position sole property for the fever-swamp Kent Courtney types or the Rev. MacKentires [sic] who get on a New York radio station and say that Nixon's foreign policy is being shaped by 'the dupes and fellow travelers ... of communism'?"[51]

Docksai's resolve to continue projecting a stance contradictory to that of campus anti-war critics did little to ignite a consensus among YAF leaders. Thompson warned that YAF's chapter chairmen, "the backbone of our organization," were troubled by the organization's apparent move away from a victory policy to one of "saying, 'Yes, Mr. President.'"[52] His opposition to the policy of Vietnamization may have determined Thompson's position, but the national board's failure to articulate a consistent stand regarding Vietnam undercut the coherence and implementation of its

Vietnam-related strategies on campus. Neither Norton nor the opponents of his strategy addressed the same issues, however. Both camps argued over the importance of Vietnam to national security, and both alluded to the role of YAF on campus. Yet neither acknowledged the reality that to be of any value in building popular student support for the war, a pro-Nixon stance was the only available option by late 1970. The extent to which this reality was fully understood by YAF activists on campus is unclear, but it manifested itself, largely because of the pro-administration positions of conservative leaders, in their chapter activities.

YAF's subtly contradictory position on Vietnam was determined as well by a factor peculiar to pro-war students who did not serve in Vietnam. As a veteran, Norton was one of only a few YAF members who did so, and he was the only veteran on the national board. In questioning YAF's Vietnam position, he asserted that "frankly, it offends hell out of me that so many YAF leaders make Vietnam sound like a holy crusade, while judiciously doing everything they can to avoid serving there themselves."[53] Dan Joy offered a weak response, but one that pinpointed the changes in YAF's war position. He acknowledged that Vietnam was no longer a "holy crusade" but affirmed this did "not mean that we ought not to be fighting the war or more desirably supporting those who are fighting the war."[54] Joy's position reflected the pro-war campaign's focus on supporting American troops in Vietnam but did little to reconcile the paradox of supporting American troops but failing to join them. Norton denied the claim offered by YAF pro-war activists that their domestic campaign was vital to the war effort. "Rationalize it however one can," he said, "what these YAF leaders do is help keep in effect a policy that others may have to die for, while being unwilling to die for it themselves."[55]

The contradiction haunted YAF activists even after the war. In 1977, during an exchange between the liberal commentator Jeff Greenfield and several members of YAF on Buckley's television show *Firing Line*, Greenfield accused the conservative activists of being hypocritical because of their failure to serve in Vietnam. John Buckley, YAF's newly elected national chair, insisted that YAF members had made sacrifices in order to show their loyalty to the war effort. He said that a strong commitment to the war "wouldn't necessarily require that we individually go out and wage the war physically." Buckley was unrepentant in his insistence that YAF activists and others who had favored the "U.S. position in the war certainly revealed the extent of that sacrifice in terms of grades and in terms of being active in the battle on campuses." Greenfield was unconvinced and quickly retorted, "No, I'm sorry, John. I don't think getting a C-plus instead of an A is equivalent to slogging through the mud in Vietnam."[56] The paradox was not lost on YAF members in 1970. The rationalization that a domestic pro-war drive was necessary ultimately led YAF to adopt campaigns that not only supported the troops but also endorsed the president's policies for the de-Americanization of the war. The debate sparked by Norton's memorandum brought into high relief the ambiguities and contradictions inherent in YAF's official policy and the distinctions between national policy and local activism. But it did little to resolve these contradictions, in part because the Vietnam issue per se had been declining in importance with the implementation of the more wide-reaching anticommunist Freedom Offensive. In this regard YAF activists mirrored the broader conservative movement and national trends; as they acknowledged that talk of victory was no longer politically viable, *any* talk of the war became politically poisonous.

From Victory to Peace with Freedom

YAF's preoccupation with the volatility of the Vietnam issue and with defining victory was certainly not unique. The concept of outright victory seemed misplaced considering Nixon's focus on peace with honor.[57] On August 16, 1970, the NSCVV was publicly relaunched as the Student Coordinating Committee for Freedom in Vietnam and Southeast Asia and claimed to include Young Republicans, Democrats, independents, conservatives, and liberals. Pledging to serve as the coordinating body for the distribution of literature and the organization of speakers and debates around the country, the new group promised to "actively support U.S. commitments in Southeast Asia."[58]

While many of the activities and personnel of the Coordinating Committee were continuations of those of the NSCVV, its name change was of great practical and ideological significance. It reflected the increasing prominence within the group of individuals such as Turner and Dan Teodoru, who were more concerned with the Vietnam War and foreign policy issues than with espousing a consistent conservative political philosophy. As YAF moved away from support for Nixon's Vietnam strategies during early 1971, the Coordinating Committee launched a vociferous defense of the president's Vietnamization policy. Although individual members of the committee, including one of its most prominent faculty advisers, Charles Moser of George Washington University, insisted on military escalation to achieve victory in Vietnam, the organization's overall standpoint was one of support for Nixon. YAF maintained a working interest in the activities of the committee, but it was no longer the dominant voice in determining policy. The fifteen people who composed the three fact-finding teams that visited Vietnam and Cambodia in August, October, and November 1970 included none of the figures prominent within YAF, an indication of the committee's new breed of leaders and YAF's practical reduction of its Vietnam-related activism. Nonetheless, the Coordinating Committee retained a rationale for American involvement in Vietnam similar to that of the NSCVV and continued to focus on disputing the arguments of the anti-war movement. Its name change was a response to changes in the administration's rhetoric and recognition that the pursuit of victory, as commonly understood, was no longer a viable means of harnessing student support for the Vietnam campaign. In altering its focus to freedom for Southeast Asia, the Coordinating Committee widened its scope for success and broadened the basis on which individuals could demonstrate backing for its agenda.

Projecting a naiveté similar to that of YAF envoys about what could be gained from short fact-finding visits to Southeast Asia, the members of the Coordinating Committee who visited Vietnam in November said, "At no time did we find the growing anti-Americanism the press speaks of or hatred for the Saigon government." Having "[ridden] public buses, stopped at tens of roadside villages, and walked into hundreds of homes seeking the views of the Vietnamese people," the committee's heralds reported that "complaints were many and the sorrows of war were abundantly clear, but nevertheless hope was ever present." Vietnamization, they concluded, was working.[59] The team members later denounced the media's negative portrayal of Nixon's strategies, each claiming to have been skeptical of the progress engendered by the policy before visiting Southeast Asia because of the news media's reporting on Vietnam. Those who had visited Vietnam previously, the report claimed, "found the progress staggering."

The reports on Vietnamization and on the situation in Cambodia drew remarkably positive conclusions and conveyed a faith in the president's assurance that peace with honor could be plausibly achieved through existing mechanisms. Hinting at their preference for escalation, the committee affirmed that "the one point on which we found unanimity among Americans in Vietnam is that Allied incursions into Cambodia are responsible for the present lull in fighting and for the weakness of the enemy." Those areas bordering Laos, "where the enemy has yet to be denied his safe bases," were, by contrast, still under threat.[60] Such faith in administration policy, albeit genuine, served the committee's practical preoccupation with disputing the anti-war movement and the allegedly misleading press coverage. Touting the success of White House policy was the only viable means of building support for the war while undermining the appeal of Nixon's anti-war critics. In light of Nixon's agreement to meet with members of the Coordinating Committee in the Oval Office in February 1971, the pro-administration stance provided a much-needed political and publicity boost to the student organization. Sven Kraemer, a White House liaison with student groups, stated that the meeting "marked a high point in this student group's unsung efforts on the Vietnam issue" and afforded it media attention.[61]

Teodoru assured Nixon that the campus problem was, in essence, one of the silent majority, of too few pro-Vietnam students being willing to publicly express themselves.[62] It was a theme that favored the Coordinating Committee's position but hardly one that appeared likely to stimulate greater support for their cause.

As became common among pro-war student groups during 1970 and 1971, the Coordinating Committee was forced to elicit support for its Vietnam position through a demonization of the enemy and those whom they claimed aided the enemy's effort at conquest of Southeast Asia. During the spring of 1971 this effort took the form of a campaign of opposition to the People's Peace Treaty, which was circulated on university campuses by the NSA. The NSA had long been the target of conservative and pro-war student groups—from 1965 on YAF concentrated much of its campus energies on replacing student governments with rightward leaning or moderate student leaders. In December 1970 the NSA sent a sixteen-member delegation to North Vietnam, where a so-called peace treaty was negotiated and signed between students supposedly representing the United States, North Vietnam, and South Vietnam. While the treaty was little more than an instrument of propaganda and publicity, it was submitted to student governments and city councils for ratification, and the NSA engaged in campus and community referenda around it.

Decidedly favoring the North Vietnamese and PRG positions, the treaty demanded that a date for complete U.S. withdrawal from Vietnam be announced immediately, that the Vietnamese agree to enter discussions to secure the release of POWs once this date had been publicly set, that the United States "pledge to end the imposition of Thieu-Ky-Khiem on the people of South Vietnam," that a coalition government be established to organize democratic elections, and that both sides agree to respect the neutrality of Laos and Cambodia.[63] Having violated two of the canons of pro-war approval of a negotiated settlement—that no date for withdrawal be announced and that no coalition government be introduced for South Vietnam—the treaty earned the wrath of pro-Vietnam student groups. The Coordinating Committee called it a "Declaration of war on the American people" and said its strenuous attacks on Vietnamization served only to embolden the pro-war actions for Nixon.[64] The NSA officially declared that Nixon's policy of Vietnamization allowed continuation of the war through the use of U.S. airpower, a position that reflected positive pro-war assessments of Nixon's strategy.[65] The unusually high degree of similarity in organizational opposition to the treaty was determined not simply by a mutual rejection of its provisions. Groups that included YAF, the Coordinating Committee, American Youth for a *Just* Peace, and the ad hoc group Stop NSA determined to launch public campaigns of opposition to the treaty as a means of devastating the NSA's credibility along with that of the anti-war student campaign.

Rather than pose a challenge to the pro-war efforts of student groups, the People's Peace Treaty became a rallying point for unified action against its anti-war provisions and the supposedly clandestine, antidemocratic way it was created. Describing the NSA endeavor, the pro-war group American Youth for a *Just* Peace declared that the treaty "embodies the double fault of representing a minuscule minority in America bidding for dictatorial power, on behalf of a minuscule minority in North Vietnam which already exercises dictatorial control."[66] The Coordinating Committee attempted to win popular backing by charging that the means by which the treaty came into being revealed that the "new politics" of the NSA "are nothing but the stale backroom maneuvers many of us rebelled against in the course of our struggle for student power and student rights." To undermine moderate students' support for the treaty, YAF simply labeled its campaign Don't Sell Out. Denying that the treaty represented the opinion of students in South Vietnam and alleging that the Saigon-based National Student Union was nothing more than "new left fiction," the Coordinating Committee echoed YAF's position by maintaining that the People's Peace Treaty highlighted nothing more than the cut-and-run policies advocated by the New Left in the name of peace, ultimately to the benefit of Hanoi. Showing little restraint in censuring the key groups endorsing the NSA's treaty, the Coordinating Committee contended that championing of individuals prominent in the radical anti-war movement epitomized the underlying principles of the treaty. Rather than simply seeking peace, the committee charged, advocates of the treaty were "ideologically and organizationally bound to Viet Cong victory."[67]

Based principally on the eight-point peace proposal introduced at the Paris plenary talks by the NLF delegation, the treaty can be understood to reflect anti-war sentiment, yet it was in no way a mirroring of the extreme anti-war viewpoint. The extremist anti-war activists energetically worked for the treaty's ratification by student councils and for a vote in its favor in campus referenda, but they had little to do with its original formulation. Perhaps because of its association with the extremist element of the anti-war movement or perhaps because of the combined pro-war student campaign to vilify its proponents, the treaty's acceptance in campus polls and referenda was less pronounced than initially expected. Rather than signifying a resurrection of its campus activism, however, the anti-NSA campaign stood as the Coordinating Committee's final large-scale campus endeavor on Vietnam.

The committee continued to produce literature that vilified the enemy, particularly in regard to the treatment of POWs. It also proclaimed the success of Nixon's policies, despite the misgivings of committee leaders about the implications of his concessions to Hanoi. Its activist campaign of opposition to the treaty was, indeed, predicated on enhancing support for the Nixon administration regarding Vietnam. Continuing a process that began in earnest with the committee's visits to Southeast Asia in late 1970, from mid-1971 until the end of the war committee leaders focused primarily on analyzing administration policy rather than on initiating campus programs. That focus was partly owing to the personal and professional interests of Teodoru and Turner, but it also was a function of YAF's reduced interest in funding and proselytizing the Vietnam issue on campus. In fact, by mid-1971 the Coordinating Committee had a new function as an alternative student voice to that of YAF with regard to administration policy.

Although the two groups concurred on many issues, the committee adopted a decidedly less confrontational approach toward the Nixon administration. Its analysis, in July 1971, of the NLF's seven-point peace proposal resolved that "militarily the North Vietnamese effort in South Vietnam has suffered tremendous setbacks." While the allied pacification program had made "major advances," the North Vietnamese were obligated to accept "that the tide has turned against them." With such a perceptible, undisputed faith in the military and functional achievements of administration policy, the committee's position descended into a rallying cry for Nixon to remain firm and for his opponents to endorse his policies. "Only now," they proclaimed, "can we appreciate the full meaning of North Vietnam's Premier Pham Van Dong's words—'Our victory will be won not in Vietnam but in America.'"[68] Unlike YAF, which determined that Nixon's policies vis-à-vis the PRC wholly undercut his Vietnam strategy, the Coordinating Committee determined to refrain from dismissing the president's Vietnam strategy. Instead, they issued only qualified support for his overall foreign policy after July 1971.[69] Rather than be a distinctively prowar voice coming from student ranks, the committee replicated the function of existing think tanks along the lines of the American Security Council. Although never a mass membership or chapter-based organization, the committee had, in cooperation with YAF and other student groups, reached a mass student audience, but by early 1972 its proclamations aimed to influence political opinion, not that of the student community. Echoing the ideas of patriotic groups and veterans' organizations, the committee was convinced a bloodbath would follow U.S. withdrawal, and it moved toward promotion of the POW issue to sustain support for a continuation of an increasingly unpopular war.

Student Success: VIVA and the POWs

VIVA was founded at the University of California, Los Angeles, in 1966, ostensibly to "bring both sides of the Viet Nam question to the students."[70] VIVA was designed to focus on creating member chapters "to support the men in our American armed forces" and to "support and encourage our American government and our American servicemen wherever they might be involved in a struggle against aggression, most specifically at this time in Vietnam."[71] VIVA's founders took part in and were inspired by a counterdemonstration against peace protestors at the Oakland naval terminal in November 1965.[72] The organization was incorporated as a nonprofit, nonpolitical, nonideological corporation on March 9, 1967, with the "specific and primary purpose" of educating students about the Vietnam War and anticommunism.

Several members of the early leadership, notably Steve Frank,

Carol Bates, and Richard Thies, dominated the organization throughout its existence. At the age of fourteen Frank worked on Nixon's presidential campaign of 1960 and later served on the Nixon for Governor Speakers Bureau. During VIVA's early days he served as state field representative for YAF and was drafted into the army in 1966, serving in Texas and subsequently in the military police in Vietnam. He later chaired the organization of YES-IN, a rally "dedicated to the reaffirmation of America's traditional values," held at the Hollywood Bowl, and intended as a loud response to the anti-war teach-ins sweeping the country in 1967.[73] Frank's work on behalf of conservative causes, far from waning when he joined VIVA, contributed greatly to the goals and methods adopted by the group. While not a YAF conservative ideologue, Frank's political views were representative of the burgeoning social and political conservatism that was becoming evident in southern California. Frank's service in Vietnam strengthened VIVA's emphasis on supporting those who served their country, a factor that advanced the group's endorsement of the American system of government and American values.

Bates, who became a prominent figure in the POW/MIA movement in the post-Vietnam period, had a similar record of achievement in conservative politics. During her teenage years she served as a staff member of Youth for Yorty, working in 1965 and 1969 on the campaigns of the flamboyant conservative Democrat Sam Yorty for mayor of Los Angeles. She also attended the Republican convention of 1968 and stated her intention to work on political campaigns throughout her tenure at VIVA.[74] During 1968, Thies, the executive director of VIVA, was also involved with YAF,[75] while Bill Saracino, the future chair of CalYAF, referred to VIVA's leaders as "fellow conservatives."[76] In describing VIVA's position, Thies stated, "In as much as we maintain a federal tax exemption, we are prohibited from taking a stand on how the war should be concluded, so we have essentially been engaging in programs and activities which would enable one to arrive at the conclusion that the war should be won without our organization actively stating or promoting that conclusion."[77]

Gloria Wells Coppin, the wife of the Los Angeles industrialist

Douglas Coppin and the mother of three teenage children, was pivotal in guiding VIVA through its early development and in determining its character. Having met the students at a party in October 1966, Coppin took them under her wing, moving the headquarters to her home in the Bel Air area of Los Angeles. She instituted the Salute to the Armed Forces formal dinner, an annual VIVA event that began in 1967. Organized by the Ladies Auxiliary, a group of wives of wealthy businessmen and political leaders, the dinner lent prestige and financial reward to the youth movement.[78] The first dinner was attended by such renowned figures as Goldwater, Haig, Hope, Perot, Yorty, and Reagan, a guest list that fostered the legitimacy of VIVA and enabled the opening of an office in Los Angeles.

Having rejected the purely reactionary efforts of past student groups, VIVA determined to establish an educational offensive, to be undertaken by the approximately seventy campus chapters founded by 1969. Stressing positive programs of action rather than simply responding to the anti-war movement, VIVA encouraged activists to adopt methods that would "build a constructive and productive offensive student force by channeling youthful idealism into tangible activities." Students needed to engage in activities "which are imaginative and innovative—which involve, educate and encourage—which dramatically demonstrate the strength and potential of the American system." Certain ventures focused on campus issues, but all had wider political objectives. Project Education, designed to enable older students to teach and offer moral support to freshmen, was intended to undermine the appeal of the New Left and to construct an image of responsible citizenship, maturity, and respect for academic integrity. VIVA hoped thereby to reduce the legitimacy of anti-war teach-ins. VIVA's speakers' bureau, composed mainly of the group's board members, was modeled on that of YAF. Operation Ombudsman asked students to use VIVA as an intermediary in negotiating the resolution of campus grievances and complaints with college administrations. By proving that administrations would respond to legitimate grievances, VIVA expected to "gain the trust and the confidence of responsible students while discrediting radical elements who employ destructive tactics on the claim that the administration will *not* respond to student initiated action."⁷⁹

One of VIVA's primary goals was to project the Vietnam War in positive terms, an objective that could be secured by highlighting the barbarity and immorality of the Vietnamese enemy. This implied a dichotomy between good American troops serving in Vietnam and an evil, corrupt enemy. One of VIVA's most widely publicized initiatives, titled Your Friendly VC or Friendly Viet Cong, presented photographic evidence of alleged communist atrocities in Vietnam. This campaign animated VIVA's campus demonstrations and tutorials and in one instance formed the basis for the University of Houston's Vietnam Fact Day.⁸⁰ According to VIVA, "This presentation has had profound results in that it establishes that terror is necessary for political control by the Viet Cong." The "graphic evidence of Viet Cong crimes," they said, led to many students becoming converts to VIVA.⁸¹ Its literature dwelled on the barbaric nature of the enemy in Vietnam and challenged the "allegation made by 'anti-war' groups that America [was] engaged in 'reckless' and 'wholesale' napalming of Vietnamese civilians."⁸²

This line of argument became more pronounced in response to the large-scale anti-war demonstrations of 1969. VIVA emulated National Unity Week activities in November 1969, calling on individuals to "wear red, white and blue armbands, fly the American Flag and turn on their porch and car lights" and to demonstrate their support for the Nixon administration through community activities.⁸³ Judy Davis of VIVA accused protestors of betraying their fellow youth serving in Vietnam: "To have Hanoi publicly endorse the moratorium and offer congratulations to the participants must certainly be the highest insult ever paid an American serviceman."⁸⁴ VIVA called on Americans to avoid demonstrations by channeling their energies into such positive programs as its own Operation Mail Call, the sending of letters and packages to American servicemen. While such programs reflected VIVA's continuing dedication to the armed forces, the group's rhetoric was couched in terms of support for the U.S. military engagement. The anti-war demonstrations would surely be interpreted, according to VIVA, "as tantamount to calling for an American surrender in Vietnam without regard for the reason forty thousand Americans have given their lives."[85] Although VIVA often failed to explicitly state the reasons for which these men had died, the organization manifestly endorsed the idea that the war served a noble and important foreign policy objective. Such rhetoric would continue to dominate VIVA, even as its name and purpose changed.

VIVA officially changed its name on April 11, 1969, becoming Voices in Vital America. The renaming acknowledged the new political environment, in which talk of victory seemed not only unrealistic and unpopular but also politically embarrassing.[86] VIVA's new statement of principles did not refer directly to Vietnam, although the group continued to stress approval of "our American form of government and our military in their stand against aggression." Justifying America's military efforts, VIVA stated, "We believe that as no sphere of influence is remote, the responsibility of our commitments to other free nations must be fulfilled if we intend to enjoy freedom ourselves. We believe that a totalitarian government which advocates the overthrow of other sovereign governments constitutes a threat to world peace."[87] VIVA's goals and methods remained almost unchanged. If anything, they more closely reiterated the moral integrity and responsibility of administration policy in the face of the enemy's aggression and intransigence at the Paris talks.

As VIVA continued under the auspices of a nonpolitical, nonideological organization, its leaders privately became involved in the Student Action Committee (SAC), a "committee of the American Security Council [ASC] insofar as its decisions [were] subject to the approval by the Board of that organization." Refusing to dilute its vision of the threats to the security of the United States and the need for greater military strength, the ASC reaffirmed its political agenda: it denied the civil war characteristics of the Vietnam War, arguing that it was part of the global, continuous war against communist expansion and that success in the conflict was essential to the position of the United States in the international arena and to the viability of future American foreign policy objectives. ASC became a leading group in the development of conservative think tanks, and VIVA's role in the SAC cannot be viewed as anything other than overtly political. The minutes of the pivotal meeting on August 9, 1970, that established the practical makeup of the organization reinforced the fact that the SAC was not itself to be a "member organization" and that its founding was plainly intended to facilitate cooperation among like-minded leaders of various groups.[88] Not surprisingly perhaps, its chairman was Dan Joy, a national board member of YAF. Although the name of the group was "chosen for its practical usefulness in presenting the organization according to its purposes," it hardly revealed its purpose. The SAC was not designed simply to coordinate student activity. It existed "to attack the concrete situation of the advancement of revolutionary communism in South and North America, marked by romanticization of revolution on American campuses and by a general lack of appreciation of the Cuban situation." Frank subsequently sought to contact local expatriate Cuban leaders, tying the goal of antiradicalism on campus to specific foreign policy and political objectives.[89]

VIVA's abiding convergence on war-related issues, especially its opposition to the Moratorium of 1969 and its adoption of Nixon's silent majority theme, showed intransigence, not transformation. The group had come to prominence only a month earlier, when President Nixon personally commended Frank for VIVA's stand against demonstrators at Los Angeles City College. Nixon wrote, "There is no substitute for the firm will of an academic community . . . in defending its own rights against disruptive, coercive or repressive elements." Again, VIVA pointed out the violence of those trying to "overthrow the Government."[90] VIVA was determined to tie its aims and methods to those of the administration, and it was through its pursuit of its twin objectives of opposing aggression (both in the domestic and foreign realms) and championing the American system that VIVA stumbled on the operation for which it would become renowned and wealthy. In 1968 and 1969 the State of California's Registry of Charitable Trusts indicated that VIVA grossed below thirty thousand dollars per annum. In July 1970 Frank wrote to a friend at YAF, "Our on campus picture is rosy, it is the financing that keeps us up nights."[91] Within a year the financial situation and much else had been dramatically and permanently altered.

In September 1970 Bryce Harlow, the deputy assistant to President Nixon for congressional affairs, met with several members of VIVA in San Diego. Frank wrote that the purpose of the meeting was to discuss "the problems of the Prisoners of War and the men Missing in Action."[92] VIVA had only recently become a player in this effort, but the group's initiatives with regard to the POW cause soon dominated its actions. At a fundraising event in California in late 1969 Bates and Kay Hunter, members of VIVA's national board, were introduced to three POW wives by Bob Dornan, an air force veteran who hosted a radio talk show and produced the *Robert K. Dornan Show* for television between 1969 and 1973. Dornan hoped VIVA would highlight the POW issue on campus. His commitment to the issue was prompted by his friendship with David Hrdlicka, the well-known POW who had been held in Laos, and by his approval of Nixon's policies in Vietnam. Opening a new way for VIVA to appeal to students through a positive program, the POW campaign also helped solve its funding problems. And so, the POW bracelet campaign was born.

Having originally hoped to acquire bracelets from Vietnam, Bates and Hunter turned to a more practical alternative. Failing to obtain loans of seed capital from either Perot or Howard Hughes, both of whom were sympathetic to the cause, VIVA was forced to rely on copper donated by Douglas Coppin. Dornan suggested that the names of an American POW or MIA be printed on each bracelet, along with his rank and the date on which he went missing. Thus began a process by which individual Americans were asked to undertake personal journeys with missing American servicemen. Originally VIVA stated, "It is to be worn with the vow that it not be removed until the day that the Red Cross is allowed into Hanoi to assure his family of his status and that he receives the humane treatment due all men." This instruction was modified as Hanoi, under international pressure, began to use anti-war forces in the United States to answer demands for information on American POWs. The bracelets were later expected to be worn until the prisoner was returned or an accounting was made, thus upping the demands and the stakes in the POW/MIA cause. By creating "a level of personal involvement and a visible display of Americans uniting behind a common cause"

VIVA again tied its backing of the war to its twin themes of encouraging demonstrative faith in the American system and promoting anticommunism abroad.[93]

Having sold out its first batch of twelve hundred bracelets and received orders for five thousand more, VIVA was soon absorbed in the distribution and sale of the bracelets. It had initially been assumed that only students would be interested in wearing such bracelets, but VIVA's first sales were made at the national convention of the National League in September 1970, a factor that contributed greatly to the organization's ever-increasing association with the league. Within a year the bracelets were being worn by a number of celebrities, and Bob Hope and Martha Raye agreed to become honorary cochairs of the bracelet campaign, giving legitimacy to the program while also popularizing it. Celebrities who publicly wore the bracelets included Charlton Heston, Bill Cosby, Steve Allen, Fred Astaire, Robert Stack, John Forsythe, Willie Shoemaker, and Don Drysdale. Hope was presented with a specially inscribed bracelet honoring all POW/MIAs at the departure ceremony of the Bob Hope–Round the World Christmas Tour in December 1970. At the time, VIVA stated that the organization's members were "devoting all their energies toward alerting the public to the P.O.W. issue."[94]

Such was the success of the fledgling bracelet campaign that it became the primary activity of the group within a matter of months, although the campaign was originally viewed as a means of financing its other Vietnam-related educational activities. In August 1972 VIVA recorded an available income of $3,397,575, the vast majority of which had been made through the sale of bracelets at $2.50 each. This income enabled the organization to distribute 18,728,000 brochures, 13,808,000 bumper stickers, 11,892,000 form letters, and approximately 11,000,000 additional materials. VIVA "purchased space on 186 million match books which [were] distributed throughout the country to inform the people of the POW/MIA plight."[95] A full-time, paid staff was required to deal with the thousands of letters VIVA received every day in 1971 and 1972. Both Frank and Bates became permanent staff members, committing themselves yet further to VIVA's success not simply as an educational institution but as a viable and profitable organization.

By 1972 VIVA had established sixty-eight offices across the United States, most of which were managed by volunteers, and had approximately one hundred people on its payroll.[96] Dependent on the POW issue in order to maintain its high public profile, VIVA's maneuverability was sharply reduced. The brochures, bumper stickers, and form letters referred almost exclusively to the POW/MIA campaign. VIVA continued to emphasize the need for national unity and the importance of opposing aggression, but by 1972 it had become almost a single-issue advocacy group. This single issue had come to symbolize its wider goals and its concept of victory in Vietnam.

The rapid increase in VIVA's involvement with other POW/MIA groups exacerbated this trend. It cultivated its relationship with the National League and was the principal source of materials and literature for nascent POW groups throughout the United States, even aiding the development of a citizens' POW/MIA group in the Panama Canal Zone. As the cause became truly national, so too did VIVA. Stretching beyond its mandate as a student organization, it began to form community chapters and established a consignment department to allow individual POW/MIA families to sell and distribute the bracelets. By 1972 most of VIVA's volunteers and members were not student activists. They were generally citizens who believed in the group's humanitarian objective and its faith in the American system. Patriotism and the POW cause had become essentially synonymous. Senators, congressmen, governors, and President Nixon were soon declaring that they owned a POW/MIA bracelet.

The group's newfound prominence prompted the Nixon administration's interest in assessing VIVA's position regarding the POW issue. The White House had no need to worry about VIVA, however, for the group continued to promote Nixon's policies for concluding the war and the administration's focus on the POW issue at the plenary peace talks in Paris. That the issue was not a prominent subject of Kissinger's then-secret talks with officials of the DRV would have shocked the members of VIVA. VIVA's opposition to POW/MIA Families for Immediate Release was indicative of its faith in the American objective in Vietnam and of its overwhelming objection to trusting the North Vietnamese negotiators. The organization, in fact, took a hard-line stance on this issue. Largely because of its tax-exempt status and its appeal to as many people as possible, VIVA refrained from challenging specific government policies, but it endorsed groups like Concern for POWs, which demanded that the government adopt a more uncompromising policy toward North Vietnam. VIVA distributed bracelets through Concern for POWs and joined it in imploring Congress to ensure that all POWs were returned before troop withdrawal had been completed.[97] VIVA, while not politically neutral, maintained its veneer of being nonpolitical through the development of a series of POW-related programs.

The initiation and direction of the Freedom Tree project were indicative of the growing influence of nonstudent individuals in the group. The project, originally devised by a POW wife and full-time VIVA volunteer, Shirley Stavast, involved the planting of trees by individuals and groups in honor of a POW or missing person as "living tribute[s]" to them.[98] VIVA provided the bronze plaque, which read as follows:

> THE FREEDOM TREE
> WITH THE VISION OF FREEDOM FOR ALL MANKIND
> THIS TREE IS DEDICATED TO — — — — —
> AND ALL PRISONERS OF WAR MISSING IN ACTION[99]

The syndicated columnist Henry J. Taylor paraphrased VIVA's vision: "Trees have sheltered men for countless centuries. It is an unending story. A tree struggles to grow. So does freedom. If a tree does not struggle, it will die. So, too, freedom. A tree is alive, and so is freedom. When our prisoners come home they will know that love and agonized concern for them have never diminished—not for a single hour—in the stricken communities that make up America."[100] The theme of freedom was intended to symbolize respect not simply for the armed forces in Vietnam but also for the cause for which they had been called to serve and for which so much had been sacrificed. It was a theme repeated in VIVA's instructions for the format of the Freedom Tree dedication ceremony. Brig. Gen.

John Schweizer Jr., USAF (Ret), who in 1972 became executive director of VIVA, informed people who were interested in dedicating a Freedom Tree to contact local POW/MIA, veterans', service, or civic organizations. He recommended that civic dignitaries and military guests be invited to the event and insisted that the ceremony include a presentation of colors, recitation of the pledge of allegiance, a dedication prayer, and patriotic songs.[101] This reflected broader pro-war activism in which traditional symbols of patriotic expression and alliances with military practices were used.

The theme of patriotic duty was repeated in VIVA's Adoption program, in which individuals or groups officially "adopted" a POW through VIVA. The program, which in many instances involved the adoption of individuals by school classes, furthered VIVA's goal of fostering emotional attachments to the POW cause. It served as well to increase the common belief that many more live POWs existed than Hanoi admitted to holding. Owing largely to escalating international pressure and the rise of the POW cause in the United States, North Vietnam began to release additional information about the prisoners it held and provided information on those known to have died. They did so primarily via the plenary talks at Paris and American anti-war organizations. By January 1973 Hanoi had testified to holding 591 American servicemen, all of whom were returned to the United States by March 1973. The U.S. Defense Department, while listing almost 2,000 more servicemen as MIA, did not seriously dispute Hanoi's figure. But, writing in a letter to Congress that "our government is still attempting to secure information on the 389 men whom they had evidence were prisoners" in Korea, VIVA warned against repeating "the shocking tragedy of having not demanded a full accounting of our men prior to the cessation of hostilities as we did in North Korea."[102] Communists, VIVA protested, could not be relied on to proffer accurate information about prisoners.

VIVA's programs served as powerful means for individuals opposed to anti-war protesters to convey their continued faith in the American purpose in Vietnam. Continuous reference to the communists' violation of the Geneva Convention could only diminish faith in the integrity of North Vietnam, implicitly enhancing the honor associated with the American cause in Vietnam. It was this cause, not YAF's promotion of an alternative military strategy, that activated pro-war student support during 1972 and that both contributed to and reflected the national mood regarding Vietnam by the final year of direct American involvement in the war.

For Country and Party: The Campus Republican National Committee

Young Republicans were no less aware of the public mood by 1972 and were determined to orchestrate a campaign that would also emphasize a positive interpretation of America's Vietnam experience among America's youth. In October Karl C. Rove, the executive director of the CRNC, proclaimed that the American public had recently "been subjected to one of the most crass and cynical deceptions in the history of politics." He referred to the recent Vietnam address of Sen. George McGovern and assured his audience that help was available from two key sources: the first, a publication that "contains all you wanted to know about the fallacies in McGovern's speech, but didn't want to ask"; and the second, Nixon's reelection.[103] Rove's enthusiastic endorsement of Nixon's Vietnam policies reflected the CRNC's consistent position of support for the president, a factor that grew inexorably from the committee's function as the "third official auxiliary" of the Republican Party. His stance also reflected the CRNC's three-year campaign to promote the Republicans as the true Peace Party.

The CRNC was founded in 1892 and had been associated with the Young Republican National Federation until 1970 when, under the direction of Chairman Joseph Abate, Executive Director Rove, and College Director Morton Blackwell, the CRNC sought greater autonomy and recognition for its independently organized and recently successful Get-Out-The-Vote campaigns on campus. The CRNC continued to receive approximately one hundred thousand dollars a year from the Republican National Committee (RNC) and amplified its function as a way of securing the youth vote after the voting age was reduced to eighteen.

While the Young Republicans remained prominent among conservative-leaning students, particularly in the run-up to midterm and presidential elections, the CRNC was the dominant Republican voice on campus. Its function as an arm of the party did little, however, to enhance its leverage with the RNC or the White House regarding its Vietnam campaigns. These campaigns were concerned with developing an independent or nonpartisan voice in favor of Nixon's Vietnamization strategy. Despite this slight by the White House and the CRNC's own emphasis on prioritizing projects that would increase its membership, the CRNC was wedded to heralding the success of Nixon's Vietnam strategy. Like YAF and VIVA, the CRNC relied heavily on demonizing the enemy and responded with vigor to the mainstream student body's antipathy toward radical anti-war protesters. Preoccupied with its struggle for autonomy during 1969, the CRNC's Vietnam campaign grew rapidly during 1970. As Rove's comment regarding McGovern suggests, however, this campaign was at all times a function of the group's wider goal: maximizing mass political support for the party.

The CRNC developed a campaign titled the New Student Politics, which aimed to nourish student activism in politics. Calling for "mass based clubs," the campaign was predicated on founding long-term membership organizations rather than on short-term collective action projects. If its target audience was novel, the campaign's emphasis was determinedly traditional, focusing not on addressing student-oriented issues but on "conventional campaign volunteer work." "We have found," the CRNC board declared in 1969, "that success of student political organization is determined by the organizational technique employed, not by the issues, Party, personality, or philosophy. You can run a dirty dishrag up a flagpole on any college campus and somebody will salute. If organized properly, a great many will salute."[104]

Carrying through on its ideal of organization first, policy second, the CRNC aided in the organization of the Leadership Training School (LTS), a weekend of presentations and debate that took place in Washington in February 1971 and was heavily sponsored by the White House.[105] Dolf Droge, an NSC member who was the administration's spokesman on Vietnam in college debates, offered the young Republican activists a talk titled "A Look at Vietnam," while the Veterans Affairs administrator, Don Johnson, hosted a "prayer breakfast for POWs and MIAs." Droge's lecture on Vietnam was the only one that addressed a contemporary policy issue. The other presentations focused on such topics as convention politics, offered by F. Clifton White, and how to attract press coverage for youth issues, presented by Jeb Magruder. As the presentation by Richard Scammon and Ben Wattenberg, "The Role of Issues in the Campaign," implied, the primary purpose of the LTS was to publicize issues that were likely to garner political support for the party.

The CRNC's campaigns around Vietnam were a function of these overarching political and organizational goals and divulged the political ambitions of the organization's leadership. This is not to suggest that Abate and Rove and indeed the organization's mass membership were not committed to success in Vietnam. But policy and strategy in Vietnam were unmistakably of less concern to the CRNC than how to enhance approval of Nixon's policies and of the party. From 1970 on, the CRNC was firmly enveloped in promoting the image of the Republican Party as the party of peace, exemplified by the committee's campaign GO•PEACE. Its posters declared, "Republicans in this century have had a continuing experience of inheriting wars, bringing about peace and maintaining peace during their administrations. President Nixon's administration is no exception."[106] While unlikely to convert anti-war students and avoiding those advocating total victory, the campaign appealed to less radical elements of the study body.

CRNC officials did not aim to attract specifically students advocating an alternative policy to that of the administration, and its emphasis actually echoed Nixon's peace with honor. Returning from a trip to Vietnam in October 1971 designed to legitimize the CRNC's pronouncements on the war, Abate issued a public report that contained little of the spirited praise for Vietnamization proffered by YAF in April 1970 and by the Coordinating Committee in November 1970. His assessment of the South Vietnamese presidential election, though positive, was measured, in part because of his audience's wariness about the Thieu regime and in part because the CRNC was not prone to making policy judgments. Thieu "may not be the adored leader of his people," Abate said, but he had "restored a much longed-for stability to Vietnam." As the South Vietnamese appeared more confident of their ability to handle North Vietnamese aggression, Abate concluded simply that "Nixon's Vietnamization program *is* working."[107] As the GO•PEACE campaign implied and as the CRNC's constant reference to Vietnamization as an exemplar of the success of the Nixon Doctrine demonstrated, the committee wished to reduce students' focus on Vietnam as a political issue, subsuming Nixon's ending of the war within a wider foreign policy framework of success. In a commentary on anti-war demonstrations of April 1971, the CRNC claimed, "The truth about the public's attitude . . . is that virtually everybody is 'anti-war.' It is now a question of who is for a real peace." "What Administration backers can rightly call themselves," the CRNC said, "is 'peace people.' Those of us who defend the President's end-the-war policies see behind the protesters' demands the dangers of an extended war—not the President's 'full generation of peace.' . . . We peace people want peace—not for awhile—but forever." "All we are saying," Abate said in summing up, "is give peace a chance." That immediate withdrawal would not result in peace remained the CRNC's only policy judgment.

Having focused during 1971 on developing the Washington Campus News Service (WCNS), a resource used to transmit radio broadcasts and issue press releases, the CRNC turned its attention during 1972 to its primary purpose: the amassing of youth votes for Republican candidates.[108] Rove was nominated chair of Operation: Open Door, a program to maximize youth interest in the Republican Party. Vietnam could hardly be ignored, but, recognizing its divisiveness on campus, the CRNC concentrated its national effort on delegitimizing the position of those who called for a radical change in Vietnam policy by emphasizing that the war was ending. Urging its chapters to campaign for local Republican candidates, Rove and Abate set about appealing to moderate students wary of the anti-war positions of leading Democrats. They also attacked YAF's opposition to Nixon's reelection in March 1972, contending that YAF's chairman was "out of step with the nation's young conservatives."[109]

Abate did, however, join YAF and the Coordinating Committee

in denouncing the NSA's People's Peace Treaty and its call for student strikes to protest the bombing of North Vietnam in April 1972. Yet the CRNC used its attack on the NSA to further promote the effectiveness of Nixon's withdrawal policies, a position that differed greatly from YAF's recent questioning of the administration's implementation of Vietnamization. While stating that Nixon's action was hopefully a "temporary resumption of the bombing," the CRNC declared that the bombing policy "makes it clear that the South Vietnamese people will be aided in their struggle to resist the imposed rule of the North."[110] Thus while the CRNC remained moderate in its assessment of a military solution to the war, its leaders, appealing to potential student supporters, stressed that the United States would continue to play a role in Southeast Asia after troop withdrawals. Although it is difficult to determine to what extent this issue resonated with students who had recently come of voting age, the literature of the CRNC leaves no doubt that its leaders believed a successful conclusion to the war and the promise of continued South Vietnamese freedom to be potential sources of support for Nixon and the Republican Party. Coupled with the highlighting of Nixon's ending of the draft, the Vietnam issue appeared sufficiently salient and potentially popular to form a key aspect of CRNC's campaign in 1972.

A Diverse Coalition

The various pro-Vietnam student campaigns had a number of similarities and were more effective in uniting in opposition to the anti-war movement than any other sector of the pro-war movement. As the experiences of YAF, NSCVV, VIVA, and CRNC demonstrate, however, there was no single or unified conservative or pro-war student response to the government's evolving Vietnam policies. VIVA and CRNC proved more able to gain the support of the mainstream student body, but they did so at the expense of focusing specifically on the basic issues of U.S. policy toward Southeast Asia. By appealing to the patriotism of those students who were reluctant to accept the ideas or actions of anti-war pro-testors, both organizations succeeded in establishing bodies of support that gave them an effective pro-war voice on campus. The CRNC drew on the political lessons of the war that had been lost on the more rabidly pro-war elements, including YAF. Although VIVA and CRNC were, therefore, able to reach their respective goals of encouraging faith in the American system and prompting support for the Republican president, both groups were ultimately forced to rely on nonstudent issues and to avoid dealing with matters of strategy and principle regarding Vietnam. In doing so, they contributed to the national environment in which victory was being redefined, in which patriotism, support of the president, and concern for POWs assumed dominance over debating the necessity or justification of the war.

YAF's concentration on responding to government policy in Vietnam rather than on mounting a lasting pro-war campaign on campus reflected its role as the youth wing of the *National Review* circle. Its leaders were committed to the war and to encouraging backing for it on campus, but they were stymied by the national board's questioning of Nixon's policies, particularly from early 1971 on. While they understood the benefits and indeed the necessity of accentuating the significance of the war among the student body, YAF leaders recognized the difficulty of establishing a campaign that asked students to demand measures in excess of those being implemented by the administration. Its Tell it to Hanoi drive revealed the popularity of programs on campus that contested the anti-war position, prompting YAF and NSCVV to dwell on positive programs of support for the president rather than on initiatives that challenged the rationale of Vietnamization and withdrawal. YAF's reluctance to do even this after 1971 fundamentally weakened its effectiveness in promoting support for the war. Having helped alter the way in which students were expected to deal with the Vietnam issue, focusing on patriotism rather than policy, YAF was unable to establish a student lobbying campaign in opposition to the administration's Vietnam strategy once withdrawal accelerated.

The student campaigns that gripped the attention of the media and government were primarily those of the anti-war New Left. Pro-war student groups were neither as demonstrative nor as willing to abandon traditional means of achieving political leverage. The student campaigns of the organizations discussed here reveal the concentration of pro-war groups on encouraging patriotism and on demonizing the enemy in order to undermine the messages and validity of their anti-war counterparts. In doing so they somewhat inadvertently undermined the significance of their original rationale for supporting American engagement in Southeast Asia and ultimately promoted support for the president's policies of withdrawal. Students' shifts in emphasis reflected popular attitudes and political realities, but how the broader pro-war movement responded to this changed public environment during 1972 led only to greater tensions among conservatives and to their eventual abandonment of the Vietnam War.

CHAPTER 7

Snatching Victory

The Endings of a War

> A strong President, willing to take bold action, literally snatched victory from the jaws of defeat for our objectives in Indo-China.... [I]n dealing with the communists ... our primary tools must be military strength, and the willingness to use it in a just cause involving the peace of the world and our own strategic national interests.
>
> Barry Goldwater, January 24, 1973

Grassroots and student activism in support of Vietnam reduced the need for the government to rationalize the continuation of the war on the basis of national security considerations. Public and congressional pressures to hasten the process of Vietnamization made any talk of outright military victory politically irrelevant. Nixon's preoccupation with the impact of the war on the election of 1972 and Kissinger's determination to secure a peace agreement that would allow him to further the broader purposes of détente therefore prompted the White House to continue the process of winding down direct U.S. military engagements in Southeast Asia.

National Review conservatives never accepted the notion that American success in Vietnam was anything other than essential, for both international and moral reasons. Yet their commitment to the war had practical limitations as well. In 1972 they questioned the success of the administration's Vietnam policies largely as a means of challenging the far greater threats associated with détente. But even this continued ideological commitment to the war was impacted by the recognition that pro-war stalwarts among veterans and patriotic groups and within the labor movement were now wedded to backing the president's policies of withdrawal. Conservative political leaders, particularly those in the Republican Party, realized that their continued push for escalation was unpopular. This exacerbated the divisions between Republicans such as Goldwater and Reagan and conservative activists at the ACU and *National Review*. But just as social conservatives had long queried the utility of American engagement in Vietnam, given the wider threats of Soviet rearmament, conservative leaders as a whole also demonstrated an increasingly limited commitment to the war during 1972. They were loath to adopt the patriotic tropes that characterized the pro-Vietnam campaigns of unions, student groups, and ad hoc citizens' groups. Ultimately, however, conservatives enjoyed broader support for their foreign policies precisely because they focused on questions of morality. As Phyllis Schlafly would declare, Kissinger's greatest crime was his "total inability to understand or appreciate what might be called typical American values."[1] The final year of America's war in Vietnam saw conservatives push for a true peace with honor, but the ending of the war also convinced them of the power of harnessing popular support for foreign policy endeavors.

Hard-line Democrats also focused on other issues at this time. Sen. Henry "Scoop" Jackson of Washington demonstrated that the Vietnam War was no means of popularly challenging détente. His embrace of neoconservative critiques of détente led him to focus on matters such as Soviet restrictions on Jewish emigration to Israel as a way of highlighting the immorality of Kissinger's Realpolitik. Legislation that would become the Jackson–Vanik amendment was introduced in October 1972 by Jackson and Rep. Charles A. Vanik, a Democrat from Ohio. It was designed to stop communist bloc countries from charging citizens high fees for education reimbursement when they petitioned to leave their country of origin and stipulated that countries wishing to avail of most favored nation status must comply with free emigration policies. The impact of this legislation, which was eventually passed with overwhelming congressional support in 1974, on superpower relations was extremely limited.[2] Its effect on popular support for détente was considerably more dramatic.[3] It signaled a new way of challenging the Nixon administration's foreign policy, based largely on appeals to morality and American exceptionalism in international relations. This shift was barely perceptible in 1972, but hard-liners in both the Democratic and Republican parties were evidently losing interest in the Vietnam War.

Politically savvy conservatives like William Rusher argued that the probable defeat of the United States in Vietnam should be highlighted to rally pro-war activists to oppose the president's foreign policies. Within five years Rusher's vision would become political reality, as conservatives were able to use the abandonment of Vietnam to challenge the morality of détente. In 1972, however, the more politically minded conservatives in the Republican Party believed it was essential to show support for the president's Vietnam policies, in part because of the political traction created by popular emphasis on POWs and the need to appeal to grassroots activists. Despite their disillusionment with the president, conservatives identified with the unity campaigns organized by pro-Nixon activists during 1969 and 1970. They identified further with the moral certainty of the campaigners, whose unambiguous celebration of American valor resonated with their own vision of America's role in the continuing Cold War. Their vision of unity had its limitations, however. It may have conditioned conservative leaders in the Republican Party to continue to champion the president's handling of the war, but it did not extend to conservatives' acknowledgment of the legitimacy of arguments against the war. To that degree, the theme of national unity served a divisive political purpose. It was intended to bring various groups of Americans together behind a particular vision of American purpose in Vietnam, one that celebrated American goals while seeing the war as a tragedy for American society. It was not clear at the time, but this shared interpretation of the war aligned intellectual conservatives with social conservatives who would form the bedrock of the New Right in the 1970s. In 1972 it influenced the ways in which conservatives responded to the ending of the Vietnam War.

Conservative politicians and activists were not able to abandon their worry over *how* the war would end. The way the United States would extricate itself from Vietnam thus became an issue of fierce debate among conservatives during 1972. Division over whether or not to sanction the Nixon administration's foreign policies was limited, however, by a shared belief that the United States needed to implement substantial demonstrations of force against North Vietnam before any settlement of the war could be accepted. The decreased focus on victory notwithstanding, conservatives had not forgotten about the Vietnam War, and, despite Nixon's best efforts to the contrary, the public would not be allowed to forget it during the bloody year of 1972. North Vietnam's Easter Offensive, which began on March 30, 1972, was the largest conventional military offensive undertaken by the PAVN during the war. Its purpose was to secure territorial gains in the South as U.S. forces withdrew, demonstrate the ineffectiveness of the ARVN, and improve Hanoi's negotiating position. The offensive was welcomed by conservatives as evidence that their hawkish military strategies and understandings of the enemy had been correct. Conservative leaders emphasized the Soviet role in orchestrating the invasion, and they were joined by the commanders of the veterans' organizations in accusing dovish members of Congress of aiding the cruel assault on South Vietnam. The wider population, once a source of useful opposition to the anti-war movement, was notably silent during this period, having become war-weary and pacified by Nixon's assurances that he would achieve both deescalation and peace with honor. Nixon's response to the invasion was determined by foreign policy considerations, notably the necessity of appearing strong before embarking on his forthcoming summit with Soviet leaders in Moscow. But he was also swayed by the dictates of electoral politics, which demanded that the United States at least appear to succeed in Vietnam before the election in November.

At this crucial juncture in the war it was obvious to both administration officials and pro-war leaders that the minimal objective, assuring South Vietnam's freedom, was in severe jeopardy. During this time the pro-war movement floundered. Patriotic organizations and veterans' groups were close to completing the process by which success in Vietnam would be determined by the return of POWs and a settlement that afforded the United States some (undefined) measure of credibility. Popular protests like those that had occurred in 1969 and 1970 were noticeably absent, and largely as a result of these initiatives patriotic support of the war had become tied to support of the president. While Nixon was right to worry about the impact of an obvious loss in Vietnam on his electoral chances, Colson could confidently state in March, "We are out of the woods now on Vietnam." So long as the White House appeared to be making progress toward peace with honor, the public was unlikely to oppose the process of winding down the war. Colson remained vigilant and urged Nixon to attend the forthcoming VFW annual convention, but he was confident there was little need to be worried that such groups would break from administration policy on Vietnam.[4] Hawks within the Republican Party, furthermore, revealed their preferences for ending the war sooner rather than later. Nixon, Andrew Johns asserts, actually "underestimated the burgeoning support—especially within the GOP—for hastening the disengagement process."[5] Nonetheless, the administration's failure to respond positively to conservatives' demands for changes to its foreign policies during late 1971 revealed that even Nixon believed conservatives could be managed and their threat to the administration limited.

In large measure Nixon took this stance because the conservative political movement, long the dominant force in pressing for victory in Vietnam, was unable to mount a concerted challenge to his policy of withdrawal and negotiation. Nixon's confidence that he could withstand conservative challenges to his Vietnam strategies had been buoyed by his weathering of the storm created by his bold China initiative. He was determined to ensure that loyal Republican hawks remained in his camp, but his fears of a right-wing backlash were certainly not as great as they had been at the outset of the Vietnamization process. Democratic hawks like Stennis were noticeably quiet on Vietnam and accepted the necessity of ending the war as quickly as possible. More important, the conservative movement was, in Rusher's words, in disarray.[6]

Conservatives sharply divided over whether or not to endorse

Ashbrook's campaign for the Republican presidential nomination. Celebrated by activists such as Rusher as a demonstration of conservatives' continued political strength, the congressman's campaign was derided by Goldwater as foolhardy, disloyal, and unnecessary. Division over the Ashbrook candidacy proved detrimental to a unified, concerted effort on Vietnam. This split was most obvious between *National Review,* the ACU, and YAF on the one hand and the Republican Right on the other. The ACU and YAF were especially critical of Goldwater's unwavering support of Nixon.[7] Goldwater publicly downplayed YAF's recent criticism of him and to a certain extent misrepresented YAF's position regarding Nixon: "There has been a growing split in the YAF ranks for the last three or four years but the anti-Nixon forces are decidedly in the minority. I have made no plans to resign as Honorary Chairman. I am hoping that the day will come that the organization can be unified again because in its present condition they are greatly weakened and much less effective."[8] Goldwater was right about the impact of internal divisions, but he could as easily have been talking about the conservative movement as a whole. The ACU/ *National Review* challenge to Nixon had undoubtedly highlighted conservative anxieties but had also brought into relief the weaknesses of bifurcated conservative political pressure.

The broad popularity of Nixon's pursuit of détente, most noticeably via his visit to China, ensured that foreign policy was not a major political problem for the White House. Indeed, David Greenberg comments that "Nixon's China breakthrough touched off an infectious giddiness." His "foreign policy triumphs," Greenberg writes, "were emerging as the cornerstone of the case for Nixon's reelection."[9] But conservatives were rallied by their opposition to détente and challenged the mainstream policy of the Republican Party. The Spring Offensive gave conservatives a unique opportunity to mobilize in justification of their preferred Vietnam policies. The offensive pinpointed the apparent intransigence of the communist world and seemed to undermine Nixon's claims that his opening to communist China and his use of triangular diplomacy would help bring an end to the Vietnam War. Certainly the Republican Right privately demanded that Nixon undertake more forceful military measures. On the whole, however, conservative leaders did not mount a vociferous pro-war campaign during this period. They chose instead to challenge the administration's overall conception of foreign policy, citing the mistakes made in Vietnam to further justify and popularize their own policy prescriptions. Nixon's eventual use of force against North Vietnam did little to dampen conservatives' efforts.

Demanding Conventional Warfare

Nixon's visit to China and the potential disarmament resulting from SALT preoccupied conservatives' attention during early 1972, not least because such issues deepened the divide between those who endorsed Nixon and those who, however timorously, supported Ashbrook's challenge. There was a pronounced dichotomy among conservative political leaders at this time. Writing to Buckley in March, Rusher said he could not "recall a time when American conservatism was in greater disarray" and blamed disagreement over Nixon as the primary cause of schism.[10] The ACU accused Goldwater and Reagan, the "conservative leadership," of "dancing attendance on Richard Nixon" and labeled such figures "partisan apologists for Cold War accommodation."[11] Ashbrook and James Burnham feared that Goldwater was too eager to satisfy the moderate, or so-called regular wing of the Republican Party. They argued that Goldwater was too concerned with politics and did not recognize the potential of pushing the party to the right, from the outside if necessary. Goldwater, in turn, called on conservatives to be realistic, but he conveyed a personal faith in Nixon that had often characterized his attitude toward the president. "If I cannot believe my president," he wrote of his meeting with Nixon in February, "then I have lost all my faith in men, in friends and in leadership." In reference to Nixon's assurances that nothing was compromised by the visit to China, Goldwater noted, "I think he has told us the truth."[12] Neither the *National Review* conservatives nor Reagan were quite convinced of that, although Reagan was willing to refrain from publicly voicing his anxieties and expressed his faith in the president's bold international initiatives.

Writing before Nixon's "capitulation at Peking," Buckley queried the outcome of the trip vis-à-vis South Vietnam.[13] "What concessions," he demanded to know, "will [Nixon] make, at the expense of South Vietnam? It is an interesting psychological point, that no one ever wonders what might be the concessions, at the expense of North Vietnam, that will be made at Peking by Chou En Lai? Because the general mood, not only in South Vietnam but elsewhere, is conditioned by a generation of Communist intransigence, and western accommodation." South Vietnam, Buckley maintained, was now slowly being "abandoned, under the aesthetic of Vietnamization."[14] This charge exhibited a change in tone regarding Vietnamization, which was the culmination of a process begun by Nixon's initiatives of July 1971.

Conservatives like Buckley were jubilant that their hard-line attitude toward Hanoi seemed justified by the Easter Offensive and were quietly hopeful that, in order to retain a semblance of credibility in the Vietnamization strategy, Nixon would augment the U.S. military campaign. Buckley stated on April 13 that "this time around, the North Vietnamese have conveniently disdained the old fiction that the South Vietnamese war is primarily a civil war. The blitzkrieg from the North, across the Demilitarized Zone, is of a wholly conventional character—tanks, infantry, artillery: it might as well be the Wehrmacht, marching into Poland."[15] Yet Nixon's attempts to keep his enemies guessing as to his possible actions also had the undesirable effect of reducing his reliability among his conservative constituency.

Nixon, in fact, agreed with conservatives that the invasion demonstrated that the "pretense of the Vietnam conflict as a 'people's war' ... was over." Kissinger fittingly noted Nixon's wariness, in light of the invasion, over continued negotiations to end the war.[16] Haldeman made note of the president's determination to respond with force. Nixon not only berated Admiral Moorer for the air force's seeming inability to quickly organize a bombing campaign but also suggested for the first time that B-52's be used to bomb the North. According to Haldeman, Nixon was "massing a huge attack force."[17] In a meeting with Kissinger in early May Nixon talked of wishing to demoralize and devastate the North Vietnamese and said, "We are going to cream 'em good."[18] Such language manifested his personal frustration with the war but also indicated his continued fear of a conservative backlash. Given Ashbrook's dismal failure to mount a challenge to Nixon in the primaries, Nixon was less worried about conservatives' political pressure than he was about the long-term credibility of his desired peace with honor. Ever since the beginning of the invasion he had been concerned with the potential for "total frustration from the right," in light of the invasion and the proposed Moscow summit meeting.[19] Kissinger later commented that Nixon was "afraid that Hanoi—as well as his conservative constituency—might confuse negotiations with weakness."[20] Such fears were hardly unwarranted, and the president was determined to ensure that conservatives would endorse the final outcome of the war. As early as April 4 Haldeman said that the president intended to "base the bombing on the violation of the DMZ and move in hard." Nixon apparently felt, according to Haldeman, this would give "us a fairly good chance of negotiations, which he has never really felt we've had up to now." Believing the enemy offensive to be a "desperation move," both Nixon and Kissinger concluded that North Vietnam "will go to negotiate."[21]

Despite Nixon's anger at the unexpected invasion, his conservative critics persisted in questioning the likelihood of his using the occasion to strike a decisive blow against Hanoi. Their public statements of early April were designed, again and perhaps finally, to push Nixon to the right. Buckley wrote that Nixon's "determination to use air power to stay the enemy's juggernaut is not simply a point of pride" but "derives from a commitment to history, annealed by the experiences that led to the second world war." The "fabric of peace and stability" was ruptured, Buckley claimed, by allowing "a military power which is strong enough to disturb the peace of the whole world underwrite armed aggression against a little power." He was referring not to North Vietnam but to the administration's failure to fully acknowledge the offensive as an "outburst . . . planned and authorized in the Kremlin," an invasion designed to fulfill the "Kremlin's dream of receiving Richard Nixon in Moscow . . . with North Vietnamese soldiers marching through the streets of the capital city towards whose defense the United

States offered up 50,000 American lives." Buckley contended that, under the circumstances, the meeting between Nixon and Premier Alexei Kosygin of the USSR in Washington "might as well be a meeting between Hitler and Pétain."[22]

Goldwater expressed his admiration for Nixon's courage "in finally taking the steps so necessary to bringing about a quick end to the war in Indochina," but he echoed the conservative theme of thinking about the war in terms of Soviet expansionism. The North Vietnamese invasion of the South was, he opined, comparable to the North Korean invasion of South Korea and the Cuban Missile Crisis, that is, "another instance of the Soviet Union attempting to alter the world balance of power by remote control."[23] Conservatives were not placated by Nixon's decision to initiate a broad, continued bombing campaign against North Vietnam. The initial operation was aimed at areas around the DMZ and did not include attacks on Hanoi until April 16. At this stage there were no public plans to bomb the symbolically important Haiphong harbor. The campaign was more extensive than anything the administration had previously implemented, "the best ever in the war," as far as Nixon was concerned, but it was not the bold strike against the war-making capabilities of North Vietnam that either conservatives or Nixon desired. Haldeman noted that the president was "knocking off" the bombing while Kissinger made a secret visit to Moscow.[24]

Rather than offer unlimited praise for the bombing, conservatives asked why the president had allowed the slow negotiating process to continue for so long. There is strong evidence that Nixon was deeply worried by hawkish opposition to his Vietnam strategy, particularly in light of his upcoming summit meeting in Moscow.[25] Also clear, however, is that his policies during late April led only to greater conservative disillusionment. On April 25 the White House made public Kissinger's recent, secret trip to Moscow, which had not resulted in a Soviet promise to accommodate American efforts to end the war. On the same day, it was announced that the plenary talks in Paris would resume. The White House's attempt to present such policies in a positive light to conservatives was futile. Haldeman urged his aides to assure pro-war leaders that "the President has flatly rejected the North Vietnamese demand that we discontinue the bombing in order to resume the talks." "They sold us that package in 1968," Haldeman said, "we're not going to buy it again."[26]

Through publications, speeches, and private channels conservatives intensified their pressure on the administration in the buildup to Nixon's national address on May 8. Thurmond warned that the "people of South Carolina do not want to see South Vietnam go down the drain." Reiterating his praise for the "necessary military measures" recently authorized by the president, Thurmond ended by advising Nixon "to step up the bombing of all strategic targets in North Vietnam, as well as other courses of action, such as closing the port of Haiphong in order to bring this war to an early end."[27] The president was bent on heading off the possibility of such criticisms being leveled against him once the much-desired peace agreement was finally reached. It was therefore vital to ensure that he appear bold and forthright in this hour of obvious aggression by Hanoi. In his speech that evening Nixon stressed the role of "other Communist nations" in enabling the offensive, highlighted the intransigence of the enemy in recent negotiations, and announced that "all entrances to North Vietnamese ports will be mined."[28] Such attacks on the North and its sponsors were essential in order to secure conservatives' endorsement of Nixon's policies; they were also, however, the minimum objectives conservatives had sought.

This is not to underestimate the great import of the mining of Haiphong harbor, which, coupled with continued air attacks on communications networks and bombing of "military targets," reduced the hostility of pro-war forces toward the administration's insistence on a negotiated settlement. Yet the mining did not fully restore conservative acquiescence in the president's policy of phased withdrawal. Vietnamization was, according to Buckley, Nixon's "principal doctrinal contribution to the post-cold-war age," but it was possibly a "chimera" and was certainly so if American "stability . . . power, and . . . resolution" proved unreliable.[29] Buckley did not simply question whether or not Vietnamization could prevail; he probed the very basis of the administration's foreign policy. He thereby challenged the architects of Vietnam policy to reprioritize victory in the war, the means by which such success should be achieved, and its relationship to overall foreign policy. While both Goldwater and Buckley endorsed Nixon's Vietnam policies, each exploited the invasion to reinforce conservatives' principal reason for supporting the war, namely, its association with international communist expansion. While they had drastically reduced their terms for victory and had embraced elements of populist campaigns in favor of the war, conservative leaders still pointed up the importance of making a strong show of force to demonstrate America's commitment to anticommunism.

It was in this context that the Linebacker bombing operations were conceived. The Right's potential dismissal of the anticipated peace agreement proved powerful at this time. Despite the public's desire for the war to come to an end, many close to Nixon understood that a conservative attack on his ending of the war might harm his long-term legacy as a peacemaker. Colson urged the White House to accentuate the restrained nature of the president's recent policies because of his fear of a resurgence of anti-war activism on the scale of the response to the Cambodian incursion. Haldeman's rejoinder to Colson's suggestion was forceful. Evidently thinking about the need to project an image of national determination, he stated, "No, absolutely not—go strong, not weak."[30] Nixon had already conveyed this sentiment to Republican leaders when he said during a meeting that if the "United States fails at this point, no President can go to Moscow, except crawling." In this regard the president sounded remarkably like his conservative critics. He concluded by saying, "If we fail [in Vietnam], we won't have a credible foreign policy."[31] This position was repeated in the wake of his speech on May 8. During a cabinet meeting Nixon explained the bombing of North Vietnam and blockade of Haiphong in terms of his planned summit meeting: "An American P[resident]" couldn't be in Moscow while Soviet guns and tanks were in Hué and we should say we're prepared to go forward and negotiate or to continue with the Summit. The responsibility now is with the Russians."[32] Such sentiment may have complemented conservatives' understanding of Vietnam, but faith in Nixon's conception of foreign policy priorities was sufficiently diminished to preclude full support even with the initiation of the Linebacker bombing campaign. Rather than enter pro-war lore, the Linebacker campaign was met by conservatives with expansive applause but also with an ample measure of anxiety. Nixon could no longer rely simply on his image as an arch–cold warrior to overcome conservatives' fears that military campaigns were being severely restricted and that withdrawal now took precedence over success in Vietnam.

Goldwater tried to undermine conservatives' criticisms and willingly acted on White House efforts to encourage administration partisans to lambaste liberals' failure to see the bombings and mining as "necessary actions to make sure that the remaining 60,000 American troops can be withdrawn from the war zone without being slaughtered."[33] Many of Goldwater's speeches and press releases during this period were based on attacking liberals' supposed opposition to affording a successful withdrawal. He utilized the populist methods ordinarily employed by the patriotic groups and invoked the images of communist slaughter of vulnerable American troops, a postwar bloodbath, and POWs. Goldwater's efforts were representative of the actions being undertaken by conservatives during this period but also derived from a concerted campaign by the White House to encourage its supporters to denounce liberal opponents of the war. As soon as the invasion began Nixon held several meetings in which he highlighted the need to attack people like Sen. Edmund Muskie of Maine, the 1968 Democratic vice presidential candidate who appeared likely to win the presidential nomination in 1972 on an antiwar platform. The president demanded that such individuals be labeled defeatists because they held that the United States should not react to the "Vietnam attack by the enemy."[34]

Goldwater too attacked opponents of the war for criticizing the president: "To hear 'doves' talk about it, you would think President Nixon, for some dark mysterious reason of his own, all at once decided to escalate the war and bomb innocent civilians as far North as Hanoi and Haiphong." He voiced his anger at those who failed to criticize the "North Vietnamese invaders" who were responsible for "slaughter of innocent civilians in the South." Goldwater had long reflected on the brutality of the enemy, but his focus on this issue became more pronounced as conservatives adopted the formula of grassroots supporters of the war. He sarcastically framed his position in contrast to that of the "righteous gentlemen who criticize the President."³⁵ Human decency and American values were decidedly on his side, Goldwater made clear, reflecting the position that had worked so well for organizations such as VIVA.

Goldwater spoke to his conservative critics as well and was effusive in his praise of the military actions. He saw the expanded measures as foils to Soviet expansion and perhaps to détente rather than simply as inducements to Hanoi to negotiate. "What Mr. Nixon did," Goldwater wrote, "when he ordered the closing of North Vietnam's ports to war supplies from Russia was to place this nation on a collision course with the Soviet Union on a matter involving American lives as well as American honor."³⁶ The ASC, in its endorsement of Nixon's actions, said the mining of Haiphong harbor was of "watershed importance—much more important than any previous decision on Vietnam." It was so primarily because it "denied the USSR the '*free ride*' it has enjoyed in southeast Asia since the beginning of the conflict." "The President has now," the ASC went on, "inserted a risk factor for Moscow which has always been lacking until now. Had similar bold action been taken by Mr. Nixon's predecessors, when the United States commitment in Vietnam was expanding, the many long years of conflict might well have been avoided."³⁷ The administration's Vietnam policies thus had the desired effect of emboldening its overall foreign policy in the eyes of conservative supporters of the administration.

The encouraging assessments of conservative organizations and Goldwater's calls for full support of the president's "heroic" actions were insufficient to enable conservative Republicans to bring the entire conservative movement into the administration's realm.³⁸ *Human Events*, reverting to its earlier, more extreme position on how to end the war, continued to stress the necessity of initiating a full-scale attack on North Vietnam. Relying on military experts who avowed that the war had assumed more conventional characteristics, the editors offered an analysis under the title "How Nixon Can Make Vietnamization Work." They counseled the administration "to destroy all military targets, including the Red River dikes, all military storage areas, even those north of the Hanoi/Haiphong area, air bases, bridges, rail nets and related targets enabling the North Vietnamese to maintain their external aggression." The editors called on Nixon to encourage an amphibious attack on North Vietnam by the South Vietnamese, to augment the provision of artillery to the ARVN, and to supply them with antitank weapons. Although *Human Events* noted with encouragement the hawkish nature of Nixon's speech announcing the blockading of Haiphong harbor, it assessed Nixon's ambiguous language as conveying too much eagerness to negotiate with Hanoi. The editors dismissed his reliance on "threatening rhetoric" and directed him to listen to his military advisers in their calls for escalation. Such proposals duplicated those favored by the journal ever since the war's beginning. By 1972 they assumed the additional function of rejecting détente: "Today . . . Saigon teeters on the edge of disaster as a result of a Soviet-instigated offensive. . . . Thus, hawkish observers in Washington are urging the President to put aside thoughts of summitry and accommodating the Soviets and get on with the business of defeating the North Vietnamese invasion."[39]

National Review also refused to fully back the administration. While acknowledging that Nixon's speech had been praised by all sectors, Buckley commented that "inevitably, analysis sets in." He argued, "We have drastically reduced our peace terms," which now "appear to be open-ended, so that there seems to be nothing to stand in the way of the North Vietnamese continuing their offensive until the opportune moment and then announcing they will go for cease-fire."[40] *Human Events*, mirroring conservative anxieties about the proposed peace terms, had already expressed the "major fear that the Administration might now accept a cease fire with masses of North Vietnamese troops stationed in the South." The front-page story concluded that "the President would seem to be committed to his goal of Vietnamization. If he fails here, history will mark him a failure as well. But the President will need more than tough rhetoric to make it work successfully."[41] The administration's apparent eagerness to negotiate an end to the war left open the possibility that a ceasefire-in-place might ultimately be conceded to the enemy. Both sides of the conservative divide distanced themselves from the policy of Vietnamization, arguing that either the Nixon foreign policy strategy was fundamentally flawed or the liberal establishment had so severely undercut Nixon's Vietnam policies as to make Vietnamization untenable.

Although the Republican Right remained publicly behind the president, conservative activists outside the party began to more determinedly move away from the policy of phased withdrawal they had initially backed. In light of the generous peace terms offered by Nixon on May 8, it seemed highly improbable that the South Vietnamese would be left with the military advantage in Vietnam once the United States completed its full withdrawal of forces. Because of détente it now seemed questionable whether Nixon could be relied on to guarantee a return to bombing if the North Vietnamese violated the settlement. In such circumstances, South Vietnam's future existence was not only fraught but seemingly doomed.

The Road to November

Grassroots activism in favor of the war had decreased markedly by mid-1972. As the POW campaign flourished, popular opinion swung in favor of securing the return of American prisoners and away from the original rationale for American engagement in Southeast Asia. South Vietnam's freedom increasingly became an abstraction, one which could be defined or distorted simply by presidential decree. Despite conservatives' private focus on policy matters, this popular interpretation of the purpose and meaning of the war was echoed by conservative politicians. The views earlier expressed by conservatives like Schlafly, namely, that the war drained America's resources and undermined American diplomatic strength, were widely entertained among conservative activists. This weakened even the most ardent pro-war commitment to continued military engagement in Vietnam.

Supporters of the war were preoccupied with disputing the arguments of the anti-war faction in Congress, an effort made all the more vital because of doves' increasing strength in gaining support for the War Powers Resolution. Conservatives consistently maintained that the resolution was not only an unconstitutional piece of legislation but also a highly dangerous and far-reaching one. It would weaken the president's ability to deal with unexpected international crises and also, perhaps more significant, send a message of divided government and general national permissiveness to the communist world. Opposition to measures set forth by congressional doves, which included withdrawal-for-prisoners resolutions and amendments affording amnesty for draft evaders, became the primary project of both the Republican Right and conservative activists more critical of the administration's current Vietnam strategies. Conservatives' concentration on Congress was a way of uniting against the liberal onslaught, but it was also the obvious action in light of their view that the handling of the war might soon be out of the president's hands. The drive to gain greater power in Congress helped build conservatives' strength during the 1970s, as they pursued control of crucial committees, most notably the Senate Armed Services Committee, with greater vigor. While this had the effect of limiting congressional activism in foreign policy in the long term, it helped enhance conservatives' political power.[42] The summer of 1972, however, brought little relief to conservatives, as end-the-war amendments were introduced in Congress with greater frequency and were more restrictive with regard to presidential action in Southeast Asia.

Such anti-war initiatives brought conservatives together on Vietnam, and by early August the conservative machine was fully involved in the campaign to limit the anti-war resolutions. Charging that amendments to cut off funding for the war in Southeast Asia would fundamentally weaken the president's ability to negotiate an end to the war, Goldwater asserted that because of such action "there is a very real possibility that the war in Vietnam will be prolonged." Goldwater attested that the United States had acted fairly toward the enemy in negotiations but could not simply abandon South Vietnam. He allied the issues of patriotic duty and American values with security considerations. Such "immoral and unwise action," he said, would "mark the United States as an unstable, inconsistent and weak nation who could not be relied upon by its other allies to honor its commitments to them, or indeed even to protect its own interests." While attacking liberals for giving "false encouragement to our enemies," Goldwater used the occasion to reiterate his belief in the significance of the war's outcome to future American credibility.[43]

Conservatives resorted to the motif of liberals having aided the enemy to delegitimize the anti-war interpretation of American interests and win popular backing for escalated military initiatives. As the negotiating process intensified in September and October, conservatives were keen to highlight liberals' role in comforting the enemy and undermining negotiations for the benefit not only of wavering congressional figures but also of the administration. The fear that the presidential election might encourage Nixon to succumb to the demands of his liberal critics hardened conservatives' efforts to shore up both conservative and popular support for the president's policies, despite their private anxieties over the possible outcome of the negotiating process.

Nixon's steadfastness in the face of congressional attacks gained him a certain measure of credibility and support among conservatives, but he did not possess a free rein. The reduced fervor of the pro-war movement notwithstanding, the nature of the Vietnam settlement remained of great concern, above all among conservative leaders. Goldwater believed Nixon had staked too much of his personal and political credibility on successfully concluding the war to contemplate imposing a weak solution on the South Vietnamese. But by 1972, having endorsed Vietnamization and encouraged support for the administration's Vietnam strategy, Goldwater and leading conservatives had staked a great deal of their own credibility on Nixon's achieving his peace with honor. Having contributed much legitimacy to Nixon's doctrine for responding to the defense needs of smaller allies, conservatives found it difficult, when it came to Vietnam, to disentangle their political fortunes from those of Nixon. As Stanton Evans noted, with not a small degree of despondency, "Conservative political leaders have large investments of energy and emotion in the Nixon presidency." Evans summed up as follows: "What Frank Meyer has called the conservative 'failure of nerve' in the wake of the 1964 Goldwater loss, plus a dose of wishful thinking about Nixon, has issued in calamity for the conservative cause.

... Having handed the GOP over to the Nixon pragmatists, the Republican right will be quite awhile in recapturing it. The power they had in '68 they will not have again in '72 or '76."[44] Rather than result in absolute backing of Nixon's continuation of Vietnamization, such investments led conservatives to again demand that the United States undertake a symbolic knockout blow against North Vietnam to force negotiations.

In late 1972 conservative leaders relied on the pro-war symbols and methods that had traditionally been employed by more populist agents such as the veterans' organizations. Employing the popular image of a brutal enemy, Buckley argued for the bombing of the Red River dikes on the grounds not only that the North Vietnamese had shown no restraint in acts of "terrorism, mass executions and sabotage" but also that to do so would be a reasonable humanitarian endeavor by the United States. "Wars should be fought as humanely as they can be fought," he stated, "but we ought to know from the experience of the last seven years that it is hardly humane to drag out a war so that people get killed and inconvenienced not over a period of months but a period of years."[45] Buckley continued to voice his frustration with Nixon's refusal to undertake such measures, a position that spoke not to a fundamental difference of opinion over the most prudent means of ending the war but to the public divide in conservative ranks. Buckley's terminology reflected his rejection of the anti-war movement's claim to the moral high ground, but the language and sentiments invoked by pro-war adherents of the administration implied that Nixon's separation from the anti-war position might not be wide enough to sustain the support of such key figures as Goldwater and Thurmond. Both men distinguished the success of Nixon's policies in relation to those proposed by their anti-war counterparts in Congress, yet both prescribed that military measures beyond those being considered by the administration were necessary to end the war on terms acceptable to the United States and its ally.

Goldwater remarked that Nixon, with the announcement of troop reductions in May, "was, in effect, announcing the virtual disengagement of American forces from all Indochina areas of war except the air."[46] He continued to believe the air campaign would be the determinant in assuring the success of Vietnamization and the collapse of the North Vietnamese campaign of aggression. During September and October he repeated conservatives' unbending position that the United States would have to keep up an air role in Vietnam or at the very least unmistakably threaten a return to bombing if the agreement was violated. While he had seemingly accepted the administration's policy of assuring South Vietnam the chance of survival, Goldwater's rhetoric emphasized the necessity of forcing Hanoi and by extension its foreign supporters to accept an American-imposed settlement. The senator appeared willing to accept a great deal less than conservatives had originally deemed the minimum outcome in Vietnam, but he was still worried about the final means by which settlement was reached.

Conservatives were united in their demands that additional military measures be brought to bear to strengthen South Vietnam before the American withdrawal was completed. Thurmond's spate of announcements and resolutions on Vietnam were prompted by White House requests but also signaled his demand for a final military push. He praised Nixon's "bold action in blockading the ports and interdicting the supply lines." In his eyes, that such action "would threaten us with reprisals by the Soviet Union or China" had been unequivocally proved to be a myth. His position reflected his requirement that no further concessions be offered to North Vietnam, particularly in light of the apparent effectiveness of the recent bombing campaign. The ostensibly "courageous military action of the South Vietnamese" only advanced Thurmond's predilection for a bold strike to achieve some measure of victory.[47]

Division within conservative ranks was acute during this period, but the leaders of the political movement reached a measure of consensus on Vietnam. Both those who publicly supported Nixon and those who vociferously challenged his foreign policies pressured the administration to negotiate with Hanoi only after additional militaristic attacks had been undertaken. The positions of both groups intimated potential disdain for the final agreements on ending the war. Kissinger was confident about the prospects of a negotiated settlement during October 1972, in part because of Hanoi's willingness to separate the military and political issues.

By this time it therefore seemed possible that conservatives might reject the settlement.

Nixon, worried by the possibility of a preelection turn by Thieu, warned his chief negotiator, "We must have Thieu as a willing partner in making any agreement." "It cannot," he said, "be a shotgun marriage."[48] Kissinger was supremely proud of his achievements, writing to Haig, "The first thing to keep in mind is that we have an excellent agreement within our grasp." While acknowledging some "soft spots," an inevitable feature of a settlement that was "short of total victory," Kissinger promised it would be "clear to the public who made the major concessions."

By this time, Kissinger's interpretation of success did not harmonize with that of the South Vietnamese government or indeed that of conservatives. In a telegram to Haig, which was to be discussed with the president, Kissinger remarked that there was "no conceivable way to make the GVN [government of Vietnam] enthusiastic about the withdrawal of American forces and the beginning of a political contest that they have been dreading for many years." Thieu was advised to claim the settlement "as a victory." Kissinger averred that "half the battle will be for the GVN to act confidently and boldly in political and psychological terms."[49] Despite Kissinger's optimistic language and Nixon's politically motivated assurances of his commitment to securing a successful agreement, the administration's exasperation with the Thieu government threatened to exceed its anger at its enemies' intransigence. Having managed to secure popular support for his withdrawal policies, Nixon faced a severe problem with the Saigon regime. Thieu threatened not only to unravel the fabric binding many pro-war conservatives to the administration but also to utterly discredit Nixon's proclamations of peace with honor.

Conservatives wanted reassurances on two particular issues: Thieu's support of the agreement; and the certainty of postwar American support of South Vietnam. Nixon's clandestine warning to Thieu that even his most ardent adherents in the United States, namely, Goldwater and Stennis, would publicly call for the abandonment of Thieu if he failed to sanction the agreements reached by Kissinger and Le Duc Tho was, in fact, exaggerated.

While Stennis was determined to see an end to the war, Goldwater and the Republican Right continued to privately pressure Nixon to force the North Vietnamese to comply with terms more acceptable to the South Vietnamese. Kissinger may have been somewhat disingenuous when he commented in 1979 that "requiring a ceasefire before withdrawal had become a conservative proposal," particularly in Congress, by 1972. Yet the White House stressed the pressures emanating from Congress, and Kissinger later noted that amendments requiring a ceasefire prior to withdrawal were consistently defeated in both houses.[50] However unlikely, the possibility that Congress would demand an end to the war through resolution and achieve this aim through budgetary constraints severely undermined the proclivity of figures such as Goldwater and Thurmond to allow the war to continue and encouraged rosy analyses of Hanoi's willingness to capitulate in the wake of U.S. military action since April. Speaking in October 1972, Goldwater asserted, "I think Hanoi is about to give up. They realize they can't win this war. . . . I feel it in my bones."[51]

One of the principal concerns of conservatives was that the proposed settlement was vague in its articulation of how the treaty was to be overseen and implemented. Nixon assured wary conservatives like Walter Judd that "I will never be pressured into approving any agreement which I find in any respect to be unclear or unsatisfactory."[52] Judd had earlier been buoyed by reports that Nixon had refused anti-war pressures to force President Thieu to accept a coalition government before open elections took place in South Vietnam.[53] The White House propaganda machine was used to fortify the pro-administration stances of people like Reagan and Buckley. Reagan promisingly said to Buckley, "Having talked to Henry Kissinger . . . I am inclined to believe that our faith will be vindicated."[54] Buckley's acute anxiety was tempered in an October meeting with Kissinger, and he proceeded to loudly support the Nixon campaign. He commented that "others who rely on my judgment" had also been relieved by Kissinger's assurances. He restated his personal commitment to Kissinger but said he had been anxious the administration might have been forced to succumb to "force majeure." Still, during the final days of the presidential campaign, Buckley spoke in support of Nixon in a number of European capitals.[55]

The White House's assurances were not entirely unfounded, as both Nixon and Kissinger were positive about the potential agreement at this time. Conservatives were keen, however, to avoid a settlement before the election, believing that Nixon's domestic victory would undermine Hanoi's supposed reliance on American politics and social division to pressure the administration to negotiate an end to the war. While some, particularly Rusher, believed Nixon might lose interest in Southeast Asia once his electoral success had been secured, the majority of conservatives held that the American negotiating position would be stronger after November 6. Speaking on October 28, 1972, Rusher said that Nixon had not yet "surrendered any essential points." He claimed that Nixon would have a free hand after the election but was unclear as to what course the president would follow. Rusher hoped Nixon would stick to his guns and "insist upon a self-determined future for the people of South Vietnam," but he was pessimistic.[56] Only with the collapse of the negotiating process was conservatives' skepticism marginally allayed. It now seemed clear the administration would honor its commitment to South Vietnam. Thus Nixon did not face an outright ultimatum from his conservative backers; the existence of a common enemy in the form of George McGovern resuscitated a great deal of conservative approval of Nixon. But the waning fortitude of conservatives' general support for his Vietnam strategy augured the very real possibility that they would question and possibly reject the final settlement.[57] Given the widespread popularity of Nixon's peace with honor among grassroots pro-war activists, conservatives did not hold a great deal of political power at this time. Their opposition to the settlement could, however, reveal the weaknesses in Nixon's alleged peace.

Indeed, once the liberal bogeyman had been disposed of in the election, Nixon faced a resurgent pro-war lobby determined to take advantage of the relief from electoral politics. From sources such as *National Review* and *Human Events* as well as veterans' organizations and the conservative caucus in Congress, Nixon heard earnest calls for introducing military measures to finally secure compromise from the North Vietnamese. Although Nixon could take a measure of comfort in popular opinion during this period, he and his advisers could not be certain of evading a reactionary conservative lobby. Only days after Nixon's electoral victory Goldwater reiterated his assertion that he would "make a mud puddle of Vietnam" given the chance.[58] Furthermore, while the administration waited until after the election to address the possibility of a settlement, Nixon's actions during November seemed only to result in additional concessions to the enemy. His declaration that he would not accept an "unsatisfactory" settlement, coupled with his steady emphasis on securing the return of POWs, persuaded the wider population that he could achieve peace with honor. While not immune to such popular contentment, conservative leaders ultimately proved harder to satisfy.

Conservatives' unease was substantiated in the November report of the Freedom Leadership Foundation. While acknowledging that the United States had secured important concessions, particularly Hanoi's acceptance that a coalition government would not be imposed on South Vietnam, a number of doubts were outstanding. The report claimed there had been inadequate participation by the South Vietnamese government in the negotiations, that the provisions for enforcement of the agreement's protocols were limited, and that the United States failed to fulfill its political commitments to Saigon. North Vietnam, for its part, failed to acknowledge the extent of its military presence in South Vietnam, Cambodia, and Laos. The tone of partiality in the agreement was especially troubling. "The language of the cease-fire document," the report lamented, "is phrased to imply much guilt on the part of the U.S. while North Vietnam emerges completely guiltless." The "world can only regard the document," it concluded, "as a *mea culpa*."[59]

The October peace terms, therefore, not only challenged conservatives' strategic and security concerns regarding Vietnam but also undermined the moral commitment undertaken by the United States. Thieu's offer to resign one month before the elections, furthermore, suggested his illegitimacy as the head of government, while conservatives were convinced that the planned elections would allow the communists to eventually usurp the Saigon government. Goldwater strongly, albeit privately, criticized the White House for its failure to declare its continued backing of President Thieu. He referenced Sen. Charles Percy's recent threat to President Thieu that the entire Senate would cease its support for the war if Thieu refused to accept the president's peace proposals.[60] In response to Goldwater, Haig claimed that Percy was not speaking on behalf of the administration. Haig assured Goldwater that "the survival and independence of our ally have been the central purpose of the President's policy all along, both in Vietnamization and in negotiations."[61]

Yet conservatives were dismayed by the administration's willingness to accept a ceasefire-in-place and were appalled by the suggestion that the United States pay reparations, as they deemed postwar aid, to North Vietnam. At the Conservative Awards Dinner in November, Vice President Agnew assured his disillusioned audience that the United States would end its involvement in Vietnam only when North Vietnam stopped its aggression. Agnew's speech spoke to conservatives' anxieties but also hinted at their willingness to accept a negotiated settlement should it be couched in appropriate language and should it suggest that South Vietnam's survival was secure. In the face of détente, the proposed settlement was unpalatable. Reached by negotiation and compromise, it was unfavorable. In the absence of unfaltering and unrestricted U.S. aid to South Vietnam it was unacceptable. But with a dramatic show of force by the United States, the agreement proved tolerable and, for some, even a meaningful victory over communism.

Snatching Victory: Operation Linebacker II

The administration needed to persuade the military too to fall in line. Addressing the JCS on November 30, Nixon tried to subvert General Westmoreland's recent insistence that a total withdrawal of North Vietnamese troops from South Vietnam was necessary. Nixon had met with Westmoreland on October 20 in order to get his views on the proposed agreement. Westmoreland stated that "the political framework provided for a ceasefire in place without commitment, and this amounted to a de facto cessation by Thieu of sovereignty over substantial portions of South Vietnamese territories." He concluded that Thieu could not accept such a settlement. Nixon stated that the existing agreement offered "a fair chance to the people of South Vietnam to retain their freedom" but assured Westmoreland that "within this framework, the United States would do all that was necessary by way of support, including strong military action if required, should violations occur."[62] The issue of complete North Vietnamese withdrawal, long the bedrock of any settlement that conservative leaders said they would endorse, now appeared beyond reach. Nixon tried to calm the anxieties of the JCS and win their concerted approval by categorically vowing that "if Hanoi violates the agreement, the U.S. response will be all out."

Nixon claimed that because Hanoi would be unable to launch an offensive in the South without additional manpower the removal of existing troops was an unnecessary precondition for settlement. Kissinger said, "Hanoi cannot keep its army in the South. It must either attack or withdraw." Claiming the matter was simply one "of principle with Hanoi," he denied that any such attack would occur—"we have provided de facto arrangements." Hanoi, Nixon and Kissinger confirmed, "has fallen off from what had been its long standing political demands." Success had been achieved.

Such positive interpretations of the real, long-term effects of the proposed agreements aside, in order to win the support of the JCS and conservative leaders the administration was forced to rely heavily on the assumption that Congress would discontinue funding the war once it reconvened in January. The United States had, according to Nixon, "stayed one step ahead of the sheriff, just missing fund cutoffs." The American people, he continued, were also demanding an end to the war on terms commensurate with those already reached by Kissinger in Paris. He appealed for the total support of the JCS by claiming the moral high ground and accentuating the cultural significance of portraying the negotiations in positive terms. "It is important," Nixon declared, "that America's military express pride in the accomplishment of the proposed agreement. If all of the sacrifices are not to be in vain, the military cannot criticize it. The American left will do this with the view of making it appear that the war itself was useless."[63] National pride demanded a united, positive response.

Pro-war activists were quick to point out the concessions made by the enemy, invariably as part of an attack on anti-war critics. Still, there was no denying the outstanding weaknesses of the proposed accords and no denying Thieu's obvious doubts about the implications of the agreement. The attitudes of pro-war conservatives had, if anything, hardened since the lull in the negotiating process in October. Once the negotiating process broke down almost entirely on December 13, the conservatives' position seemed fixed.

The Linebacker II bombing campaign, a devastating sustained attack against North Vietnam, was initiated on December 18.[64] It was not intended to fundamentally weaken the Hanoi government, although it was expected that the North Vietnamese proclivity to negotiate would increase. While militarily significant, Linebacker II was principally designed to reassure both Thieu and Nixon's most ardent pro-war constituency, his conservative supporters, that the proposed accords would bring peace with honor. Believing the bombings were necessary to enhance his personal integrity, Nixon looked, as so often before, to his place in history. The bombing was a last-ditch boon to Vietnamization, although it was not expected to fundamentally weaken the North's potential to secure its power in the South in the long term. It was, rather, intended to magnify Nixon's legacy vis-à-vis Vietnam and to afford pro-war advocates of both Vietnamization and military escalation final justification for their policies. Conservatives did not fail to take the opportunity to warrant their position, despite the waves of domestic and international outrage the bombings provoked. Widespread fears that Nixon intended to use the interruption in the negotiating process to facilitate the bombing of the dikes and other points of strategic interest in North Vietnam simply fueled the pro-war movement's campaign in support of the president.

Human Events, which had strongly criticized the proposed agreements, came out in full support of the bombing and contended that an acceptable treaty might be forthcoming as a direct result of the military campaign. The air war, a front-page editorial claimed, "underscores the President's desire to prevent Hanoi from exploiting a 'stall' during the peace talks for the purpose of rebuilding its military machine." Claiming that the military campaigns of April and May had brought the North Vietnamese back to the negotiating table, *Human Events* noted the significance of Hanoi's refusal to formally break off the talks, "a sure sign that Hanoi is desperate to get out from under American bombing raids." While acting as a "solid signal . . . that the U.S. is likely to make a similar massive retaliation if the Communists flagrantly violate any cease-fire agreement that is finally reached," the bombings were considered necessary simply because the peace terms of October had been "extremely generous, far too generous as far as we were concerned." The editors noted that since October "some critical parts of the agreement were apparently tentatively revised in Saigon's favor in the December negotiations." They remained skeptical, however.[65]

The pattern of support for the bombings was also evident at *National Review* and in the proclamations and speeches of veterans' organizations and conservative politicians. Almost all such sources of endorsement of the president's actions, however, exhibited the belief that the campaign would continue until North Vietnam at least stated its intention to withdraw its forces from the South. Strenuously insisting that the bombing was the logical and "honorable . . . consequence of the breakdown of the negotiations in Paris as a result of the North Vietnamese mickey mouse," Buckley held that Hanoi's refusal to allow realistic supervision of the withdrawal led directly to the breakdown of negotiations.[66] Citing Gen. Maxwell Taylor, who stated, "We're a long way from peace in Southeast Asia if the North Vietnamese forces are left with arms in their hands in South Viet Nam," *Human Events* concluded that this long-term goal was within reach: "With the resumption of the bombing, perhaps the Administration will eventually be able to produce an agreement with Hanoi that is neither vague, nor allusive, nor indirect, but very specific, even on the subject of getting Hanoi to promise to evacuate its troops in the South."[67] Goldwater was eager to use the bombing campaign to vindicate his philosophical objections to limited war. He lambasted those who challenged the administration: "I insist there is no such thing as a limited war. . . . When you go into a war, the more effort and power you put into it the quicker you win it—and at less cost and fewer casualties. President Nixon understands this but his predecessors apparently did not."⁶⁸

No matter such positive pronouncements, the fear of a cease-fire-in-place remained. Thurmond warned Nixon of the danger of allowing enemy troops to stay in the south: "This could be the foundation for North Vietnam to take over South Vietnam after our final withdrawal in the future. In such an outcome, history will judge that the sacrifice of American lives was in vain."⁶⁹ Buckley pushed the administration to fully implement Vietnamization. American pilots should be viewed as technicians, to be eventually replaced by South Vietnamese pilots, while Saigon made all decisions to use them in bombing the North. While it may have been too late for Nixon "to turn to his advantage . . . the appeal of a true Vietnamization," it was not too late to engage in the real motions of "sharing military authority with Saigon," in such a way as to give Saigon "the principal tactical authority over the use of such military weapons as are needed to accomplish the objective."⁷⁰ This statement hinted at the conservative belief that the potential agreements were largely a means of achieving the handover of military authority to the South Vietnamese and to afford U.S. withdrawal before the fighting between the two Vietnams resumed.

The tenor of the patriotic campaigns of the previous three years severely undercut conservatives' ability, and desire to mount a strong challenge to the administration. Thurmond's emphasis on the legacy of American sacrifice therefore proved more compelling than Buckley's analysis of policy. Congressional opposition to Nixon's policies only served to heighten conservatives' willingness to accept the limited gains the administration had made. Members of Congress such as Goldwater demanded a united conservative response to the bombing, largely because of the threat from the Left. Judd said Nixon must ignore the "denunciations" of the scorned "peace-dreamer." Your "high place in history," he wrote to the president, "will be won not by yielding to short-range desires or demands, but by patiently sticking to principle and integrity as you are doing."⁷¹ Goldwater, fearing that the year-long divide within the ranks of the conservative movement might inhibit vociferous praise for the bombing, wrote to Buckley on December 21 to "get behind the President in his decision to forge peace in Vietnam."⁷² Buckley assured Goldwater that he agreed with this position, pointing to his recent and forthcoming columns as evidence of his approval of the president's peace.⁷³ While neither Goldwater nor Buckley was entirely candid in his statement of unambiguous support for the president, they were both swayed by the intensity of opposition to the bombing campaign. It spurred both camps of the conservative political divide and more populist pro-war groups such as the VFW to rally to the administration's defense.

Popular opposition to the bombing led, perhaps inevitably, to conservatives' acceptance that the wider public simply would not countenance further military measures. Aware of the likelihood that Congress would further limit resources for the continuation of the war, Goldwater, Thurmond and others were intent on reaching a settlement. This position was reinforced by the increasingly vocal and troublesome demands for immediate settlement emanating from the ranks of the POW/MIA campaign. POW/MIA organizations, including the National League of Families, pressured the president to secure a settlement and release of prisoners with speed. In the last months of 1972 the patience of these organizations was wearing thin, and Nixon could no longer count on them to back a continuation of the war. In many respects the movement Nixon had helped create for his administration's benefit became something of a Frankenstein's monster and was ultimately beyond government influence. Having persuaded the public that the POW issue was a priority in the war, it was difficult to call for patience when this noble goal was in sight.

While conservative leaders in Congress faced the possibility of further alienating their core constituencies by supporting a settlement that did not achieve victory, they faced potentially more damaging foes in a weary public and disaffected POW movement. This pattern of opposing anti-war critics was matched by a curtailment of minimum objectives on the part of pro-war activists. This resulted in the rallying of pro-war support for the accords eventually reached after North Vietnam asked for the cessation of bombing as a precondition for a return to negotiations. While certainly not the victory that advocates of military escalation had envisioned, this apparent concession on the part of the North Vietnamese seemed exactly the quid pro quo in favor of the Americans they had demanded as a precondition for any achievement of peace with honor. By January 1973 it was clear the administration would not or could not continue the war for much longer. Conservatives were unwilling to be seen as extreme in matters of foreign policy and knew that such would be the result of a continued commitment to the war. Despite all their protests of October and November, in January 1973 conservatives aided the Nixon administration's subtle abandonment of South Vietnam.

Withdrawal ... with a Smile and a Whimper

The popular pro-war campaigns that began with such rallies as the Support Our Boys in Vietnam march in New York in 1967 and that culminated in the POW awareness programs of VIVA and the Project Appreciation activities of YAF boosted confidence in Nixon's policies of withdrawal from Vietnam. While not necessarily the intended consequence of such endeavors, support for the troops, veterans, and POWs helped popularize Nixon's efforts to secure complete U.S. troop withdrawal. Public confidence in withdrawal was also conditioned by two additional factors: widespread rejection of assertions that it had been essential for the United States to intervene in Vietnam in order to maintain its national security interests; and Nixon's foreign policy successes in 1971 and 1972. Vietnamization, when tied to the recent bombardment of North Vietnam, seemed to imply the saving of America's honor, which by 1972 had become the measurement of success or victory in Vietnam at a popular level. Attention focused on the internal dynamics of division within America, such that local veterans' organizations and patriotic groups, taking the lead of national organizations like the American Legion and VFW, pushed their members to work to secure postwar victory on the domestic front. Recognizing that the war had brutalized American society, many who characterized themselves as supporters of the war welcomed the likelihood of peace in late 1972.

The conservative political movement also found itself brutalized by the upheavals of the Nixon years and brutalized as well by the divisiveness of foreign policy issues, once the terrain on which conservatives could reliably reach widespread unity. Formal consultations among conservative leaders did not take place in January 1973 as they had during the summer of 1971. While coverage of the agreement was offered in both *Human Events* and *National Review*, neither publication seemed capable of mustering the enthusiasm for the bold stands, either positive or negative, that had previously characterized the editors' attitudes to matters of foreign policy.

In the final week of negotiations *Human Events* reiterated its position of November that North Vietnamese troops must be withdrawn from the South, arguing that the importance of this issue "should not be underestimated." The editors said that the "final wording ... must eliminate all innuendo that the United States is somehow guilty of aggression in Indochina" and held that the foreign aid package could still be understood as reparations. Asserting that the United States must make clear its intention to "unleash its bombers and warships if the North Vietnamese flagrantly violate the conditions of the peace agreement," *Human Events* concluded, "The United States is now writing what could be the closing chapter of the Viet Nam war, but whether that chapter will have a happy and honorable ending is still very much up in the air."[74] The final agreement was most certainly not in keeping with the *Human Events* line, and yet the journal was largely uncritical of it.

Rather than list its faults, the lead editorial in the issue published after the announcements of January 23 highlighted "what these accords are not." "They are *not* a sell-out," the editors pronounced, "in the McGovern style." *Human Events* subsequently offered details of the numerous ways in which the accords contradicted the demands of anti-war critics. While asserting that the forced withdrawal of North Vietnamese troops from the South would have been the preferred outcome, the journal's editors conceded that "the agreement hammered out in Paris looks far better than we dared imagine after hearing Dr. Kissinger's statement last October." Rather than dwell entirely on the specifics of the agreement, conservatives again insisted that the United States must clarify its resolve to resume the air war if violations became evident. Prompting Nixon to remain vigilant in his unwavering support for the South Vietnamese and in the oversight of the agreements, the editors defined their understanding of the accords: "The fact is . . . that this prospect [renewed American involvement] should be very thinkable, for precisely down that path lies the only chance of preserving that freedom of South Vietnam, Cambodia and Laos. For, as the most recent B-52 strikes over Hanoi have so clearly demonstrated, the North Vietnamese leaders are perfectly willing to listen to reason when faced with severe and painful punishment."[75]

By renewed involvement, *Human Events* meant air attacks, not a return of U.S. ground forces to Southeast Asia. The ACU/*Human Events* line thus offered conditional support for the accords, support that no doubt would have been very unlikely had the Nixon administration not administered a supposedly decisive blow to the North Vietnamese during the final month of negotiations. Considering the power of the anti-war lobby in Congress, the likelihood that the administration would be willing, or indeed able, to facilitate a return to the air war over Vietnam was very low. Although Nixon may have shared conservatives' willingness to upholding the agreement in this way, Stephen Randolph accurately notes that any such expectation was highly speculative and indeed improbable, given the domestic mood.[76] Despite this reality, conservatives helped legitimize the accords by suggesting that they could secure South Vietnam's future.

This position was evident among both pro-war supporters and detractors of the administration's policies. Thurmond publicly voiced his respect for the president's achievement of "worthy peace goals" and said that "capitulation on lesser terms would not have insured an honorable peace and protected the freedom of the people of South Vietnam and Southeast Asia."[77] Thurmond, invariably more concerned with the domestic implications of an apparent defeat for the United States, focused primarily on the return of American POWs and lambasted the anti-war movement for its role in prolonging the war. His preoccupation with the North

Vietnamese capability of returning to warfare was never wholly assuaged, but, like much of the Republican Right, he retained faith in the proposition that the United States would continue to ensure South Vietnam's survival via the threat of a resumption of the air war that had recently appeared so successful.

Goldwater's response to the accords was similarly positive: he offered unambiguous praise for the administration's achievement of a peace treaty that he believed could not have been secured without Nixon's bold military measures: "The ceasefire and peace agreement in Vietnam marks one of the most important victories the United States has ever scored over Communist aggression. . . . [It] is a tribute to the concept of firmness, strength and realism in the conduct of American foreign policies and armed intervention." The agreement, Goldwater further contended, could not have been reached "even four weeks earlier" because Hanoi "stubbornly refused to settle until it became clear that the peace movement in America had failed."[78] When questioned on January 24, Kissinger explicitly stated that the air campaign had broken the deadline and made peace possible.[79] While the accords may not have been entirely harmonious with the requirements of conservatives, having been irrevocably tied to the bombing of North Vietnam they were sufficiently reasonable to afford conservatives the opportunity to hold that "weak-kneed American pacifists" had been defeated.[80] Rather than offer detailed analyses of the accords, conservatives in Congress touted the peace achieved through bold military measures, castigating their liberal predecessors for having pursued a policy of limited war.

Among mainstream conservatives there was general acceptance that the accords were far preferable to anything Johnson could have achieved and widespread acknowledgment that they constituted peace with honor. Having offered only grudging support for the peace terms of October, *National Review* lauded the bombing, and Buckley offered resounding praise for the accords. Burnham and Rusher were less effusive in their praise of Nixon, but neither pronounced the settlement a failure.[81] Rather, *National Review* believed that peace with honor was secure so long as the United States remained vigilant in its oversight of the treaty's terms and continued to support South Vietnam in any future military campaigns. In the end, both men offered nothing but outright praise for Nixon's achievement of peace with honor.

Where opposition to the accords existed within conservative circles it emanated primarily from groups that had already fully broken with the administration. Nixon's inability to secure the endorsement of the pro-war student communities proved highly disadvantageous. In the main, VIVA, by now dominated by the National League of Families, offered hearty praise for the administration's role in securing the return of American POWs, but in the long term the POW movement's growing suspicions of Nixon and Kissinger overshadowed their achievements in 1973. YAF, in a bellicose move that further divided the conservative movement, initially questioned the terms of the settlement and offered a cutting indictment of the accords after its February board meeting. Seeing the agreement as a reward to North Vietnam's aggression, YAF officially stated that the settlement prepared the way for a quick renewal of war: "We have reaped at best something slightly worse than a stalemate in the war, and more likely an ultimate defeat, at a high price in blood, treasure, domestic discontent and radicalization, and a weakening of anti-communist sentiment. It was a high price for a bankrupt policy, and conservatives might want to ask themselves if they made the distinction as clear as they should have between that policy and the one of victory they preferred."

YAF leaders believed, as did much of the conservative movement, that liberals in Congress and the anti-war movement were principally responsible for thwarting the American effort. YAF was disheartened by the fact that North Vietnamese troops were permitted to remain in South Vietnam but acknowledged the argument made by conservatives that "this is the best the U.S. can get, that treaty or no treaty, the possibility is strong that Congress would have ended the war this session by ending appropriations for it."[82] The potential opposition of the anti-war movement to any American response to North Vietnamese violations of the accords determined the level of YAF's opposition in early 1973. They were, again, attempting to push Nixon to the right by highlighting the futility of trying to assuage liberals in foreign policy matters. Much of YAF's concern with the accords, however, related to its fierce opposition to demands in Congress that amnesty be granted to draft resisters. It was mainly as a result of the possibility that Congress would stipulate this provision as a precondition for passage of the agreement that YAF protested at Capitol Hill and organized anti-amnesty groups.[83] Indeed, the larger pro-war movement, detrimentally divided since 1971, managed to unite in opposition to amnesty and to postwar aid to North Vietnam.

Rather than challenge the specifics of the agreements, therefore, conservative political leaders and organizations joined the wider pro-war movement in haranguing liberals for thwarting the president's efforts in Southeast Asia. In opposing amnesty for draft resisters, they attempted to usurp the moral high ground from those who had apparently made good use of it during the war. In focusing on this issue, they revealed the weak state of their genuine commitment to South Vietnam. In the words of YAF, the final month of the war "proved correct" the conservatives' argument "that America's aim in the war should have been to *win*, with maximum use of force in minimum amount of time."[84] Throughout 1973 conservative leaders paid more attention to the righteousness of their wartime position than to ensuring that South Vietnam received necessary aid. The war, with conservatives' acquiescence, was over, and what was left was the need to refute the liberal opinion that the war was an unnecessary and unjust cause.

The Postwar Challenge

Among much of the pro-war movement the Paris accords, the withdrawal of U.S. troops, and the greatly vaunted return of American POWs brought the Vietnam conflict to a conclusion of sorts. Veterans' groups and patriotic organizations especially promoted welcome home parades for veterans and concentrated their lobbying efforts on highlighting the financial, educational, and medical needs of U.S. servicemen. In so doing, the organizations publicized the sacrifices made by Vietnam veterans and implicitly advanced the image of the war as a just cause, one misrepresented by a biased media and misunderstood by the public at large. The

American Legion and VFW recommended that all local posts organize parades to welcome the last troops from Vietnam, as they had done throughout the war, and also that celebratory events be held in honor of the American POWs who were released in March 1973.

The Committee for Responsible Patriotism, which was associated with the original Support Our Boys in Vietnam Parade Committee, organized a parade in New York City on March 31, 1973. The Home with Honor parade on Broadway was intended to pay tribute to those who had served in Southeast Asia. It was billed as a patriotic event, and those who participated were said by Raymond Gimmler to have turned their backs on the VVAW. Some 60,000 people took part in the parade, and 250,000 people were estimated to have watched from the sidelines. The parade did not receive the same level of media coverage as the original parades. In the postwar period Gimmler and the Committee for Responsible Patriotism became more and more involved with the POW/MIA issue and in 1983 launched a series of lawsuits against the PBS documentary series *Vietnam: A Television History*. They, along with Accuracy in Media, maintained that the episode "Homefront USA" portrayed only anti-war demonstrators and paid insufficient attention to prowar activities. This reflected the committee's claims that the news media had misrepresented America's military progress during the war and had therefore stimulated anti-war sentiment at home.

Veterans' organizations were joined by populist conservatives, including such individuals as Helms and Reagan, in centering public attention on the faults of liberals in the handling of the war. Rather than delve into the accords, these individuals and organizations seemed remarkably unwilling to subject the agreement ending a war for which they had so vigorously campaigned to anything more than the most perfunctory public criticism and questioning. The war itself had been lost in the domestic arena long before January 1973, and all that remained of the victory for which pro-war activists had struggled was the possibility of defining the war's meaning in the popular imagination and using the mistakes of Vietnam to redirect future foreign policymaking. During the late 1970s conservative leaders like Reagan demonstrated that they had ably learned the public opinion lessons of Vietnam.

They understood that redirecting foreign policy was dependent on interpreting the Vietnam experience positively for the American people. Ultimately, they would focus on the ideals perpetuated by campaigns such as the We Support Our Boys rallies, the National Unity Week of 1969, YAF's Tell it to Hanoi initiatives, and VIVA's POW drives in order to construct a positive interpretation of Vietnam. While conservatives certainly emphasized the possibility that a military victory could have been achieved, politically savvy leaders like Reagan identified the greater utility in highlighting the patriotism associated with honoring those who served and denigrating the anti-war movement. Indeed, the lost cause became a powerful source of unity in the conservative movement as a whole. Having disagreed over whether or not to support Nixon's policies, traditionalist conservatives could unite in lambasting liberals' failure to support South Vietnam after 1973. Perhaps more important, the sharp differences in how intellectual and social conservatives viewed the importance of Vietnam became less relevant once the war was over. Surprisingly, the message of social conservatives that military intervention had been mistaken became powerful within the movement. Furthermore, political leaders who had for so long dwelled on the national security considerations at stake in Vietnam increasingly domesticated their interpretations of the war's meaning. For conservatives, it rapidly became a war that had been fought between Americans; this interpretation of Vietnam helped polarize American opinion in ways that ultimately benefited the conservative political movement.

Few pro-war leaders did an about-face in the wake of America's failure in Southeast Asia. Meaney, who in early 1973 declared that the enemy's goals had been thwarted, later publicly admitted his regret at having supported Nixon's policies. Meaney was unusual among pro-war leaders; unlike conservatives, he expressed his belief that the continuation of the war had been a mistake.[85] His views were shared by many Americans who questioned the necessity of engaging in a land war in Asia in the first place. Goldwater, too, became acutely disillusioned with the president in the wake of the Watergate scandal and in turn questioned Nixon's resolve toward Vietnam.[86] He continued to argue, however, that the bombing campaign of December 1972 led directly to the peace settlement and insisted that the Paris accords "were not a defeat."[87] Discussing the accords in 1979, Goldwater admitted that they could not be "considered a victory for the free world," but neither did they represent defeat. The accords had "appeared to ensure the independence of South Vietnam," secured the release of American POWs, and recognized the integrity of Laos and Cambodia.[88] In many respects Goldwater's analysis of the agreement continued to be ambiguous and conditioned by his long-standing commitment to the war and the president. Rather than disavow Nixon's policies of Vietnamization and withdrawal, Goldwater laid the blame for the American debacle in Southeast Asia firmly at the door of the Johnson administration and those doves in Congress who refused to provide postwar aid to the beleaguered Saigon regime.[89] The process of blaming liberals for America's failure began during the war, but it became the dominant motif of conservatives' responses to Vietnam after 1972.

The Linebacker campaigns of May and December 1972 earned conservatives' praise. But they also made it clear that neither the public nor the White House was willing to endorse a full-scale bombing campaign for an indefinite period. Having supported the process of Vietnamization since 1969, conservatives were unable to delegitimize the policy that increasingly meant abandonment of the South Vietnamese. Through their backing of Nixon's strategies and their related promotion of patriotic support for the president, conservative leaders helped create an environment which made it easier for the United States to withdraw from its commitment to Vietnam. Despite conservatives' continued allegiance to the war, the events of 1972 convinced them that the Nixon administration was intent on withdrawal. Conservative leaders thus began demanding a final military push in order to justify their preferred policies and to shore up the Saigon regime in the short term. Linebacker II allowed conservatives to claim a measure of victory in Vietnam, even if that victory related more to challenging the liberals' policy of limited war than to securing the future of South Vietnam.

Conclusion

Defining the Vietnam War

The Watergate scandal in 1972–74 undercut what remained of the Nixon administration's commitment to South Vietnam. It also convinced conservative leaders that the provisions of the Paris accords that were designed to ensure North Vietnam's compliance were in fact hollow. Although individuals like Goldwater, Reagan, and Buckley became disillusioned with Nixon during this period, their reasons for supposing that the accords would ultimately fail to ensure South Vietnam's independence were not entirely related to the president or even to the details of the agreement ending the war. In part, this was because they had not fully expected the accords to end the war in Vietnam; in the months after the U.S. troop withdrawal it became clear that the struggle between the two Vietnams would continue. Primarily, however, conservatives lost faith in the accords because of their perception that Congress was undermining the Americans' ability and obligation to uphold the agreement by supplying aid to South Vietnam and the realistic threat of a resumption of the air war once violations occurred. Stressing almost exclusively Hanoi's transgressions rather than acknowledging that Saigon and Washington also violated the agreement, conservatives lambasted Congress's refusal to extend additional military aid to South Vietnam.

They steadfastly failed to engage in any serious analysis of the political weaknesses that defined the Saigon government. Nixon echoed this line in his memoirs. What Nixon dismissed and conservatives ignored between 1973 and 1975 was the reality that the administration did not wish to raise the Vietnam issue again. The "decent interval" means of facilitating the U.S. troop withdrawal had become dominant in administration policy during the final year of engagement. Whether or not conservatives were publicly willing to acknowledge the fact, they too had come to accept the probability that South Vietnam might not be able to withstand the expected North Vietnamese attack. Few, however, thought that the fateful day would come so soon after Nixon and his conservative backers declared peace with honor in Southeast Asia.

As the situation in South Vietnam deteriorated rapidly during early 1975, conservatives launched an ad hoc attack on Congress and the Ford administration. They claimed that the War Powers Act of 1973 had dangerously undermined the president's room for maneuver and was indicative of liberals' policies of appeasement toward the communist world. Although Ford appealed for $522 million in military aid for South Vietnam and Cambodia in January 1975, conservatives continued to challenge the administration's response to the Vietnam problem. On January 11, 1975, the State Department sent diplomatic notes to the governments of the Soviet Union, the PRC, Britain, France, Hungary, Poland, Indonesia, and Iran and to Secretary General Kurt Waldheim of the United Nations; the notes requested aid for South Vietnam and detailed North Vietnam's violations of the Agreement on Ending the War and Restoring the Peace in Vietnam. Over the next several weeks the State Department continued to issue statements highlighting violations of the agreement. This seemingly half-hearted diplomatic approach did little to satisfy conservatives' demands that the administration threaten to use force in order to stop the North Vietnamese advance.

Conservative leaders, particularly the Republican Right and the *National Review* circle, certainly wished to push Congress to extend additional military aid to Saigon and anticipated that such aid would enable the South Vietnamese to forestall the immediate communist advance. The ASC commented that the $300 million of aid for South Vietnam "will not end the war. It will not even permit the South Vietnamese to drive the invaders out of their country. It will only buy time—and not much of that." Conservatives had no real expectations that either Congress or the administration would launch campaigns in support of the beleaguered South Vietnamese sufficient to ensure the country's survival. Their efforts of early 1975 were designed to expose the fallacies of détente and to shore up their own positions in having endorsed the accords in 1973. The ASC, asserting that South Vietnam had not violated the agreement, charged that for "Congress to refuse to give South Vietnam the military aid it needs will amount to the adoption by the U.S. of punishing its former ally for abiding by the Agreement and rewarding its former enemy for violating it." In failing to provide immediate military assistance, Congress was not only dooming the army of South Vietnam to "ultimate defeat" but was also condemning "quite possibly millions" of civilians to "brutal death." "No water from the bowl of Pontius Pilate," they concluded, "will suffice to wash our hands of that blood."[1]

Once Saigon fell on April 30, 1975, the conservative attack intensified. Doves in Congress and a biased media were blamed for having turned Americans against South Vietnam and having ignored the international implications of the American ally's fall to communism. Clare Booth Luce, a longtime anticommunist activist and associate of the staff at *National Review*, contended that the "anti-Vietnam media" were responsible for Americans' widespread hostility to the waves of Vietnamese refugees seeking asylum. The media, "in their long campaign to end U.S. involvement in the Vietnam war, found it expedient to poison the minds of Americans against the South Vietnamese people, denigrate their patriotism, and blacken their character."[2] This idea became more prominent in the decade after the war. One of the original activists associated with the We Support Our Boys in Vietnam parades, Charles Wiley, later set in motion a campaign against network news coverage of the Vietnam War and became a prominent member of Accuracy in Media in the 1980s and 1990s.

Conservatives, partly to assuage their own failure to push for additional aid to South Vietnam between 1973 and 1975, affirmed that an honorable peace had been established but was subsequently lost by Congress. This pattern proved common among the ranks of the pro-war movement, and as a result the demise of the Republic of Vietnam in 1975 only boosted the postwar pro-Vietnam cause, particularly among those who had advocated a more militaristic policy. The un-won war became a far more powerful motif in promoting the righteousness of pro-war arguments than even the supposed peace with honor and stalemate of 1973 had been. Indeed, the memory of defeat after 1975 was far more useful to conservatives than its anticipation in 1972; Americans seemed willing to sacrifice more for Vietnam in retrospect, and with the passage of time it was more politically acceptable and useful to argue that the United States should have gone all out to win in Vietnam. Operation Linebacker II became a symbol of how the war could have been won, with little sacrifice in lives, as early as 1965. "Our own restraint," Tower claimed, "cost us Vietnam. We forced Hanoi to the Paris accords by choking off its lifeline through the mining of Haiphong and through interdicting the supply routes from southern China into North Vietnam." At the very least, he said, the status quo should have been maintained: "That is to say: a friendly South Vietnam, a hostile North Vietnam, and a more or less neutralized Laos and Cambodia. But we failed to do that because Congress mandated that there should be no military assistance after a certain point."[3] The sacrifice of more than fifty thousand lives mandated such an outcome.

Scholars have noted the significance of the impact of the war on conservatives' interpretations of post-Vietnam foreign policy. The so-called lessons of Vietnam became fundamental to both traditionalist and neoconservative understandings of how U.S. policy should be constructed, implemented, and sold to the American people. Intellectuals of varying conservative stripes had in fact been preoccupied with rearmament from at least the early 1970s, and Vietnam was a sideline issue when compared to the overarching menace of international détente. Yet the war continued to play a leading part in locating conservatives' cultural interpretations of how foreign policy should be conducted. This position was furthered by the Americans' defeat, demonstrating the supposed weaknesses inherent in policies of limited war, negotiation, and unilateral concession. That the war could and should have been won became the cornerstone of the lessons that conservatives drew from Vietnam. During the late 1970s, however, conservative leaders put forward more ambiguous lessons about whether or not the United States should have engaged in direct military intervention in Southeast at all. As Tower commented in 1980, the irony of Vietnam was that "we could have won it." He followed this typical hawkish refrain with the more surprising assertion that the failure to win was an "even bigger mistake than getting involved in Vietnam in the first place."[4]

Writing in 1979, Goldwater declared, "It seems impossible that we could have been drawn into a land war in Asia." He concluded that "it is impossible to overstate the destructive impact on American institutions, American self-confidence, and our constitutional government resulting from that twelve-year tragedy."[5] Goldwater expressed his regret about Vietnam in the context of the eventual loss of the war and the limited military means employed, for it is impossible to say he considered it to be an unnecessary aspect of U.S. foreign policy during the early 1960s. The very use of the term "drawn into" belies the active role conservatives played in dynamically pursuing direct military intervention in Southeast Asia. The Powell or Weinberger Doctrine that became synonymous with conservatives' reluctance to engage in limited or "no-win" wars was undoubtedly a result of exasperation over the circumstances in which the United States had gone to war in 1964 and 1965. It reflected the widely held belief among conservative political leaders that the Johnson administration had not only misrepresented its plans for the level of American engagement but also deliberately pursued a style of warfare that could never have brought about military victory. It had done so, furthermore, against the express wishes of military leaders. Conservatives' focus on establishing preconditions for U.S. military intervention revealed their understanding of the military's frustration with its Vietnam experiences more than it did conservatives' beliefs about the necessity or utility of American engagement during the early 1960s. It therefore indicated a postdefeat evaluation of America's entry into the war that sought to distance conservative leaders from responsibility for their part in pushing for military intervention to uphold the Saigon government.

In many respects the question of whether or not conservatives had supported initial engagement epitomized the internal divisions among conservatives regarding foreign policy priorities during the Vietnam War. When activists such as Goldwater and Tower recalled their wartime position of limited commitment to intervention, they were in fact remembering the position that nonelite conservative actors had held. Social conservatives and activists like Schlafly had questioned the utility of intervention far more than political leaders in the Republican Party and the conservative journals. This alternative recollection of conservatives' activism was pursued not simply to disavow their active role in seeking war in Vietnam but also to advance two postwar objectives: capitalizing on the patriotic campaigns undertaken by grassroots conservatives, who defined the war in noble terms, and firmly laying blame for defeat at the feet of the anti-war movement.

If conservative leaders were not united in their opinions on intervention, they found greater political utility in defining the reasons for defeat. Several suspects came under intense attack: Johnson administration officials; a liberal news media biased toward the anti-war position; a dovish Congress; and the amorphous anti-war movement. Many conservative intellectuals also pointed to Nixon officials, especially Kissinger, for having abandoned America's erstwhile ally in South Vietnam. This line of argument was valuable in establishing why Saigon fell after the signing of the Peace accords in 1973, but it posed substantial problems for conservative Republicans and their allies at organizations such as *National Review*, who had actively supported and thereby legitimized Nixon's policies of Vietnamization and negotiation. Forgetting this particular chapter in conservative activism became an essential element in reconstructing a politically viable past. Blaming anti-war critics and their supposed allies in the news media and Congress also distracted from conservatives' emphasis on how the United States could have won the war militarily. While this remained a core tenet of conservatives' memory of the war, it seemed incredible to a public that had experienced the war and that was wary of future military interventions. The noble cause motif put forward by Reagan became an alternative means of attacking anti-war critics. By focusing on the heroism of veterans' service and by implicitly tying it to a positive interpretation of the war's meaning for Americans, conservative leaders attempted to delegitimize anti-war opinion and thereby create positive popular understandings of their own foreign policy preferences. American heroism, conservative leaders held, mandated rejection of détente on the basis of the exceptionalist credo. The heroism of the lost cause thereby became a conservative mantra as conservatives worked to construct a politically viable memory of the Vietnam War.

In addition, conservatives' virulent opposition to Congress during 1975 and their record of opposition to Nixon's pursuit of détente served to foster the Right's postwar interpretations of their actions during the conflict. The popular belief that conservatives had consistently opposed limited war served this purpose, despite the fact that they had helped legitimize Nixon's failed policy of Vietnamization. In the wake of American defeat reference to Nixon's once lauded peace with honor was replaced by claims that the war simply should have been won by military victory. Conservatives such as Goldwater, Reagan, and Buckley were intent on playing down their earlier endorsement of Vietnamization and their praise for the president's handling of the war. Instead they highlighted the consequences of defeat, most notably the negative implications of what pundits were soon referring to as the Vietnam syndrome. They did so in order to raise domestic morale and popular faith in military interventions rather than simply to continue the worn strategy of attacking the policies of limited war pursued by successive administrations.

Despite widespread disillusionment with the management and outcome of America's war in Southeast Asia, the conservative political movement was not initially able to capitalize on popular discontent and anxiety. In part this was because conservatives remained divided and seemed unable to offer a promising alternative to current foreign policy. To a greater extent conservative political leaders were too closely associated with a stringent form of anticommunism that seemed less relevant to the international scene in the mid-1970s. By the end of the decade, however, the conservative political movement had learned certain lessons from its Vietnam experience, lessons that resonated with a populace influenced by the patriotic campaigns of the Vietnam years. Like much of American society, conservative political activists of the post-Vietnam era sought to learn the so-called lessons of Vietnam without a great deal of engagement with the actual events of the war. In particular, Americans looked to their own society to understand the reasons for North Vietnam's victory and failed to appreciate either the enemy's resilience or the legitimacy of Johnson's and Nixon's concerns that expanding the military operations would have widened the conflict.

While conservatives' campaigns to alter U.S. policy in Vietnam had been the most conspicuous of the pro-war endeavors undertaken, theirs was not the campaign that proved the most enduring. This accolade goes to those often unremarkable, subtle activists who campaigned in favor of the war on the basis of supporting the troops and the president. Tinged with the supposition that the United States was engaged in a just cause in Southeast Asia, their arguments assumed heightened potency as the American mission irrevocably faltered in 1975. Despite its ongoing internal debate about the efficacy of having supported the Nixon strategies in Vietnam, the conservative political movement benefited from the popular framework for viewing the war that these patriotic campaigns created. Coupled with increased support for a more hardline foreign policy, conservatives' wartime opposition to anti-war factions invigorated its claim to patriotism during the late 1970s. In the postwar political environment, by connecting two distinct issues—intellectual challenges to the policy of limited war and grassroots activism that portrayed American policy as just—conservatives were able to politically utilize Vietnam and to thereby inform a broader, perhaps even national, memory of the Vietnam experience. In this respect, memories of Vietnam served to advance a conservative political agenda.

The *National Review* circle and the Republican Right faced an unexpected challenge in the form of the New Right during the

1970s. Activists associated with social conservative issues had never been as ideologically committed to the war as their political counterparts in the Republican Party. Intellectual conservatives' preoccupation with foreign policy meant that the war was of far greater significance to them than issues such as school prayer, abortion, and the equal rights agendas of the feminist and gay movements. Initially their concern with the anti-war movement between 1964 and 1973 related largely to its impact on government policy, not to what its radical elements signified about a newly permissive American society. This changed over time, as the messages enunciated by Agnew exposed the power of political polarization and its implicit benefits to the conservative movement. While some in the New Right rejected older heroes like Goldwater, who were dismissed by younger Republicans as being lazy and soft in challenging domestic liberalism, others like Thurmond, Reagan, and newly minted conservative Republicans like Helms were better at realizing the potential of harnessing public anger about America's place in the world.[6] The international and the domestic, they recognized, could be subsumed within a social interpretation of American values. On no occasion was this more evident than during the debates over the Panama Canal Treaty.

Dominic Sandbrook writes that "what lay behind the Panama issue, of course, was Vietnam."[7] Certainly the war, or rather America's defeat, determined the power of grassroots conservatives' responses to Kissinger's efforts to reshape the relationship between the United States and Panama with regard to the canal. But as Natasha Zaretsky astutely notes, "The treaty fight crystallized a debate in the mid to late 1970s about the future of U.S. foreign policy after Vietnam." Opponents of the treaty viewed the willingness of the Gerald Ford and, later, Jimmy Carter administrations to concede ownership of the canal as evidence of American weakness in the wake of Vietnam. Schlafly, Zaretsky notes, described this process as a "pattern of surrender."[8] Such conservatives were less interested in refighting the Vietnam War than in demonstrating how international retreat had contributed to domestic turmoil. Vietnam served a powerful function in accentuating the implications—moral, cultural, and political—that derived from international weakness. The

Panama issue was a simple means of grappling with the complex legacies of the war. While there was certainly no conservative consensus on the question of the Panama Canal—indeed, such diverse representatives of the movement as Buckley and John Wayne opposed conservative challenges to renegotiation—the Panama issue proved a compelling means of conflating two strands of conservative memories of the war: intellectuals' emphasis on the policy legacies that resulted from America's failure to secure victory; and grassroots social conservatives' interest in polarizing opinion on the meaning of American patriotism. That social conservatives had been among the least committed to intervention in Vietnam was evidence of how distorted memories of Vietnam were put to use in the debates on Panama to drive conservatives' political and cultural agendas. It signified further the potent legacy of the patriotic campaigns undertaken in favor of the war and of supporting the troops vis-à-vis conservatives' identity after the war.

Divisions over Nixon in particular weakened the unity of the *National Review* circle and afforded the New Right the opportunity to enhance its standing in the conservative movement of the 1970s. Reagan was able to relate to the New Right crusade better than his fellow ideologues at *National Review* and could present his anticommunist foreign policies in a populist framework that originated in opposition to the anti-war movement during the 1960s and early 1970s. This is not to suggest that intellectual conservatives were paralyzed after the war. Indeed, they used the war as attestation of the failure of liberal policies and thereby set about reinvigorating anticommunism as the basis of U.S. foreign policy. Burnham and others recognized the necessity of resurrecting popular confidence in America's international missions. Writing in January 1975, he cautioned that the "most damaging result" of South Vietnam's fall to communism "would be the still further loss of confidence in (and fear of) U.S. integrity and power." Burnham was referring to international perceptions of the United States, but he also understood the importance of domestic confidence.[9]

While reluctant to fully endorse the nationalism of the New Right, *National Review* conservatives were more receptive to neoconservatives' emphasis on the danger of post-Vietnam isolationism. The war had been crucial to the organizational development of the neoconservatives, who in turn were instrumental in the rise of conservative political fortunes in the late 1970s and 1980s.[10] The Committee on the Present Danger, one of the most prominent conservative think tanks of the 1970s, was a successor of the ASC and preserved the original organization's ethos. While the Republican Right embraced the argument that intervention had been a mistake, they continued to espouse the view that its failure had dramatic international consequences and was testimony to liberals' flawed conception of international relations, especially their seemingly unlimited faith in détente. Goldwater persisted in his belief that the fall of Saigon and the process of communist expansion in the region validated conservatives' interpretation of the domino theory, and conservatives consistently argued that South Vietnam's collapse emboldened the Soviet Union elsewhere.[11] Buckley claimed that détente did not bring peace with honor to South Vietnam. "What has détente brought for us," he queried, "except to provide a backdrop for the exchange of toasts between American Presidents and Communist tyrants?" He preferred a return to Cold War tensions over the continuation of "diplomatic hypocrisy" and contended that increased defense expenditure was the only means of resurrecting the United States from its dire position in the international arena.[12]

Again, however, there was a social dimension to conservatives' interpretation of the legacy of the Vietnam War. In decrying détente, Clare Booth Luce wrote in 1977 that the "long, ill-conceived, badly fought, bloody, costly war in Vietnam was the test of capitalist America's ideological staying power. America failed the test."[13] Indeed, in the fraught political environment of the late 1970s, in which competing visions of American exceptionalism vied for popular support, conservatives needed to do more than simply bemoan American weakness and present frightening assessments of its future. They needed to appeal to moderates, to build an effective alliance with neoconservatives, and to offer a positive, uplifting image of America's future. If the war itself did not help conservatives reach these symbiotic goals, then emphasizing its social dimensions could prove more useful.

The legacy of America's failed military engagement in Southeast

Asia as it pertained to the conservative movement was complex and diverse. Overwhelmingly, conservatives believed that engagement in Vietnam was necessary and just, and they professed that the weakened American position of the 1970s demonstrated the perilous implications of failing to secure victory in the war. In denying official recognition of Vietnam, ostensibly because of the POW/MIA issue, and in elevating the war to noble status, conservatives did much to build their political base and to reframe the meaning of the Vietnam War for Americans. But the themes enunciated by Reagan in his address to the VFW in 1980, when he articulated the idea of the war as a noble cause, helped shape popular understandings of the issues at the heart of the divisions between liberals and conservatives regarding foreign policy. While intellectual conservatives and the Republican Right had focused their wartime efforts on promoting the international significance of the Vietnam experience, their postwar initiatives to domesticate it were considerable. In part the method suited the former goal: by reimagining Vietnam as something positive, conservatives could overcome popular anxieties about future military campaigns. But in part this was also an initiative designed to subvert liberals' characterization of the war as immoral and unnecessary. Reagan's description of Vietnam as a noble cause was merely the climax of this extended campaign, which had begun with a reconstruction of conservatives' active engagement in America's intervention and which was symbolized by the debates over the Panama Canal Treaty.

As Patrick Hagopian's study of Americans' commemorations of the Vietnam War has ably demonstrated, Reagan's characterization of the war did not secure the national consensus he hoped to achieve. It was the more widespread, bipartisan concentration on healing and honoring veterans' service that allowed Vietnam memorials to play "a part in the hegemonic politics of Reaganism."[14] Yet Reagan's rhetoric showed the success conservative leaders enjoyed in tying together two strands of wartime activism that favored the war. Reagan stressed the international imperatives of fighting the war, but he also celebrated the activism of such organizations as the VFW, which during the war had unwaveringly backed the troops and proclaimed the cause of American POWs.

The American Legion, for instance, had financially and logistically aided the mammoth We Support Our Boys in Vietnam parades that took place in New York City in 1967 and 1969. While each of these parades proclaimed its purpose to be to unite people behind the troops—and to avoid political commentary on the war—they also manifestly proffered a pro-war political agenda. Veterans' groups later allied themselves with conservative patriotic organizations that during the last two years of the war declared the POW issue to be the most important topic of the Vietnam experience.

Reagan was therefore building on an existing history of pro-war activism that reconfigured the Vietnam War as one fought between Americans rather than between the United States and a foreign enemy. Conservative leaders thus treated the war itself as an abstraction. They engaged in little analysis and no true public discussion of how the North Vietnamese or the NLF had contributed to America's defeat. Furthermore, the language of unity belied a considered effort to delegitimize and marginalize anti-war opinions. Rather than acknowledge the considerable extent to which most Americans had turned against the war by its final years, Reagan presented a narrative of popular support for America's noble effort.

Just as many Americans had rejected conservatives' fixation on the possibility of military victory in Vietnam, many disregarded Reagan's interpretation of America's purpose in the war. Yet his message was one of redemption. The war could be redeemed by collective contemplation of America's sacrifice in Vietnam and on the tragedy wrought by liberals' refusal to allow American servicemen to attain a deserved military victory. This message gained political traction for many varied reasons, not least of which was the fact that President Carter had already sounded the trumpet of revisionism in July 1980. Carter had unequivocally rejected the concept that honoring the troops meant honoring the war, but he did acknowledge that it was important to dignify "the freedoms that they fought to preserve." Carter, Robert McMahon writes, in thus "implicitly repudiating all of his earlier, critical insights about the Vietnam War" set the stage for Reagan's more radical revisionism.[15] Reagan's ability to coalesce conservatives' retrospective account of their wartime record, that is, their opposition to intervention and limited war, with a broader, popular emphasis on patriotic support of the troops and America's innocence as represented by the POW issue was notable. Grassroots conservative, patriotic, and veterans' groups had consistently pressed these issues during the war. Conservative leaders succeeded in pushing them onto the national agenda during 1980 and thereby created the means for new ways of remembering America's Vietnam War experiences.

Writing in 1985, Kissinger argued that "Reagan's election itself was part of the national reaction to Vietnam." The war, he said, "put in motion such a weakening of America and created so many frustrations that a reaction to the right was inevitable."[16] Kissinger's perspective had elements of truth, but he underestimated the extent to which Reagan's carefully crafted remembering of the war offered Americans more than simply a reaction to American defeat. For Americans who had directly witnessed the war, simply repeating the idea that victory could have been achieved with ease offered limited relief and, for many, was wholly implausible. By elevating the war to noble status, conservatives took strides to build their political base and to reframe the meaning of the Vietnam War for Americans. This change in how conservatives publicly articulated the meaning of the war reflected changes in how they presented their foreign policies. As one commentator noted in 1979, Reagan was determined to demonstrate he "was not another Barry Goldwater."[17] This populist framework was intended to secure public support for conservatives' foreign policies; while it included a novel emphasis on patriotic themes, conservatives did not abandon their core resolve on the anticommunist agenda that had conditioned their positions during the war.

Speaking at the dedication ceremony for the Unknown Soldier of the Vietnam War, Reagan queried whether the man in question ever played on an American city street or worked with his father on a farm in America's heartland. He wondered if the man had married, had children, or expected to return to a bride. "We'll never know," Reagan stated, "the answers to these questions about his life." "We do know, though" the president continued, "why he died. He saw the horrors of war but bravely faced them, certain his own cause and his country's cause was a noble one; that he was fighting for human dignity, for free men everywhere."[18] National healing was possible, Reagan claimed, by thanking those who served. "We can," he said, "be worthy of the values and ideals for which our sons sacrificed, worthy of their courage in the face of a fear that few of us will ever experience, by honoring their commitment and devotion to duty and country." The fight for freedom, indeed, the war itself, had been just according to conservatives, and the tragedy rested with America's failure to secure victory.

While the broader public might draw different conclusions about the utility of future military engagements, the conservative memory of Vietnam was firmly incorporated into the public consciousness and facilitated broader interpretations of American victimhood and noble sacrifice, interpretations that gained much resonance in certain elements of popular culture during the 1980s. The debates over Vietnam would continue to rage, most demonstrably over the design of the Vietnam Veterans Memorial, and there could be no consensus on the policy lessons of Vietnam. But conservatives' efforts to reconstruct their own history of the war not only helped their political fortunes during the late 1980s but also contributed to a national celebration of popular innocence regarding the war. If hawks had neither endorsed peace with honor nor pushed for military intervention in 1964 and 1965, then the wider public could hardly be held to account for the nation's role in intervening in a disastrous military conflict. Conservatives thereby helped to fashion Vietnam as a conflict between polarized elements of American society, a tragedy befitting national remorse for the failure to secure victory, but a tragedy that could be overcome by collective healing and collective celebration of America's role in international affairs. If future foreign policy debates continued to be influenced by a Vietnam syndrome, it was not a syndrome predicated on the weaknesses and contradictions of America's global intentions. This was not the victory for which conservatives had struggled throughout the long, disappointing, and divisive years of the Vietnam War. It was a limited victory, a result that had come at great cost to conservatives' unity and the influence of intellectuals within the broader movement, but one that could be celebrated as a victory nonetheless.

NOTES

INTRODUCTION
Conservatives and the Vietnam War

1. Ronald Reagan, address at the Veterans of Foreign Wars Annual Convention, Chicago, Illinois, August 18, 1980.
2. Reagan, quoted at the candlelight vigil of the National Salute to Vietnam Veterans, National Cathedral, Washington, D.C., November 10, 1982, Kurt Anderson, "A Homecoming at Last," *Time*, November 22, 1982.
3. Patrick Hagopian, *The Vietnam War in American Memory: Veterans, Memorials, and the Politics of Healing* (Amherst: University of Massachusetts Press, 2009), 12–13.
4. Telegram, Support Our Boys in Vietnam Parade Committee to General William C. Westmoreland, April 16, 1967, We Support Our Boys in Vietnam, Inc. Archive, Hoover Institution Archives, Stanford, California, box 6.
5. Frank Costigliola's examination of George Kennan is a prime example of the cultural turn in diplomatic history and details the influence of cultural perception on policymakers' early interpretations of hostilities with the Soviet Union. "'Unceasing Pressure for Penetration': Gender, Pathology, and Emotion in George Kennan's Formation of the Cold War," *Journal of American History* (March 1997), 1309–39. Steven Casey details President Franklin D. Roosevelt's cautious approach, determined by domestic politics, to direct engagement in the Second World War and emphasizes how public opinion influenced the timing of military decisions. *Cautious Crusade: Franklin D. Roosevelt, American Public Opinion, and the War against Nazi Germany* (New York: Oxford University Press, 2001). Casey examines the limitations on President Harry Truman's ability to sell limited war in *Selling the Korean War: Propaganda, Politics, and Public Opinion in the United States, 1950–1953* (New York: Oxford University Press, 2008). In relation to Vietnam, Fredrik Logevall and Melvin Small have demonstrated the necessity of considering how concerns about domestic backlash and personal

prestige influenced policymakers' understanding of the priorities that should be attached to victory in Vietnam. Logevall, *Choosing War: The Lost Chance for Peace and Escalation of the War in Vietnam* (Berkeley: University of California Press, 1999). Small, *At the Water's Edge: American Politics and the Vietnam War* (Chicago: Ivan R. Dee, 2005).

6. Colin Dueck, *Hard Line: The Republican Party and U.S. Foreign Policy since World War II* (Princeton: Princeton University Press, 2010).

7. Andrew Johns, *Vietnam's Second Front: Domestic Politics, the Republican Party, and the War* (Lexington: University Press of Kentucky, 2010).

8. Robert David Johnson, *Congress and the Cold War* (New York: Cambridge University Press, 2006). Julian Zelizer, *Arsenal of Democracy: The Politics of National Security—From World War II to the War on Terrorism* (New York: Basic Books, 2010).

9. Until the 1990s historians of the 1960s largely focused on conservatism only insofar as it represented a social and cultural backlash against Great Society liberalism and the New Left. More recent accounts of the era have incorporated discussions of the origins of the modern conservative movement. See Maurice Isserman and Michael Kazin, *America Divided: The Civil War of the 1960s* (New York: Oxford University Press, 2000), and Mark H. Lytle, *America's Uncivil Wars: The Sixties Era from Elvis to the Fall of Richard Nixon* (New York: Oxford University Press, 2005). Isserman and Kazin comment, "Blessed with hindsight, we can better appreciate the significance of the '60s Right.' *America Divided*, 206. Early histories of conservatism emphasized the significance of philosophical change among intellectual conservatives. George Nash's thorough examination of the postwar conservative intellectual movement remained the authoritative account of modern conservative thought until the mid-1990s. Nash, *The Conservative Intellectual Movement in America since 1945* (New York: Basic Books, 1976). The breadth and depth of scholarship since 1994, however, signifies a new phase in historical analysis of the Right. In focusing on the organizational development and political campaigns of the Right during the 1960s, Mary Brennan, Rick Perlstein, Kurt Schuparra, and Matthew Dallek have contributed much to our understanding of the policy priorities and organizational techniques of the conservative movement. Mary C. Brennan, *Turning Right in the Sixties: The Conservative Capture of the GOP* (Chapel Hill: University of North Carolina Press, 1995); Rick Perlstein, *Before the Storm: Barry Goldwater and the Unmaking of the American Consensus* (New York: Hill and Wang, 2001); Kurt Schuparra, *Triumph of the Right: The Rise of the California Conservative Movement, 1945–1966* (Armonk, N.Y.: M. E. Sharpe, 1998); Matthew Dallek, *The Right Moment: Ronald Reagan's First Victory and the Decisive Turning Point in American Politics* (New York: Free Press, 2000). Others have chosen to explore the youth wing of the Right in order to analyze and understand conservatives on their own terms. John A. Andrew III, *The Other Side of the Sixties: Young Americans for Freedom and the Rise of Conservative Politics* (New Brunswick: Rutgers University Press, 1997); Gregory Schneider, *Cadres for Conservatism: Young Americans for Freedom and the Rise of the Contemporary Right* (New York: New York University Press, 1999); Rebecca Klatch, *A Generation Divided: The New Left, the New Right, and the 1960s* (Berkeley: University of California Press, 1999); and Wayne Thorburn, *A Generation Awakes: Young Americans for Freedom and the Creation of the Conservative Movement* (Ottawa, Ill.: Jameson Books, 2010). Social histories of the origins of conservatism emphasize the importance of grass-roots activism: Lisa McGirr, *Suburban*

Warriors: The Origins of the New American Right (Princeton: Princeton University Press, 2001); Donald T. Critchlow, *Phyllis Schlafly and Grassroots Conservatism: A Woman's Crusade* (Princeton: Princeton University Press, 2005); Michelle Nickerson, "Moral Mothers and Goldwater Girls," in *The Conservative Sixties*, ed. David Farber and Jeff Roche (New York: Peter Lang, 2003), 51–62; Jeff Roche, "Cowboy Conservatism," in *Conservative Sixties*, 79–92. Several historians point to demographic and economic shifts in order to explain the heightened political significance of the Sunbelt: Matthew Lassiter, *The Silent Majority: Suburban Politics in the Sunbelt South* (Princeton: Princeton University Press, 2006). Elizabeth Tandy Shermer examined the importance of conservatives' antilabor positions in boosting conservative political strength: "Origins of the Conservative Ascendancy: Barry Goldwater's Early Senate Career and the De-legitimization of Organized Labor," *Journal of American History* (December 2008), "Counter-Organizing the Sunbelt: Right to Work Campaigns and Anti-Union Conservatism, 1943–1958," *Pacific Historical Review* (February 2009), 81–118. The varied responses in the North and South to civil rights and racial integration have also been examined by historians to explain the development of modern conservatism: Joseph Crespino, *In Search of Another Country: Mississippi and the Conservative Counterrevolution* (Princeton: Princeton University Press, 2007); Kevin M. Kruse, *White Flight: Atlanta and the Making of Modern Conservatism* (Princeton: Princeton University Press, 2005); Thomas Sugrue, *The Origins of the Urban Crisis: Race and Inequality in Postwar Detroit* (Princeton: Princeton University Press, 1996).

10. Julian Zelizer, "Reflections: Rethinking the History of American Conservatism," *Reviews in American History* 39, no. 2 (2010), 367–92. See also Kim Phillips-Fein, "Conservatism: A State of the Field," *Journal of American History* 98, 3 (December 2011), 723–43.
11. See Robert Mason and Iwan Morgan, eds., *Seeking a New Majority: The Republican Party and American Politics, 1960–1980* (Nashville: Vanderbilt University Press, 2013).
12. See McGirr, *Suburban Warriors*, chap. 1.

1. NO SUBSTITUTE FOR VICTORY
The Beginnings of a War

1. Governor Mark O. Hatfield, Keynote Address, Republican National Convention, San Francisco, July 13, 1964.
2. Andrew Johns, "Doves among Hawks: Republican Opposition to the War in Vietnam, 1964–1968," *Peace & Change* 31, no. 4 (October 2006), 585–628.
3. Colin Dueck, *Hard Line: The Republican Party and U.S. Foreign Policy since World War II* (Princeton: Princeton University Press, 2010), 137; Andrew Johns notes that Dirksen was President Johnson's staunchest ally in the Republican Party until 1968, *Vietnam's Second Front: Domestic Politics, the Republican Party, and the War* (Lexington: University Press of Kentucky, 2010), 72.
4. Congressman Robert Wilson (R-CA), cited in Johns, *Vietnam's Second Front*, 37.
5. Donald T. Critchlow, *The Conservative Ascendancy: How the GOP Right Made Political History* (Cambridge: Harvard University Press, 2006).
6. Memorandum, William Rusher to Senator John Ashbrook, William F. Buckley Jr., Tom Winter, Al McKay, Dave Jones, John Jones, and Bob Bauman, March 4,

1969, William A. Rusher papers, Library of Congress, Washington, Manuscript and Archives Division, box 7, folder General Correspondence, Ashbrook, John, 1967–1982. Hereafter cited as Rusher papers.

7. Ronald Reagan, cited in Rick Perlstein, *Nixonland: The Rise of a President and the Fracturing of America* (New York: Scriber, 2008), 91.

8. See, for example, "Cuba: JFK Leaves Much Unanswered," December 1, 1962; "Senators Still Have Doubts on Cuba," January 12, 1963; "Cuba: New Crisis Looms," February 2, 1963; "Cuba: Another Soviet Hoax," March 2, 1963; "We May Be Creating More Cubas," April 13. 1963; all *Human Events*.

9. Sara Diamond, *Roads to Dominion: Right-wing Movements and Political Power in the United States* (New York: Guildford Press, 1995), 9.

10. George H. Nash, *The Conservative Intellectual Movement in America since 1945*, 2d ed. (Wilmington: Intercollegiate Studies Institute, 1996), 114. More recently, James Hijiya has noted that although "everybody seems to agree that it was anticommunism that enabled conservatives to stick together . . . unanimous agreement . . . does not make a proposition correct." James Hijiya, "The Conservative 1960s," *Journal of American Studies* 37 (2003), 216.

11. David Farber, *The Rise and Fall of Modern American Conservatism: A Short History* (Princeton: Princeton University Press, 2010), 37.

12. Meyer's ideas were articulated in his books *The Moulding of Communists: The Training of the Communist Cadre* (New York: Harcourt, Brace, 1961) and *In Defense of Freedom: A Conservative Credo* (Chicago: Regnery, 1962). For a discussion of the origins of neoconservatism, see Jacob Heilbrunn, *They Knew They Were Right: The Rise of the Neocons* (New York: Doubleday, 2008), Murray Friedman, *The Neoconservative Revolution: Jewish Intellectuals and the Shaping of Public Policy* (New York: Cambridge University Press, 2005), and Justin Vaïsse, *Neoconservatism: The Biography of a Movement* (Cambridge: Harvard University Press, 2010).

13. See Nash, *Conservative Intellectual Movement*, 161; Murray Rothbard, "Frank Meyer and Sidney Hook," in *The Irrepressible Rothbard: The Rothbard–Rockwell Report Essays of Murray N. Rothbard*, ed. Llewellyn H. Rockwell Jr. (Burlingame, Calif.: Center for Libertarian Studies, 2000), 20–25.

14. Statement of principles of the American Conservative Union, April 1965, Thomas A. Lane Papers, Hoover Institution Archives, Stanford, California, box 5, folder American Conservative Union.

15. Rothbard, "Frank Meyer," in Rockwell, *Irrepressible Rothbard*.

16. William F. Buckley Jr., cited in Rick Perlstein, *Before the Storm: Barry Goldwater and the Unmaking of the American Consensus* (New York: Hill and Wang, 2001), 155.

17. Michelle M. Nickerson, *Mothers of Conservatism: Women and the Postwar Right* (Princeton: Princeton University Press, 2012), 138–39.

18. Jonathan Schoenwald, *A Time for Choosing: The Rise of Modern American Conservatism* (New York: Oxford University Press, 2001), 234–35.

19. Lisa McGirr, *Suburban Warriors: The Origins of the New American Right* (Princeton: Princeton University Press, 2001), 77–79.

20. Nash, *Conservative Intellectual Movement*, 81.

21. Editorial, "Hungary and Human Rights," *National Review*, December 15, 1956.

22. Nash, *Conservative Intellectual Movement*, 81.

23. Dueck, *Hard Line*, 129.

24. Paul Gottfried, *The Conservative Movement*, 2d ed. (New York: Twayne, 1993), 16. Sandra Scanlon, "A Dangerous Illusion: The Nixon Administration and the

American Conservative Response to Détente," in *Reform and Renewal: Transatlantic Relations during the 1960s and 1970s*, ed. Catherine Hynes and Sandra Scanlon (Newcastle: Cambridge Scholars Publishing, 2009), 105–26.
25. Barry Goldwater, *The Conscience of a Conservative* (Shepherdsville, Ky.: Victor Publishing, 1960), 123.
26. Frank Meyer, cited in East, *American Conservative Movement*, 93, taken from Meyer, *The Moulding of Communists*.
27. Kevin Smant, *How Great the Triumph: James Burnham, Anticommunism and the Conservative Movement* (Lanham, Md.: University Press of America, 1992), 66.
28. For details of U.S. domestic support for Ngo Dinh Diem, see Seth Jacobs, *America's Miracle Man in Vietnam: Ngo Dinh Diem, Religion, Race and U.S. Intervention in Southeast Asia* (Durham: Duke University Press, 2004).
29. Joseph Morgan, *The Vietnam Lobby: The American Friends of Vietnam, 1955–1975* (Chapel Hill: University of North Carolina Press, 1997).
30. Nash, *Conservative Intellectual Movement*, 238.
31. Johns, *Vietnam's Second Front*, 35.
32. Conservatives had lambasted Truman's approach to preparing the American people for the war in Korea and, in line with their own rejection of limited war, failed to take note of the Truman administration's difficulties in selling the ongoing war to an increasingly weary American public. See Steven Casey, *Selling the Korean War: Propaganda, Politics, and Public Opinion in the United States, 1950–1953* (New York: Oxford University Press, 2008).
33. Letter, Walter Judd to David Lawrence, journalist for the *Washington Post*; May 14, 1969, Walter Judd Papers, Hoover Institution Archives, Stanford, California, box 250, folder Vietnam, general, 1969, Jan.–Oct. Hereafter cited as Judd papers.
34. "JFK Losing Cold War," *Human Events*, January 26, 1963. The editors also claimed that such military measures, and "choking off these supply centers" were in fact necessary to "prevent escalation."
35. "More 'No-win' Policy," *Human Events*, June 8, 1963. This editorial originally appeared in the *Nashville Banner* and was republished in *Human Events* as one of several "outstanding editorials."
36. Ibid.
37. Barry Goldwater, *Why Not Victory?: A Fresh Look at American Policy* (New York: Macfadden, 1963), 30.
38. Editorial, "Who Pulled the Rug in Viet Nam?," *Chicago Tribune*, reprinted in *Human Events*, November 16, 1963.
39. "Our Country's Inglorious Role in the Final Days of the Diem Regime," *Human Events*, March 7, 1964.
40. Johns, *Vietnam's Second Front*, 37.
41. Senator Barry Goldwater speech, Republican fundraising event, Seattle, October 24, 1964, Free Society Association Records, Hoover Institution Archives, Stanford, California, box 4, folder Campaign speeches.
42. David Levy, *The Debate over Vietnam*, 2d ed. (Baltimore: Johns Hopkins University Press, 1995), 110; Donald T. Critchlow, "Conservatism Reconsidered: Phyllis Schlafly and Grassroots Conservatism," in *The Conservative Sixties*, ed. David Farber and Jeff Roche (New York: Peter Lang, 2003), 123–24.
43. Critchlow, *Conservative Ascendancy*, 83; Johns, *Vietnam's Second Front*, 76.
44. Governor William Scranton, cited in Johns, *Vietnam's Second Front*, 56.
45. "Lyndon's 'No-Win' Foreign Policy," *Human Events*, July 11, 1964.
46. GOP platform, 1964, as cited in *Human Events*, August 1, 1964.

47. Fredrik Logevall, *Choosing War: The Lost Chance for Peace and Escalation of the War in Vietnam* (Berkeley: University of California Press, 1999); Sylvia Ellis, *Britain, America and the Vietnam War* (Westport: Praeger, 2004).
48. Senator Barry Goldwater, "Where I Stand on the Issues," *Human Events*, October 24, 1964.
49. Goldwater, cited in Johns, *Vietnam's Second Front*, 63.
50. Goldwater quotation from Harold K. Smith's television show *Issues and Answers*, May 24, 1964, Goldwater, *With No Apologies: The Personal and Political Memoirs of United States Senator Barry M. Goldwater* (New York: Morrow, 1979), 176.
51. Goldwater, cited in Perlstein, *Before the Storm*, 346–48.
52. American Conservative Union task force study: "Vietnam," Strom Thurmond papers, Strom Thurmond Institute, Clemson University, South Carolina, Special Preparedness Investigating Committee series, box 20, folder Vietnam II.
53. Senator Strom Thurmond, cited in Johns, *Vietnam's Second Front*, 69.
54. American Security Council report, *Guidelines for Cold War Victory*, reprinted in *Human Events*, September 19, 1964.
55. Seth Jacobs, "'No Place to Fight a War': Laos and the Evolution of U.S. Policy toward Vietnam," in *Making Sense of the Vietnam Wars: Local, National, and Transnational Perspectives*, ed. Mark Bradley and Marilyn Young (New York: Oxford University Press, 2008).
56. "War of Liberation: Strategy for Southeast Asia," *Human Events*, September 19, 1964.
57. "Viet Nam Begins to Look Like Cuba," *Human Events*, January 9, 1965.
58. Senator Barry Goldwater, cited in "Goldwater Says Periled Pilots in Vietnam," *New York Times*, August 20, 1964.
59. Johns, *Vietnam's Second Front*, 5.
60. "Uprising Creates a New GOP Issue," *New York Times*, September 14, 1964.
61. Senator Barry Goldwater, speech at Madison Square Garden, cited in "Goldwater Exhorts 18,000 in Garden 'Victory' Rally; Hits Johnson Daddyism," *New York Times*, October 28, 1964.

2. The Loyal Opposition?
The Push for Victory, 1965–1968

1. Andrew Johns, *Vietnam's Second Front: Domestic Politics, the Republican Party, and the War* (Lexington: University Press of Kentucky, 2010), 96, 105.
2. Senator John Tower, quoted in Johns, *Vietnam's Second Front*, 109.
3. Francis Bator, "No Good Choices: LBJ and the Vietnam/Great Society Connection," *Diplomatic History*, May 2008, 309–40.
4. President Lyndon B. Johnson to George Ball, cited in Joseph A. Fry, *Debating Vietnam: Fulbright, Stennis, and Their Senate Hearings* (Oxford: Rowman and Littlefield, 2006), 87.
5. Ibid., 20.
6. ACU statement on Vietnam, April 1965, Thomas A. Lane Papers, Hoover Institution Archives, Stanford, California, box 5, folder American Conservative Union. Hereafter cited as Lane papers.
7. Letter, General Thomas Lane (Ret.) to Frank Meyer, March 10, 1965, Lane papers, box 5, folder ACU.
8. ACU statement on Vietnam, April 1965, Lane papers, box 5, folder ACU.
9. Ibid.

10. Senator Stuart Symington cited in "Calls for Knockout Air Strikes," *Bowling Green* [Ky.] *Park City Daily News*, February 1, 1966.
11. "Military Chiefs Ask for Bombing," *Spokane Spokesman-Register*, March 29, 1966.
12. "Tough Line on Hanoi, Peking," *Chicago Daily News*, March 28, 1966.
13. Letter, Senator Barry Goldwater to Frederick Ayer, November 22, 1966, Barry M. Goldwater Papers, Arizona Historical Foundation, Arizona State University, Tempe, Arizona, Congressional papers, box 90, folder Misc. 1967–1968, At–Ay. Hereafter cited as Goldwater papers.
14. Letter, Senator Barry Goldwater to Richard E. Yoder, June 1, 1967, Goldwater papers, Congressional papers, box 90, folder Young Americans for Freedom.
15. Letter, Judd to Richard Nixon, December 15, 1967, Walter Judd Papers, Hoover Institution Archives, Stanford, California, box 31, folder Correspondence, Nixon, Richard, M., 1952–1984.
16. Letter, Senator Barry Goldwater to Richard E. Yoder, June 1, 1967, Goldwater papers, Congressional papers, box 90, folder Young Americans for Freedom.
17. Admiral U. S. G. Sharp, "We Could Have Won in Vietnam Long Ago," *Readers' Digest*, May 1969.
18. William F. Buckley Jr., "On the Right: Vietnam and Partisan Politics," Universal Press Syndicate, February 8, 1967.
19. The report was written by a subcommittee of the ASC led by Lieutenant General Edward Almond, Rear Admiral Chester C. Ward, who coauthored foreign policy analyses with Phyllis Schlafly, and Professor Stefan Possony. ASC report cited: "The Crucial Importance of Haiphong," *Cincinnati Enquirer*, August 23, 1967.
20. "Carrying the War to North Vietnam: Time to Strike the Red River Dike System," *Washington Report* (weekly ASC publication), February 19, 1968, Goldwater Papers, 'SP' series, box 3, folder 34.
21. Gregory Schneider, *Cadres for Conservatism: Young Americans for Freedom and the Rise of the Contemporary Right* (New York: New York University Press, 1999), 96.
22. William F. Buckley Jr., "On the Right: Vietnam Amen," December 10, 1966.
23. William Rusher speech notes on Vietnam, 1968, William A. Rusher papers, Library of Congress, Washington, Manuscript and Archives Division, box 208, folder Speaking engagements, miscellaneous notes and research materials, Vietnam War, 1968, n.d. Hereafter cited as Rusher papers.
24. Senator Barry Goldwater, cited in Robert A. Goldberg, *Barry Goldwater* (New Haven: Yale University Press, 1995), 249.
25. Fry, *Debating Vietnam*, 95; Senator Richard Russell, cited in ibid., 94.
26. See Seth Jacobs, *America's Miracle Man in Vietnam: Ngo Dinh Diem, Religion, Race and U.S. Intervention in Southeast Asia* (Durham: Duke University Press, 2004).
27. Joseph Morgan, *The Vietnam Lobby: The American Friends of Vietnam, 1955–1975* (Chapel Hill: University of North Carolina Press, 1997), 13–14.
28. William F. Buckley Jr., "On the Right: Vietnam Amen," December 10, 1966.
29. Spellman, cited in David Levy, *The Debate over Vietnam*, 2d ed. (Baltimore: Johns Hopkins University Press, 1995), 97.
30. John B. Judis, *William F. Buckley, Jr: Patron Saint of the Conservatives* (New York: Simon and Schuster, 2001), 246–47.
31. Levy, *Debate over Vietnam*, 141.
32. "Police Break Up Anti-war Rally," *New York Times*, August 9, 1964.
33. Support Our Boys in Vietnam Parade Committee statement, issued early May 1967, We Support Our Boys in Vietnam, Inc. Archive, Hoover Institution Archives, Stanford, California, box 7, folder Letters, 1967–1968. Hereafter cited as WSOBV archive.

34. Letter, Herbert C. Brain to Raymond W. Gimmler, April 25, 1967, WSOBV archive, box 3, folder Letters from organizations, 1967–1968.
35. "70,000 Turn Out to Back U.S. Men in Vietnam War," *New York Times,* May 14, 1967.
36. Buckley won 13.4 percent of the vote. Judis, *Buckley,* 255.
37. New York Conservative Party poster, WSOBV, box 8.
38. YAF *Action Line II* memorandum, WSOBV archive, box 10, scrapbook: Support Our Men in Vietnam Parades, 1967–1968.
39. Taped coverage of the parade is available at the Hoover Institution Archives.
40. "70,000 Turn Out to Back U.S. Men in Vietnam War," *New York Times,* May 14, 1967. PBS broadcast live coverage of the parade for several hours on May 13, 1967. The footage from this coverage was incorporated into a documentary film funded by the American Legion and developed by the original parade committee and the associated Citizens Committee for Responsible Patriotism. In 1968 Ray Gimmler, on behalf of the filmmakers, accepted a financial prize from the Freedoms Foundation at Valley Forge that enabled the committee to reproduce and disseminate copies of the documentary among patriotic groups and conservative youth groups.
41. Barry Goldwater cited in "Goldwater Says Johnson Plays Politics with War," *New York Times,* May 6, 1966.
42. Senator Barry Goldwater cited in Barry Goldwater and Jack Casserly, *Goldwater* (New York: Doubleday, 1988), 305.
43. Recent scholarship has convincingly argued that the anti-war movement, by its actions and the radicalism of its most prominent figureheads, actually prolonged the war by undermining the growth of mainstream questioning of the war. Gerard DeGroot, *A Noble Cause? America and the Vietnam War* (New York: Longman, 2000); Rhodri Jeffreys-Jones, *Peace Now! American Society and the Ending of the Vietnam War* (New Haven: Yale University Press, 1999); Adam Garfinkle, "No Discharge from that War: Aftermath of the Anti-war Movement," in *The Vietnam Anti-War Movement,* ed. Walter L. Hixson (New York: Garland Publishing, 2000), 181–84. Jeffreys-Jones emphasizes the significance of anti-war protest in sustaining mainstream working-class and labor union support for the war.
44. Levy, *Debate over Vietnam,* 86.
45. John A. Andrew III, "Pro-War and Anti-Draft: YAF and the War in Vietnam," in *The Vietnam War on Campus: Other Voices, More Distant Drums,* ed. Marc Jason Gilbert (Westport, Conn.: Praeger, 2001), 6.
46. Ronald Reagan, quoted in Rick Perlstein, *Nixonland: The Rise of a President and the Fracturing of America* (New York: Scribner, 2008), 91; ibid., 95.
47. YAF national convention statement, 1968, cited in Andrew, "Pro-War and Antidraft," 11.
48. Schneider, *Cadres for Conservatism,* 98.
49. YAF Issues Paper Number 4, "East-West trade: committing national suicide," Patrick Dowd Papers, Hoover Institution Archives, Stanford, California, box 2, folder YAF/National Board—memoranda, circulars and printed material. Hereafter cited as Dowd papers. See also Schneider, *Cadres for Conservatism,* 101–8.
50. Rebecca Klatch, *A Generation Divided: The New Left, the New Right, and the 1960s* (Berkeley: University of California Press, 1999), 101.
51. YAF Issues Paper Number 4, "East-West Trade: Committing National Suicide," Dowd papers, box 2, folder YAF/National Board—memoranda, circulars and printed material.

52. "The Case against East-West Trade," *New Guard*, April 1968, Dowd papers, box 2, folder YAF/national board—memoranda, circulars and printed matter.
53. Klatch, *Generation Divided*, 87, 81.
54. James Burnham, *National Review*, January 10, 1967.
55. Frank Meyer, "Principles and Heresies: Republican Bug-out," October 31, 1967, Frank S. Meyer Papers, Hoover Institution Archives, Stanford, California, box 17, folder Columns, book II. Hereafter cited as Meyer papers.
56. Paul Douglas statement at press conference, October 25, 1967, Robert F. Turner Papers, Hoover Institution Archives, Stanford, California, box 7, folder Citizens Committee for Peace with Freedom in Vietnam. Hereafter cited as Turner papers.
57. Mary B. Lord testimony before the Republican Platform Committee, July 30, 1968, "The Struggle for Peace with Freedom," CCPFV publication, Turner papers, box 7, folder Citizens Committee for Peace with Freedom in Vietnam.
58. David Levy has argued that the Vietnam War did not create a substantial divide in the Republican Party during the 1960s but was used as a means of attacking the Democratic Party. Levy, *Debate over Vietnam*, 77. Republicans recognized the power of a public show of unity in opposition to the Johnson administration, but in fact the signs of intraparty division were evident from the first stages of the war. For a further discussion of the Republican Party and the war, see Terry Dietz, *Republicans and the Vietnam War, 1961–1968* (Westport, Conn.: Greenwood Press, 1986), and Johns, *Vietnam's Second Front*.
59. Meyer, "Principles and Heresies: Republican Bug-out," *National Review*, October 31, 1967.
60. Kevin J. Smant, *How Great the Triumph: James Burnham, Anticommunism and the Conservative Movement* (Lanham, Md.: University Press of America, 1992), 106.
61. William Rusher speech notes on Vietnam, 1968, Rusher papers, box 208, folder Speaking engagements, miscellaneous notes and research materials, Vietnam War, 1968, n.d.
62. David Schmitz, *The Tet Offensive: Politics, War, and Public Opinion* (Oxford: Rowman and Littlefield, 2005), xv.
63. Ibid., 53, 112. Donald Critchlow notes that conservatives, namely, George Will in 1981, painted the Tet Offensive as a great victory for the United States. But, as Critchlow accurately remarks, at the time this signaled a considerable decline in public support for the war. *The Conservative Ascendancy: How the GOP Right Made Political History* (Cambridge: Harvard University Press, 2006), 83.
64. Perlstein, *Nixonland*, 153.
65. Johns, *Vietnam's Second Front*, 49.

3. CONSERVATIVES FOR NIXON
The Domestic Politics of Vietnam, 1968–1969

1. Richard Nixon, statement to Richard J. Whalen, Ray Price, and Patrick Buchanan, March 29, 1968, cited in Richard Whalen, *Catch the Falling Flag: A Republican's Challenge to His Party* (Boston: Houghton Mifflin, 1972), 137.
2. A. James Reichley, *Conservatives in an Age of Change: The Nixon and Ford Administrations* (Washington: Brookings Institution, 1981), 106.
3. Sarah Katherine Mergel, *Conservative Intellectuals and Richard Nixon: Rethinking the Rise of the Right* (New York: Palgrave Macmillan, 2010), 22.
4. Rick Perlstein, *Before the Storm: Barry Goldwater and the Unmaking of the American Consensus* (New York: Hill and Wang, 2001), 357–59.

5. Richard Nixon, cited in ibid., 358.
6. "Richard Nixon: Republican Candidate," *Human Events*, September 28, 1968.
7. Richard Nixon, quoted in Perlstein, *Before the Storm*, 515.
8. Robert A. Goldberg, *Barry Goldwater* (New Haven: Yale University Press, 1995), 251.
9. Andrew L. Johns, "A Voice from the Wilderness: Richard Nixon and the Vietnam War, 1964–1966," *Presidential Studies Quarterly* 29, no. 2 (June 1999), 318.
10. Richard Nixon, "Needed in Vietnam: The Will to Win," *Readers' Digest*, August 1964.
11. Richard Nixon, quoted in Jeffrey Kimball, *Nixon's Vietnam War* (Lawrence: University Press of Kansas, 1998), 49.
12. Richard Nixon, address to the Sales Executive Club of New York, January 26, 1965, quoted in Johns, "Voice from the Wilderness," 321.
13. Letter from Nixon to Goldwater, February 10, 1956, reprinted in Herbert S. Parmet, *Richard Nixon and His America* (Boston: Little Brown, 1990), 453.
14. Richard Nixon, cited in Dan T. Carter, *The Politics of Rage: George Wallace, the Origins of the New Conservatism, and the Transformation of American Politics* (Baton Rouge: Louisiana State University Press, 1995), 327.
15. President Johnson's attack on Nixon's Vietnam position in September 1966 did little to damage Nixon's position among the ranks of the hawks. See Johns, "Voice from the Wilderness," 327.
16. Walter Judd Papers, Hoover Institution Archives, Stanford, California, box 239, folder Nixon, Richard, 1963–1968. Hereafter cited as Judd papers.
17. Richard M. Nixon, "Asia after Vietnam," *Foreign Affairs*, October 1967.
18. Carter, *Politics of Rage*, 326, 327–29.
19. George H. Nash, *The Conservative Intellectual Movement in America since 1945*, 2d ed. (Wilmington: Intercollegiate Studies Institute, 1996), 275–76.
20. Carter, *Politics of Rage*, 335.
21. Ibid., 359.
22. "George Wallace: Humphrey's Secret Weapon," *Human Events*, August 3, 1968.
23. Strom Thurmond statement, "Endorsing former Vice President Richard M. Nixon for President," Strom Thurmond Papers, Strom Thurmond Institute, Clemson University, South Carolina, box 31, folder Statement, 'Endorsing former Vice President Richard M. Nixon for President,' Columbia, SC, June 22, 1968. Hereafter cited as Thurmond papers.
24. John B. Judis, *William F. Buckley, Jr.: Patron Saint of the Conservatives* (New York: Simon and Schuster, 2001), 282.
25. William Rusher, "What Happened at Miami Beach?" *National Review*, December 1968.
26. Goldwater diary account, June 8, 1966, Barry M. Goldwater Papers, Arizona Historical Foundation, Arizona State University, Tempe, Arizona, 'PPI' series, box 8, folder Correspondence. Hereafter cited as Goldwater papers.
27. Examples: Letter, Barry Goldwater to Ronald Reagan, August 31, 1967, Goldwater papers, Congressional series 91, box 66, folder 6; Letter, Barry Goldwater to Thomas Reed, April 25, 1968, ibid.; Letter, Barry Goldwater to Thomas Reed (copy also sent to R. Nixon), May 19, 1968, 'PPI' series, box 8, folder 20; Letter, Barry Goldwater to Ronald Reagan, 19 June 1968, Congressional series 91, box 66, folder 6.
28. Letter, Barry Goldwater to Ronald Reagan, June 19, 1968, Goldwater papers, Congressional series 91, box 66, folder 6.
29. "Why Nixon Should Abandon Kissinger's Plan," *Human Events*, August 9, 1968.

30. See, Arthur W. Radford, with Stephen Jurika Jr., *From Pearl Harbor to Vietnam: The Memoirs of Admiral Arthur W. Radford* (Stanford: Hoover Institution Press, 1980).
31. John Chamberlain, "Why the Reagan Drive Failed in the South," *Human Events*, August 24, 1968.
32. William Rusher, "What Happened at Miami Beach?" *National Review*, December 1968.
33. *Human Events*, August 24, 1968.
34. Mergel, *Conservative Intellectuals and Richard Nixon*, 35. Andrew Johns notes that a "memorandum in the files of the Republican National Committee acknowledges that Nixon did indicate that he had definite ideas on how to end the war through what would become known as Vietnamization. Yet he did not reveal his thoughts to even his closest confidants." Andrew Johns, *Vietnam's Second Front: Domestic Politics, the Republican Party, and the War* (Lexington: University Press of Kentucky, 2010), 198.
35. "Richard Nixon: Republican Candidate," *Human Events*, September 28, 1968.
36. Richard Nixon, speech before the Committee on Resolutions, Republican National Convention, August 1, 1968, cited in "Richard Nixon: Republican Candidate," *Human Events*, September 28, 1968.
37. Ronald Reagan, speech before Platform Committee, Republican National Convention, July 31, 1968, Ronald Reagan Subject Collection, Hoover Institution Archives, Stanford, California, box 2, unidentified folder.
38. Jeffrey Kimball, *The Vietnam War Files: Uncovering the Secret History of Nixon-era Strategy* (Lawrence: University Press of Kansas, 2004), 61; Stanley Karnow, *Vietnam: A History* (New York: Penguin, 1984), 597–98.
39. Richard Nixon, cited in transcript of meeting with southern Republicans, August 6, 1968, "What Dick Nixon Told Southern Delegates," *Miami Herald*, August 7, 1968, reprinted in Kimball, *Vietnam War Files*, 64–65.
40. "How Nixon Now Views the Viet Nam War," *Human Events*, December 28, 1968.
41. Richard Nixon speech before the Committee on Resolutions, Republican National Convention, August 1, 1968, cited in "Richard Nixon: Republican Candidate," *Human Events*, September 28, 1968.
42. Kimball, *Vietnam War Files*, 64–65.
43. In 1971 Roland Evans and Robert Novak stated that by 1968 Nixon was no longer an "unequivocal hawk" on Vietnam, but Nixon's policies and certainly his rhetoric remained preoccupied with the premise that American credibility would be determined by the outcome of the war. Evans and Novak, *Nixon in the White House: The Frustration of Power* (London: Random House, 1971), 75. Recent scholars attest to changes in Nixon's understanding of Vietnam by 1967, Kimball, *Nixon's Vietnam War*, 29–30; Robert Schulzinger, *A Time for War: The United States and Vietnam, 1941–1975* (New York: Oxford University Press, 1997), 287–300, Reichley, *Conservatives in an Age of Change*, 106. The conservative political activist Lee Edwards later claimed that there was no reason in 1968 to anticipate the "accommodationist" foreign policy adopted by the Nixon administration. Edwards, *The Conservative Revolution: The Movement that Remade America* (New York: Free Press, 1999), 165.
44. Kimball, *Nixon's Vietnam War*, 40.
45. Letter, Richard Nixon to William F. Buckley Jr., April 8, 1968, William F. Buckley Jr. Papers, Sterling Memorial Library Manuscripts and Archives, Yale University, New Haven, Connecticut, box 52, folder Nixon, Richard M. Hereafter cited as Buckley papers.

46. Kimball, *Nixon's Vietnam War*, 29.
47. Report of debate between William Rusher and Mark Anderson, affiliated with JBS, Salt Lake City, October 15, 1968, *Daily Utah Chronicle*, October 15, 1968.
48. Letter, Strom Thurmond to Mrs. Gale Griffin, constituent, July 5, 1968, Thurmond papers, Subject Correspondence Series, Subject correspondence box 15, folder Foreign relations 7 (War in Vietnam) folder VII; June 19–July 26, 1968. Thurmond had endorsed Nixon's candidacy for president on June 22, 1968.
49. Buckley papers, box 57, folder Young Americans for Freedom (YAF), Sep–Dec 1968.
50. William A. Rusher papers, Library of Congress, Washington, Manuscript and Archives Division, box 131, folder ACU, Aims and principles, 1965. Hereafter cited as Rusher papers.
51. Letter, John Mitchell to William F. Buckley Jr., October 11, 1968, Buckley papers, box 52, folder White House suggestions and recommendations for Administration positions in 1969.
52. William Rusher, "What Happened at Miami Beach?" *National Review*, December 1968.
53. Colin Dueck, *Hard Line: The Republican Party and U.S. Foreign Policy since World War II* (Princeton: Princeton University Press, 2010), 148.
54. See Kent G. Sieg, "The 1968 Presidential Campaign and Peace in Vietnam," in *Leadership and Diplomacy in the Vietnam War*, ed. Walter L. Hixson (New York: Garland, 2000), 275–76. Sieg contends that "Republicans and the general public were convinced that the war had to be pursued with more vigor, or the United States should get out; consequently, they were not necessarily dissatisfied with LBJ's hard line in 1968. Nixon personally kept a 'low profile' during the campaign on Vietnam because he also did not oppose the president's policies."
55. "Richard Nixon: Republican Candidate," *Human Events*, September 28, 1968.
56. Evans and Novak, *Nixon*, 75.
57. Kimball, *Nixon's Vietnam War*, 41. Kimball continued, "For doves and moderates, he [Nixon] spoke less of escalating military measures and protecting vital interests and more of taking *non-military* steps toward *peace*; for hawks and conservatives, he continued to talk about putting *pressure* and *winning* the peace. For all Americans, he spoke of a peace with *honor*."
58. See Larry Berman, *No Peace, No Honor: Nixon, Kissinger, and Betrayal in Vietnam* (New York: Touchstone, 2001), 32–36; Kimball, *Nixon's Vietnam War*, 56–62; Anthony Summers, *The Arrogance of Power: The Secret World of Richard Nixon* (New York: Penguin, 2000), xiv, 298–305.
59. Kimball, *Nixon's Vietnam War*, 58.
60. Telephone conversation between President Johnson and Richard Nixon, September 30, 1968, *Foreign Relations of the United States* (FRUS), 1964–1968, vol. 7, Vietnam, September 1968–January 1969, Doc. 38.
61. Sieg, "The 1968 Presidential Election and Peace in Vietnam," 279.
62. Governor Ronald Reagan, quoted in Johns, *Vietnam's Second Front*, 228; Senator John Tower, quoted in Johns, *Vietnam's Second Front*, 230.
63. AFL-CIO platform proposals, 1968, released July 29, 1968, Jay Lovestone Papers, Hoover Institution Archives, Stanford, California, box 10, folder The AFL-CIO Platform Proposals, 1968. Hereafter cited as Lovestone papers.
64. AFL-CIO platform proposals, 1968, released July 29, 1968, Lovestone papers, box 10, folder The AFL-CIO Platform Proposals, 1968.
65. Secretary Clark Clifford outlined the possibility that the halt would be misconstrued as a purely political maneuver. Telephone conversation between

President Johnson and Secretary of Defense Clifford, October 22, 1968, *FRUS, 1964–1968*, vol. 7, Vietnam, September 1968–January 1969, Doc. 106.
66. Telephone conversation between President Johnson and Senator Richard Russell, October 23, 1968, *FRUS, 1964–1968*, vol. 7, Vietnam, September 1968–January 1969, Doc. 109.
67. "Air Force Association Plan for Ending the War," Ralph de Toledano, *Human Events*, October 19, 1968.
68. "North Viet Nam Rebuilds Supply Routes during Bomb Pause," *Human Events*, October 19, 1968.
69. "What Viet Nam Has Taught Us," *Human Events*, November 9, 1968 (column written before the election).
70. Senator Strom Thurmond press release, October 31, 1968, Thurmond papers, Speeches subseries A, box 31, folder Press release, [On the cessation of bombing in Vietnam]; Washington, D.C., October 31, 1968.
71. "Election of Nixon, Defeat of HHH Vital after Bombing Halt," *Shreveport Times*, November 4, 1968.
72. "Air Force Association Plan for Ending the War," Ralph de Toledano, *Human Events*, October 19, 1968.
73. Judis, *Buckley*, 297.
74. Johnson administration report, early December 1968, Nixon Presidential Materials, National Archives, College Park, Maryland, National Security Council files, Henry A. Kissinger Office Files, HAK administrative and staff files, box 3, folder Vietnam. Hereafter cited as Kissinger files.
75. Tower's response to a Johnson administration report: "Current Vietnam Situation (beginning of December)," Nixon–Agnew Key Issues Committee, December 6, 1968, Kissinger files, box 3, folder Vietnam.
76. Confidential report, Current Vietnam Situation (beginning of December), Nixon–Agnew Key Issues Committee, December 6, 1968, Kissinger files, box 3, folder Vietnam.
77. "How Nixon Now Views Viet Nam War," *Human Events*, December 28, 1968.
78. Evans and Novak, *Nixon*, 83.
79. Writing in the *New York Times*, Max Frankel described Nixon's cabinet as "a team of moderates." Chester Lewis, Godfrey Hodgson, and Bruce Page, *An American Melodrama: The Presidential Campaign of 1968* (New York: Viking Adult, 1969), 778.
80. ACU newsletter, January 1969, Rusher papers, box 134, folder ACU–Newsletter, ACU Report, 1965–69.
81. "Mr. Nixon, Thus Far, Disappoints," *Republican Battle Line*, February/March 1969, Rusher papers, box 135, folder ACU, Newsletter, Republican Battle Line, printed versions, 1969–70.
82. Senator Barry Goldwater, speech in the Senate, early March 1969, reported by Bob Kephart, *Human Events*, in letter to William Rusher, mid-March 1969, Rusher papers, box 41, folder Human Events.
83. *Republican Battle Line*, April 1969, Rusher papers, box 135, folder ACU, Newsletter, Republican Battle Line, printed versions, 1969–70.
84. Letter, William F. Buckley Jr. to Senator Barry Goldwater, March 18, 1969, copy of column attached, Buckley papers, box 61, folder Goldwater, Barry.
85. Buckley, "On the Right: Restiveness on the Right," Buckley papers, box 435, folder Buckley columns, *On the Right*, Jan–Jun 1969.
86. Barry Goldwater diary entry, February 8, 1969, Goldwater papers, Personal/Political I series, box 9, folder Senator's personal.

87. Letter, Barry Goldwater to J. Nelson, March 26, 1969, Goldwater papers, Congressional series 91, box 48, folder Various subjects, legislative miscellaneous correspondence, 1969–70.
88. Letter, Barry Goldwater to Bryce Harlow, April 15, 1969, Goldwater papers, Congressional series 91, box 77, folder 4.
89. Letter, Barry Goldwater to Harry Dent, June 3, 1969, Goldwater papers, Congressional series 91, box 88, folder 2.
90. Joan Hoff, *Nixon Reconsidered* (New York: Basic Books, 1994), 158.
91. Evans and Novak, *Nixon*, 20.
92. Reichley, *Conservatives in an Age of Change*, 67. Together with Kissinger's reorganization of the National Security Council (NSC) and interagency role in the development of foreign policy, the NSC assumed a new level of importance in the formulation of policy.
93. See Reichley, *Conservatives in an Age of Change*, 64–67, Gerard DeGroot, *A Noble Cause? America and the Vietnam War* (New York: Longman, 2000), 201, Hoff, *Nixon Reconsidered*, 159–60, Henry Kissinger, *White House Years* (London: Phoenix Press, 1979), 11.
94. *National Review*, May 6, 1969.
95. Kimball, *Nixon's Vietnam War*, 71.
96. Ibid., 75. See also Reichley, *Conservatives in an Age of Change*, 109, 115–18.
97. *Chicago Tribune*, March 3, 1969.
98. Judis, *Buckley*, 302.
99. Writing to Henry Kissinger on October 22, 1969, Buckley claimed that Frank Shakespeare, head of the United States Information Agency, had said the following to Buckley: "If you [Buckley] never do another thing for your country, your introducing Henry Kissinger to the Nixon people will still qualify you as a hero." Buckley papers, box 67, folder White House (1969), Kissinger, Henry A. Writing to the academic Henry Paolucci in defense of his support of Kissinger, Buckley stated, "It is worse than you suppose—I introduced him to Nixon during the '68 campaign." January 4, 1971, Buckley papers, box 214, folder Paolucci, Henry, 1969–73. Kissinger also mentioned the fact that Buckley had introduced him to Mitchell in early October 1968. *White House Years*, 10.
100. Letter, Allan Ryskind to William F. Buckley Jr., December 10, 1968, Buckley papers, box 65, folder Ryskind, Allan.
101. Letter, William Buckley Jr. to Professor Henry Paolucci, January 2, 1969, Buckley papers, box 219, folder Paolucci, Henry, 1969–73. Paolucci consistently urged *National Review* to cease its support of Kissinger and wrote in 1980 that the "so-called respectable right of the Buckley conservatives' were fearful of accusations of anti-Semitism 'to the level of paranoia.'" Henry Paolucci, *Kissinger's War: 1957–1975* (New York: Griffon House, 1980), 36. While *National Review* was eager to avoid any association with anti-Semitic views, which had dominated the *American Mercury* during its final years, there is no evidence that this was the reason Buckley endorsed Kissinger's foreign policies.
102. Letter, Henry Kissinger to William F. Buckley Jr., December 10, 1968, Buckley papers, box 65, folder White House, suggestions and recommendations for positions in the Nixon administration (Oct 1968–April 1969).
103. Judis, *Buckley*, 300.
104. Reichley, *Conservatives in an Age of Change*, 110.
105. Ralph de Toledano, "Later Reflections on the Nixon Cabinet," December 14/15, 1968, Ralph de Toledano Papers, Hoover Institution Archives, Stanford,

California, box 2, folder King Features Column, Sept–Dec 1968. Hereafter cited as De Toledano papers. Writing in 1969, the journalists Lewis Chester, Godfrey Hodgson, and Bruce Page described Laird as a "supple right-wing politician." Chester et al., *American Melodrama*, 778.
106. Memorandum, H. R. Haldeman to Patrick Buchanan, March 13, 1969, Nixon Presidential Materials, National Archives, College Park, Maryland, White House Special Files, Staff Member and Office Files, H. R. Haldeman, 1969–73, box 49, folder Memos/Pat Buchanan (March 1969). Hereafter cited as Haldeman files.
107. Memorandum, Patrick Buchanan to the President, March 6, 1969, Nixon Presidential Materials, National Archives, College Park, Maryland, White House Special Files, Staff Member and Office Files, President's office files, box 77, folder March 2, 1969. Hereafter cited as President's office files.
108. Tom Wells, *The War Within: America's Battle over Vietnam* (Berkeley: University of California Press, 1994), 287–88.
109. Kissinger, *White House Years*, 261.
110. Ibid., 253.
111. Memorandum of president's meeting with participants of the 1969 TIME News Tour of the Far East and representatives of TIME, Inc., composed by Alexander Butterfield for the president's file, March 11, 1969. President's office files, 1969–74, box 77, folder March 9, 1969.
112. Memorandum, Patrick Buchanan to the President, March 4, 1969, President's office files, box 77, folder March 2, 1969.
113. Richard Nixon, *RN: The Memoirs of Richard Nixon* (New York: Grosset and Dunlap, 1978), 391.
114. "What Now in Vietnam?," *National Review*, May 6, 1969.
115. President Richard Nixon, "Address to the Nation on Vietnam," May 14, 1969, *Public Papers of the Presidents of the United States, Richard Nixon, 1969* (Washington: Government Printing Office, 1971), Doc. 195.
116. "Joint statement following the meeting with President Thieu," June 8, 1969, *Public Papers, Nixon, 1969*, Doc. 232.
117. Memorandum, Patrick Buchanan to the President, May 13, 1969, Subject: One observer's notes of legislative leadership meeting, May 13, 1969, President's office files, box 78, folder 11 May 1969.
118. Memorandum, Patrick Buchanan to the President (notes on meeting with Congressional leaders, 15 May 1969), May 16, 1969, President's office files, box 78, folder 11 May 1969.
119. Nixon, "Address to the Nation on Vietnam," May 14, 1969, *Public Papers, Nixon, 1969*, Doc. 195.
120. Kimball, *Nixon's Vietnam War*, 104.
121. "What Now in Vietnam?," *National Review*, May 6, 1969.
122. Walter Judd handwritten notes on *National Review* editorial on Vietnam, May 6, 1969, Judd papers, box 250, folder Vietnam, general, 1969, January–October.
123. Congressman Gerald Ford, May 15, 1969, *Congressional Record*, House, vol. 115, 12645.
124. Congressman Carl Albert (D-OK), May 15, 1969, *Congressional Record*, House, vol. 115, 12648.
125. Congressman Edward J. Derwinski (R-IL), May 15, 1969, *Congressional Record*, House, vol. 115, 12662.
126. H. R. Haldeman, *The Haldeman Diaries: Inside the Nixon White House* (New York: G. P. Putnam's Sons, 1994), diary entry for June 8, 1969, 64.

127. Evans and Novak, *Nixon*, 80.
128. Haldeman, *Diaries*, entry for June 19, 1969, 65.
129. Kimball, *Nixon's Vietnam War*, 150.
130. Haldeman, *Diaries*, entry for June 20, 1969, 65.
131. Melvin Small argues that Vietnamization was meant to assure the American people that the war was not endless and to convince Hanoi of the full American support for administration policy but had the effect, he concludes, of convincing Hanoi to hold out longer. Small, *Johnson, Nixon, and the Doves* (New Brunswick: Rutgers University Press, 1988), 191–92, 230. Robert McNamara has observed that the Nixon administration fell victim to its own illusion of Vietnamization: "The idea that the United States could withdraw completely and that the South Vietnamese government would successfully defend itself against the NLF and North Vietnamese forces." Robert S. McNamara, James G. Blight, Robert K. Brigham, Thomas J. Biersteher, and Col. Herbert Y. Schlandler, *Argument without End: In Search of Answers to the Vietnam Tragedy* (New York: Public Affairs, 1999), 367. George Donelson Moss claims that Vietnamization "rested on a fantasy" that the "motley home guards" of South Vietnam "could be molded into a modern strike force that would be able to hold its own against the disciplined, battle-tested units of the NVA." Moss, *Vietnam: An American Ordeal* (Englewood Cliffs: Prentice Hall, 1990), 307. Gerard DeGroot assumes a similar approach, although he also argues that the administration was aware that Vietnamization was not going to work, concluding that it "did not actually need to work, as long as it *appeared* that progress was made." The "charade," as DeGroot described it, "worked too well; many Americans began to believe that Nixon had found the magic formula to get the United States out of the war *and* defeat the communists." DeGroot, *Noble Cause*, 211.
132. Kimball, *Nixon's Vietnam War*, 137–39, 154–55, Kimball, *Vietnam War Files*, 11–13, 82–83.
133. Berman, *No Peace, No Honor*, 50–51, 261–62.
134. Joan Hoff discusses Vietnamization in this context,, and asserts that Laird played a prominent role in the development of the Nixon Doctrine. See Hoff, *Nixon Reconsidered*, 163–65.
135. Kimball, *Nixon's Vietnam War*, 155.
136. Haldeman, *Diaries*, entry for July 24–25, 1969, with additional notation, 74–75. Haldeman originally referred to the Apollo moon landing.
137. Michael Miles describes the Nixon Doctrine as a "renewal of Eisenhower Dulles foreign policy." *The Odyssey of the American Right* (New York: Oxford University Press, 1980), 312.
138. Parmet, *Nixon*, 566–67.
139. President Richard Nixon, commencement address at the Air Force Academy, June 4, 1969, *Public Papers, Nixon, 1969*, Doc. 225.
140. Memorandum, Alexander Butterfield to Henry Kissinger and Herb Klein, cc. to John Ehrlichman, Ron Ziegler, and Bud Keogh, June 30, 1969, Haldeman files, box 50, folder Memos Dr [Henry] Kissinger (June 1969).
141. Haldeman, *Diaries*, diary entry for July 7, 1969, 69–70.
142. Sir Robert Thompson, cited in Karnow, *Vietnam*, 612.
143. Memorandum of conversation, Nixon, Thompson, and Kissinger, October 17, 1969, reprinted in Kimball, *Vietnam War Files*, 122–24.
144. Lien-Hang Nguyen, "Waging War on All Fronts: Nixon, Kissinger, and the Vietnam War, 1969–1972," in *Nixon in the World: American Foreign Relations,*

1969–1977, ed. Fredrik Logevall and Andrew Preston (New York: Oxford University Press, 2008), 192.
145. Sir Robert Thompson, cited in Kimball, *Vietnam War Files*, 122.
146. Thomas A. Lane press release, "War Requires More than Troop Withdrawal," June 17, 1969, Thurmond papers, Military Assistant Series, box 18, folder Vietnam.
147. Lane, cited in W. Wood, "While Brave Men Die," *American Opinion*, June 1967.
148. Thomas A. Lane press release, "War Requires More than Troop Withdrawal," June 17, 1969, Thurmond papers, Military Assistant Series, box 18, folder Vietnam.
149. Caroline Page, *United States Official Propaganda during the Vietnam War, 1965–1973: The Limits of Persuasion* (London: Leicester University Press, 1996), 254.
150. Senator Strom Thurmond press release, "On the Withdrawal of American Troops in Vietnam," June 16, 1969, Thurmond papers, Speeches subseries A, box 36, folder 03075.
151. Letter, Barry Goldwater to constituent, June 23, 1969, Goldwater papers, Congressional series 91, box 40, folder Vietnam War—pro- June–Sept 1969, legislative-general correspondence, 1969–1970.
152. Letter, Barry Goldwater to G. Hawkins, April 7, 1969, Goldwater papers, Congressional series 91, box 40, folder Vietnam War—pro- January–May 1969, legislative-general correspondence, 1969–1970.
153. Letter, Barry Goldwater to B. Oberg, July 8, 1969, Goldwater papers, Congressional series 91, box 40, folder Vietnam War—pro- June–Sept 1969, legislative-general correspondence, 1969–1970.
154. Barry Goldwater diary entry, July 4, 1969, Goldwater papers, Personal/political I series, box 9, folder Senator's private.
155. Senator Strom Thurmond, July 2, 1969, *Congressional Record*, Senate, vol. 115, 18264.
156. General Thomas Lane, "No Viet Nam Victory in Sight: Why Nixon Should Abandon Kissinger's Plan," *Human Events*, August 9, 1969.
157. *ACU News*, June 6, 1969, Rusher papers, box 135, folder ACU—Press releases, 1965–73.
158. CCPFV, "The Choice in Vietnam," October 29, 1969, Buckley papers, box 179, folder Vietnam—Today Show. The CCPFV used Nixon's own words, of February 8, 1968, to support this point: "The Viet Cong and the North Vietnamese . . . cannot and should not count on American division to gain politically in the United States what they cannot gain militarily in Vietnam."
159. CCPFV, "The Choice in Vietnam," October 29, 1969, Buckley papers, box 179, folder Vietnam—Today Show.
160. General Earle Wheeler, chair of the JCS, press conference on departure from Saigon, October 6, 1969.
161. "Turning Point in Viet Nam: Will Nixon Heed His Own Advice?" Senator Strom Thurmond, *Human Events*, October 11, 1969.
162. Letter, Barry Goldwater to Charles R. Whitmer, July 30, 1969, Goldwater papers, Congressional series 90, box 40, folder Vietnam War—pro- Nov–Dec 1969, legislative-general correspondence, 1969–1970.
163. Goldwater diary, July 4, 1969, Goldwater papers, Personal/Political I, box 5, folder 9, Senator's private.
164. Goldwater diary, July 4, 1969, Goldwater papers, Personal/Political I, box 5, folder 9, Senator's private.
165. Letter, Goldwater to Helen R. Fennell, October 6, 1969, Goldwater papers,

Congressional series 90, box 40, folder Vietnam War—pro- October 1969, legislative-general correspondence, 1969-1970.
166. Letter, Goldwater to George Bott, September 10, 1969, Goldwater papers, Congressional series 90, box 40, folder Vietnam War—pro- June-Sept 1969, legislative-general correspondence, 1969-1970.
167. Andrew Johns convincingly argues that throughout the war Congress as a whole took only limited steps to impact administration policy in Vietnam. "Through their actions and—perhaps more important—inaction, members of Congress played an essential part in the escalation and duration of the Vietnam conflict." Johns, *Vietnam's Second Front*, 3.
168. Memorandum, H. R. Haldeman to Bryce Harlow, Henry Kissinger, and John Ehrlichman, October 1, 1969, Haldeman files, box 53, folder Memos/Henry Kissinger (October 1969).
169. "After the Stalemate, What?," *Human Events*, October 11, 1969.
170. Kimball, *Nixon's Vietnam War*, 139.
171. Ibid., 165-66.
172. William Burr and Jeffrey Kimball, "Nixon's Secret Nuclear Alert: Vietnam War Diplomacy and the Joint Chiefs of Staff Readiness Test, October 1969," *Cold War History* 2, no. 2 (2003), 113-56.
173. President Nixon, "Address to the Nation on Vietnam," November 3, 1969, *Public Papers, Nixon, 1969*, Doc. 425.
174. "'Vietnamization' Causes Growing Problems," *Human Events*, December 13, 1969.
175. White House release, November 5, 1969, Goldwater papers, Congressional series 91, box 77, folder 4.
176. Frank Meyer, "October 15, 1969 v. November 5, 1968," *National Review*, November 4, 1969.

4. From Victory to Honor
Making Peace with Withdrawal, 1969-1972

1. Edmund F. Wehrle, "Labor's Longest War: Trade Unionists and the Vietnam Conflict," *Labor's Heritage* 11, no. 4 (Winter/Spring 2002), 50-65.
2. "Right Wing Unhappy with Nixon," *Detroit, Michigan News*, November 19, 1969, copy in William A. Rusher papers, Library of Congress, Washington, Manuscript and Archives Division, box 131, folder ACU-Articles and newspaper clippings, 1965-73. Hereafter cited as Rusher papers.
3. *Republican Battle Line*, November 1969, Rusher papers, box 135, folder ACU, Newsletter, Republican Battle Line, printed versions, 1969-1970.
4. William F. Buckley Jr., "On the Right: Summing it Up," December 18, 1969, William F. Buckley Jr. Papers, Sterling Memorial Library Manuscripts and Archives, Yale University, New Haven, Connecticut, box 435, folder Buckley columns, On the Right, Nov-Dec 1969. Hereafter cited as Buckley papers.
5. Kevin J. Smant, *How Great the Triumph: James Burnham, Anticommunism and the Conservative Movement* (Lanham, Md.: University Press of America, 1992), 107.
6. William F. Buckley Jr., "On the Right: Summing it Up," December 18, 1969, Buckley papers, box 435, folder Buckley columns, On the Right, Nov-Dec 1969.
7. Letter, Senator Barry Goldwater to Master Sergeant F. N. Steele, USAF (Ret.), January 2, 1970, Barry M. Goldwater Papers, Arizona Historical Foundation,

Arizona State University, Tempe, Arizona, Congressional Series 91, box 28, folder Nixon's speech on peace in Vietnam, legislative-general correspondence, 1969–1970. Hereafter cited as Goldwater papers.

8. Letter, Senator Barry Goldwater to F. W. Osborne, January 21, 1970, Goldwater papers, Congressional Series 91, box 39, folder Vietnam War, legislative-general correspondence, 1969–1970 [2].
9. Letter, Senator Barry Goldwater to R. Adair, January 6, 1970, Goldwater papers, Congressional Series 91, box 39, folder Vietnam War, legislative-general correspondence, 1969–1970 [2].
10. Memorandum, Patrick Buchanan to the President, December 18, 1969, Nixon Presidential Materials, National Archives, College Park, Maryland, White House Special Files, Staff Member and Office Files, H. R. Haldeman, box 56, folder Memos/Pat Buchanan (January 1970). Hereafter cited as Haldeman files.
11. Memorandum, Henry Kissinger to H. R. Haldeman, December 27, 1970, Haldeman files, box 56, folder Memos/Pat Buchanan (January 1970).
12. Walter Judd Papers, Hoover Institution Archives, Stanford, California, box 218, folder Subject file—American Council for World Freedom 1970–1972; Letter, Walter Judd to Lady Malcolm Douglas-Hamilton, April 4, 1972, Judd papers, box 225, folder Subject file, Communism and anticommunism, correspondence, 1961–1975. Hereafter cited as Judd papers. Letter, Lee Edwards, David Rowe, Dr. Lev Dobriansky, Dr. Stefan T. Possony, Rev. Raymond de Jaeger, S.J., Walter Chopiwskyj, January 14, 1970, Rusher papers, box 29, folder Edwards, Lee, 1969–85.
13. Letter, Allan H. Ryskind to Harry Dent, 19 December 1969, Nixon Presidential Materials, National Archives, College Park, Maryland, White House Special Files, Staff Member and Office Files, Harry S. Dent Files, 1969–1970, box 2, folder Staff memos, October 1969–January 1970.
14. "Will Administration End Vacillation? Cambodia Needs U.S. Military Aid," *Human Events*, May 2, 1970.
15. "Nixon Administration Split on Cambodia Question," *Human Events*, April 25, 1971.
16. President Richard M. Nixon, "Address to the Nation on the Situation in Southeast Asia," April 30, 1970, *Public Papers of the Presidents of the United States, Richard Nixon, 1970* (Washington: Government Printing Office, 1971), Doc. 139.
17. Roland Evans and Robert Novak, *Nixon in the White House: The Frustration of Power* (London: Random House, 1971), 245.
18. President Richard M. Nixon, "Address to the Nation on the Situation in Southeast Asia," April 30, 1970, *Public Papers, Nixon, 1970*, Doc. 139.
19. Evans and Novak, *Nixon*, 245.
20. Memorandum, Charles Colson to H. R. Haldeman, May 1, 1970, Nixon Presidential Materials, National Archives, College Park, Maryland, White House Special Files, Staff Member and Office Files, Charles Colson, box 34, folder American Legion. Hereafter cited as Colson files.
21. Memorandum, Charles Colson to H. R. Haldeman, May 1, 1970, Colson files, box 34, folder American Legion.
22. Senator Barry Goldwater, cited in Robert A. Goldberg, *Barry Goldwater* (New Haven: Yale University Press, 1995), 263; Senator Barry Goldwater form letter, May 1970, Goldwater papers, Congressional Series 91, box 11, folder Cambodian War—For, Armed Services Comm., Legislative–general, correspondence, 1969–70; Senator Barry Goldwater cited in "Anarchists Blasted by Goldwater,"

Arizona Republic, May 6, 1970, Goldwater papers, Personal/political III, box 2, folder Newspaper articles, May 1970; Letter, Senator Barry Goldwater to J. M. Collier, September 17, 1970, Goldwater papers, Congressional Series 91, box 39, folder Vietnam War, legislative-general correspondence, 1969–1970.

23. Senator Strom Thurmond press release, May 5, 1970, Strom Thurmond Papers, Strom Thurmond Institute, Clemson University, South Carolina, box 40, folder Press release, "Nixon's Actions against North Vietnamese Sanctuaries," Washington, DC, May 5, 1970. Hereafter cited as Thurmond papers.

24. AFL-CIO Department of Public Relations press release, Statement of AFL-CIO President George Meaney, 1 May 1970, Colson files, box 20, folder AFL-CIO Executive Council Meeting with President, 5/12/70.

25. Memorandum, Charles Colson to the President, May 11, 1970, Colson files, box 20, folder AFL-CIO Executive Council Meeting with President, 5/12/70.

26. Memorandum, Henry Kissinger to U. Alexis Smith, Undersecretary of State for Political Affairs, David Packard, Deputy Secretary of Defense, Adm. Thomas H. Moorer, Acting Chairman, Joint Chiefs of Staff, Richard Helms, Director, Central Intelligence Agency, June 17, 1970. Nixon Presidential Materials, National Archives, College Park, Maryland, National Security Council files, Henry A. Kissinger Office Files, HAK administrative and staff files, box 13, folder Cambodia. Hereafter cited as Kissinger files.

27. Lien-Hang Nguyen, "Waging War on All Fronts: Nixon, Kissinger, and the Vietnam War, 1969–1972," in *Nixon in the World: American Foreign Relations, 1969–1977,* ed. Fredrik Logevall and Andrew Preston (New York: Oxford University Press, 2008), 194.

28. Gerard DeGroot, *A Noble Cause? America and the Vietnam War* (New York: Longman, 2000), 222; Jeffrey Kimball, *Nixon's Vietnam War* (Lawrence: University Press of Kansas, 1998), 217.

29. Colin Dueck, *Hard Line: The Republican Party and U.S. Foreign Policy since World War II* (Princeton: Princeton University Press, 2010), 160.

30. Andrew Johns, *Vietnam's Second Front: Domestic Politics, the Republican Party, and the War* (Lexington: University Press of Kentucky, 2010), 294.

31. Senator Strom Thurmond, Press release, June 30, 1970, Thurmond papers, box 40, folder Press release, "Thurmond's opposition to the passage of the Cooper–Church amendment," Washington, D.C., June 30, 1970.

32. "Shameful Day in the Senate," *Human Events,* July 11, 1970.

33. Senator Strom Thurmond, Press release, May 14, 1970, Thurmond papers, Speeches subseries A, box 40, folder Press release, "Passage of the Cooper–Church Amendment would be a Tragic Mistake," Washington, D.C., May 14, 1970.

34. "For the Short War and the Long War," *Human Events,* May 16, 1970 (Kilpatrick column, *Washington Star Syndicate*).

35. ACU's *Republican Battle Line,* May 1970, Rusher papers, box 135, folder ACU, Newsletter, Republican Battle Line, printed versions, 1969–1970.

36. ACU official statement on the allied attack on enemy sanctuaries in Cambodia, May 1, 1970, copy printed in *Republican Battle Line,* May 1970, Rusher papers, box 135, folder ACU, Newsletter, Republican Battle Line, printed versions, 1969–1970.

37. Letter, Senator Barry Goldwater to the President, May 6, 1970, Goldwater papers, Congressional series 91, box 81, folder 6.

38. Senator Barry Goldwater confidential memorandum, May 1970, Goldwater papers, Personal, box 5, folder 3.

39. Letter, Senator Barry Goldwater to the President, May 6, 1970, Goldwater papers, Congressional series 91, box 81, folder 6.
40. Smant, *How Great the Triumph*, 107.
41. "The Cooper–Church Amendment, Is it Constitutional?" C. Dickerman Williams, *National Review*, July 14, 1970.
42. William F. Buckley Jr., "On the Right: The Stakes in Cambodia," May 2/3, 1970, Buckley papers, box 435, folder Buckley columns, On the Right, May 1970.
43. James Buckley, cited in an article by Lester Abelman, "Dem Candidates Rap Nixon," May 1970, Rusher papers, box 169, folder Political campaigns, Buckley, James, articles and newspaper clippings, 1970.
44. Letter, Garry Wills to Bill Buckley, May 18, 1970, Buckley papers, box 279, folder Wills, Garry.
45. Letter, William F. Buckley Jr. to Garry Wills, June 8, 1970, Buckley papers, box 279, folder Wills, Garry.
46. Letter, William Rusher to Patrick Buchanan, July 21, 1970, Rusher papers, box 13, folder General Corr., Buchanan, Patrick J., 1969–1988.
47. Garry Wills column, "Nixon, the Fifties President," July 1, 1970, Buckley papers, box 279, folder Wills, Garry.
48. Morrie Ryskind, "The Wailing Wall," *Human Events*, June 20, 1970.
49. Vice President Spiro Agnew, excerpts from speech before group of Ohio Republicans at Sheraton Cleveland Hotel, Cleveland, Ohio, June 20, 1970, reprinted in *Human Events*, July 4, 1970.
50. Henry Kissinger, *White House Years* (London: Phoenix Press, 1979), 508.
51. Memorandum, Henry Kissinger to U. Alexis Smith, Undersecretary of State for Political Affairs, David Packard, Deputy Secretary of Defense, Adm. Thomas H. Moorer, Acting Chairman, Joint Chiefs of Staff, Richard Helms, Director, Central Intelligence Agency, June 17, 1970. Kissinger attached a "summary of the President's views on Cambodia, which Nixon had expressed at the June 15 WSAG meeting." Kissinger files, box 13, folder Cambodia.
52. Department of State publication 8545, Pamphlet, "A Conversation with the President," transcript of a television interview that Nixon conducted with representatives of the three major television networks: John Chancellor, NBC News; Eric Sevareid, CBS News; Howard K. Smith, ABC News. The interview was televised live from Los Angeles on July 1, 1970. Copy of pamphlet in Jay Lovestone Papers, Hoover Institution Archives, Stanford, California, box 172, folder U.S. Department of State. Hereafter cited as Lovestone papers.
53. Morrie Ryskind, "The Wailing Wall," *Human Events*, June 20, 1970.
54. Letter, Ralph de Toledano to William F. Buckley Jr., August 26, 1970, Buckley papers, box 126, folder de Toledano.
55. For a fuller discussion of conservatives' responses to Nixon's domestic and economic policies, see Sarah Katherine Mergel, *Conservative Intellectuals and Richard Nixon: Rethinking the Rise of the Right* (New York: Palgrave Macmillan, 2010).
56. Memorandum, Patrick Buchanan to the President, January 6, 1971, Colson files, box 52, folder Conservatives.
57. John B. Judis, *William F. Buckley, Jr.: Patron Saint of the Conservatives* (New York: Simon and Schuster, 1988), 304.
58. David Keene, quoted in ibid.
59. William F. Buckley Jr., *Playboy*, May 1970.
60. Memorandum, Patrick Buchanan to the President, January 6, 1971, Colson files, box 52, folder Conservatives.

61. See Gregory Schneider, *Cadres for Conservatism: Young Americans for Freedom and the Rise of the Contemporary Right* (New York: New York University Press, 1999), 131–41.
62. Senator John Tower, "The Priority of Defense: Safeguard and the Balance of Power," *The New Guard*, September 1970 (10th anniversary special edition), Rusher papers, box 212, folder Speaking engagements, presentations, speeches and lectures, May–Sept 1970.
63. Kissinger, *White House Years*, 513, 969.
64. Richard Nixon, cited in record of cabinet meeting, October 7, 1970, Memorandum, James Keogh for the President's file, October 7, 1970, Nixon Presidential Materials, National Archives, College Park, Maryland, White House Special Files, Staff Member and Office Files, President's office files, 1969–74, box 82, folder October 4, 1970. Hereafter cited as President's office files.
65. Memorandum, Charles Colson to the President, October 13, 1970, President's office files, box 82, folder October 11, 1970.
66. "Bombing Operations and the Prisoner-of-War Rescue Mission in North Vietnam," Hearing before the Committee on Foreign Relations, United States Senate, Honorable Melvin Laird, Secretary of Defense, November 24, 1970.
67. William F. Buckley Jr., "On the Right: The Bombing," November 28/29, 1970, Buckley papers, box 436, folder Buckley columns, On the Right, Nov–Dec 1970.
68. "The Prison Raid Raised Hopes," *New York Times*, December 8, 1970.
69. "A New Bombing Policy: Nixon Redefines the 'Understanding' with Hanoi," *Newsweek*, December 21, 1970.
70. Memorandum, Patrick Buchanan to the President, January 6, 1971, Colson files, box 52, folder Conservatives.
71. Memorandum, Patrick Buchanan to H. R. Haldeman, January 14, 1971, Colson files, box 52, folder Conservatives.
72. Frank Meyer, "Mr. Nixon's Course?" *National Review*, January 26, 1971.
73. Nick Thimmesch, "Conservatives Complain about Nixon," *Newsday*, January 5, 1971.
74. Confidential memorandum, Senator Barry Goldwater, "My Visit with the President, December 14, 1970," Goldwater papers, Personal, box 5, folder 9.
75. Goldwater confidential memorandum, January 27, 1970, Goldwater papers, Personal, box 5, folder 9.
76. Memorandum, Patrick Buchanan to the Committee of Six (Middle America Group), February 3, 1971, Haldeman files, box 73, folder Pat Buchanan, February 1971.
77. Memorandum, "Observations at the Conservative Awards Dinner," Patrick Buchanan to H. R. Haldeman, February 8, 1971, Colson files, box 52, folder Conservatives.
78. Evans and Novak, *Nixon*, 390.
79. Jeffrey Kimball, *The Vietnam War Files: Uncovering the Secret History of Nixon-era Strategy* (Lawrence: University Press of Kansas, 2004), 144–50.
80. Letter, Walter Judd to Ambassador Ellsworth Bunker, March 2, 1971, Judd papers, box 251, folder Vietnam, General, 1971.
81. Senator Strom Thurmond weekly radio broadcast, February 28–March 1, 1971, Thurmond papers, Speeches, box 44, subseries IIA, no. 03766.
82. Senator Strom Thurmond, "The Stakes in Vietnam," April 19, 1971, Thurmond papers, Speeches, subseries IIA, box 45, no. 03817.
83. General Thomas Lane, "Why Doves Are Wrong on Laos," *Human Events*, February 20, 1971. Emphasis added.

84. Mergel, *Conservative Intellectuals and Richard Nixon*, 44.
85. "Laos: The Other Shoe Falls," *Battle Line*, February 1971, Rusher papers, box 135, folder ACU, Newsletter, Republican Battle Line, Printed versions, 1971–72.
86. Copy of background briefing, Saigon, March 21, 1971, sent to Senator Barry Goldwater by Richard G. Capen Jr., assistant to the Secretary of Legislative Affairs, Office of the Secretary of Defense, late March 1971, Goldwater papers, Congressional series 92, box 18, folder 8.
87. Department of State briefing, issued by Robert J. McCloskey, February 8, 1971, Colson files, box 77, folder Lam Son 719, Laos.
88. Telegram, Walter Judd to President Richard Nixon, March 26, 1971, Judd papers, box 31, folder Correspondence, Nixon, Richard M., 1952–1984.
89. Letters, with attached reports, Henry Kissinger to Governor Ronald Reagan, April 2 and 3, 1971, Nixon Presidential Materials, National Archives, College Park, Maryland, National Security Council files, Names files: Reagan, Ronald. Hereafter cited as NSC Reagan file.
90. Letter, Henry Kissinger to Governor Ronald Reagan, April 2, 1971, NSC Reagan file.
91. Randal Teague statement withdrawing YAF support of President Nixon, c. March 1971, cited in *Exclusive* (published by Special Reports, Inc.), April 23, 1971, Goldwater papers, Congressional series 92, box 26, folder 1.
92. Letter, Governor Ronald Reagan to Ron Docksai, national chairman of YAF, May 21, 1971, NSC Reagan file.
93. Letter, William Rusher to William F. Buckley Jr., February 24, 1971, Rusher papers, box 121, folder Staff correspondence and memoranda, Buckley, William F., Jr., 1971.
94. Sir Robert Thompson cited in advance release for "The Advocates," a television debate program cohosted by William Rusher, June 21, 1971, Rusher papers, box 222, folder Television programs, "The Advocates," 1970–1974.
95. "Country Should Rally behind Nixon War Stand,' *Human Events*, April 17, 1971.
96. *Battle Line*, January 1971, Rusher papers, box 135, folder ACU, newsletter, Republican Battle Line, Printed versions, 1971–72.
97. Memorandum, Patrick Buchanan to the President, April 1, 1971, Haldeman files, box 76, folder Patrick Buchanan, April 1971.
98. Memorandum, Ken BeLieu for the president's file, April 21, 1971, Nixon Presidential Materials, National Archives, College Park, Maryland, White House Special Files, Staff Member and Office Files, President's Personal Files, 1971, box 84, folder April 18, 1971. Hereafter cited as President's personal files.
99. Memorandum, Patrick Buchanan to the President, March 30, 1971, Nixon Presidential Materials, National Archives, College Park, Maryland, White House Special Files, Staff Member and Office Files, Patrick J. Buchanan, 1969–72, box 1, folder Chronological files, March 1971. Hereafter cited as Buchanan files.
100. William F. Buckley Jr., "On the Right: The Pentagon Papers," June 22, 1971, Buckley papers, box 210, folder National Review "Hoax," 1971.
101. *First Monday*, October 4, 1971, copy in Buckley papers, box 210, folder National Review "Hoax," 1971.
102. Memorandum, Alexander Haig to Patrick Buchanan, June 23, 1971, Nixon Presidential Materials, National Archives, College Park, Maryland, National Security Council files, Names files: Vice President Spiro Agnew (1971 and 1972), box 837.

103. *National Review* news release on publication of the Vietnam documents, July 1971, Buckley papers, box 210, folder National Review "Hoax," 1971.
104. *National Review* document, Memorandum from the Joint Chiefs of Staff to Secretary of Defense McNamara, January 13, 1962, transmitted to President Kennedy on January 27 without endorsement, published in *National Review*, July 27, 1971.
105. *National Review* document, Memorandum from Head, Division of Psychological Assessment, CIA, to the Secretary of Defense, December 11, 1963, published in *National Review*, July 27, 1971.
106. *National Review* document, handwritten note by Secretary of State summarizing the results of a high-level departmental meeting at which the advisability of seeking a declaration of war had been discussed, February 10, 1965, published in *National Review*, July 27, 1971.
107. "Even White House Believed Buckley's Vietnam Secrets," *Washington Star*, July 24, 1971.
108. Writing of the *National Review* papers, Buckley declared, "In at least five identified cases, the individual [alleged to have written the document] refused to disavow the paper. Their refusals were interpreted by the press as suggesting that we were dead on target. i.e., that the gentlemen could not confidently disavow seven-year-old memoranda, because it was altogether possible that the memoranda were genuine." William F. Buckley Jr., "On the Right: The *National Review* Papers," July 27, 1971, Buckley papers, box 221, folder 1793.
109. William F. Buckley Jr., "On the Right," July 30, 1971.
110. Paraphrase of William F. Buckley's discussion of the hoax with Bill Jorgensen on 10.00 p.m. news, WNEW-TV, July 21, 1971, Radio TV Reports, Inc, Buckley papers, box 210, folder 1671.
111. William Rusher cited in WCBS-TV report, July 31, 1971, Buckley papers, box 220, folder National Review "Hoax," 1971.
112. Letter, William F. Buckley Jr. to Roger A. Moore, Ropes and Gray, July 14, 1971, Buckley papers, box 220, folder National Review "Hoax," 1971.
113. WCBS news report from "Newsradio 88," July 23, 1971, Buckley papers, box 210, folder National Review "Hoax," 1971.
114. WCBS-TV and CBS Television Network report, July 22, 1971, Buckley papers, box 210, folder National Review "Hoax," 1971. Beyond the major television networks and national newspapers the *National Review* hoax received more positive coverage.
115. Letter, William H. Hornby, editor of the *Denver Post*, to *National Review*, July 23, 1971, Buckley papers, box 220, folder "Pentagon Papers," *National Review's*, 1971 July 23–July 24.
116. Mark R. Winchell, *William F. Buckley, Jr* (Boston: Twayne, 1984), 35.
117. "Inside Washington: Expert on USSR Defense Warns of SALT Dangers," *Human Events*, June 19, 1971.
118. "Joint Chiefs Warn of USSR Superiority by Mid-'70s," *Human Events*, March 20, 1971.
119. Senator Strom Thurmond radio address, June 13, 1971, Thurmond papers, Press Assistant Series, box 44, folder Address (radio) "Trade with Red China," Washington, D.C., June 13, 1971.
120. Memorandum, H. R. Haldeman to Patrick Buchanan, June 3, 1971, Haldeman files, box 80, folder Pat Buchanan, June 1971.
121. Memorandum, H. R. Haldeman to Henry Kissinger, June 8, 1971, Haldeman files, box 80, folder Pat Buchanan, June 1971.

122. News release, "Prominent Conservative Leaders 'Suspend' Support of President Nixon," issued by William Rusher, July 29, 1971, Rusher papers, box 168, folder Nixon, Richard, conservative suspension of support, press releases, 1971.
123. William F. Buckley Jr., cited in Winchell, *Buckley*, 22.
124. William F. Buckley Jr., "On the Right: Notes on the China Visit," July 20, 1971, Buckley papers, box 437, folder Buckley columns, *On the Right*, Jul–Aug 1971.
125. News release, "Prominent Conservative Leaders 'Suspend' Support of President Nixon," issued by William Rusher, July 29, 1971, Rusher papers, box 168, folder Nixon, Richard, conservative suspension of support, press releases, 1971.
126. Memorandum, Jeff Bell to "Signers of July 26 Statement (Manhattan Twelve)," Re.: Possible next steps, September 16, 1971, Rusher papers, box 167, folder Nixon, Richard, Conservative suspension of support, correspondence and related materials, 1971–1972.
127. Memorandum, J. Daniel Mahoney to The Manhattan Twelve and Allied Outriders, c. late September 1971, Rusher papers, box 167, folder Nixon, Richard, Conservative suspension of support, correspondence and related materials, 1971–1972.
128. Memorandum, Frank Meyer to the Manhattan Twelve, October 16, 1971, Buckley papers, box 193, folder The "Manhattan 12," 1971.
129. Memorandum, Neil McCaffrey to the Manhattan Twelve, October 22, 1971, Buckley papers, box 193, folder The "Manhattan 12," 1971.
130. Letter, Allan Ryskind to William F. Buckley Jr., November 2, 1971, Buckley papers, box 193, folder The "Manhattan 12," 1971.
131. "Manhattan Twelve" points submitted to Colson, November 1, 1971, Nixon Presidential Materials, National Archives, College Park, Maryland, National Security Council files, Names files, box 811, folder Colson, Charles. Hereafter cited as NSC Colson file.
132. Memorandum, Charles Colson to Al Haig, November 2, 1971, NSC Colson file.
133. Memorandum, Patrick Buchanan to H. R. Haldeman and Charles Colson, October 26, 1971, Buchanan files, Staff memos 1971, folder Haldeman (1 of 2).
134. List of demands submitted to the Nixon administration, November 1, 1972, NSC Colson file.
135. News release, "Prominent Conservative Leaders 'Suspend' Support of President Nixon," issued by William Rusher, July 29, 1971, Rusher papers, box 168, folder Nixon, Richard, conservative suspension of support, press releases, 1971. Charles Moser, *Promise and Hope: The Ashbrook Presidential Campaign of 1972* (Washington: Institute for Government and Politics of Free Congress Research and Education Foundation, 1985), 5. As the public positions of leading conservatives indicated, however, opposition to Nixon's Vietnam policies did not become prominent until after his China announcement and remained subordinate to concerns over disarmament after this time.
136. List of points submitted to Charles Colson by the "Manhattan Twelve," November 1, 1971, NSC Colson file. The conservatives asked the administration to reply to their points, offering a deadline of November 25, 1971.
137. James Burnham, cited in Smant, *How Great the Triumph*, 107–8.
138. Letter, William F. Buckley Jr. to Henry Kissinger, c. mid-September 1971, Nixon Presidential Materials, National Archives, College Park, Maryland, National Security Council files, Names files, box 809, folder Buckley, William F. Hereafter cited as NSC Buckley file.

139. Frank Meyer, "Peace in Our Time," *National Review,* August 10, 1971.
140. James Burnham, cited in Smant, *How Great the Triumph,* 108.
141. Letter, Ernst van den Haag to William Rusher, August 9, 1971, Rusher papers, box 94, folder van den Haag.
142. Press release, Senator James Buckley, August 1, 1971, Rusher papers, box 13, folder Buckley, James L., 1959, 1969–1971.
143. Press release, Senator Barry Goldwater, 29 December 1971, Colson files, box 52, folder Conservatives.
144. Memorandum, Patrick Buchanan to the Attorney General and H. R. Haldeman, December 3, 1971, Buchanan files, Staff memos 1971, folder Haldeman (1 of 2).
145. American Legion resolution no. 462, Subject: Presidential visit to Communist China, National Convention, August 31–September 2, 1971, Houston, Texas, Colson files, box 34, folder American Legion.
146. Memorandum for the President's file, Subject: Meeting with Alfred Chamie, July 27, 1971, President's office files, box 85, folder July 25, 1971.
147. Memorandum for the president's file, Subject: The president's meeting with Senator Barry Goldwater, August 31, 1971, President's office files, box 86, folder August 26, 1971.
148. Senator Strom Thurmond, weekly broadcast, July 25–26, 1971, Thurmond papers, Speeches, box 44, folder 03772.
149. Congressman John Ashbrook, "The Current U.S. Diplomacy Toward Communist China: A Critical Appraisal," John M. Ashbrook Papers, Ashbrook Center for Public Affairs at Ashland University, Ohio, C/C, box 22, folder Red China.
150. *National Review Bulletin,* January 28, 1972.
151. Letter, William F. Buckley Jr. to Henry Kissinger, c. mid-September 1971, NSC Buckley file.
152. Letter, Senator Barry Goldwater to Henry Kissinger, January 26, 1972, Nixon Presidential Materials, National Archives, College Park, Maryland, National Security Council files, Names files: Barry M. Goldwater.
153. Senator Barry Goldwater diary report, January 3, 1972, Goldwater papers, Personal/political series I, box 5, folder Vietnam media.
154. Memorandum, Patrick Buchanan for the president's file, January 26, 1972, President's office files, box 87, folder January 23, 1972.
155. Memorandum, Patrick Buchanan for the president's file, January 26, 1972, President's office files, box 87, folder January 23, 1972.
156. Senator Barry Goldwater diary report, January 26, 1972, Goldwater papers, Personal/political series I, box 5, folder 2.
157. *Battle Line,* January 1972, Rusher papers, box 135, folder ACU newsletter, Republican Battle Line, printed versions, 1971–1972.
158. "Viet Peace Offers Chancy Gamble," *Human Events,* February 5, 1972.
159. *National Review Bulletin,* January 28, 1972.
160. Letter, Senator Barry Goldwater to Andre Doyon, February 1, 1972, Goldwater papers, Congressional series 92, box 34, folder Vietnam (1), S. 3409, SR 294, Foreign relations.
161. Kimball, *Vietnam War Files,* 203.
162. William F. Buckley Jr., "On the Right: Capitulation in Peking," mailed from Peking, February 28, 1972, Buckley papers, box 437, folder Buckley columns, On the Right, Jul–Aug 1971.

5. THE SEARCH FOR A NEW MAJORITY
Popular Support for the War

1. Mrs. W. H. Neans, quoted in "Cause for Anguish: Their Missing Men," *The State*, Columbia, S.C., October 1969.
2. David Levy, *The Debate over Vietnam*, 2d ed. (Baltimore: Johns Hopkins University Press, 1995), 140.
3. "Nixon Supporters Planning War Rallies," *New York Times*, November 9, 1969.
4. *Nhan Dan*, cited in the *New York Times*, October 15, 1969.
5. Governor Ronald Reagan speech at a dinner commemorating the 79th birthday anniversary of the late President Eisenhower, Washington, D.C., October 9, 1969, "Reagan Urges Nixon Not to be Swayed by Mass Demonstrations," *Sacramento Bee*, October 10, 1969, Voices in Vital America, Inc. Archive, Kent State University Special Collections and Archives, Ohio, box 8. Hereafter cited as VIVA papers.
6. Bob Hope, cited in "Bob Hope Head of Patriotism Week in U.S.," *Chicago Tribune*, November 7, 1969.
7. "Drive Started to Back Nixon Vietnam Policy," *Los Angeles Times*, November 9, 1969; "Nixon's Unsilent Supporters," *Time*, November 21, 1969.
8. Quotations taken from "Nixon's Unsilent Supporters," *Time*, November 21, 1969.
9. "Patriotism Stressed," *Chicago Tribune*, November 10, 1969.
10. "Week-long Program Backs President," *New York Times*, November 12, 1969.
11. "Massive Protest of Vietnam War Expected Today," *New York Times*, October 15, 1969.
12. "Week-long Program Backs President," *New York Times*, November 12, 1969.
13. National Committee for Responsible Patriotism, Inc. brochure, We Support Our Boys in Vietnam, Inc. Archive, Hoover Institution Archives, Stanford, California, box 8. Hereafter cited as WSOBV archive.
14. Charles W. Wiley, reply to WCBS-TV broadcast (October 15, 1969), October 22, 1969, copy of Wiley's statements in WSOBV archive, box 8.
15. "Nixon Supporters Planning War Rallies," *New York Times*, November 9, 1969.
16. "Call Response to Viet Unity Bid Fantastic," *Chicago Tribune*, November 12, 1969.
17. "Massive Protest of Vietnam War Expected Today," *New York Times*, October 15, 1969; "'Honor America Week' Set to Counter War Protest," *New York Times*, November 7, 1969; "Nixon Supporters Planning War Rallies," *New York Times*, November 9, 1969; "5 Days of Patriotism Beginning with Salute to Veterans Today," *New York Times*, November 11, 1969; "The 'Silent Majority' Speaks Out on Veterans Day," *Human Events*, November 22, 1969.
18. "Many in U.S. Back Nixon War Stand on Veterans Day," *New York Times*, November 12, 1969.
19. Ibid.; "The 'Silent Majority' Speaks Out on Veterans Day,' *Human Events*, November 22, 1969.
20. "Nixon Supporters Planning War Rallies," *New York Times*, November 9, 1969.
21. "15,000 Rally Behind Nixon's War Policy," *Chicago Tribune*, November 12, 1969.
22. "Nixon's Unsilent Supporters," *Time*, November 21, 1969.
23. "15,000 Rally Behind Nixon's War Policy," *Chicago Tribune*, November 12, 1969.
24. "The 'Silent Majority' Speaks Out on Veterans Day," *Human Events*, November 22, 1969.
25. "Many in U.S. Back Nixon War Stand on Veterans Day," *New York Times*, November 12, 1969.

26. Senator John Tower, cited in "The 'Silent Majority' Speaks Out on Veterans Day," *Human Events*, November 22, 1969.
27. Memorandum, Charles Colson to Alexander Butterfield, December 15, 1969, Nixon Presidential Materials, National Archives, College Park, Maryland, White House Special Files, Staff Member and Office Files, Charles Colson, box 41, folder Businessmen—Ross Perot—Personal. Hereafter cited as Colson files.
28. "Many in U.S. Back Nixon War Stand on Veterans Day," *New York Times*, November 12, 1969.
29. "The 'Silent Majority' Speaks Out on Veterans Day," *Human Events*, November 22, 1969.
30. National Committee for Responsible Patriotism, Inc. brochure, WSOBV archive, box 8.
31. "Capital Prepares for July 4 Event; Up to 400,000 Expected for Honor America Day," *New York Times*, July 3, 1970.
32. Honor America Day material, Colson files, box 72, folder Honor America Day—July 1971.
33. Stewart Meacham, cited in "Capital Prepares for July 4 Event; Up to 400,000 Expected for Honor America Day," *New York Times*, July 3, 1970.
34. "Capital Prepares for July 4 Event; Up to 400,000 Expected for Honor America Day," *New York Times*, July 3, 1970.
35. "Nearly 400,000 Honor America," *Human Events*, July 18, 1970. Although not involved in the organization of Honor America Day, approximately five hundred members of YAF served as crowd marshals on the day of the rally.
36. "Credit Due Police in Capital Rally," *Chicago Tribune*, July 10, 1970.
37. *Washington Post*, April 5, 1970.
38. "March in Capital Tomorrow to Back Vietnam War," *New York Times*, April 3, 1970.
39. Letter, Senator Strom Thurmond to Mr. James E. Carter, April 1, 1970, Strom Thurmond Institute, Clemson University, South Carolina, Strom Thurmond papers, Subject correspondence series, box 9, folder Foreign relations 7 (War in Vietnam), folder II; April 1–May 29, 1970. Hereafter cited as Thurmond papers.
40. Letter, Senator Barry Goldwater to C. Keith Hones, 22 April 70, Barry M. Goldwater Papers, Arizona Historical Foundation, Arizona State University, Tempe, Arizona, Congressional series 91, box 38, folder Victory March, legislative—correspondence, 1969–1970. Hereafter cited as Goldwater papers.
41. Letter, Senator Barry Goldwater to C. Keith Hones, April 22, 1970, Goldwater Papers, Congressional series 91, box 38, folder Victory March, legislative—correspondence, 1969–1970.
42. "Ky to Out-Agnew Agnew at Rally, McIntire Says," *New York Times*, September 15, 1970.
43. "Kissinger Seeks to Deter Visit by Ky," *New York Times*, September 26, 1970.
44. "McIntire Criticizes Nixon on Ky's Plans," *New York Times*, September 30, 1970.
45. "Monthly 'Victory' Marches Planned as Prod to Nixon," *New York Times*, October 15, 1970.
46. "Throng Forecast by 'Victory Now,'" *New York Times*, May 5, 1971; "15,000 Rally in Capital to Urge Vietnam Victory," *New York Times*, May 9, 1971.
47. American Legion Resolution no. 46, "Vietnam Policy Statement," 55th National Convention, September 1–3, 1970, copy in Colson files, box 33, folder American Legion.
48. Memorandum, Charles Colson to the President, re. Commander Vicites' meeting with the President, October 5, 1971, Colson files, box 22, folder Commander Vicities—VFW, with President, 10/5/71.

49. Statement of support for the administration, Joseph Vicites, Commander-in-Chief, VFW, April 1972, copy attached to letter from C. Colson to Frank Fitzsimmons of the Teamsters Union, April 19, 1972, Colson files, box 53: folder Continued North Vietnamese Invasion, April 1972.
50. Draft of President Nixon's speech before the convention of the American Legion, August 24, 1972, Nixon Presidential Materials, National Archives, College Park, Maryland, White House Special Files, Staff Member and Office Files, Patrick J. Buchanan, 1969–72, Chronological files, folder Haldeman memos, 1972 (folder 2 of 4). Hereafter cited as Buchanan files.
51. For an analysis of the conservative movement's successful exploitation of union members' opposition to labor leaders, see Elizabeth Tandy Shermer, "Origins of the Conservative Ascendancy: Barry Goldwater's Early Senate Career and the Delegitimization of Organized Labor," *Journal of American History* (December 2008), 678–709.
52. Levy, *Debate over Vietnam*, 113.
53. Frank Koscielski, *Divided Loyalties: American Unions and the Vietnam War* (New York: Garland, 1999), 3–16, 11.
54. Christian Appy, *Working-Class War: American Combat Soldiers and Vietnam* (Chapel Hill: University of North Carolina Press, 1993), 38.
55. Ibid., 39–40, David Farber, "The Silent Majority and Talk about Revolution," in *The Sixties: From Memory to History*, ed. David Farber (Chapel Hill: University of North Carolina Press, 1994), 291–316. Appy also indicates high levels of opposition to the anti-war movement among U.S. soldiers serving in Vietnam, *Working-Class War*, 220–23.
56. Appy, *Working-Class War*, 39–40, Farber, "The Silent Majority."
57. Farber, "The Silent Majority," 296–97. Such opposition to elite opinion had also contributed to the rise of grass-roots conservatism, particularly in the Southwest. Lisa McGirr, *Suburban Warriors: The Origins of the New American Right* (Princeton: Princeton University Press, 2001), 147–86. Meaney's desire to be part of the elite and to ensure the labor movement was represented among elite circles had, according to Jeffreys-Jones, reinforced his anticommunism and his commitment to supporting the president on the Vietnam issue. Rhodri Jeffreys-Jones, *Peace Now! American Society and the Ending of the Vietnam War* (New Haven: Yale University Press, 1999), 181.
58. YAF flyer, issued in 1970, Patrick Dowd Papers, Hoover Institution Archives, Stanford, California, box 1, folder YAF/California State Chapter, memoranda & circulars. Hereafter cited as Dowd papers.
59. Memorandum, Tom Charles Huston to Bryce Harlow, Harry Dent, Lyn Nofziger, Murray Chotiner, H. R. Haldeman and John Ehrlichman, May 13, 1970, Harry S. Dent Papers, Strom Thurmond Institute, Clemson University, South Carolina, box 5, folder Middle America. Hereafter cited as Dent papers (Clemson).
60. Joshua B. Freeman, "Hardhats: Construction Workers, Manliness, and the 1970 Pro-war Demonstrations," *Journal of Social History* 26 (Summer 1993), 725–39.
61. " . . . Violence on the Right," *New York Times*, May 9, 1970.
62. Jeffreys-Jones, *Peace Now!*, 200.
63. Anthony Summers, *The Arrogance of Power: The Secret World of Richard Nixon* (New York: Penguin, 2000), 358–59; Philip S. Foner, *U.S. Labor and the Vietnam War* (New York: International, 1989), 104–5.
64. "2 Protest Groups Meet on Wall St.," *New York Times*, May 13, 1970; "Huge City Hall Rally Backs Nixon's Indochina Policies," *New York Times*, May 21, 1970.

65. "Huge City Hall Rally Backs Nixon's Indochina Policies," May 21, 1970; "For the Flag and for Country, They March," *New York Times*, May 21, 1970.
66. Koscielski, *Divided Loyalties*, 19.
67. "At War with War," *Time*, May 18, 1970.
68. Peter Brennan, cited in "Nixon Meets Heads of 2 City Unions; Hails War Support," *New York Times*, May 27, 1970.
69. Peter Brennan, cited in "Nixon Thanks Hardhat Workers for Support on His Viet Policy," *Chicago Tribune*, May 27, 1970.
70. Herbert S. Parmet, *Richard Nixon and His America* (Boston: Little Brown, 1990), 568.
71. Memorandum, Harry Dent to the President, October 16, 1969, quoted in Richard Reeves, *President Nixon: Alone in the White House* (New York: Simon and Schuster, 2001), 139. Memorandum, Tom Huston to Harry Dent, August 11, 1970, Dent papers (Clemson), box 5, folder Middle America.
72. See Caroline Page, *United States Official Propaganda during the Vietnam War, 1965–1973: The Limits of Persuasion* (London: Leicester University Press, 1996), 274.
73. Reeves, *Nixon*, 235.
74. Tom Charles Huston memoranda, cited in "National Security, Civil Liberties, and the Collection of Intelligence: A Report of the Huston Plan," supplement to the "Final Report of the Select Committee to Study Government Operations with Respect of Intelligence Activities," United States Senate, April 23, 1976.
75. Cover showing Agnew in the White House, *Life*, May 11, 1970.
76. "Citizens Panel Backs Nixon on Viet Policy," *Chicago Tribune*, November 1, 1970.
77. Transcripts of CCPFV meetings with President Thieu, April 15, 1970, and Vice President Ky, April 13, 1970, Jay Lovestone Papers, Hoover Institution Archives, Stanford, California, box 580, folder Vietnam—history, conflict, 1967–1975, general. Hereafter cited as Lovestone papers.
78. CCPFV publication, "Vietnam Revisited," April 1970, copy in Lovestone papers, box 579, folder Vietnam—history, conflict, 1967–1975, general.
79. Robert O'Neill, WCBS-TV editorial, December 16, 1969, 6.55 p.m., Subject: Year end—Vietnam, copy in Colson files, box 33, folder American Friends of Vietnam, Inc.
80. Draft of William F. Ward's reply to WCBS-TV editorial, issued by William Henderson on December 30, 1969, and presented by Ward on January 5, 1970, Colson files, box 33, folder American Friends of Vietnam, Inc.
81. The National Strategy Information Center (NSIC), founded in 1962, was one of the first rightward-leaning think tanks to focus on matters of foreign policy. Founded with seed money from the Joseph Coors organization, the group's early members included Frank Barnett, who became prominent in the Committee for the Present Danger during the late 1970s, Frank Shakespeare of the U.S. Information Agency, and William Casey, who later became director of the CIA. The vice president of NSIC, Gene Bradley, was the president of Americans for Winning the Peace, a nominally independent pro-Nixon organization founded in 1970 at the initiation and direction of Colson. While not promoted as a specifically right-wing organization during the 1960s, NSIC established links with Irving Kristol's neoconservative lobbying effort in the 1970s.
82. Letter, Frank Barnett to Charles Colson, January 12, 1970, Colson files, box 33, folder American Friends of Vietnam, Inc.
83. For an analysis of AFV's management and organizational activity between

1969 and 1975, when it formally ceased to operate, see Joseph Morgan, *The Vietnam Lobby: The American Friends of Vietnam, 1955–1975* (Chapel Hill: University of North Carolina Press, 1997), 137–52.
84. AFV press release, March 6, 1970, copy in Colson files, box 33, folder American Friends of Vietnam, Inc.
85. Letter, Charles Colson to William Henderson, April 3, 1970, Colson files, box 33, folder American Friends of Vietnam, Inc.
86. Letter, William Henderson to Charles Colson, April 10, 1970, Colson files, box 33, folder American Friends of Vietnam, Inc.
87. Letter, George Bell to William J. Baroody, July 13, 1970, Colson files, box 33, folder American Friends of Vietnam, Inc.
88. Memorandum, George Bell to Charles Colson, August 17, 1970, Colson files, box 33, folder American Friends of Vietnam, Inc.
89. Charles Colson handwritten notes on AFV in Colson files, box 33, folder American Friends of Vietnam, Inc.
90. Memorandum, Charles Colson to Dwight Chapin, November 27, 1970, Colson files, box 36, folder Americans for Winning the Peace (3 of 7).
91. Sample questions re. Americans for Winning the Peace, "For internal use only, for answering questions," Summer 1970, Colson files, box 36, folder Americans for Winning the Peace (3 of 7).
92. Americans for Winning the Peace position paper on the "McGovern Hatfield amendment 'to end the war,'" August 19, 1970, Colson files, box 36, folder Americans for Winning the Peace (4 of 7).
93. Letter, Gene Bradley to Charles Colson, October 26, 1970, Colson files, box 36, folder Americans for Winning the Peace (5 of 7).
94. Memorandum, Charles Colson to H. R. Haldeman, December 30, 1971, Colson files, box 36, folder Americans for Winning the Peace (2 of 7).
95. Memorandum, Charles Colson to Dwight Chapin, January 4, 1971, Colson files, box 36, folder Americans for Winning the Peace (2 of 7).
96. Memorandum, Charles Colson to H. R. Haldeman, December 30, 1970, Colson files, box 36, folder Americans for Winning the Peace (2 of 7).
97. Memorandum, Gene Bradley to Charles Colson, October 6, 1970, Colson files, box 27, folder Americans for Winning the Peace (7 of 7).
98. Memorandum, Gene Bradley to Charles Colson, December 1, 1970, Colson files, box 36, folder Americans for Winning the Peace (2 of 7).
99. Memorandum, Charles Colson to Gene Bradley, January 14, 1971, Colson files, box 27, folder Americans for Winning the Peace (7 of 7).
100. "White House Briefs Pro-Nixon Unit," *Washington Post*, February 6, 1971.
101. "Calley: Soldier or Killer?" *New York Times*, July 11, 1971. For a detailed explication of this theme, see Bernd Greiner, *War Without Fronts: The USA in Vietnam* (New Haven: Yale University Press, 2009).
102. "Taught to Obey Orders: Calley," *Chicago Tribune*, February 23, 1971.
103. Vice President Spiro Agnew, cited in "Agnew Says War Critics Apply Double Standard," *Chicago Tribune*, April 1, 1971.
104. Rick Perlstein, *Nixonland: The Rise of a President and the Fracturing of America* (New York: Scribner, 2008), 556.
105. Roland Evans and Robert Novak, *Nixon in the White House: The Frustration of Power* (London: Random House, 1971), 394.
106. William F. Buckley Jr., "On the Right: Calley Is No Scapegoat," c. April 1971, copy in Donald M. Dozer Papers, Hoover Institution Archives, Stanford, California, box 134, folder U.S. politics—organizations, YAF, general, 1970–1973.

107. Memorandum, Jon Huntsman to Patrick Buchanan, April 15, 1971, response to Buchanan's memorandum to the president, April 5, 1971, Buchanan files, Chronological files, Staff memos received, folder Action memos—1971.
108. "After Decades, Renewed War on Old Conflict: (O'Neill & Nixon vs. Kerry)," *Washington Post*, August 28, 2004; Transcript of President Nixon's meeting with H. R. Haldeman, Oval Office, June 2, 1971, "Conversations Reveal Nixon's Desire to Discredit John Kerry in 1971," MSNBC Nightly News, March 15, 2004.
109. Statement of formation, Vietnam Veterans for a Just Peace, June 1971, Robert F. Turner Papers, Hoover Institution Archives, Stanford, California, box 31, folder Vietnam Veterans for a Just Peace. Hereafter cited as Turner papers.
110. Press conference statement of Bruce Kessler, June 1, 1971. Copies of statement and flyer in Christopher Emmett Papers, Hoover Institution Archives, Stanford, California, box 55, folder Vietnam Veterans for a Just Peace. Hereafter cited as Emmett papers.
111. VVJP flyer, Turner papers, box 31, folder Vietnam Veterans for a Just Peace.
112. Kesler and O'Neill statements, June 1, 1971, Emmett papers, box 55, folder Vietnam Veterans for a Just Peace.
113. Buckley, "On the Right: John Kerry's Speech—I," June 12, 1971.
114. Buckley, "On the Right: John Kerry's Speech—II," June 15, 1971.
115. Transcript of John O'Neill/John Kerry debate on *Dick Cavett Show*, June 30, 1971.
116. See Jerry Lembcke, *The Spitting Image: Myth, Memory, and the Legacy of Vietnam* (New York: New York University Press, 1998), and Richard Moser, *The New Winter Soldiers: GI and Veteran Dissent during the Vietnam Era* (New Brunswick: Rutgers University Press, 1996).
117. Congressman Roman C. Pucinski (D-IL), speech in House of Representatives, April 3, 1969, *Congressional Record*, 8585–88. Pucinski had served as the chief investigator for the Congressional Special Committee to Conduct an Investigation and Study of the Facts, Evidence, and Circumstances of the Katyn Forest Massacre, in 1952.
118. Michael J. Allen, *Until the Last Man Comes Home: POWs, MIAs, and the Unending Vietnam War* (Chapel Hill: University of North Carolina Press, 2009), 15.
119. Secretary of Defense Melvin Laird, press conference, Washington, D.C., May 19, 1969, cited in POW/MIA report of the Select Committee on POW/MIA Affairs, U.S. Senate, January 1993.
120. Open letter, "Public Opinion Influences Hanoi—You Are Public Opinion," 1969, copy in Shirley Mae Stark Papers, Hoover Institution Archives, Stanford, California, box 3. Hereafter cited as Stark papers.
121. Open letter from Sybil Stockdale, c. mid-1969, Stark papers, box 6, folder National League.
122. H. Bruce Franklin, *M.I.A., or Mythmaking in America: How Belief in Live POWs Has Possessed a Nation* (New Brunswick: Rutgers University Press, 1992), 53.
123. Testimony of H. Ross Perot before the Senate Select Committee on POW/MIA Affairs, November 8, 1992.
124. "Super-rich Texan Fights Social Ills," *New York Times*, November 28, 1969.
125. Perot, cited in "Nixon's Unsilent Supporters," *Time*, November 21, 1969.
126. Memorandum, Charles Colson to Larry Higby, December 3, 1969, Colson files, box 41, folder Businessmen—Ross Perot—Personal.
127. Senator Barry Goldwater, speech in the Senate, August 5, 1969, *Congressional Record*.

128. Senator John Tower, speech in Senate, June 2, 1969, *Congressional Record*, 14500–14502.
129. Letter, Rear Admiral D. H. Guinn, acting chief of naval personnel to navy wives and families, to Shirley Mae Stark, board member of the National League, December 16, 1969, Stark papers, box 4, folder Personal.
130. Frank Borman, address to Congress, September 22, 1970.
131. Memorandum, Gene Bradley to Charles Colson, December 1, 1970, Colson files, box 36, folder American Friends of Vietnam (2 of 7).
132. American Legion resolution no. 123, Subject: American POWs in Southeast Asia, National Convention, September 1–3, 1970, Colson files, box 33, folder American Legion.
133. Statement of purpose, Council for the Civilized Treatment of P.O.W.s, WSOBV archive, box 8.
134. Letter, Lt. Robert Frischman, Concern for Prisoners of War, to all members of U.S. Congress, April 28, 1971, VIVA papers, box 17, folder VIVA Headlines.
135. Concern for Prisoners of War, Inc. brochure, circa early 1971, VIVA papers, box 25.
136. President Richard M. Nixon, "Address to the Nation about a New Initiative for Peace in Southeast Asia," October 7, 1970, *Public Papers of the Presidents of the United States: Richard Nixon, 1971* (Washington: U.S. Government Printing Office, 1972), Doc. 335.
137. "The Prison Raid Raised Hopes," *New York Times*, December 8, 1970.
138. Open letter from Herbert Klein, December 1, 1970, Colson files, box 104, folder Prisoners of War (POW).
139. Memorandum, George Bell to H. R. Haldeman, December 8, 1970, Colson files, box 104, folder Prisoners of War (POW).
140. Governor Ronald Reagan speech before POW/MIA International Inc. dinner, June 4, 1971, copy of speech in VIVA papers, box 4, folder POW/MIA International.
141. Letter, David Dellinger and Cora Weiss to Shirley Mae Stark, January 6, 1971, Stark papers, box 5, folder Committee of Liaison.
142. Cybil Stockdale, "Questions and Answers," Stark papers, box 3.
143. Peace proposal of the Provisional Revolutionary Government of South Vietnam, July 1, 1971, translated by Robert K. Brigham and Le Phuong Anh.
144. Franklin, *M.I.A.*, 6.

6. Tell It to Hanoi
Student Pro-War Campaigns

1. M. Stanton Evans, *Revolt on the Campus* (Chicago: Regnery, 1961), preface.
2. Tom Wells, *The War Within: America's Battle over Vietnam* (Berkeley: University of California Press, 1994), 320. For a discussion of YAF's opposition to the NSA, see Wayne Thorburn, *A Generation Awakes: Young Americans for Freedom and the Creation of the Conservative Movement* (Ottawa, Ill.: Jameson Books, 2010), 82–88.
3. H. R. Haldeman and Ray Price, cited in Wells, *War Within*, 316.
4. David Levy, *The Debate over Vietnam*, 2d ed. (Baltimore: Johns Hopkins University Press, 1995), 103. James Hijiya, "The Conservative 1960s," *Journal of American Studies* 37, 2 (2003), 201–27.
5. Hijiya comments, "One salient distinction between the New Right and the

New Left was the former's emphasis on organization: the history of conservatism in the 1960s is essentially institutional history." "Conservative 1960s," 203.
6. National Student Committee for Victory in Vietnam, Memo #1, written by Michael W. Thompson, 1967, Robert F. Turner Papers, Hoover Institution Archives, Stanford, California, box 22, folder National Student Committee for Victory in Vietnam. Hereafter cited as Turner papers.
7. M. Stanton Evans article "Student Majority Speaks Out," included in the *Congressional Record* by Congressman John Ashbrook, March 17, 1969, *Congressional Record*, House, 6648.
8. See John A. Andrew III, "Pro-War and Anti-Draft: YAF and the War in Vietnam," in *The Vietnam War on Campus: Other Voices, More Distant Drums*, ed. Marc Jason Gilbert (Westport, Conn.: Praeger, 2001), 1–19.
9. Report of the meeting of the National Board of YAF, Washington, D.C., February 5–7, 1971, Patrick Dowd Papers, Hoover Institution Archives, Stanford, California, box 22, folder Subject files, YAF/National Board—memoranda, circulars, and printed matter. Hereafter cited as Dowd papers.
10. Letter, P. Gayman, schedule secretary to Governor Reagan, to Patrick Dowd, February 25, 1969, Dowd papers, box 1, folder Correspondence, letters received, 1968–1969.
11. "Anti-War Office Invaded by Anti-Antis," *Boston Herald Traveler*, reprinted in *YAF in the News*, April 1969, Dowd papers, box 3, folder Subject file, YAF/Newsletter, "YAF in the News."
12. Gregory Schneider, *Cadres for Conservatism: Young Americans for Freedom and the Rise of the Contemporary Right* (New York: New York University Press, 1999), 116.
13. Letter, Ron Docksai to Arnie Steinberg and William F. Buckley Jr., April 26, 1969, William F. Buckley Jr. Papers, Sterling Memorial Library Manuscripts and Archives, Yale University, New Haven, Connecticut, box 76, folder Young Americans for Freedom, (YAF), Mar–Sep 1969. Hereafter cited as Buckley papers.
14. Letter, William F. Buckley Jr. to Ron Docksai, May 6, 1969, Buckley papers, box 76, folder Young Americans for Freedom, (YAF), Mar–Sep 1969.
15. Memorandum, Alan McKay, YAF national chair, and Randal Teague, YAF director of regional and state activities, to all YAF leaders, January 21, 1969, Dowd papers, box 1, folder YAF/California State Chapter—memoranda and circulars.
16. Memorandum, Alan McKay, YAF national chair, and Randal Teague, YAF director of regional and state activities, to all YAF leaders, January 21, 1969, Dowd papers, box 1, folder YAF/California State Chapter—memoranda and circulars.
17. Memorandum, Alan McKay and Randal Teague to all YAF leaders, January 21, 1969, Dowd papers, box 1, folder YAF/California State Chapter—memoranda and circulars.
18. Schneider, *Cadres for Conservatism*, 121.
19. Memorandum, Randal Teague to YAF's Board of Directors, October 21, 1969, Dowd papers, box 2, folder Subject file, YAF/National Board—minutes of meetings, 1970.
20. Memorandum, Michael Thompson to NSCVV members, Fall 1968, Turner papers, box 22, folder National Student Committee for Victory in Vietnam.
21. "Memo # 1," Michael W. Thompson on behalf of NSCVV, 1967, Dowd papers, box 22, folder National Student Committee for Victory in Vietnam.
22. Memorandum distributed by NSCVV directors to interested parties, Spring 1968, Turner papers, box 22, folder National Student Committee for Victory in Vietnam.

23. Robert Turner, Vietnam Cliché #1: "Ho Chi Minh is the George Washington of Vietnam." Turner papers, box 13, folder Ho Chi Minh—File I (DRV File).
24. Turner, Vietnam Cliché #4, "The U.S. should allow the United Nations to consider the Vietnam question." Turner papers, box 22, folder National Student Committee for Victory in Vietnam.
25. Robert Turner, *Myths of the Vietnam War: The Pentagon Papers Reconsidered* (New York: American Friends of Vietnam, 1972), 1.
26. Robert Turner, "Expert Punctures 'No Bloodbath' Myth," *Human Events*, November 11, 1972.
27. Memorandum distributed by NSCVV directors to interested parties, Spring 1968, Turner papers, box 22, folder National Student Committee for Victory in Vietnam.
28. Minutes of national board meeting of YAF, February 28–March 2, 1969, New York City, Dowd papers, box 2, folder Subject file, YAF/National Board—printed matter and reports.
29. Handwritten notes, YAF Board meeting, October 5, 1969, Hotel Sonesta, Washington, D.C., Dowd papers, box 2, folder Subject file, YAF/National Board—minutes of meetings, 1970; Minutes of meeting of the YAF national board, October 3–5, 1969, Dowd papers, box 2, folder Subject file, YAF/National Board—minutes of meetings, 1970.
30. Letter, Randal Teague to the Board of Directors, October 21, 1969, Dowd papers, box 2, folder Subject file, YAF/National Board—minutes of meetings, 1970.
31. Memorandum, Philip Abbott Luce to all YAF chapter chairmen, September 25, 1969, Dowd papers, box 2, folder Subject file, YAF/National Board, memoranda and circulars.
32. Randal Teague cited in "Young 'Freedom' students oppose anti-war groups," *Tennessean*, reprinted in YAF's newsletter, *YAF in the News*, December 1969, Dowd papers, box 3, folder Subject file, YAF/Newsletter, "YAF in the News." Teague also cited in *Omaha Evening World-Herald*, "Young Freedom Americans fight 'Defeatism,'" reprinted in YAF's newsletter, *YAF in the News*, December 1969, Dowd papers, box 3, folder Subject file, YAF/Newsletter, "YAF in the News."
33. YAF memorandum, cited in "Young 'Freedom' students oppose anti-war groups," *Tennessean*, reprinted in YAF's newsletter, *YAF in the News*, December 1969, Dowd papers, box 3, folder Subject file, YAF/Newsletter, "YAF in the News."
34. David Keene, cited in YAF news release, "Young Americans for Freedom to Push 'Tell it to Hanoi' Movement for Peace," released in late November 1969, Dowd papers, box 2, folder Subject files, YAF/National Board, memoranda and circulars.
35. "YAF Leads March Against Moratorium," *St. Louis Post-Dispatch*, November 14, 1969, reprinted in YAF's newsletter, *YAF in the News*, November 1969, Dowd papers, box 3, folder Subject file, YAF/Newsletter, "YAF in the News."
36. Ron Dear, YAF news release, "Young Americans for Freedom to Push 'Tell it to Hanoi' Movement for Peace," released in late November 1969, Dowd papers, box 2, folder Subject files, YAF/National Board, memoranda and circulars.
37. "2,500 Rally on Common to Support U.S. on War," *Boston Herald Traveler*, December 8, 1969.
38. Ibid.
39. Congressman Page Henry Belcher, speech in House of Representatives, December 9, 1969, *Congressional Record*.

40. Letter, Randal Teague to the Board of Directors, January 28, 1970, Dowd papers, box 2, folder Subject file, YAF/National Board—minutes of meetings, 1970.
41. Barry M. Goldwater Papers, Arizona Historical Foundation, Arizona State University, Tempe, Arizona, Congressional series 91, box 88, folder 10. Hereafter cited as Goldwater papers.
42. "YAF Team, Back from Viet, to Fight Unilateral Pullout," *Honolulu Advertiser*, reprinted in "YAF in the News," April 1970, Dowd papers, box 3, folder Subject files, YAF/Newsletter, "YAF in the News."
43. David Keene, cited in "Shun Anti-War Rally, YAF Leader Urges," *Chicago Tribune*, May 8, 1970.
44. YAF full-page advertisement in *Washington Star*, May 3, 4, 1970, copy sent from Randal Teague to Charles Colson on May 2, 1970, Nixon Presidential Materials, National Archives, College Park, Maryland, White House Special Files, Staff Member and Office Files, Charles Colson, box 43, folder Cambodian (2 of 2), Memoranda re. Cambodia. Hereafter cited as Colson files.
45. YAF reply to WCBS editorial on Kent State University incident, May 10, 1970, copy in Colson files, box 125, folder Young Americans for Freedom.
46. Ron Kimberling, "Vietnam: A Libertarian View," *Forty-Niner*, October 15, 1969, Dowd papers, box 2, folder YAF/National Board—printed matter and reports.
47. Letter, Randal Teague to National Board of Directors, September 19, 1969, Dowd papers, box 2, folder YAF/National Board—printed matter and reports.
48. Rebecca Klatch, *A Generation Divided: The New Left, the New Right, and the 1960s* (Berkeley: University of California Press, 1999), 119.
49. Memorandum, Jerry Norton to Randal Teague, c. October 1970, Dowd papers, box 3, folder YAF/National Board—memoranda, circulars, and printed matter.
50. Memorandum, Michael W. Thompson to the National Board, c. October 1970, Dowd papers, box 3, folder Subject file, YAF/National Board—memoranda, circulars, and printed matter.
51. Memorandum, Ron Docksai to Jerry Norton and the National Board, October 22, 1970, Dowd papers, box 3, folder Subject file, YAF/National Board—memoranda, circulars, and printed matter.
52. Memorandum, Michael W. Thompson to the National Board, c. October 1970, Dowd papers, box 3, folder Subject file, YAF/National Board—memoranda, circulars, and printed matter.
53. Memorandum, Jerry Norton to Randal Teague, c. October 1970, Dowd papers, box 3, folder YAF/National Board—memoranda, circulars, and printed matter.
54. Memorandum, Dan Joy to Jerry Norton, c. October 1970, Dowd papers, box 3, folder YAF/National Board—memoranda, circulars, and printed matter.
55. Memorandum, Jerry Norton to Randal Teague, c. October 1970, Dowd papers, box 3, folder Subject file, YAF/National Board—memoranda, circulars, and printed matter.
56. Alan Crawford, *Thunder on the Right: The 'New Right' and the Politics of Resentment* (New York: Pantheon Books, 1980), 18–19.
57. In February 1970 Thompson reported that the NSCVV had more campus representatives than ever before and promised a victory march in Washington sometime in April. The group's failure to organize this march reflected its move toward a less conspicuous focus on victory. Minutes of meeting of the national board of YAF, February 6–8, 1970, Dowd papers, box 3, folder Subject file, YAF/National board—memoranda, circulars, and printed matter.
58. Student Coordinating Committee for Freedom in Vietnam and Southeast Asia

press release, "National Pro-Vietnam Student Group Launched—Challenges Sens. McCarthy and McGovern to Debate," August 16, 1970, Turner papers, box 22, folder NSCVV.
59. Letter, from Group II of the National Coordinating Committee for Freedom in Vietnam and Southeast Asia fact-finding mission to Vietnam and Cambodia, November 13, 1970, to President Nixon, Turner papers, box 22, folder National Coordinating Committee for Victory in Vietnam and Southeast Asia.
60. Report on Vietnamization, National Coordinating Committee for Freedom in Vietnam and Southeast Asia, issued in February 1971, Turner papers, box 22, folder National Coordinating Committee for Victory in Vietnam and Southeast Asia.
61. Memorandum, Sven Kraemer to General Alexander Haig, February 9, 1971, Nixon Presidential Materials, National Archives, College Park, Maryland, White House Special Files, White House Central Files, Confidential Files, 1969–74, box 42, folder [CF] NO18/165 [Vietnam] [1971–74]. Hereafter cited as White House confidential files.
62. Press release issued by the National Coordinating Committee for Freedom in Vietnam and Southeast Asia after meeting with President Nixon, February 2, 1971, Turner papers, box 22, folder National Coordinating Committee for Victory in Vietnam and Southeast Asia.
63. Copy of the Joint Treaty of Peace Between the People of the United States, South Vietnam, and North Vietnam (People's Peace Treaty), Turner papers, box 22, folder National Student Committee for Victory in Vietnam.
64. Pamphlet distributed by the National Coordinating Committee for Peace with Freedom in Vietnam and Southeast Asia, copy in Walter Judd Papers, Hoover Institution Archives, Stanford, California, box 251, folder Vietnam, General, 1971. Hereafter cited as Judd papers.
65. "Campaigning for a People's Peace Treaty," promotional package of the NSA, Douglas Pike collection, Texas Tech University, Vietnam Archive, Lubbock, Texas, Unit 03-Anti-war Activities, People's Peace Treaty, 1970, folder 10, box 08.
66. "The NSA 'Peace Treaty' versus the People," an analysis by American Youth for a Just Peace, Turner papers, box 22, folder National Student Committee for Victory in Vietnam.
67. The individuals named were David Dellinger, Sidney Peck, Ron Young, Cora Weiss, and Rennie Davis. National Student Coordinating Committee for Freedom in Vietnam and Southeast Asia, "Report on the NSA People's Peace Treaty," Turner papers, box 22, folder National Student Coordinating Committee for Victory in Vietnam.
68. National Student Coordinating Committee for Freedom in Vietnam and Southeast Asia report, "On Viet Cong 7-point 'peace' proposal," July 3, 1971, Turner papers, box 22, folder National Student Committee for Victory in Vietnam.
69. National Student Coordinating Committee for Freedom in Vietnam and Southeast Asia press release, "Nixon and Red China," July 1971, Turner papers, box 22, folder National Student Committee for Victory in Vietnam.
70. Steve Frank, one of the founders of VIVA and its director of operations, cited in a letter to Bernard Direnfeld, national commander of Jewish War Veterans of America, July 6, 1970, Voices in Vital America, Inc. Archive, Kent State University Special Collections and Archives, Ohio, box 5, folder Steven Frank, director of operations (includes his bio). Hereafter cited as VIVA papers.
71. Articles of incorporation of Victory in Vietnam Association, 1967, box 1, folder

Articles of incorporation, amendments and registration of a charitable organization, VIVA papers.
72. H. Bruce Franklin, *M.I.A., or Mythmaking in America: How Belief in Live POWs Has Possessed a Nation* (New Brunswick: Rutgers University Press, 1992), 55. Franklin quotes an article written by Russell Kirk that appeared in *National Review* in 1966. Kirk advertised the organization as a courageous new student–faculty coalition dedicated to countering anti-war feeling on American campuses.
73. Letter, Steve Frank to Arnold Steinberg, VIVA's public relations team and former YAF leader in California, July 14, 1970, VIVA papers, box 5, folder Steven Frank, director of operations (includes his bio).
74. Biography of Carol Bates for VIVA Speakers Bureau, VIVA papers, box 16, folder Speakers Bureau.
75. Jerry Norton correspondence, VIVA papers, box 33.
76. Saracino thanked VIVA for purchasing a table at the Parade of Stars for Rafferty dinner and donating that table to YAF. Letter, Bill Saracino to VIVA, April 1, 1968, VIVA papers, box 33.
77. Letter, Richard Thies to Dan Johnson, spokesman for the Committee for a *Lasting* Peace, March 19, 1970, VIVA papers, box 5, folder Correspondence with National Committee for a *Lasting* Peace. Thies was responding to Johnson's request for VIVA to distribute his organization's literature; the National Committee for a *Lasting* Peace assumed a more hard-line position than VIVA.
78. Franklin, *M.I.A,* 55.
79. Prospectus, Positive Student Action on Campus, VIVA papers, box 1, folder Prospectus, 1970–71.
80. *VIVA Headlines* (the group's quarterly publication), Spring 1970, VIVA papers, box 17, folder VIVA Headlines.
81. VIVA pamphlet, "On-Campus Programs Designed to Attract the Support and Participation of the Student 'Silent Majority,'" c. mid-1970, VIVA papers, box 25.
82. VIVA statement of purpose, quoted in "Problems hit POW-MIA organization," *The Tennessean,* March 11, 1973, VIVA papers, box 1, folder Prospectus, 1970–71.
83. "Drive Started to Back Nixon Vietnam Policy," *Los Angeles Times,* November 9, 1969.
84. VIVA press release, 15 October 1969, VIVA papers, box 33.
85. Ibid.
86. Franklin, *M.I.A.,* 55–56.
87. VIVA pamphlet, "On-Campus Programs Designed to Attract the Support and Participation of the Student 'Silent Majority,'" c. mid-1970, VIVA papers, box 25.
88. Minutes of the Student Action Committee, Sunday, August 9, 1970, VIVA papers, box 5, folder Student Action Committee (aka Student Action Council and SAC).
89. Letter, Steve Frank to Dan Joy, August 20, 1970, VIVA papers, box 5, folder Student Action Committee (aka Student Action Council and SAC).
90. Nixon and Frank, quoted in "The Quiet Majority: Other Side of Campus Revolt," *U.S. News and World Report,* May 26, 1969.
91. Letter, Steve Frank to Arnold Steinberg, who was then working on the "Buckley for Senate" staff, July 21, 1970, VIVA papers, box 5, folder Stephen Frank, director of operations (includes his bio).

92. Letter, Steve Frank to Bryce Harlow, December 7, 1973, VIVA papers, box 33, folder Government officials.
93. VIVA press release, c. mid-1970, VIVA papers, box 17, folder VIVA publicity, Steve Frank personal.
94. VIVA press release, "P.O.W. Bracelets Worn around the World," December 12, 1970, VIVA papers, box 17, folder Publicity.
95. VIVA Annual Report Year Ended August 31, 1972, VIVA papers, box 2, folder VIVA Annual Report.
96. Gloria Coppin, excerpt in Christian Appy, *Patriots: The Vietnam War Remembered from All Sides* (New York: Viking, 2003), 490.
97. Letter, VIVA, Concern for POWs, Inc., POW/MIA International, National League of Families, Mrs. Donald Bloodworth, and Support Our MIAs/POWs, to all members of Congress, c. late 1972, VIVA papers, box 25.
98. VIVA sample news release, c. June 1971, VIVA papers, box 15, folder Freedom Tree Kit.
99. VIVA Freedom Tree Kit, c. July 1972, VIVA papers, box 15, folder Freedom Tree Kit.
100. "Plea for Freedom Trees," by Henry J. Taylor, United Features Syndicate, Inc. (188 newspapers), 1972, VIVA papers, box 15, folder Freedom Tree Kit.
101. Such patriotism was prevalent in the first Freedom Tree dedication, which paid tribute to Shirley Stavast's husband, a POW, in Claremont, California, on July 4, 1972. Form letter, John M. Schweizer, Jr, c. July/August 1972, VIVA papers, box 15, folder Freedom Tree Kit.
102. Letter, VIVA, Concern for POWs, Inc., POW/MIA International, National League of Families, Mrs. Donald Bloodworth, and Support Our MIAs/POWs, to all members of Congress, c. late 1972, VIVA papers, box 25.
103. General mailing, Karl C. Rove to CRNC members, October 17, 1972, Campus Republican National Committee Collection, Hoover Institution Archives, Stanford, California, box 36, folder CRNC memoranda and mass mailings, 1972. Hereafter cited as CRNC collection.
104. CRNC instruction manual, "The New Student Politics," 1969, CRNC collection, box 8.
105. The LTS was primarily organized by the YRNF and included keynote speeches by Senators Bob Dole, James Buckley, Strom Thurmond, and Bill Brock. LTS brochure, CRNC collection, box 31, folder CRNC board meeting, February 1971 (at Young Republican LTS).
106. GO•PEACE brochure, which included a chart indicating Nixon's record of troop withdrawal since 1969, CRNC collection, box 35, folder 1971 Mailings—July–December.
107. Report on his visit to Vietnam, Joseph Abate, October 1971, CRNC collection, box 24, folder Chairman, 1971.
108. "Proposal for Expansion of Washington Campus News Service," CRNC, January 18, 1971, CRNC collection, box 32, folder WCNS correspondence, 1971–1972.
109. CRNC press release, "GOP College Leader Attacks YAF Chairman,' March 22, 1972, CRNC collection, box 43, folder YAF, 1971–1974.
110. CRNC press release, "NSA Strike Call Grounded in 'Demagoguery,' College Leader Charges," April 20, 1972, CRNC collection, box 36, folder CRNC memoranda: 1972.

7. Snatching Victory
The Endings of a War

1. Phyllis Schlafly, cited in "Introduction: The Adventurous Journey of Nixon in the World," *Nixon in the World: American Foreign Relations, 1969–1977*, ed. Fredrik Logevall and Andrew Preston (New York: Oxford University Press, 2008), 8. The quotation was taken from Schlafly's book, coauthored with Chester Ward, *Kissinger on the Couch* (1975).
2. Robert David Johnson, *Congress and the Cold War* (New York: Cambridge University Press, 2006), 199.
3. For discussion of the declining popularity of détente and the impact of the Jackson–Vanik amendment on Kissinger's thwarted use of linkage diplomacy to induce Soviet concessions, see Mike Bowker and Phil Williams, *Superpower Détente: A Reappraisal* (London: Institute for Public Affairs, 1988), chap. 7; Mario Del Pero, *The Eccentric Realist: Henry Kissinger and the Shaping of American Foreign Policy* (Ithaca: Cornell University Press, 2010); Julian Zelizer, "Détente and Domestic Politics," *Diplomatic History* 33 (September 2009), 653–70.
4. Memorandum, Charles Colson to H. R. Haldeman, March 3, 1972, Nixon Presidential Materials, National Archives, College Park, Maryland, White House Special Files, Staff Member and Office Files, Charles Colson, box 120, folder patriotic and veterans groups, VFW [1 of 3]. Hereafter cited as Colson files.
5. Andrew Johns, *Vietnam's Second Front: Domestic Politics, the Republican Party, and the War* (Lexington: University Press of Kentucky, 2010), 296.
6. Letter, William Rusher to William F. Buckley Jr., March 9, 1972, William A. Rusher papers, Library of Congress, Washington, D.C., Manuscript and Archives Division, box 121, folder Staff correspondence and memoranda, William F. Buckley, 1971. Hereafter cited as Rusher papers.
7. Columns in Rusher papers, box 121, folder Staff Correspondence and memoranda, William F. Buckley, 1971.
8. Goldwater press release, March 22, 1972, Barry M. Goldwater Papers, Arizona Historical Foundation, Arizona State University, Tempe, Arizona, SP series, box 8, folder Remarks by Barry M. Goldwater, press releases, 1972. Hereafter cited as Goldwater papers.
9. David Greenberg, "Nixon as Statesman: The Failed Campaign," in *Nixon in the World*, ed. Logevall and Preston, 55, 58.
10. Letter, William Rusher to William F. Buckley Jr., March 9, 1972, Rusher papers, box 121, folder Staff correspondence and memoranda, William F. Buckley, 1971.
11. *Battle Line*, April 1972, Rusher papers, box 135, folder ACU newsletter, Republican Battle Line, printed versions, 1971–1972.
12. Senator Barry Goldwater, cited in Robert A. Goldberg, *Barry Goldwater* (New Haven: Yale University Press, 1995), 266.
13. William F. Buckley Jr., "On the Right: Capitulation at Peking," February 28, 1972, William F. Buckley Jr. Papers, Sterling Memorial Library Manuscripts and Archives, Yale University, New Haven, Connecticut, box 437, folder Buckley columns, On the Right, January 1972. Hereafter cited as Buckley papers.
14. William F. Buckley Jr., "On the Right," January 27, 1972, Buckley papers, box 437, folder Buckley columns, On the Right, February 1972.
15. Buckley, "On the Right: Hour of Decision," April 13, 1972, Buckley papers, box 437, folder Buckley columns, On the Right, April 1972.
16. Henry Kissinger, *White House Years* (London: Phoenix Press, 1979), 1097, 1102.
17. H. R. Haldeman diary entry, April 4, 1972, H. R. Haldeman, *The Haldeman*

Diaries: Inside the Nixon White House (New York: G. P. Putnam's Sons, 1994), 435.
18. President Richard Nixon, cited in Jeffrey Kimball, *The Vietnam War Files: Uncovering the Secret History of Nixon-era Strategy* (Lawrence: University Press of Kansas, 2004), 219.
19. Memorandum, President Richard Nixon to Henry Kissinger, April 20, 1972, copy in Kimball, *Vietnam War Files*, 207–9.
20. Kissinger, *White House Years*, 1102.
21. H. R. Haldeman diary entry, April 4, 1972, *Haldeman Diaries*, 435.
22. William F. Buckley Jr., "On the Right: Hour of Decision," April 13, 1972, Buckley papers, box 437, folder Buckley columns, On the Right, Apr 1972.
23. Senator Barry Goldwater, address to the Senate, April 17, 1972, *Congressional Record*.
24. Nixon, cited in Haldeman's diary entry, April 16, 1972, *Haldeman Diaries*, 441.
25. See Jeffrey Kimball, *Nixon's Vietnam War* (Lawrence: University Press of Kansas, 1998), 309–16.
26. Memorandum, H. R. Haldeman to Charles Colson and Clark MacGregor, April 25, 1972, Colson files, box 53, folder Continued North Vietnam Invasion April 1972.
27. Telegram, Senator Strom Thurmond to President Richard Nixon, May 8, 1972, Strom Thurmond Papers, Strom Thurmond Institute, Clemson University, South Carolina, Military Assistant Series, box 15, folder Vietnam, Mar 23, 1971–1972. Hereafter cited as Thurmond papers.
28. President Richard Nixon, Address to the nation on the situation in Southeast Asia, May 8, 1972, *Public Papers of the Presidents of the United States, Richard Nixon, 1972* (Washington: Government Printing Office, 1973), Doc. 147.
29. William F. Buckley Jr., "On the Right: Hour of Decision," April 13, 1972, Buckley papers, box 437, folder Buckley columns, On the Right, April 1972.
30. H. R. Haldeman note, written on memorandum from Charles Colson to H. R. Haldeman, May 9, 1972, Colson files, box 122, folder Vietnam speech, 5/8/72 [1 of 4].
31. Patrick Buchanan, memorandum of GOP leadership meeting, for the president's file, April 12, 1972, Nixon Presidential Materials, National Archives, College Park, Maryland, White House Special Files, Staff Member and Office Files, President's personal files, 1972, box 88, folder April 9, 1972. Hereafter cited as President's personal files.
32. Haldeman diary entry, May 8, 1972, *Haldeman Diaries*, 456–57.
33. Senator Barry Goldwater, column #156, mid-May 1972, Goldwater papers, Speech series, box 8, folder 3.
34. Haldeman diary entry, April 2, 1972, *Haldeman Diaries*, 435.
35. Goldwater column # 153, c. mid-May, Goldwater papers, SP series, box 8, folder 3.
36. Senator Barry Goldwater, column #156, mid-May 1972, Goldwater papers, Speech series, box 8, folder 3.
37. American Security Council, *Washington Report*, May 12, 1972, copy in Walter Judd Papers, Hoover Institution Archives, Stanford, California, box 251, folder Vietnam, general, 1972. Hereafter cited as Judd papers.
38. Senator Barry Goldwater, column #156, mid-May 1972, Goldwater papers, Speech series, box 8, folder 3.
39. "How Nixon Can Make Vietnamization Work," *Human Events*, May 13, 1972.
40. William F. Buckley Jr., "On the Right: Nixon's Last Stand," May 13/14, 1972, Buckley papers, box 437, folder Buckley columns, On the Right, May–June 1972.

41. "Nixon's speech good, but . . . South Viet Nam must have modern weaponry," *Human Events*, May 6, 1972.
42. See Johnson, *Congress and the Cold War*, 230–58.
43. Senator Barry Goldwater, remarks on the Senate floor, "The Amendment to Prolong the War," August 2, 1972, Buckley papers, box 178, folder Vietnam and war powers.
44. M. Stanton Evans, Report for conservative leaders, "Submerging the Republican Majority: The First 1,000 Days of the Richard Nixon Presidency," copy in Rusher papers, box 30, folder Evans, M. Stanton, 1969–1987.
45. William F. Buckley Jr., "On the Right: Bomb the Dikes?" August 17, 1972, Buckley papers, box 438, folder Buckley columns, On the Right, August 1972.
46. Senator Barry Goldwater, column #143, circa May 1972, Goldwater papers, speech series, box 8, folder 3.
47. Senator Strom Thurmond, weekly radio broadcast, "Vietnam Progress," September 24–25, 1972, Thurmond papers, Speeches series, box 49, subseries IIA, folder 04154.
48. Telegram, Alexander Haig to Henry Kissinger, with direct message from President Richard Nixon to Henry Kissinger, October 20, 1972, Nixon Presidential Materials, National Archives, College Park, Maryland, National Security Council files, Henry A. Kissinger Office Files, HAK administrative and staff files, box 104, folder HAK's Saigon Trip. Hereafter cited as Kissinger files.
49. Telegram, Henry Kissinger to Major General Alexander Haig, October 21, 1972, ibid.
50. Kissinger, *White House Years*, 1307.
51. Senator Barry Goldwater, cited in "Goldwater Smells Vietnam Accord," *Tacoma News Tribune*, October 19, 1972.
52. Letter, President Richard Nixon to Walter Judd, November 29, 1972, Judd papers, box 31, folder Correspondence, Nixon, Richard M., 1952–1984.
53. Letter, Walter Judd to President Richard Nixon, October 22, 1972, Judd papers, box 31, folder Correspondence, Nixon, Richard M., 1952–1984.
54. Letter, Ronald Reagan to William F. Buckley Jr., November 2, 1972, Buckley papers, box 227, folder Reagan, Mr. and Mrs. Ronald and staff, 1972–1974.
55. Letter, William F. Buckley Jr. to Henry Kissinger, October 25, 1972, Buckley papers, box 274, folder White House, 1972.
56. William Rusher, interview with CBS News, copy of interview in Rusher papers, box 212, folder Speaking engagements, presentations, radio broadcasts, 1965–1974.
57. Henry Paolucci proclaimed in 1980 that the administration delayed ending the Vietnam War, particularly in October 1972, because officials feared a right-wing backlash. Paolucci, *Kissinger's War: 1957–1975* (New York: Griffon House, 1980), 45. Jeffrey Kimball comments that Nixon "backed away from the [October] agreement in the face of President Nguyen Van Thieu's objections and right-wing criticism from within and without his administration." Kimball, *Nixon's Vietnam War*, 8.
58. Senator Barry Goldwater, cited in *National Observer*, November 11, 1972.
59. Report by the Freedom Leadership Foundation, November 1972, copy in Thurmond papers, Subject Correspondence Series, 1972, box 6, folder Vietnam War.
60. Letter, Senator Barry Goldwater to Major General Alexander Haig, deputy assistant to the president for national security affairs, December 6, 1972, Nixon Presidential Materials, National Archives, College Park, Maryland, National Security Council files, Names files: Barry M. Goldwater. Hereafter cited as NSC Goldwater file.

61. Letter, Major General Alexander Haig to Senator Barry Goldwater, December 18, 1972, NSC Goldwater file.
62. Memorandum, "Meeting between President Nixon, General Westmoreland and General Haig," prepared by Major General Alexander Haig Jr., October 20, 1972, President's office files, box 90, folder October 15, 1972.
63. Memorandum, "The President's Meeting with the Joint Chiefs of Staff," prepared by Major General Alexander Haig Jr., November 30, 1972, President's office files, box 90, folder November 26, 1972. For further discussion of Nixon's efforts to sell the peace terms to the JCS, see Stephen P. Randolph, *Powerful and Brutal Weapons: Nixon, Kissinger, and the Easter Offensive* (Cambridge: Harvard University Press, 2007), 331–32.
64. For details of the military campaign, see Ronald B. Frankum Jr., *Like Rolling Thunder: The Air War in Vietnam, 1964–1975* (Oxford: Rowman and Littlefield, 2005), 164–66.
65. "Americans Should Back President: Stepped-up Air War Could Produce Sound Viet Peace," *Human Events*, December 30, 1972.
66. William F. Buckley Jr., "On the Right," December 26, 1972, Buckley papers, box 438, folder Buckley columns, On the Right, November–December 1972.
67. "Americans Should Back President: Stepped-up Air War Could Produce Sound Viet Peace," *Human Events*, December 30, 1972.
68. Senator Barry Goldwater press release, December 21, 1972, Goldwater papers, SP series, box 1, folder 88: Press release: the increased bombing campaign in North Vietnam, December 21, 1972.
69. Telegram, Senator Strom Thurmond to President Richard Nixon, January 2, 1973, Thurmond papers, White House series, Nixon administration, box 1, folder Nixon presidential, folder III; January 10, 1972–August 19, 1973.
70. William F. Buckley Jr., "On the Right: The End of Vietnamization," January 2, 1973, Buckley papers, box 438, folder Buckley columns, On the Right, Jan–Feb 1973.
71. Telegram, Walter Judd to President Richard Nixon, December 19, 1972, Judd papers, box 31, folder Correspondence, Nixon, Richard M., 1952–1984.
72. Telegram, Senator Barry Goldwater to William F. Buckley Jr., December 21, 1972, Buckley papers, box 147, folder Goldwater, Barry, 1972–1975.
73. Letter, William F. Buckley Jr. to Senator Barry Goldwater, December 29, 1972, Buckley papers, box 147, folder Goldwater, Barry, 1972–1975.
74. "Have Critical Changes Been Made in New Viet Pact?" *Human Events*, January 27, 1973.
75. "Only Nixon Resolve Can Make Pact Work," *Human Events*, February 3, 1973.
76. Randolph, *Powerful and Brutal Weapons*, 336.
77. Senator Strom Thurmond, press release, January 23, 1973, Thurmond papers, Military Assistant series, box 15, folder Vietnam, January 23–December 5, 1973.
78. Senator Barry Goldwater, article for Associated Press on the Vietnam Ceasefire Agreement, January 24, 1973, Colson files, box 120, folder Vietnam January Ceasefire, 1973.
79. Frankum, *Like Rolling Thunder*, 165.
80. Senator Barry Goldwater, article for Associated Press on the Vietnam Ceasefire Agreement, January 24, 1973, Colson files, box 120, folder Vietnam January Ceasefire, 1973.
81. Kevin J. Smant, *How Great the Triumph: James Burnham, Anticommunism and the Conservative Movement* (Lanham, Md.: University Press of America, 1992), 108.
82. YAF official statement on the Vietnam settlement, *New Guard*, February 1973.

83. Gregory Schneider, *Cadres for Conservatism: Young Americans for Freedom and the Rise of the Contemporary Right* (New York: New York University Press, 1999), 155.
84. YAF official statement on the Vietnam settlement, *New Guard*, February 1973.
85. Frank Koscielski, *Divided Loyalties: American Unions and the Vietnam War* (New York: Garland, 1999), 45.
86. Goldberg, *Goldwater*, 281–82.
87. Barry M. Goldwater, *With No Apologies: The Personal and Political Memoirs of United States Senator Barry M. Goldwater* (New York: Morrow, 1979), 250.
88. Ibid.
89. Indeed, Goldwater's postwar memoirs (1979) discuss Vietnam almost wholly in terms of the Johnson administration. Although Goldwater's memoir offered some criticism of Nixon, particularly of the president's policies toward China, he reserved much of his criticism regarding Vietnam for Robert McNamara and the Kennedy and Johnson administrations. Goldwater, *No Apologies*, 200–250. Goldwater's collaboration with Jack Casserly in 1988 offered a more extensive condemnation of the Democrats and McNamara. Of the thirty-five pages devoted to a discussion of Vietnam, Nixon's policies were noted on only two. Goldwater and Casserly, *Goldwater*, 282–317. Goldwater's failure to address his position during the Nixon years was reflected in Robert A. Goldberg's biography, which devotes twenty pages of discussion to Goldwater's position on Johnson's handling of the Vietnam War and fewer than two pages to analysis of Nixon's policies. Goldberg, *Goldwater*, 243–64.

Conclusion
Defining the Vietnam War

1. ASC report, "South Vietnam—Test of U.S. Will and Greatness," published in *Washington Report*, February 1975, copy in Elizabeth Churchill Brown Papers, Hoover Institution Archives, Stanford, California, box 41, folder Vietnam War—printed material, c. 1970–1977.
2. Clare Booth Luce, "Media Hypocritical on South Vietnam," *Honolulu Advertiser*, May 15, 1975.
3. Senator John Tower, "Not to Win Was Biggest Vietnam Error," *Rock Hill* (South Carolina) *Herald*, April 26, 1980.
4. Ibid.
5. Barry M. Goldwater, *With No Apologies: The Personal and Political Memoirs of United States Senator Barry M. Goldwater* (New York: Morrow, 1979), 148.
6. Dominic Sandbrook, *Mad as Hell: The Crisis of the 1970s and the Rise of the Populist Right* (New York: Alfred A. Knopf, 2011), 336.
7. Ibid., 338.
8. Natasha Zaretsky, "Restraint or Retreat? The Debate over the Panama Canal Treaties and U.S. Nationalism after Vietnam," *Diplomatic History* 35 (June 2011), 537.
9. James Burnham, "The Protracted Conflict: Go East, Old Man," *National Review*, January 21, 1975.
10. See Gregory Schneider, *Conservatism in America since 1930: A Reader* (New York: New York University Press, 2003), 275–78; Jacob Heilbrunn, *They Knew They Were Right: The Rise of the Neocons* (New York: Doubleday, 2008); Mario Del Pero, *The Eccentric Realist: Henry Kissinger and the Shaping of American Foreign Policy* (Ithaca: Cornell University Press, 2010).

11. Robert A. Goldberg, *Barry Goldwater* (New Haven: Yale University Press, 1995), 288; Michael Lind, *Vietnam, the Necessary War: A Reinterpretation of America's Most Disastrous Military Conflict* (New York: Free Press, 1999), 25.
12. William F. Buckley Jr., cited in John Wesley Young, "William F. Buckley, Jr.: Conservatism with Class," in *American Conservative Opinion Leaders*, ed. Mark J. Rozell and James F. Pontuso (Boulder: Westview Press, 1990), 55.
13. Clare Booth Luce, "The High Human Price of Détente," *National Review*, November 11, 1977.
14. Patrick Hagopian, *The Vietnam War in American Memory: Veterans, Memorials, and the Politics of Healing* (Amherst: University of Massachusetts Press, 2009), 15, 17.
15. Robert J. McMahon, "Contested Memory: The Vietnam War and American Society, 1975–2001," *Diplomatic History* 26 (Spring 2002), 168.
16. *Wall Street Journal* (eastern edition), January 14, 1985, 1.
17. Mary McGrory, "Reagan Finds Moderation," *Boca Raton News*, January 31, 1979.
18. President Ronald Reagan, Speech Honoring the Vietnam War's Unknown Soldier, May 28, 1984.

Index

Abate, Joseph, 282, 284–86
Abrams, Creighton, 92, 123
Accuracy in Media, 325, 330
Acheson, Dean, 66
Achilles, Theodore C., 217
Action Line (newsletter), 60
ACU. *See* American Conservative Union (ACU)
Adoption program, 281
AFL-CIO (American Federation of Labor/Congress of Industrial Organizations), 66–67, 90–91, 134–35
AFV (American Friends of Vietnam), 54, 215–17, 252
Agnew, Spiro: anticommunism of, 126, 164; attacks on anti-war movement, 125–26, 210, 212–13, 232; attempts to pacify conservatives, 177; Buchanan on possible speech for, 128; on Calley conviction, 221–22; on Cambodian invasion of 1970, 132; at gala for POWs at Constitution Hall in May 1970, 232; on Humphrey's proposed bombing halt, 90; Keene as aide to, 243; McIntire compares Ky with, 200; on North Vietnamese support for anti-war movement, 189; on not letting Communists make the rules, 143; on Pentagon papers, 164; on polarization, 137, 336; on Vietnam War ending only with end of North Vietnamese aggression, 313; Young Americans for Freedom praise, 257
Albert, Carl, 107
Alexander, Holmes, 39
All American Conference to Combat Communism, 253
Allen, Michael, 227
Allen, Richard, 82, 89
Allott, Gordon, 102, 148, 149
Alternative Weekend (Boston), 257, 258
American Conservative Union (ACU), 23–24; *Battle Line* magazine, 139, 156, 182; broad attack on Nixon's foreign policy by, 152–53; on Cambodian invasion of 1970, 139; Citizens Committee for Peace with Freedom in Vietnam contrasted with, 68; de Toledano's animosity toward, 146; division between Republican politicians and, 290, 295; in Draft Goldwater drives, 6; fusionism of, 23; increasingly public challenges to Nixon's policies, 147; John Birch Society opposed by, 26–27; at July 26, 1971, conservative meeting, 170; Kissinger fails to blunt animosity of, 177; on Kissinger's appointment as national security adviser, 99–100; on Lam Son 719 operation, 156; on mining of Haiphong harbor, 302; 1965 plan to win the war, 45–48; on Nixon appointees, 97–98; Nixon endorsed in 1968 by, 86–87; Nixon's Vietnam policy criticized by, 126–27; on Nixon's visit to China, 171; on Paris peace accords, 321; on polarization, 161–62; Possony as member of, 29; Rusher's criticism of, 160; and split over Ashbrook's presidential

[389]

ACU (*continued*)
campaign of 1972, 294; on Vietnamization, 115, 124, 126, 139, 153, 156, 159; Young Americans for Freedom allied with, 23, 245, 246
American Conservative Union Speakers Bureau, 253
American Council for World Freedom (ACWF), 129
American Enterprise Institute, 216
American Federation of Labor/Congress of Industrial Organizations (AFL-CIO), 66–67, 90–91, 134–35
American flag, 191, 192, 193, 206, 208, 210, 274
American Friends of Vietnam (AFV), 54, 215–17, 252
American Legion: on anti-war movement as giving comfort to enemy, 201; on Cambodian invasion of 1970, 134; on domestic consequences of Vietnam War, 319; "For God and Country Support Our Boys in Vietnam" slogan, 188–89; Honor America Week endorsed by, 193; and New York City Veterans Day parade, 1969, 196; in Nixon's flag-waving drive, 210; on Nixon's visit to China, 178; patriotic drives sponsored by, 7; positive means of seeing the war of, 189; in POW campaign, 233–34; supporting-the-troops theme of, 56; welcome home parades organized by, 325; and "We Support Our Boys in Vietnam" parades, 57, 58, 59, 60, 340
American Opinion (journal), 25, 55–56
American Security Council (ASC): on attacking Red River dike system, 51; on blocking Haiphong harbor, 50–51; on bombing North Vietnam, 49; Committee on the Present Danger as successor to, 338; on Cuba as threat, 20; on key to successful defense of Southeast Asia, 17; on military aid to South Vietnam in 1975, 330; on Soviet aid to North Vietnam, 50; strategy for victory in Vietnam, 38–39; Student Action Committee, 275–76; Student Coordinating Committee for Freedom in Vietnam and Southeast Asia compared with, 271
Americans for Winning the Peace (AWP), 217–20
American Students for a *Just* Peace, 269
amnesty for draft evaders, 305, 324
Anderson, Martin, 82, 210
anti-ballistic missile (ABM) system, 102, 109, 173
anticommunism: of AFL-CIO, 67, 90, 135; of Agnew, 126, 164; of American Conservative Union, 24; anti-war movement as threat to, 14; Catholic fervor in, 54; grassroots activists accuse Democrats of limited commitment to, 41; intellectual conservatives seek to reinvigorate, 337; liberal, 215; of McIntire, 198; *National Review* urges stronger anticommunist foreign policy, 14–15, 19, 20; of Nixon, 72, 75–76, 78–79, 124; nuclear test ban treaty opposed by anticommunists, 90; pro-war rallies compared with those of, 8; of Reagan, 337; in reemergence of conservatism, 13; on the right, 20–30; Schwarz's criticism of anticommunists in government, 35; seems less relevant by mid-1970s, 335; in southern California, 35; unifying significance of, 22, 25; of Victory in Vietnam Association, 271, 278; Vietnam War associated with, 5, 14, 18–19, 21, 30, 59, 65–66, 240, 300; of Young Americans for Freedom, 63–64, 65, 247
anti-war movement: Agnew's attacks on, 125–26, 210, 212–13, 232; alliance with North Vietnam attributed to, 189–90; anti-war congressmen, 143, 148, 162, 210, 218, 304–5; April 15, 1967, demonstration in New York City, 58–59, 60; April 24, 1971, march in Washington, 200–201; August 1964 rally in New York City, 57–58;

on Cambodian invasion of 1970, 133, 136, 141–42, 207; changes over time, 185; Citizens Committee for Peace with Freedom in Vietnam on, 117; communist influence seen in, 78, 211–12; conservative opposition to, 6, 10, 14, 183, 335, 340; conservative support for Vietnamization as response to, 161; defeat in Vietnam blamed on, 323, 333–34; demands become extreme, 151; dissent seen as challenge to patriotism, 58, 61–62; Goldwater on, 181; grassroots opposition to, 5; Haldeman on motivation of, 244; high point of popular activism against, 190; Honor America Day Rally of 1970 opposes, 198; Humphrey supported by, 90; investigations and infiltrations of, 211–12; Lam Son 719 operation opposed by, 156; and libertarian Young Americans for Freedom, 260; mainstream dissent emerges, 141–42; as marginalized in public opinion, 58; as minority of students, 244; national rallies sent for autumn 1969, 121; National Student Committee for Peace with Freedom in Southeast Asia opposes, 252; Nixon and, 73, 123, 137, 143, 147, 151, 158, 202, 211–12; Nixon's "Silent Majority" speech galvanizes opposition to, 125; North Vietnam releases information on prisoners of war to, 277, 281; opposition to Vietnam War in evidence since earliest days, 57; patriotism limits acceptance of, 185; and Pentagon papers, 163, 168; People's Peace Treaty, 268–70; permissiveness associated with, 197; polarization aids, 162; popular opposition to, 87, 137, 186, 189, 202, 205, 207; and POW issue, 227, 233, 234, 236–37, 238–39; protests at Democratic National Convention of 1968, 87; seen as deepening national divide, 141, 207, 244; seen as giving comfort to enemy, 7, 201, 211, 242; seen as treasonous and harmful, 9; seen as un-American, 59, 62–63, 206, 208, 213, 232; social conservatives attribute moral degeneracy to, 13; student pro-war groups oppose, 242–43; supporting the troops as reaction to, 56–57, 250; threatens to counter McIntire's Victory in Vietnam March, 200; Thurmond's criticism of, 321–22; Turner counters claims of, 251–52; Victory in Vietnam Association opposes, 271, 274–75, 281; Vietnamization as attempt to pacify, 103; Vietnam Veterans for a Just Peace on, 226; Vietnam War prolonged by, 350n43; Westmoreland on, 196; "We Support Our Boys in Vietnam" parade in New York, May 13, 1967, as response to, 57, 61; Young Americans for Freedom oppose, 242, 246–47, 249, 258, 259–60. *See also* Moratorium to End the War in Vietnam; student radicals

Appy, Christian, 203, 204
Arends, Leslie, 103
Arlington National Cemetery, 196
armbands, red-white-and-blue, 191, 193, 257, 274
Arrogance of Power, The (Fulbright), 58
ASC. *See* American Security Council (ASC)
Ashbrook, John: and American Conservative Union endorsement of Nixon in 1968, 86; on Cambodian invasion of 1970, 139; on China and Vietnam War, 179, 181; hostility between Goldwater and, 13; and Huston Plan, 212; and Manhattan Twelve statement, 170; Nixon praised by, 75; presidential campaign of 1972, 293–94, 295, 297
Asian People's Anti-Communist League, 63
Asian Speakers Bureau, 253
Association of Student Governments (ASG), 243

AWP (Americans for Winning the Peace), 217–20

Ball, George, 44
Barnett, Frank, 215
Baroody, Bill, 216
Barrett, Richard, 199
Bates, Carol, 272, 277, 278
Batista, Fulgencio, 34
Bator, Francis, 44
Battle Line (magazine), 139, 156, 182
Bay of Pigs invasion, 31, 39
Belcher, Page, 258
Bell, George, 216, 219, 235
Bell, Jeff, 161, 170, 172
Berman, Larry, 108
Birch Society. *See* John Birch Society (JBS)
Blackwell, Morton, 282
bloodbath argument, 218, 226–27, 238, 252, 271, 300
Bloody Friday (May 8, 1970), 205–7
blue button campaign, 204, 246–47
bombing North Vietnam: American Conservative Union on, 47; of April 1972, 286, 296–301; B-52s in, 296; bombing pause of December 1965, 44; Buckley on, 150–51, 179–80, 307; Burnham on, 140; Citizens Committee for Peace with Freedom in Vietnam on, 67; conservatives call for, 39–40, 47, 53, 140, 239; December 1971 campaign, 179–80, 182; Eisenhower on Nixon threatening resumption of, 96; Goldwater on, 119, 127–28, 140, 153, 180; "heavier bombing boys," 44–45, 148–49; *Human Events* calls for, 302–3; Humphrey announces support for halting, 89–91; Johnson on reciprocal nature of bombing, 40; Johnson's bombing halt before 1968 election, 91–94; Johnson's bombing halt of March 1968, 69, 94, 128; Judd on, 48–49; Kissinger on, 99, 100; Laird on, 149, 150; limited campaign of March 31, 1968 to November 1, 1968, 95; limited value of strategic, 97; Linebacker II, 313–19, 321, 322, 327, 331; new targets announced in February 1967, 49; Nixon on, 73, 77, 103, 151–52, 153, 154–55; Nixon sets November 1, 1969, deadline for negotiation or, 121; in option to the right, 145–46; as protective reaction, 149; Radford supports, 82; as retaliation for North Vietnamese escalation, 110; Rolling Thunder operation, 41, 77, 179; Sharp on, 49; Symington on, 48; Tower on, 97; Veterans Day parades urge, 196; "We Support Our Boys in Vietnam" parade in New York, May 13, 1967, urges, 61
Borman, Frank, 217, 233
Bozell, L. Brent, 23
Bradley, Gene, 217, 219, 220, 372n81
Bradley, Omar, 66, 194, 196
Brennan, Peter, 207, 208–9
Brian, Herbert, 59
Broomfield, William, 36
Buchanan, John, 195
Buchanan, Patrick: Agnew speeches written by, 213; on Cambodian invasion of 1970, 153; conservative agenda pushed by, 128–29; on conservative list of demands for Nixon, 174; on Kissinger's reaction to conservative opposition, 177; in Middle America Group, 210–11; on *National Review*'s support of Nixon, 162; on Nixon and conservative Republicanism, 146; on Nixon's commitment to conservative values, 153–54; on Nixon's conservative policy team, 82; on Nixon's May 1969 peace proposal, 106; and Nixon's views on victory in Vietnam, 73; on polarization, 137, 161; on residual U.S. forces in Vietnam, 161; on South Vietnamese action after U.S. withdrawal, 125; tough position on Vietnam of, 104; "Trouble on the Right," 147, 152
Buckley, James, 141, 154, 176–77

Buckley, John, 264–65
Buckley, William F.: on acceptance of coexistence, 171; and Agnew, 177, 213; anticommunist guerrilla groups urged by, 51; associates *National Review* with Republican Party and Goldwater, 25, 83; becomes disillusioned with Nixon, 328; on bombing North Vietnam, 150–51, 179–80, 307; on Calley conviction, 222; on Cambodian invasion of 1970, 140–41; Catholic fervor of, 55; close association with Nixon administration, 146–47; conservative consensus sought by, 22; on conservative role in Nixon's 1968 victory, 124; criticism from the right of, 147; on détente, 338; in formulating list of demands for Nixon, 174; John Birch Society opposed by, 13, 25–26; at July 26, 1971, conservative meeting, 170; on Kerry, 224–25; Kissinger reassures him about settlement, 310–11; Kissinger's appointment as national security adviser endorsed by, 99, 100–101; Kissinger seen as doing PR job on, 146; Linebacker II bombings supported by, 316, 318; mayoral campaign of 1965, 60; on Moscow summit of 1972, 298; on *National Review*'s fake secret documents, 166–68; on Nixon appointees, 98; on Nixon's April 1972 bombing of North Vietnam, 297; Nixon supported in 1968 by, 75, 82–83, 87; on Nixon's visit to China, 170, 183, 296; on Panama Canal Treaty, 337; on paradox of U.S. policy in Vietnam, 175; on Paris peace accords, 322; on Pentagon papers, 163; on rearmament, 174; on Republican objectives in 1968 election, 74; on SALT negotiations, 169; on South Vietnamese action after U.S. withdrawal, 125, 127; on Soviet aid to North Vietnam, 49–50; at tenth anniversary celebrations of Young Americans for Freedom, 147; on Vietnamization, 127, 141, 159, 296, 299–300, 317, 334; and Wills, 141, 142; on Young Americans for Freedom activities, 247

Bunker, Ellsworth, 155

Burnham, James: on Cambodian invasion of 1970, 140; conservative consensus sought by, 22; on containment policy, 27–29; on debunking communist myths, 30; on Goldwater as too eager to satisfy moderates, 295; on Hungarian revolution of 1956, 28; on John Birch Society, 26; on Kissinger's appointment as national security adviser, 101; Manhattan Twelve statement signed by, 170; on Nixon's grand strategic turn, 175; on Nixon's visit to China, 170, 176; on Paris peace accords, 322–23; on resurrecting confidence in America's international missions, 337; theoretical formulation for victory in Cold War, 27, 28; on victory as unattainable, 69; on Vietnamization, 127; on Vietnam War as historical turning point, 65

Burns, Arthur, 82
Burr, William, 122
Bursk, Edward, 217
Butterfield, Alexander, 195
Buzhardt, J. Fred, 166
Byrd, Harry, Jr., 148
Byrnes, Arthur, 66

CACC (Christian Anti-Communist Crusade), 25, 35
California YAF (CalYAF), 246–47, 260, 272
Calley, William "Rusty," 221–23
Calloway, "Bo," 83
Cambodia: Buchanan on South Vietnamese action in, 128, 129; enemy buildup in 1968, 95; Ford seeks military aid for, 329; in Manhattan Twelve's list of demands, 174–75; neutrality of, 132, 268; in Nixon's Vietnam strategy, 73;

Cambodia (*continued*)
North Vietnam moves troops in South Vietnam through, 49; in Paris peace accords, 321, 327; in People's Peace Treaty, 268; as sanctuary for Viet Cong, 114, 131, 132, 144; secret bombing campaign in, 103–4, 108, 131; Sihanoukville, 127, 131, 143, 165; South Vietnamese offensive against North Vietnamese in, 149; Tower on sanitization of, 148; worsening military situation in, 179. *See also* Cambodian invasion of 1970

Cambodian invasion of 1970, 130–45; Buchanan on, 153; Kent State University shootings, 141, 142, 206, 259; opposition to, 133, 136, 141–42, 207; public support for, 187, 208; Student Coordinating Committee for Freedom in Vietnam and Southeast Asia on, 267; troops' morale improved by, 209; Vietnam Veterans for a Just Peace on, 224; Young Americans for Freedom support, 133, 259

Campaigne, Jameson G., 24
Cannon, Howard, 45
Capen, Dick, 229
"Carrying the War to North Vietnam: Time to Strike the Red River Dike System" (American Security Council), 51
Carter, Dan, 78
Carter, Jimmy, 336, 340
Casey, William J., 220
Castro, Fidel, 20, 21
CCPFV. *See* Citizens Committee for Peace with Freedom in Vietnam (CCPFV)
ceasefire-in-place, 303, 313–14, 317
Chamberlain, John, 24, 80, 83
Chamie, Alfred, 178
Chapin, Dwight, 218
Chennault, Anna, 88
Chiang Kai-shek, 34
China: American missionaries and revolution in, 33; conservatives criticize Nixon policies toward, 152, 154; Eisenhower on U.S. withdrawal from Vietnam leading to domination by, 77; and Eisenhower's diplomacy in ending Korean War, 84–85; Goldwater on possibility of intervention by, 38; in *National Review*'s fake secret documents, 165; Nixon on, 76, 78; Nixon's visit to, 169–83, 271, 293, 294, 295; North Vietnam supplied by, 37–38, 50; Radford recommends U.S. strike on, 82; Sino-Soviet split, 29, 32, 76; U.S. failures in, 31; Vietnamization and, 123

China lobby, 31, 176
Chodorov, Frank, 22
Christian Anti-Communist Crusade (CACC), 25, 35
Citizens Committee for Peace with Freedom in Vietnam (CCPFV), 66–68; Americans for Winning the Peace compared with, 217; Nixon administration seeks support of, 214–15; on Silent Center, 67, 122, 211, 214; on Vietnamization, 214; on withdrawal of U.S. troops, 115–17
Citizens Committee for Peace with Security, 220
civil rights: backlash against, 12; communist influence seen in, 78; conservatives criticize liberal policies on, 24; grassroots conservatives' attitudes toward, 21; McIntire on, 199; Nixon as stemming tide of, 75
Clark, Peter, 217
class resentment, 187, 202–4, 206
Clifford, Clark, 91, 107, 354n65
coalition government, 105, 114, 115, 181, 268, 310, 312
Cold War: Asia seen as heart of, 31, 33; Burnham's theoretical formulation for victory in, 27, 28; consensus, 208; conservative vision of U.S. role in, 291; Democratic Party abandons core tenets of, 12; domestic issues and, 11–12; fear that U.S. was losing, 32, 34; isolationism declines

due to, 21–22; Kissinger as cold warrior, 98–99; Laird as cold warrior, 101; limited salience of appeals to, 9; Nixon as cold warrior, 301; Republican Party's hard-line stands in, 28; Vietnam War associated with, 2, 191

College Republican National Committee (CRNC), 282–86; GO•PEACE campaign, 284, 285; Leadership Training School, 283–84; New Student Politics, 283; Nixon administration and, 244; Operation: Open Door, 285; patriotism as focus of, 244, 286–87; in pro-war movement, 16; and Washington Campus News Service, 285

College Young Republicans, 243, 244, 282–83

Colson, Charles: on administration being out of the woods in Vietnam, 293; on American Friends of Vietnam, 215, 216, 217; on Americans for Winning the Peace, 218, 219, 220; and Citizens Committee for Peace with Freedom in Vietnam, 214; fear of resurgence of anti-war activism in 1972, 300; and Manhattan Twelve's demands, 173, 174; on Meany, 135; national unity theme emphasized by, 201; ostensibly independent organizations set up by, 217; on POW campaign, 231; on "Rally for Freedom in Vietnam and All the World," 195; on siege mentality in White House, 137; on Vietnam Veterans for a Just Peace, 223; on Westmoreland and Nixon's peace proposal, 149; works to keep conservatives in Nixon camp, 178; on Young Americans for Freedom supporting Nixon, 133

Committee for a Week of National Unity, 190–91, 195

Committee for Responsible Patriotism, 325

Committee of Liaison with Families of Servicemen Detained in North Vietnam, 236–37

Committee on the Present Danger, 338

Concern for Prisoners Of War, 234, 280

Conservative Awards Dinner, 153

Conservative Book Club, 170

conservatives: Agnew supported by, 125–26; on airpower, 111, 112; anticommunism of, 20–30; anticommunist guerrilla groups urged by, 51; anti-war movement opposed by, 6, 10, 14, 183, 335, 340; on attacking Haiphong harbor, 39, 48, 49–51; on bombing North Vietnam, 39–40, 47, 53, 140, 239; Buchanan pushes agenda of, 128–29; on Cambodian invasion of 1970, 130–45; coalition government opposed by, 105, 114, 115, 181; conflicted over Vietnam War in 1964, 18–19; on containment, 28, 34; continued commitment to Vietnam after Cambodian invasion, 142–43; in Democratic Party, 44, 79, 89–90, 91, 93, 142, 168, 272; détente opposed by, 4, 5, 12, 14, 169, 291, 294, 330, 334; determination to take control of Republican Party, 12, 13, 15; divisions within movement, 7, 10, 12–13, 13–14, 25, 31, 36, 127, 147, 158–62, 171, 176, 179–80, 183, 290, 295, 320, 323, 333, 334; in domestic politics of Vietnam, 1968–1969, 72–124; and ending of Vietnam War, 289–327; escalation supported by, 32, 33–34, 36–41, 45, 52–53, 140, 290, 306, 315; on extending war to North Vietnam, 38, 111; on failure of U.S. to win Vietnam War, 2, 4, 5; failure to serve in Vietnam, 264–65; fortunes as tied to Nixon's, 306–7; gradual move toward acceptance of negotiation, 73–74; growing doubts about Nixon's Vietnam policy, 126–30; Gulf of Tonkin Resolution supported by, 38, 40; humanitarian issues stressed by, 52; Johnson's war policy criticized by, 2, 15, 16, 36–37, 39–41, 43–45, 184, 332; and Lam Son 719 operation, 154–58; on land reform

conservatives (*continued*)
in South Vietnam, 52; limited support for Vietnam War by 1972, 290; on limited war policy, 9, 34, 53, 142, 147, 334, 335, 341; on Linebacker II bombings, 313–19, 327; militarized foreign policy supported by, 20; neoconservatism, 62, 215, 290, 331, 337–38; New Right, 291, 335–36, 337–38; New York Conservative Party, 60, 141, 170; Nixon and the hawks, 74–87; on Nixon appointees, 97; Nixon pushed to the right by, 145–54; on Nixon's China visit of 1972, 169–83; in Nixon's 1968 victory, 95, 124; Nixon's overall foreign policy challenged by, 294; noble cause argument endorsed by, 5, 339; on Panama Canal Treaty, 336–37, 339; on Paris peace accords, 16, 308–19, 320–24, 328; on "peace with honor," 97, 290; polarization as beneficial for, 137, 161–62, 336; policy evolution, 1965–1968, 65–71; and postwar challenge, 324–27; pro-war stance rallies, 13; on public opinion's significance, 6, 9, 127, 187; reparations opposed by, 313; "responsible conservatives," 19, 20, 26, 147; search-and-destroy policies supported by, 51; seeks to escape right-wing extremist label, 19; on Senate Armed Forces Committee, 305; on Sino-Soviet split, 76; southern, 44, 75, 80, 84, 91, 212; in southern California, 272; on symbolic value of Vietnam War, 181; and U.S. push into Southeast Asia, 31–42; on U.S. failure to provide postwar support to South Vietnam, 328–31; on victory or withdrawal, 35; on Vietnamization, 113–24, 129–30, 140, 141, 148, 159–60, 175, 178, 239, 262, 268, 303–4, 306, 327, 334; Vietnam lobby, 31, 54–63; Vietnam service by, 244; and the Vietnam War, 1–16; Vietnam War as unifying force for, 13; Vietnam War causes changes in, 10; Vietnam War policy influenced by, 9–10; Vietnam War's influence on postwar foreign policy views of, 331–42; Wallace's populist conservatism, 79–80; on War Powers Act, 329; on withdrawal of U.S. troops, 113–14, 142. *See also* grassroots activists; intellectual conservatives; John Birch Society (JBS); libertarians; pro-war movement; social conservatives; traditional conservatives

containment policy, 27–29, 34, 201
Cooper, John Sherman, 68
Cooper–Church amendment, 136, 138–39, 140, 144, 148
Coppin, Douglas, 273, 277
Coppin, Gloria Wells, 272–73
Council for the Civilized Treatment of the POWs, 234
country music, 194
Courtney, Kent, 263
Crane, Philip, 154
Critchlow, Donald, 35, 351n58
Cronkite, Walter, 167
Cuba: Bay of Pigs invasion, 31, 39; conservative concern with, 20–21, 31; embargo of, 173; Student Action Committee on, 276; Vietnam compared with, 39
Cuban missile crisis, 20–21, 30, 298
Curtis, Carl, 83

Davis, Judy, 274
Dear, Ron, 257
decent interval solution, 211, 329
Defeating Communist Insurgency (Thompson), 51
defense spending, 152, 153, 171, 173, 174, 177, 262, 338
defoliation, Goldwater proposes, 37–38
DeGroot, Gerard, 358n131
Dellinger, Dave, 236–37
demilitarized zone (DMZ): Abrams given authority to respond to violations of, 92; April 1972 bombing around, 298; Buchanan on sending U.S. troops across, 128; Goldwater on

destroying enemy material north of, 140; Humphrey on, 89; Johnson's bombing halt of October 1968 and reestablishment of, 91; Laird on responding to violations of, 150; North Vietnamese violate in 1972, 296, 297; Tower on enemy buildup near, 95

Democratic Party: abandons core tenets of Cold War, 12; anti-war Democrats, 12, 87; Byrd breaks with, 148; commitment of men and material to Vietnam in 1964 and 1965, 18; conservative Democrats, 44, 79, 89–90, 91, 93, 142, 168, 272; divisions in, 45, 119; hawk opposition to Johnson, 44–45; increasing opposition to Nixon's policies, 119–20; limited commitment to anticommunism attributed to, 41; Muskie's 1972 presidential campaign, 301; National Convention of 1968, 87; national unity theme as opportunity to divide, 202; Nixon opposes liberal Democratic domestic policies, 152; pro-war Democrats, 92, 115; Republicans as less hostile to Johnson than, 43–45; southern Democrats, 44–45, 92, 148; and Soviet Jewish emigration issue, 290–91; Vietnam War and presidential election of 1968, 87–97; Vietnam War helped end of dominance of, 10; weakened ties with working class, 187. *See also* Johnson, Lyndon; Kennedy, John F.; Stennis, John; *and others by name*

demonization of the enemy: becomes prominent, 226–27; by College Republican National Committee, 283; by conservatives, 307; Nixon's rhetoric accelerates, 202; popular, 201; in POW campaigns, 231–32, 233–34, 238–39, 240–41; by Student Coordinating Committee for Freedom in Vietnam and Southeast Asia, 268, 270; by student pro-war groups, 288; by Victory in Vietnam Association, 274; by Young

Americans for Freedom, 245, 259
Dent, Harry, 80, 97, 98, 129, 210
Derwinski, Edward, 107
détente: broad popularity of, 171, 294; Buckley on, 338; conservative opposition to, 4, 5, 12, 14, 169, 291, 294, 330, 334; future of South Vietnam seen to be in jeopardy due to, 304, 313; Goldwater opposed to, 75; *Human Events* on, 303; Jackson–Vanik amendment and support for, 291; Manhattan Twelve on, 175; Moscow summit of 1972, 292, 297–98; Nixon's visit to China, 169–83, 271, 293, 294, 295; U.S. military superiority seen as requirement for, 173; Vietnamization becomes associated with, 182, 289–91
de Toledano, Ralph, 93, 94, 101, 120, 146
Diem, Ngo Dinh: American Friends of Vietnam's support for, 54; coup against, 20, 34, 37; long-term supporters of, 31
Dien Bien Phu, 82
Dirksen, Everett, 18, 83, 90, 102, 103
disarmament, 90, 98, 169, 172, 178, 295
DMZ. *See* demilitarized zone (DMZ)
Docksai, Ron, 247, 263
Dodd, Thomas, 45
Dole, Robert, 137, 232
Dombrowski, Edmund, 190, 191
domino theory, 46, 82, 338
"Don't Forget the Eagles" (song), 233
Dornan, Bob, 277
Dos Passos, John, 24
Douglas, Paul H., 66, 67
draft, the, 128, 260, 286, 305, 324
Droge, Dolf, 233, 283
Duck Hook, Operation, 103, 120, 121
Dueck, Colin, 11, 28, 87, 137

Eagle Trust Fund, 35
Education About Communism Through Refugee Program, 253
Edwards, Lee, 129, 194, 353n43
Ehrlichman, John, 137, 207
Eisenhower, Dwight: Burnham's criticism of foreign policy of, 27, 28; on

Eisenhower, Dwight (*continued*)
Chinese domination as consequence of U.S. withdrawal from Vietnam, 77; Citizens Committee for Peace with Freedom in Vietnam supported by, 66; diplomacy in ending Korean War, 84–85; on domino effect, 46; Goldwater compares Nixon with, 98; on Johnson's Vietnam policies, 73; New Look defense policy of, 82; Nixon Doctrine compared with policy of, 109; on Nixon threatening resumption of bombing, 96; promise to go to Korea, 90; Welch's accusations against, 25

Ellsberg, Daniel, 163

Emerging Republican Majority, The (Phillips), 206

end-the-war amendments: Americans for Winning the Peace opposes, 220; Cambodian incursion produces, 136; conservative opposition in 1972, 305–6; Cooper–Church amendment, 136, 138–39, 140, 144, 148; Goodell Resolution, 120; limit conservatives' options, 310; Mansfield amendment, 168, 181; McGovern–Hatfield amendment, 136, 217, 218–19; National League of Families of Prisoners of War on, 234, 237; North Vietnamese apparent willingness to abide by provisions of, 238; POW issue used to promote, 236; widening public support for, 161

escalation of Vietnam War: Allott on, 149; American Conservative Union plan to win the war, 45–48; bombing North Vietnam as retaliation for North Vietnamese, 110; Cambodian invasion of 1970 as, 132–33; conservatives call for, 32, 33–34, 36–41, 45, 52–53, 140, 290, 306, 315; Duck Hook operation, 103, 120, 121; growing opposition to, 138; *Human Events* urges in 1972, 302–3; versus immediate withdrawal, 7; intellectual conservatives continue to support, 2, 70; Johnson's room for maneuver reduced by, 44; Kissinger on, 110–11; *National Review* on re-escalation, 106; in *National Review*'s fake secret documents, 165; Nixon on, 72, 111; Nixon sets November 1, 1969, deadline for negotiation or, 120–21; Reuther opposed to, 202; Symington calls for, 48; Thompson opposes, 111; Vietnamization and, 127, 132, 139, 141; Young Americans for Freedom support, 261. *See also* bombing North Vietnam

ethnic working-class, 203–4

Evans, M. Stanton, 170, 174, 242, 246, 251, 306–7

Evans, Rowland, 88, 97, 132, 154, 222, 353n43

exceptionalism, 291, 334, 338

Farber, David, 21, 204
Feder, Don, 257
Finch, Robert, 97
Firestone Tire and Rubber Company, 63–64
Firing Line (television program), 264
Fischer, John, 129
Fish Hook offensive, 132
Foner, Philip, 207
Ford, Gerald, 26, 34, 104, 107, 329, 336
Foreign Military Sales Act, 137
foreign policy: bipartisan approach to, 67, 100; Democrat divisions over, 45; divisiveness of issues, 320; domestic issues influence, 11; Kissinger's expertise in, 99; militarized, 20; *National Review* urges stronger anticommunist, 14–15, 19, 20; Nixon on Vietnam as opportunity for resurrection of strong, 76; Nixon's determination to dominate, 99, 102; Nixon's experience in, 86; in reemergence of conservatism, 13; Vietnam War and overall U.S., 106–7; Vietnam War's influence on postwar conservative views of, 331–42. *See also* anticommunism; détente

Foreign Policy Research Institute, 29
Fowler, Henry, 217
Frank, Steve, 271–72, 276, 277, 278
Franklin, H. Bruce, 239
Freedom Leadership Foundation, 312
Freedoms Foundation, 60
Freedom Tree project, 280–81
Freeman, Joshua, 206
Frischman, Robert, 234
Fry, Joseph, 53
Fulbright, J. William, 52, 58, 70, 76, 185, 195
fusionism, 22, 23, 24–25

Galbraith, John Kenneth, 100
Gavin, William, 82
Geneva Convention, 221, 231, 233, 234, 258, 281
Gimmler, Raymond, 57, 58–59, 325
Goldwater, Barry: accepts Republican nomination for president, 17; on airpower, 128, 307–8; on altered objective of Nixon policy in 1971, 162; on anti-war movement, 181; on April 1972 bombing of North Vietnam, 298, 300, 302; on Ashbrook's presidential campaign of 1972, 13, 294; on attacking Red River dike system, 51; as attentive to public opinion, 171; becomes disillusioned with Nixon, 326–27, 328; on bombing Haiphong harbor, 119, 152; on bombing North Vietnam, 119, 127–28, 140, 153, 180; briefing on Lam Son 719 operation, 157; on Cambodian invasion of 1970, 133, 139–40; on chances of South Vietnamese survival, 183; on conservative role in Nixon's 1968 victory, 124; on continued backing of Thieu, 313; on dealing with Communists, 289; on defense spending, 177; on dissent lending comfort to the enemy, 61; division between conservative activists and, 290, 295; on domino theory, 338; Draft Goldwater drives, 6, 12, 19, 23, 245; on ending Vietnam War within two weeks, 52; on end-the-war amendments, 305–6; as figurehead of conservative coalition, 6; at gala for POWs at Constitution Hall in May 1970, 232; and Huston Plan, 212; as intent on reaching settlement in late 1972, 318; on Johnson's bombing North Vietnam, 40, 49; on Johnson's policies as "drift, deception, and defeat," 41; on Kissinger's appointment as national security adviser, 100; liberals attacked by, 301–2, 306; and liberation of Eastern Europe, 28; Linebacker II bombings supported by, 316–18; loyalty to Nixon's Vietnam strategy, 98, 295; on McIntire's Victory in Vietnam March, 199–200; *National Review* associated with, 14, 19, 25; *National Review*'s denunciation of John Birch Society opposed by, 56, 79; New Right on, 336; on Nixon appointees, 97, 98; Nixon endorsed in 1968 by, 81–82; at Nixon's January 26, 1972, meeting with Republican leadership, 181; Nixon's policies defended against conservatives by, 153; Nixon's political support for, 74–75; Nixon supported in 1972 by, 294; on Nixon's visit to China, 176, 177, 178, 180–81, 295; on noble cause argument, 16; on North Vietnam as about to give up, 310; on no substitute for victory, 36, 37; on Paris peace accords, 322, 327; peace proposal of January 1972 endorsed by, 182; on Pentagon papers, 164; on POW issue, 231; pressures Nixon on Vietnam after election of 1972, 312; Reagan distinguishes himself from, 341; recalls his wartime position, 333, 386n89; refuses to denounce John Birch Society, 26; on Republicans as peace party, 43; at Salute to the Armed Forces dinner, 273; seeks to take advantages of Kennedy's failure in Vietnam, 32; seen as extremist, 55, 75; on South Vietnamese acceptance of any

Goldwater, Barry (*continued*)
  settlement, 309–10; on stopping Chinese supplies to North Vietnam, 37–38; on unilateral disarmament by U.S., 169; on U.S. as at war in Vietnam, 17; on use of American military power, 33–34; on Vietnam "as close as Kansas," 35; on Vietnamization, 127–28, 140, 183, 306, 308, 334; on Vietnam War's destructive impact on American society, 332; visits to Vietnam, 49, 127, 180; on withdrawal of U.S. troops, 113, 118–19; writings in special edition of *New Guard*, 147; and Young Americans for Freedom, 245, 259, 294
Goodell, Charles, 120
Goodell Resolution, 120
GO•PEACE campaign, 284, 285
Graham, Billy, 197, 198, 199
grassroots activists: activism decreases by mid-1972, 304; and anticommunism, 13, 21; anti-war movement opposed by, 5; associate patriotism with support for the war, 185; conservative movement's complex relationship with, 15; Democrats accused of limited commitment to anticommunism by, 41; Goldwater supported by, 6; humanitarian issues stressed by, 52; in John Birch Society, 26; *National Review* circle as more influential than, 15; Nixon administration attempts to manage, 16; Nixon's "Silent Majority" speech rallies, 125; Nixon supported after Cambodian invasion, 143; on Panama Canal Treaty, 336–37; patriotic campaigns of, 10, 333; "peace with honor" supported by, 311; Republicans continue to support war to appeal to, 291; Schwarz and Schlafly focus on building, 35–36; on victory or withdrawal, 35; Vietnamization supported by, 153; in Young Americans for Freedom, 245
Great Society, 44, 90
Greenberg, David, 294

Greenfield, Jeff, 264–65
Greenspan, Alan, 82
Gruenther, Alfred M., 217
Guidelines for Cold War Victory (American Security Council), 17
Gulf of Tonkin Resolution, 38, 40, 136–37

Haggard, Merle, 194
Hagopian, Patrick, 339
Haig, Alexander, 173–74, 230, 273, 309, 313
Haiphong harbor: air battles above in spring 1967, 49; American Conservative Union on blockading, 126; and April 1972 bombing, 298; Buckley on South Vietnamese action against, 127; conservatives call for bombing of, 39, 48, 49–51; failure to attack as symbol of limited war policy, 49; Goldwater on bombing of, 119, 152; in *National Review*'s fake secret documents, 165; Nixon blockades in 1972, 300, 302–3; Nixon on mining in 1966, 77; Symington on closing, 48; Thurmond calls for closing, 299; Tower on effectiveness of mining, 331
Haldeman, Bob: on anti-ballistic missile (ABM) system, 102; on anti-war movement, 244; on bombing of April 1972, 297, 298–99, 300; on Kissinger talking with conservative columnists, 169; on nation in civil war, 137; on Nixon Doctrine, 109; on Nixon's response to North Vietnamese Easter 1972 offensive, 296; on Nixon's troop withdrawals, 107–8; on positive polarization, 137; on problem of right-wing Republican unhappiness, 110; and Son Tay POW camp raid, 235; on Vietnam Veterans for a Just Peace, 223
Hanoi: air battles above in spring 1967, 49; and April 1972 bombing, 298; conservatives call for military action against, 19, 39; Red River dike system, 51, 119, 165, 302, 307, 315

hard hat riots, 202–9
Harlow, Bryce, 98, 277
Harrigan, Anthony, 170
Hatfield, Mark, 17–18, 68, 120, 136
Hayes, Wayne, 45
Helms, Jesse, 325, 336
Henderson, William, 216
Hersh, Seymour, 221
Heston, Charlton, 218
Hijiya, James, 244
Ho Chi Minh, 251
Ho Chi Minh Trail, 39, 48, 127, 140, 155, 184, 224
Honor America Day Rally (1970), 143, 197–98, 210, 240
Honor America Week (1969), 192–94, 230, 257
Hoover, J. Edgar, 212
Hope, Bob, 184, 190–91, 197, 198, 273, 278
Houffman, David Lee, 260
Howard, Richard, 207
Hrdlicka, David, 277
Hué, 149–50, 226, 300
Hughes, Howard, 277
Hukari, Harvey, 64–65, 261
Human Events (journal): American Conservative Union allied with, 23; on anti-war congressmen, 143; on Cambodian invasion of 1970, 130; on Cooper–Church amendment, 138–39; on Cuba as threat, 20, 21; on détente, 303; on Diem overthrow, 34; on Eisenhower's diplomacy in ending Korean War, 85; on full-scale attack on North Vietnam in 1972, 302–3; on Honor America Day Rally of 1970, 198; Johnson's war policy criticized by, 36–37, 93; at July 26, 1971, conservative meeting, 170; on Kennedy's failures in Vietnam, 32; on Kissinger's appointment as national security adviser, 100; on Lam Son 719 operation, 156; Lane as columnist for, 46; Linebacker II bombings supported by, 315–16; on Nixon and Paris peace talks, 88; on Nixon's support for Goldwater, 75; on Nixon's Vietnam policy, 83, 96, 114; on only solution in Vietnam, 33; on Paris peace accords, 320–21; on peace proposal of January 1972, 182; pressures Nixon on Vietnam after election of 1972, 311; on "Rally for Freedom in Vietnam and All the World," 195; on renewed involvement in Vietnam, 321; on residual U.S. forces in Vietnam, 160; on Soviet military superiority, 169; Turner's "myths" published by, 252; on Vietnamization, 123, 124, 130, 302–3; on Wheeler on bombing halt of March 1968, 93–94
humanitarian issues, 52
Humphrey, Hubert, 80, 86, 87, 89–91, 94, 95
Hungarian revolution of 1956, 27–28, 130
Hunt, H. L., 79
Hunter, Kay, 277
Huntsman, Jon, 222
Huston, Tom Charles, 63, 78, 205, 206, 210, 212
Huston Plan, 212

In Defense of Freedom (Meyer), 23
intellectual conservatives: conservative politicians contrasted with, 6; containment accepted by, 34; defeat in Vietnam as of great significance for, 336; Douglas attacks, 67; escalation supported by, 2, 70; hard-line foreign policy of, 13; isolationism abandoned by, 21–22; Johnson policies questioned by, 43; on Lam Son 719 operation, 156; lessons of Vietnam War influence on, 331; on liberation of Eastern Europe, 28; national security emphasized by, 5, 7; and Panama Canal Treaty, 337; postwar initiatives on Vietnam War, 339; rearmament as concern of, 331; seek to reinvigorate anticommunism, 337; and social conservatives share interpretation of Vietnam War, 291

Interagency Group on Domestic Intelligence and Internal Security, 212

International Relations in the Age of Conflict between Democracy and Dictatorship (Possony and Strausz-Hupé), 29

isolationism: Americans for Winning the Peace on surrender in Vietnam and, 218; attributed to anti-war movement, 213, 260; intellectual conservatives abandon, 21–22; interventionist conservatives reject, 32; neoconservative opposition to, 337–38; Roosevelt's challenge to, 219; of Welch, 25, 26

Jackson, Henry, 290–91
Jackson–Vanik amendment, 290–91
Javits, Jacob, 120
JBS. *See* John Birch Society (JBS)
JCS. *See* Joint Chiefs of Staff (JCS)
Jewish War Veterans, 56
John Birch Society (JBS): American Conservative Union opposes, 26–27; Buckley opposes, 13, 25–26; Hatfield on, 17; as loose network, 26, 27, 56; *National Review* opposes, 25–26, 55, 56, 79; Vietnam War opposed by, 55–56, 65; Wallace candidacy supported in, 79
Johns, Andrew, 11, 32, 293, 353n34
Johnson, Don, 284
Johnson, Lyndon: American Friends of Vietnam funded by, 217; anti-war movement opposes policies of, 57; attempts to rally public opinion, 184–85; bombing halt before 1968 election, 91–93; Citizens Committee for Peace with Freedom in Vietnam established by, 66, 115; conservative criticism of, 2, 15, 16, 36–37, 39–41, 43–45, 184, 332; conservative opposition constrains, 9–10; Democratic hawk opposition to, 44–45; Goldwater attributes loss in Vietnam to, 327; Goldwater describes policies as "drift, deception, and defeat," 41; Goldwater on bombing policy of, 40, 49; Great Society, 44, 90; Hatfield's criticism of, 18; and Humphrey's proposed bombing halt, 89, 91; joint communiqué with Thieu of September 1966, 105; Kissinger as consultant to, 98; Laird's criticism of, 89; large-scale deployment of troops by, 65; limited war policy of, 5, 6, 8, 19, 41, 44, 49, 52–53, 62, 245; Meyer on Republican Party policy regarding, 69; Meyer's criticism of, 65–66; negotiated settlement sought by, 53, 70; Nixon's criticism of, 72, 73, 75–77, 83, 85, 88, 105; overtures to China of, 169; partisan politics and Vietnam War policy of, 12; patriotism in responses to early initiatives in Vietnam of, 19–20, 40–42; peace initiative of March 31, 1968, 69; and Pentagon papers, 164; personal commitment to Vietnam, 44; policies as issue in presidential campaign of 1968, 70–71; political success of 1964, 44; and POW issue, 227, 228; on reciprocal nature of bombing North Vietnam, 40; search-and-destroy policies of, 51; seeks to avoid debate on Americanization of the war, 184; Tower's criticism of, 95–96; unwillingness to attack Haiphong harbor, 49, 51; and Vietnamization concept, 116; Vietnam War as Johnson's war, 19, 36; Young Americans for Freedom on, 261
Johnson, Robert David, 11, 12
Joint Chiefs of Staff (JCS): and bombing of North Vietnam, 180; on educating the public about Vietnam War, 53; escalation supported by, 48, 49, 104; at gala for POWs at Constitution Hall in May 1970, 232; Nixon urges acceptance of settlement on, 313–14; phased withdrawal opposed by, 107; on South Vietnamese capacity to invade Cambodia, 132

Joint Chiefs Readiness Test, 122
Jones, John, 170
Joy, Dan, 264, 276
Judd, Walter: in American Council for World Freedom, 129; on bombing North Vietnam, 48–49; in China lobby, 31; and Huston on pushing Nixon to the right, 78; on Korean War as object lesson, 33; on Lam Son 719 operation, 155, 157; Linebacker II bombings supported by, 317; on Nixon resisting demands of coalition government, 310; on U.S. being able to outlast North Vietnam, 106

Keene, David, 129, 146, 177, 243, 245, 256, 259
Kennedy, John F.: conservatives on foreign policy failures of, 30, 31; in Cuban missile crisis, 20, 21, 30; and Diem overthrow, 34; Laos policy, 30, 31, 32, 39; seeks to avoid debate on Americanization of the war, 184; Vietnam involvement of, 18, 31, 32
Kent State University shootings, 141, 142, 206, 259
Kerry, John, 223–25, 226
Kesler, Bruce, 223, 224
Khmer Rouge, 133
Khrushchev, Nikita, 171
Kilpatrick, James Jackson, 139
Kimball, Jeffrey, 84, 108, 121, 122, 354n57
Kirk, Russell, 22, 39
Kissinger, Henry: on Americans for Winning the Peace, 219–20; Buchanan recommendation on South Vietnamese action rejected by, 129; and Buckley on paradox of U.S. policy in Vietnam, 175; on Cambodian invasion of 1970, 143–44; on ceasefire before withdrawal, 310; commitment to Vietnam War, 99; and conservative opposition to Nixon, 177; on conservatives becoming demoralized, 148; on continuing war by alternative means, 108; on December 1971 bombing and peace accords, 322; defeat in Vietnam blamed on, 333; differences of opinion with Laird, 110, 111; on escalation to end war sooner, 110–11; Haldeman asks him to talk with conservative columnists, 169; *Human Events'* criticism of, 182; on Lam Son 719 operation, 154, 157; Lane's criticism of, 114; on Mansfield amendment, 181; on military strength as leading to negotiations, 103; *National Review* on, 99, 100, 356n101; national security staff of, 99; Nixon and tough position on Vietnam of, 104; on Nixon's May 1969 peace proposal, 106; on Nixon's troop withdrawals, 107–8; on Nixon's visit to China, 178; on North Vietnam as unable to keep its army in the South, 314; on North Vietnamese Easter 1972 offensive, 296; on North Vietnam mistaking negotiation for weakness, 297; on option to the right, 145; on Panama Canal Treaty, 336; and Paris peace accords, 320; and Paris peace talks during 1968 presidential campaign, 88; and POW issue, 230, 323; on prospects for negotiation in 1972, 308–9, 311; reactions to appointment as national security adviser, 98–101; on Reagan's election as reaction to Vietnam, 341; Schlafly's criticism of, 290; secret negotiations with North Vietnam, 230, 279; secret visit to Moscow, 298; seen as doing PR job on Buckley, 146; sees Vietnam peace related to détente, 289; on South Vietnamese accepting settlement, 309; and Soviet Jewish emigration issue, 290; Thompson meets with, 111; on Vietnamization, 115
Klatch, Rebecca, 65
Klein, Herbert, 235
Kleindienst, Richard, 82
Korean War: accounting for POWs in, 281; China lobby on, 31; Eisenhower's diplomacy in ending,

Korean War (*continued*)
84–85; Eisenhower's promise to go to Korea, 90; Goldwater on lessons of, 37; Goldwater on Truman's decision to enter, 140; *Human Events* on, 32–33; North Vietnamese invasion of 1972 compared with, 298; residual U.S. forces in Korea, 160
Koscielski, Frank, 203, 207–8
Kosygin, Alexei, 298
Kraemer, Sven, 267
Kramer, Fritz, 100
Krogh, Bud, 210
Ky, Nguyen Cao, 200, 214

labor, organized. *See* organized labor
Laird, Melvin: begins calling for withdrawal of U.S. forces, 89; on bombing of December 1971, 179; differences of opinion with Kissinger, 110, 111; escalation opposed by, 138; at gala for POWs at Constitution Hall in May 1970, 232; Goldwater's support for, 118; on Kennedy's Vietnam policy, 34; opposition to bold strike in November 1969, 111; on political fallout from continuation of the war, 149; on POW issue, 228, 229; pushes for faster withdrawal, 110; reactions to appointment as secretary of defense, 101; Senate Foreign Relations Committee testimony of, 149–50; on Vietnamization, 102, 103, 121; "win or get out" strategy supported by, 96
Lam Son 719, 154–58
land reform, 52
Lane, Thomas, 46–47, 112–13, 114, 129, 156
Laos: agreement of 1962 on, 231; Buchanan on North Vietnamese violations of neutrality of, 128; Buchanan on South Vietnamese action in, 128, 129; Kennedy's policy in, 30, 31, 32, 39; Lam Son 719 operation, 154–58; in Manhattan Twelve's list of demands, 174–75; in Nixon's Vietnam strategy, 73; in Paris peace accords, 321, 327; in People's Peace Treaty, 268; as sanctuary for Viet Cong, 39, 114, 267; Tower on sanitization of, 148; U.S. bombing of, 216, 237
law and order: anti-war movement seen as soft on, 213; libertarians on, 260; Nixon emphasizes, 75, 87, 101
Leadership Training School (LTS), 283–84
LeMay, Curtis, 79
Levy, David, 62, 203, 351n58
Lewis, Hobart, 197
liberals: abandon support for Vietnam War, 14; Agnew's opposition to, 164; American Friends of Vietnam seen as liberal, 215; and Cambodian invasion of 1970, 134; conservatives criticize civil rights policies of, 24; conservatives see impossibility of eradicating, 13; Goldwater attacks, 301–2, 306; interventionism of, 14; Meyer on threat posed by, 23; Nixon opposes liberal Democratic domestic policies, 152; Norton on Vietnam contributing to voting strength of, 262; rightward drift among, 62; social conservatives see them as unpatriotic, 7; in Student Coordinating Committee for Freedom in Vietnam and Southeast Asia, 265; Vietnam defeat blamed on, 323, 324, 325, 326, 327, 338, 340; War Powers Act as indicative of policies of, 329
libertarians: abandon conservative consensus on Vietnam, 147; Meyer as libertarian, 23; Rothbard's criticism of Meyer's fusionism, 24–25; versus traditional conservatives, 22; in Young Americans for Freedom split of 1969, 260–61
Liberty Lobby, 86
Liebman, Marvin, 78
limited war policy: in Cambodia, 133; Citizens Committee for Peace with Freedom in Vietnam accepts, 67–68;

conservative attitude toward, 9, 34, 53, 142, 147, 334, 335, 341; failure to attack Haiphong harbor as symbol of, 49; fear of right-wing backlash against, 41, 44, 52–53; of Johnson administration, 5, 6, 8, 19, 20, 41, 44, 49, 52–53, 62, 245; *National Review* opposes, 6; National Student Committee for Peace with Freedom in Southeast Asia on, 250; of Nixon administration, 5, 6, 138, 142, 147, 169, 245; public opinion on, 112; rallies in support of, 8; Reagan opposes, 62; Vietnam War seen as showing weakness of, 332; Young Americans for Freedom opposes, 245
Lindsay, John, 206, 207
Linebacker, Operation, 300–301
Linebacker II, Operation, 313–19, 321, 322, 327, 331
Linkletter, Art, 190–91
Lon Nol, 130, 131
Lord, Mary, 217
Lovell, James, 232
Lovestone, Jay, 67, 90, 125, 135, 149
Loyalty Day (VFW), 59
Luce, Clare Booth, 218, 330, 338
Luce, Phillip Abbott, 255
Lucey, Archibishop Robert, 66
Lukens, Donald, 195
Lyons, Charlton, 83

MacArthur, Douglas, 32
MacMahon, Robert, 340
Maddox, Lester, 195–96, 199
"madman theory," 84, 108
Magruder, Jeb, 284
Mahoney, J. Daniel, 170, 172
Manhattan Twelve, 170, 171–73, 174, 176
Manila formula, 105
Manion, Dean Clarence, 56, 79
Mansfield, Mike, 168
Mansfield amendment, 168, 181
Mardian, Robert, 166
Marriott, J. Willard, 197
Marsh, John, 195
Martin, David, 100

May 2nd Movement, 58
McCaffrey, Neil, 170, 173
McCain, John (admiral), 180
McCain, John (prisoner of war), 244
McCarthyism, 21
McClellan, John, 45
McCracken, Paul, 82
McElroy, Neil, 217
McGirr, Lisa, 27
McGovern, George, 120, 220, 282, 283, 311, 320
McGovern–Hatfield amendment, 136, 217, 218–19
McIntire, Carl, 198–201, 263
McKay, Alan, 245, 257
McNamara, Robert, 61–62, 110, 163, 164, 177
Meacham, Steward, 197
Meany, George: in Americans for Winning the Peace, 217; anticommunism of, 90; and bombing campaign of December 1971, 179; on Cambodian invasion of 1970, 134–36; changes his mind about Vietnam, 326; desires to be part of elite, 371n57; and Nixon dropping demand for mutual withdrawal, 149; perpetuates image of pro-war working class, 203; Reuther contrasted with, 202; Vietnamization supported by, 125; Vietnam War supported by, 66–67
media: Accuracy in Media, 325, 330; defeat in Vietnam blamed on, 330, 333
Merchant, Livingston T., 217
Mergel, Sarah Katherine, 156
Meyer, Frank, 22–23; and American Conservative Union endorsement of Nixon in 1968, 86; in American Conservative Union's founding, 23; break with Nixon urged by, 147; on conservative "failure of nerve" after 1964 election, 306; on debunking communist myths, 30; on defense spending, 152, 173; fusionism of, 22, 23, 24–25; Kissinger fails to blunt

Meyer, Frank (*continued*)
animosity of, 177; Manhattan Twelve statement signed by, 170; on Nixon's "Silent Majority" speech, 123; on Nixon's visit to China, 175–76; Reagan supported in 1968 by, 80; on Republican Party policy, 68–69; on Vietnam War and anticommunism, 65–66; on Wills, 142
MIAs. *See* missing in action (MIAs)
Middle America Group, 210–11
Milliken, Roger, 83
missing in action (MIAs): accounting for, 233, 281; local groups advocating for, 228. *See also* prisoners of war (POWs)
Mitchell, John, 87, 89, 100
Mollenhoff, Clark, 210
Moorer, Thomas, 232, 296
Moratorium to End the War in Vietnam: congressional hawks oppose, 120; Dombrowski and, 190; National Committee for Responsible Patriotism opposes, 192; Nixon administration's response to, 211; pro-war activists encourage popular opposition to, 189; pro-war campaigns in response to, 239; "Rally for Freedom in Vietnam and All the World" compared with, 194–95; Victory in Vietnam Association opposes, 274, 276; Young Americans for Freedom and National Student Coordinating Committee for Victory in Vietnam oppose, 254–57, 258, 263
Morgan, Joseph, 54
Moser, Charles, 194, 195, 266
Moss, George Donelson, 358n131
Moynihan, Daniel Patrick, 97, 137
Muskie, Edmund, 301
My Lai massacre, 221–23
Myths of the Vietnam War (Turner), 252

Nash, George, 31–32
National Committee for Responsible Patriotism (NCRP), 191–93, 195, 196, 197
National Coordinating Committee for Freedom in Vietnam and Southeast Asia, 238
National Day of Prayer and Concern for POWs (1969), 232
Nationalist Movement, 199
National League of Families of Prisoners of War and Missing in Action in Southeast Asia, 228–29; accuses North Vietnamese of holding POWs to ransom, 237; echoes anti-war sentiments, 238, 318; fails to endorse end-the-war resolutions, 237; Nixon meets with representatives of, 232, 238; Nixon's policies supported by, 234; in POW bracelet campaign, 278; on Son Tay POW prison camp raid, 151, 235; Victory in Vietnam Association and, 279, 323
National Liberation Front (NLF): anticommunist guerrilla groups urged against, 51; conservatives ignore in postwar analysis of, 340; eight-point proposal of, 269; Manila formula on, 105; Nixon on Communist colonialism of, 76; participation in free elections, 115, 181
National Review (journal): on Agnew, 213; American Conservative Union allied with, 23; anticommunist basis of war emphasized by, 14, 30, 241; anticommunist guerrilla groups urged by, 51; on Cambodian invasion of 1970, 140; Catholic fervor of, 54; conservative consensus sought by, 22; containment policy accepted by, 27; on Cuba as threat, 20; on debunking communist myths, 30; on December 1971 bombing campaign, 182; détente as concern of, 290; de Toledano's criticism of, 147; division between Republican politicians and, 290; escalation supported by, 36; extremism as concern of, 55; fake secret documents published by, 164–68; fear that U.S. was losing Cold War, 32; fusionism of, 23; Goldwater associated with, 14, 19, 25; on Hungarian

revolution of 1956, 27; John Birch Society opposed by, 25–26, 55, 56, 79; at July 26, 1971, conservative meeting, 170; Kissinger's appointment as national security adviser endorsed by, 99, 100, 356n101; on liberation of Eastern Europe, 28; limited war opposed by, 6; Linebacker II bombings supported by, 316; on military aid to South Vietnam in 1975, 329–30; on minimum objective of Vietnam War, 104; national security state as concern of, 24; and New Right, 335–36, 337–38; New York Conservative Party's stance compared with that of, 60; Nixon associated with, 83, 146, 162; on Nixon's May 1969 peace proposal, 106; on Nixon's May 1972 peace proposal, 303; on Nixon's visit to China, 176, 179, 295; on Paris peace accords, 321, 322–23; on Pentagon papers, 162–64; Possony and Strausz-Hupé distinguish themselves from, 29; pressures Nixon on Vietnam after election of 1972, 311; prominence and leadership of, 25; "Rally for Freedom in Vietnam and All the World" publicized by, 195; and Republican candidacy of 1968, 80–81, 83; Republican Party associated with, 25; and split over Ashbrook's presidential campaign of 1972, 294; stronger anticommunist foreign policy urged by, 14–15, 19, 20; takes up anti-anti-war-movement rhetoric, 202; on Vietnamization, 124, 153, 159, 179, 182, 333; Vietnam lobby contrasted with, 31; on Vietnam War as Johnson's war, 36; on Wills, 142; Young Americans for Freedom allied with, 245, 246, 287

national security: American Conservative Union on Vietnam War and, 126; Americans for Winning the Peace on peace with security, 218; becomes less important as justification for Vietnam War, 183, 211, 225, 319; conservatives' emphasis on, 6; difficulty relating Vietnam War to, 57; versus patriotism in support of Vietnam War, 6–7, 10, 187; Reagan's emphasis on, 5; state, 24; Young Americans for Freedom on, 258, 264

National Strategy Information Center (NSIC), 215, 217, 220, 372n81

National Student Association (NSA): Association of Student Governments founded in opposition to, 243; People's Peace Treaty of, 268–70

National Student Committee for Peace with Freedom in Southeast Asia, 242

National Student Coordinating Committee for Victory in Vietnam (NSCVV), 250–55; founding of, 250; functions of, 250–52; Moratorium opposed by, 254–57; patriotism as focus of, 244, 287; relaunched as Student Coordinating Committee for Freedom in Vietnam and Southeast Asia, 265, 266; "Victory in Vietnam Week," 252–53

National Student Union (South Vietnam), 269

national unity theme: American Conservative Union and, 161; bipartisan gala for POWs and their families for advancing, 232; for combating extreme right, 198; conservatives accept, 202, 291; grassroots activists advance, 5; Nixon administration emphasizes, 201, 232; Nixon as national unity candidate, 73; POW campaign advances, 233; Victory in Vietnam Association on, 279

National Unity Week (1969), 190–91, 193, 195, 274, 326

NCRP (National Committee for Responsible Patriotism), 191–93, 195, 196, 197

negotiation: American Conservative Union on, 47–48; Burnham on ineffectiveness of, 69; conservatives become unable to mount concerted challenge to, 293; conservatives

negotiation (*continued*)
demand knockout blow to force, 307; conservatives question slow progress of, 298; Cooper–Church amendment seen as jeopardizing, 139; Ford on, 107; intensifies in late 1972, 306; Johnson administration seeks, 53, 70, 91; Johnson-Thieu joint communiqué of September 1966 on, 104; Kissinger on military strength as leading to, 103; Kissinger on North Vietnam mistaking it for weakness, 297; Kissinger on prospects in 1972, 308–9; Kissinger's secret negotiations with North Vietnam, 230; Linebacker II bombings as result of breakdown in, 316; McIntire's opposition to, 199; by Nixon, 10, 73–74, 123, 138; Nixon sets November 1, 1969, deadline for, 120–21; North Vietnam asks cessation of Linebacker II bombings as precondition to resume, 318–19; North Vietnam's Easter 1972 offensive and, 292; only after additional military action, 308; and option to the right, 145–46; POW campaign and, 227, 228; pro-war movement's conditions for, 268; Thompson on bold strike and, 111; Vietnam War seen as showing weakness of, 332; while fighting, 108; withdrawal as alternative to, 149. *See also* Paris peace talks

neoconservatism, 62, 215, 290, 331, 337–38

New Deal, 12, 21

New Guard (publication), 147, 252

New Left: Committee of Liaison with Families of Servicemen Detained in North Vietnam, 236–37; Huston Plan designed to disrupt, 212; Norton on Vietnam as strengthening, 262; People's Peace Treaty associated with, 269; pro-war student groups compared with, 287; student opposition to, 16; student pro-war groups altered by rise of, 242; supporting the troops as reaction to, 250; Victory in Vietnam Association opposes, 273; Young Americans for Freedom compared with, 245; Young Americans for Freedom opposes, 246, 248, 249. *See also* Students for a Democratic Society (SDS)

New Mobilization Committee to End the War in Vietnam (New Mobe), 258

New Right, 291, 335–36, 337–38

New Student Politics, 283

New York Building and Construction Trades Union, 207

New York Conservative Party, 60, 141, 170

Nguyen, Lien-Hang, 137

Nguyen Ngoc Bich, 256–57

Nickerson, Michelle, 26

Nitze, Paul, 218

Nixon, Richard: advice on Vietnam policy after 1968 election, 96–97; Air Force Academy address of June 1969, 109–10; on airpower to interdict supplies from North, 145; ambiguity in Vietnam policy of, 86; anti-ballistic missile (ABM) system of, 102, 109, 173; anticommunism of, 72, 75–76, 78–79, 124; and anti-war movement, 73, 123, 137, 143, 147, 151, 158, 202, 211–12; appointees of, 97–102; April 30, 1969, address of, 131–32, 133; article on Vietnam of 1964, 117; attempts to control pro-war message, 202, 209, 213, 226; attempts to manage grassroots groups, 16; on bombing North Vietnam, 73, 77, 103, 151–52, 153, 154–55; "Bring Us Together" aim of, 3; and Buckley, 75, 82–83, 87, 146–47; Cambodian invasion of 1970, 130–45; China visit of 1972, 169–83, 271, 293, 294, 295; as cold warrior, 301; College Republican National Committee supports, 282, 284; comes to believe that victory is impossible, 73; commitment to Thieu government, 107, 108, 181; conservative backlash feared by, 10, 293, 297; conservative policy team of, 82–83; conservative Republican support sought in 1968, 74–75, 83–87; conservative role in 1968 victory of, 95, 124; conservatives challenge overall foreign policy of, 294; conservatives' complex relationship with, 15, 16; conservatives' growing doubts about Vietnam policy of, 126–30; conservative threats to challenge in 1972, 172, 177; on continuing war by alternative means after withdrawal, 108; development of Vietnam policy of, 97–114; divisions among conservatives over, 112, 129, 147, 158–62, 179, 261, 292, 308, 337; domestic politics of Vietnam, 1968–1969, 72–124; and ending of Vietnam War, 289–327; failure to provide postwar support to South Vietnam, 328–31; foreign policy dominated by, 99, 102; foreign policy experience of, 86; globalist perspective on Vietnam War, 77; Goldwater becomes disillusioned with, 326–27, 328; Goldwater endorses in 1968, 81–82; Goldwater's loyalty to Vietnam strategy of, 98, 295; Goldwater supported by in 1964, 74–75; on Goodell Resolution, 120; gradualism of, 120, 261; grassroots displays of support for, 143; and hard hat demonstrations, 206–7, 208–9; and the hawks, 74–87; Huston Plan approved by, 212; increasing Democratic opposition to policies of, 119–20; intends to end war in his first year in office, 102; January 26, 1972, meeting with Republican leadership, 181, and Johnson's bombing halt before 1968 election, 93, 94–95; June 1969 plan for troop withdrawal, 113, 116; June 30, 1970, address of, 144; and Lam Son 719 operation, 154–58; law and order emphasized by, 75, 87, 101; liberal Democratic domestic policies opposed by, 152; limited war policy of, 5, 6, 138, 142, 147, 169, 245; Linebacker II bombings, 313–19; "madman theory" of, 84, 108; May 1969 peace proposals of, 104–7, 113, 119; May 8, 1972, address of, 299, 300, 303–4; McIntire opposed by, 199, 200; Moscow summit of 1972, 292, 297–98, 300; National Day of Prayer and Concern for POWs declared by, 232; *National Review* associated with, 83, 146, 162; as national unity candidate, 73; negotiation by, 10, 73–74, 123, 138; nobility of veterans' service emphasized by, 4; October 1970 address, 235; O'Neill of Vietnam Veterans for a Just Peace meets with, 225; on option to the right, 145; and Paris peace accords, 319–24, 321; partisan politics and Vietnam War policy of, 12; on patriotism, 184; peace proposal of January 1972, 181, 182; on "peace with honor," 83, 86, 89, 94, 97, 162, 179, 183, 265, 267, 284, 292, 293, 297, 306, 311, 312, 315, 323; polarization used by, 162; as positive about potential agreements in late 1972, 311; and POW campaign, 227–39, 279, 312; presidential campaign of 1968, 70–71, 73, 75, 79–92; pro-war movement and administration of, 209–26; pro-war movement pressure after election of 1972, 311–12; pro-war movement supports in 1968, 80, 95; public doctrine of, 110–11; public opinion influences decision making of, 121; public opinion rallied by, 124, 185; pushed to the right, 145–54; reduction in U.S. troops accepted by, 85–86; response to North Vietnamese Easter 1972 offensive, 292, 296–304; Reuther as critical of, 202; secret plan for ending the war, 83, 88, 104; seeks to take advantages of Kennedy's failure in Vietnam, 32; sets November 1, 1969, deadline for negotiation, 120–21; "Silent Majority" speech, 122–24, 125, 191, 194, 211, 214, 276; steadfastness in face of congressional opposition, 306; Student Coordinating Committee for Freedom in Vietnam

Nixon, Richard (*continued*)
and Southeast Asia supports, 270–71; and student pro-war groups, 243–44; Thieu meets at Midway Island, 107, 115; on Thieu's agreement to any settlement, 309; Thompson meets with, 112; triangular diplomacy of, 177, 179, 294; on victory in Vietnam as essential, 43; Victory in Vietnam Association supports, 274, 276, 279; Watergate scandal, 326, 328; Young Americans for Freedom break with, 158–60, 285; Young Americans for Freedom support, 86, 259, 260, 264. *See also* détente; Nixon Doctrine; Vietnamization

Nixon-Agnew Key Issues Committee, 95

Nixon Doctrine, 108; Cambodian invasion of 1970 and, 130–31; College Republican National Committee on, 285; conservative support for, 10, 108–9, 122, 124, 130; Cooper–Church amendment seen as repudiation of, 138; Lam Son 719 operation and, 156; Nixon's China initiative and, 175; Vietnamization and, 108–9, 122, 124, 130, 285

NLF. *See* National Liberation Front (NLF)

noble cause argument: conservatives endorse, 5, 339; Goldwater on, 16; Nixon administration influenced by, 16; postwar consensus on, 7–8; Reagan on, 1, 2, 3, 7, 16, 334, 339–42

Nofziger, Lyn, 210

Non-Proliferation of Nuclear Weapons Treaty, 102

North Vietnam: aid to South Vietnam from, 77, 145; anti-war movement seen as in alliance with, 189–90; and Cambodian invasion of 1970, 132, 133, 144; on cessation of Linebacker II bombings as precondition to resume negotiation, 318–19; China provides supplies to, 37–38, 50; conservatives' attitude toward, 19, 38, 47, 118, 340; Easter 1972 offensive, 201, 292, 294, 300, 301; fails to acknowledge its military presence in South Vietnam, 312; in gradual acceptance of negotiated settlement, 74; Kissinger on, 103, 297; Kissinger's secret negotiations with, 230, 279; Lam Son 719, 154–58; Laos agreement of 1962, 231; Manila formula on, 105; moves troops in South Vietnam through Cambodia, 49; in mutual withdrawal of troops, 149, 313–14; in *National Review*'s fake secret documents, 165; Nixon sets November 1, 1969, deadline for negotiations, 120–21; Nixon's visit to China and, 296; in Paris peace accords, 320–24, 328; in People's Peace Treaty, 268, 269; and POW issue, 227, 229, 230, 231, 233–34, 236, 237–38, 241; Red River dike system, 51, 119, 165, 302, 307, 315; releases information on prisoners of war, 277, 281; response to U.S. bombing halt of November 1968, 92, 93; as sanctuary for Viet Cong, 39; Son Tay POW camp raided, 151, 153, 235–36, 237; South Vietnamese offensive against in Cambodia, 149; Soviet aid to, 49–50, 141; Turner on, 251; U.S. reconnaissance planes attacked by, 149, 151; war continues after Paris peace accords, 328–29; Young Americans for Freedom opposes trade with states supplying, 64; Young Americans for Freedom's Tell it to Hanoi campaign, 242, 256–58, 259, 262, 287, 326. *See also* bombing North Vietnam; Haiphong harbor; Hanoi

Norton, Jerry, 261–64, 265

No Substitute for Victory (film), 123

Novak, Robert, 88, 97, 132, 154, 222, 353n43

no-win policy: *Human Events* charges Johnson administration with, 37; *Human Events* charges Kennedy administration with, 32; in *National*

Review's fake secret documents, 165; Vietnam War in reluctance to engage in, 332. *See also* limited war policy
NSA. *See* National Student Association (NSA)
NSCVV. *See* National Student Coordinating Committee for Victory in Vietnam (NSCVV)
NSIC (National Strategy Information Center), 215, 217, 220, 372n81
nuclear weapons: Citizens Committee for Peace with Freedom in Vietnam on, 67; Goldwater proposes defoliation with, 37–38; LeMay and use of, 79; Nixon denies that Vietnam War could escalate to use of, 76; and Nixon Doctrine, 108; Nixon heightens readiness in autumn 1969, 121; Non-Proliferation of Nuclear Weapons Treaty, 102; Norton on shield against, 262; nuclear test ban treaty, 31, 90; SALT, 152, 154, 169, 173, 175, 295

O'Doherty, Kieran, 60
O'Donnell, Peter, 24, 75, 83
Ondrasik, Barbara, 151
O'Neill, John, 223, 225, 226
Operation Gratitude, 196
Operation Mail Call, 274
Operation Ombudsman, 273–74
Operation: Open Door, 285
organized labor: AFL-CIO, 66–67, 90–91, 134–35; on Cambodian invasion of 1970, 134–36; hard hat riots, 202–9; moves toward promotion of prisoner of war issue, 161; Nixon's withdrawal policy supported by, 290; on patriotism and supporting the war, 240; in POW campaign, 233; "Silent Majority" speech rallies, 125; Taft and conservative opposition to, 21; working-class resentment harnessed by, 187
Ostpolitik, 173

pacification, 216, 270

Panama Canal Treaty, 336–37, 339
Paolucci, Henry, 356n99, 356n101, 384n57
Paris peace accords, 319–24; failure to ensure South Vietnamese independence, 328; North Vietnamese violation of, 329; Tower on Linebacker II leading to, 331
Paris peace talks: AFL-CIO on, 90; Americans for Winning the Peace on McGovern-Hatfield amendment and, 218; break down in December 1971, 179; Buckley on, 150; Citizens Committee for Peace with Freedom in Vietnam on, 116; eight-point proposal of National Liberation front, 269; Goldwater on, 118, 119; and Johnson's bombing halt before 1968 election, 91, 92, 93, 95; Lane on, 156; and Nixon's 1968 presidential campaign, 88–89; and People's Peace Treaty, 269; and POW issue, 227, 231, 237; resume in April 1972, 298; Tower on North Vietnamese strategy regarding, 96; Victory in Vietnam Association on, 275, 279; Young Americans for Freedom petition to, 133, 258. *See also* Paris peace accords
Parmet, Herbert, 210
patriotic organizations: on anti-war movement as giving comfort to enemy, 201; bloodbath predicted by, 271; on Cambodian invasion of 1970, 133, 134; on domestic consequences of Vietnam War, 319; Goldwater adopts populist methods of, 301; Lane in, 46; minimal objective in Vietnam changes, 292–93; Moratorium opposed by, 211; moves toward promotion of prisoner of war issue, 161; Nixon administration attempts to manage, 16; Operation Rolling Thunder supported by, 41; patriotism and supporting the troops by, 186; in POW campaign, 340; student pro-war groups contrasted with, 243; symbolic value of the war

patriotic organizations (*continued*)
as emphasis of, 188; Vietnamization supported by, 124, 290; welcome home parades promoted by, 324–25

patriotism: anti-war movement support limited by, 185; in campaigns to support Vietnam War, 8, 54, 55, 56; Committee for a Week of National Unity on, 191; conservative activists resist rhetoric of, 290; country music associated with, 194; dissent seen as challenge to, 58, 61–62; grassroots campaigns for, 333; hard hat as symbol of, 206, 208; at Honor America Day Rally of 1970, 197; media in denigration of, 330; versus national security in support of Vietnam War, 6–7, 10, 187; Nixon on, 184; Nixon's "Silent Majority" speech engenders, 125; "peace with honor" associated with, 183; POW campaign and, 238, 279; "Rally for Freedom in Vietnam and All the World" on, 195; Reagan makes Vietnam War support a matter of, 4, 326; religious fervor and, 55; in responses to Johnson's early initiatives in Vietnam, 19–20, 40–42; student pro-war groups focus on, 244, 286, 288; support of Vietnam War associated with, 9, 185–86, 188, 197, 198, 207, 208, 211, 239–41; symbols of, 186; veterans' groups turn to promotion of, 262; in Victory in Vietnam Association's Adoption program, 281; victory strategy associated with, 61–62; "We Support Our Boys in Vietnam" parade in New York, May 13, 1967, promotes, 61; of working class, 203; in Young Americans for Freedom's Tell it to Hanoi campaign, 257. *See also* patriotic organizations

Patrolmen's Benevolent Society, 193

peace movement. *See* anti-war movement

"peace with honor": Buckley on détente and, 338; Citizens Committee for Peace with Freedom in Vietnam on immediate withdrawal and, 214; College Republican National Committee and, 284; Congress moves to limit time frame for, 179; conservative understanding of, 97, 290; Nixon calls for, 83, 86, 89, 94, 97, 162, 179, 183, 265, 267, 284, 292, 293, 297, 306, 311, 312, 315, 323; North Vietnamese attack soon after, 329; Paris peace accords and, 322–23; patriotism associated with, 183; POW campaign and, 234–35, 238; pro-war movement becomes associated with, 94, 120; seen as lost by Congress, 331; Tower on, 43

Pentagon papers, 162–64
People's Peace Treaty, 268–70, 286
People's Self-Defense Force, 116–17
Percy, Charles, 81, 313
Perlstein, Rick, 63, 222
permissiveness, 197, 336
Perot, H. Ross, 197, 217, 229–30, 232, 234, 273, 277
Perspectives (journal), 216
Pham Van Dong, 189, 271
Phillips, Kevin, 206
polarization, 137, 161–62, 245, 336
Politician, The (Welch), 25
Possony, Stefan, 23–24, 28–29, 129, 169
Powell, Colin, 332
POW/MIA Families for Immediate Release, 237, 279
POWs. *See* prisoners of war (POWs)
PRC. *See* China
Price, Ray, 73, 244
"Principles and Heresies" (Meyer), 22
prisoners of war (POWs): American innocence represented by, 231, 341; Americans for Winning the Peace and, 220; associated with support for Nixon's policies in Vietnam, 210, 211; Bates in campaign for, 272; bracelet campaign, 277–80; campaign over issue of, 7, 226–39, 304, 319; College Republican National Committee supports, 284; Committee for a Week of National Unity on

prayers for, 191, 193; continuation of war to secure release of, 236; Cooper–Church amendment seen as jeopardizing, 139; in demonization of North Vietnam, 231–32, 233–34, 238–39, 240–41; gala at Constitution Hall in May 1970 for, 232; Geneva Convention, 221, 231, 233, 234, 258, 281; Goldwater and, 200, 301; heightened awareness of, 183; immediate settlement sought by campaign for, 318; National Committee for Responsible Patriotism focuses on, 196; Nixon on, 202, 312; in North Vietnamese peace proposals of July 1971, 237; North Vietnam releases information on, 277, 281; in Paris peace accords, 321, 323, 324, 327; in People's Peace Treaty, 268; Perot as advocate of, 197; plight captures popular imagination, 188; political traction of issue, 291; populist focus of support for, 9; pro-war agenda of most POW groups, 235; public opinion swayed by issue of, 240; recognition of Vietnam denied due to, 339; return becomes objective in Vietnam, 293; returned, 232, 281, 325; Son Tay POW camp raided, 151, 153, 235–36, 237; Student Coordinating Committee for Freedom in Vietnam and Southeast Asia on, 270, 271; veterans' groups in campaign for, 233, 340; Veterans of Foreign Wars and, 339; Victory in Vietnam Association in campaign for, 277–81; Vietnam Veterans for a Just Peace and, 226; withdrawal of U.S. troops related to release of, 159, 161, 228, 234, 237, 280, 305, 319

Project Appreciation, 319

Project Education, 273

Proudly They Came (film), 197

pro-war movement: on Cambodian invasion of 1970, 131, 132, 133; Catholic hierarchy supports, 66, 203–4; changes over time, 183, 185, 187; conservative leadership as dominant element in, 14; conservatives rallied by, 13; détente opposed by, 169; divisions in, 210; hard hat riots, 202–9; Humphrey's proposed bombing halt alienates, 89; minimal objective in Vietnam changes, 292–93; new voices emerge in 1967, 66; Nixon administration and, 209–26; Nixon pressured after election of 1972, 311–12; Nixon's "Silent Majority" speech encourages, 125; Nixon supported in 1968 by, 80, 95; parades in support of Vietnam War, 8–9, 63; "peace with honor" becomes associated with, 94, 120; on Pentagon papers, 163; pro-war congressmen, 103, 107, 143, 231; rallies in support of Vietnam War, 5, 187, 188–202; reduced fervor by late 1972, 306; split within, 114; traditional practices and values in, 9; varied perspectives and competing affiliations in, 9; on Vietnamization, 120, 138, 139. *See also* conservatives; grassroots activists; patriotic organizations; student pro-war campaigns; veterans' organizations

Public Interest (journal), 62

public opinion, 184–241; conservatives acknowledge significance of, 6, 9, 127, 171, 187; decreasing support for Vietnam War from 1967, 87; Johnson attempts to rally, 184–85; on limited war policy, 112; National Student Coordinating Committee for Victory in Vietnam plan to poll students, 253; Nixon continues air activities despite risk to, 144; Nixon rallies, 124, 185; Nixon's decision making influenced by, 121; POW issue used for swaying, 240; Reagan as attentive to, 171, 325; realist perspective denies relevance of, 11; turns against Vietnam War in 1968, 69–70, 72–73; Vietnamization and, 123; on withdrawal of U.S. troops, 121, 151; working-class attitudes, 203

Pucinski, Roman, 226

Radford, Arthur, 82
"Rally for Freedom in Vietnam and All the World" (Washington, D.C.), 194–95
Randolph, Stephen, 321
Rarick, John, 199
Raye, Martha, 278
Reader's Digest (magazine), 197, 210
Reagan, Ronald: anti-war protesters attacked by, 62; as attentive to public opinion, 171, 325; becomes disillusioned with Nixon, 328; in blue button campaign, 247; on conservative role in Nixon's 1968 victory, 124; division between conservative activists and, 290, 295; Goldwater on, 81; Haggard pardoned by, 194; on Humphrey's proposed bombing halt, 90; and Huston Plan, 212; Kissinger on Vietnam War and election of, 341; Kissinger reassures him about settlement, 310; on Lam Son 719 operation, 157; limited war policy criticized by, 20; *National Review* circle and, 15; New Right and, 336, 337; on Nixon's visit to China, 176, 177, 180–81, 295; noble cause argument of, 1, 2, 3, 7, 334, 339–42; on North Vietnamese support for anti-war movement, 189; patriotism emphasized by, 4, 326; on POW issue, 236; and Republican candidacy of 1968, 79–81, 83; at Salute to the Armed Forces dinner, 273; threatens to resign from Young Americans for Freedom board, 159–60; Veterans of Foreign Wars speech of 1980, 1–3, 339; on Vietnamization, 159, 334; on Vietnam War, 1–4, 15, 84; on why the war was lost, 325; writings in special edition of *New Guard*, 147
rearmament, 173, 174, 331
Red River dike system, 51, 119, 165, 302, 307, 315
reparations, 313

Report of the Committee on Cold War Education (National Governors' Conference), 248
Republican Party: anti-war faction in, 12; anxieties about elections of 1970, 149; Buchanan on Nixon and conservative Republicanism, 146; Buckley's demands for 1968 election, 74; China lobby, 31; College Republican National Committee as official auxiliary, 282; College Young Republicans, 243, 244, 282–83; conservative determination to take control of, 12, 13, 15; containment policy accepted by, 27; continued support for Vietnam War in 1972, 291; divisions over Vietnam War, 12, 45, 68–69; escalation supported by, 36–41; Gulf of Tonkin Resolution supported by, 38; as less hostile to Johnson than Democrats, 43–45; on liberals as responsible for Vietnam defeat, 338; on liberation of Eastern Europe, 28; little opposition to Vietnam War in 1964 and 1965, 18; moderates, 214; *National Review* associated with, 25; New Right and, 335–36; Nixon meets with Senate loyalists in April 1971, 162; Nixon seeks support from conservative wing, 74–75, 83–87; Nixon's January 26, 1972, meeting with leadership, 181; on Nixon's visit to China, 170; as peace party to Goldwater, 43; Phillips's *The Emerging Republican Majority*, 206; on political importance of supporting Nixon, 180–81; postwar initiatives on Vietnam War, 339; presidential campaign of 1968, 70–71; seek political gains from any Johnson policy, 44; seeks political gains from Vietnam War, 12; seeks to escape right-wing extremist label, 19; seeks to take advantages of Kennedy's failure in Vietnam, 32; southern, 84; on Vietnamization, 153; on Vietnam War as Johnson's war, 36. *See also* Ashbrook, John; Eisenhower, Dwight;

Goldwater, Barry; Kissinger, Henry; Laird, Melvin; Nixon, Richard; Reagan, Ronald; Thurmond, Strom; Tower, John; *and others by name*
Reserve Officer Training Corps (ROTC), 246, 251
Resistance (anti-war group), 247
Reuther, Walter, 202
"Rights Revolution," 204
Rivers, Mendel, 45, 103, 195, 199
Rockefeller, Nelson, 32, 80, 82, 88, 98
Rogers, William, 101–2, 110, 111, 138
Rolling Thunder, Operation, 41, 77, 179
Romney, George, 74, 81
Rostow, Eugene, 217
Rostow, Walt, 49
Rothbard, Murray, 24–25
Rove, Karl C., 282, 284, 285
Rumsfeld, Donald, 138
Rusher, William: as American Conservative Union founding member, 23; in American Council for World Freedom, 129; on Ashbrook's presidential campaign of 1972, 294; on avoiding a settlement before election of 1972, 311; break with Nixon urged by, 147; on conservative movement in disarray, 293, 295; on conservative opposition to Nixon, 160; on debate between traditionalist and libertarian conservatives, 22; détente opposed by, 291; de Toledano's animosity toward, 146; Kissinger fails to blunt animosity of, 177; on Laird's appointment as secretary of defense, 101; Manhattan Twelve statement signed by, 170; on Meyer on Wills, 142; *National Review's* denunciation of John Birch Society opposed by, 56, 79; on *National Review's* fake secret documents, 166; on Nixon's Vietnam policy, 86; on Paris peace accords, 322–23; Reagan supported in 1968 by, 80–81, 83; on reform in South Vietnam, 52; on responsible conservatives, 19
Russell, Richard, 44–45, 53, 91–92, 93, 94, 103, 113

Ryskind, Allan: disillusionment with Nixon, 129; father Morrie, 143; at July 26, 1971, conservative meeting, 170; on Kissinger, 100, 101; and Manhattan Twelve demands, 173, 174; on rearmament, 174
Ryskind, Morrie, 143, 145

Safire, William, 213
Saigon: enemy mining of harbor, 50; fall of, 330
SALT, 152, 154, 169, 173, 175, 295
Salute to the Armed Forces dinners, 273
Saracino, Bill, 272
Scammon, Richard, 284
Schlafly, Fred, 129
Schlafly, Phyllis, 35–36, 290, 304, 333, 336
Schlesinger, Arthur, Jr., 99, 100
Schmitz, David, 69
Schneider, Gregory, 63
Schoenwald, Jonathan, 26–27
Schwarz, Fred, 25, 35–36
Schweizer, John, Jr., 281
Scott, Paul, 85
Scranton, William, 36
SDS. *See* Students for a Democratic Society (SDS)
search-and-destroy policies, 51
security, national. *See* national security
Senate Armed Forces Committee, 52, 305
Senate Foreign Relations Committee, 52, 58, 136, 149–50, 163, 224
Senate Preparedness Investigating Subcommittee, 52, 53
Shakespeare, Frank, 356n99
Sharp, Ulysses S. G., 49
Sheehan, Neil, 163
Shirk, Mary, 190
Sieg, Kent G., 354n54
Sihanoukville, 127, 131, 143, 165
Sikes, Bob, 45
silent majority: Agnew as mouthpiece of, 213; Americans for Winning the Peace and, 218; hard hat demonstrations and, 206; *Human Events* on power of, 195; Nixon's "Silent Majority" speech, 122–24, 125, 191,

silent majority (*continued*)
194, 211, 214, 276; as not equivalent of pro-war position, 186, 187; rallies behind Nixon over Cambodia, 208, 209; Silent Majority Division in Veterans Day parade, 194; Victory in Vietnam Association adopts theme, 276; Young Americans for Freedom appeal to, 256, 258

Small, Melvin, 358n131

Smith, Howard K., 37–38

social conservatives: and intellectual conservatives share interpretation of Vietnam War, 291; Nixon appeals to, 137; and Panama Canal Treaty, 337; query utility of Vietnam War, 290, 333, 336, 337; social issues emphasized by, 5, 7, 13, 336; on Vietnam War as Johnson's war, 36

socialism, 24

Son Tay POW camp, 151, 153, 235–36, 237

Southeast Asian Perspectives (journal), 252

Southern States Industrial Council, 170

South Vietnam: American Security Council on giving controversial operations to, 50–51; and Cambodian invasion of 1970, 132–33, 143, 144; coalition government for, 105, 114, 115, 181, 268, 310, 312; détente and prospects after U.S. withdrawal, 304, 313; deteriorating situation in early 1975, 329; elections in, 115, 181, 284–85; failure of U.S. to provide postwar support to, 309, 327, 328–31; fall of Saigon, 330; Freedom Leadership Foundation on participation in negotiations of, 312; Goldwater on chances of survival of, 183; Hué, 149–50, 226, 300; *Human Events* calls for attack on North Vietnam by, 303; Kissinger on their accepting settlement, 309; Lam Son 719, 154–58; in Manhattan Twelve's list of demands, 174–75; Manila formula on, 105, 105; neutrality for, 77, 105; newfound military strength of, 149; Nixon on giving them chance for survival, 162; Nixon's visit to China and, 296; North Vietnamese supplies to, 77, 145; North Vietnam's Easter 1972 offensive, 201, 292, 294, 300, 301; offensive in Cambodia of, 149; in Paris peace accords, 320–24, 328; in People's Peace Treaty, 268, 269; People's Self-Defense Force, 116–17; popular affection for, 55; as "rice bowl" of Asia, 46; succession of governments in, 52; in Vietnamization, 102–3, 153, 155–56, 159; war continues after Paris peace accords, 328–29; Watergate scandal undercut Nixon's commitment to, 328. *See also* Diem, Ngo Dinh; Thieu, Nguyen Van

Soviet Union: accuses China of backing U.S. policy, 178–79; aid to North Vietnam, 49–50, 141; American Conservative Union on mining of Haiphong harbor and, 302; and conservative attitude toward Vietnam War in 1964, 18–19; conservatives' apprehension about military strength of, 102, 129; in Cuban missile crisis, 21; Hungarian revolution of 1956, 27–28; Jewish emigration issue, 290; Khrushchev's visit to U.S., 171; Kissinger's secret visit to Moscow, 298; makes use of wars of national liberation, 46; Moscow summit of 1972, 292, 297–98, 300; Nixon on U.S. strength relative to, 169; in Nixon's Vietnam strategy, 73; in North Vietnam's Easter 1972 offensive, 292; SALT, 152, 154, 169, 173, 175, 295; seen as at war with U.S., 30; Sino-Soviet split, 29, 32, 76; Thurmond on Vietnam role of, 113; U.S. containment policy toward, 27–29; Vietnam War seen as Soviet-engineered distraction, 35; Young Americans for Freedom opposes trade with, 64, 245, 248

Spellman, Cardinal Francis, 54, 55

Spock, Benjamin, 195

Stavast, Shirley, 280
Steinberg, Arnold, 86
Stennis, John: accepts ending the war as soon as possible, 293; bombing of North Vietnam supported by, 45, 53; Humphrey alienates, 89–90; informed of secret bombing of Cambodia, 103; as Senate Preparedness Investigating Subcommittee chair, 52, 53; on South Vietnamese acceptance of any settlement, 309–10; on troop withdrawals of July 1969, 113
Stewart, Jimmy, 197, 220
Stockdale, Sybil, 228, 229, 237
Stop NSA, 269
Strausz-Hupé, Robert, 28–29, 100
Student Action Committee (SAC), 275–76
Student Committee for the Loyalty Oath, 62
Student Coordinating Committee for Freedom in Vietnam and Southeast Asia, 265–71; Abate joins, 285–86; as alternative voice to Young Americans for Freedom, 271; Nixon meets with, 267; People's Peace Treaty opposed by, 268–70; Vietnamization supported by, 266–67; visits to Vietnam, 266–67, 270
student pro-war campaigns, 242–88; divergent means of, 243; as diverse coalition, 286–88; as minority of students, 244; mutual reinforcement of groups, 243; patriotism as focus of, 244, 286, 288. See also College Republican National Committee (CRNC); National Student Coordinating Committee for Victory in Vietnam (NSCVV); Student Coordinating Committee for Freedom in Vietnam and Southeast Asia; Victory in Vietnam Association (VIVA); Young Americans for Freedom (YAF)
student radicals: Agnew's attacks on, 210; increasing extremism of, 244; in National Student Association, 243; petitions of, 225; student pro-war groups oppose, 243, 246; working-class attitudes toward, 204; Young Americans for Freedom on, 204–5, 246, 247. See also anti-war movement; Students for a Democratic Society (SDS)
Students for a Democratic Society (SDS): campus opposition to, 246; North Vietnamese praise for, 189; Young Americans for Freedom oppose, 64, 247, 260
Summers, Anthony, 207
supporting the troops: American Legion's "For God and Country Support Our Boys in Vietnam" slogan, 188–89; effectiveness of campaign for, 335; helps popularize Nixon's efforts to secure troop withdrawal, 319; National Committee for Responsible Patriotism's Operation Gratitude, 196; populist focus of, 9; rallies for, 8; Reagan on, 2; replaces "win the war" strategy, 135; resonates with American people, 56–57, 341; as support for the war, 187; "Support Our Boys" rallies, 189; Veterans Day parades on, 196; by veterans' groups, 55, 56; by Victory in Vietnam Association, 271, 272; by Young Americans for Freedom, 259, 264, 265. See also "We Support Our Boys in Vietnam" parades
Symington, Stuart, 45, 48

Taft, Robert, 21
Taylor, Henry J., 280
Taylor, Maxwell, 316
teach-ins: seen as unpatriotic, 62; Victory in Vietnam Association opposes, 272, 273; of Young Americans for Freedom, 246; Young Americans for Freedom opposes, 64–65
Teague, Olin, 45, 195
Teague, Randal, 133, 158, 170, 254–55, 255–56, 258–59, 261

Tell it to Hanoi campaign, 242, 256–58, 259, 262, 287, 326
Teodoru, Dan, 266, 267, 270
Tet offensive (1968), 69–70, 226, 351n58
Thanh Hoa, 93, 94
Thies, Richard, 272
Thieu, Nguyen Van: Citizens Committee for Peace with Freedom in Vietnam on supporting, 116, 214; College Republican National Committee on, 284–85; conservative concern about U.S. commitment to, 312–13; having to be willing partner in any settlement, 309; joint communiqué with Johnson of September 1966, 105; on Lam Son 719, 154; Linebacker II bombings as reassurance for, 315; Nixon meets at Midway Island, 107, 115; Nixon's commitment to, 107, 108, 181; Nixon urges him to not endorse Paris peace talks, 88; North Vietnam rejects U.S. demand that he remain in office, 179; in People's Peace Treaty, 268; Westmoreland on ceasefire-in-place as defeat for, 314
think tanks, 271, 275, 338
Thompson, Michael, 129, 245, 250, 254, 263
Thompson, Sir Robert, 51, 111–12, 156
Thurmond, Strom: on Cambodian invasion of 1970, 134; on conservative role in Nixon's 1968 victory, 124; on Cooper–Church amendment, 138, 139; demand for final military push by, 307, 308; Gulf of Tonkin Resolution supported by, 38; as intent on reaching settlement in late 1972, 318; on Johnson's bombing halt before 1968 election, 94; on Lam Son 719 operation, 155; on legacy of American sacrifice, 317; on McIntire's Victory in Vietnam March, 199; *National Review* circle and, 15; New Right and, 336; Nixon supported by, 75, 80, 83; on Nixon's visit to China, 176, 178; on Paris peace accords, 321–22; at "Rally for Freedom in Vietnam and All the World," 195; response to Nixon's May 8, 1972, speech, 299; on trade with China, 169; on using Chinese nationalist forces in Vietnam, 111; on Vietnamization, 155–56; on withdrawal of U.S. troops, 113, 117; writings in special edition of *New Guard*, 147
Tomb of the Unknown Soldier of Vietnam (Arlington National Cemetery), 3
Tower, John: on bombing North Vietnam, 97; on Humphrey's proposed bombing halt, 90; Johnson's Vietnam policy criticized by, 95–96; on Kissinger's appointment as national security adviser, 100; *National Review* circle and, 15; as Nixon-Agnew Key Issues Committee chair, 95; Nixon defended against conservatives by, 147–48; Nixon praised by, 75; on Nixon's visit to China, 176; on Non-Proliferation of Nuclear Weapons Treaty, 102; on peace with honor, 43; on POW issue, 231–32; at "Rally for Freedom in Vietnam and All the World," 195; recalls his wartime position, 333; resigns from Young Americans for Freedom board, 159; on restraint costing U.S. Vietnam War, 331, 332; writings in special edition of *New Guard*, 147
traditional conservatives: on Agnew, 164; anti-war movement opposed by, 62; lessons of Vietnam War's influence on, 331; on liberals in loss of Vietnam War, 326; versus libertarians, 22; McIntire opposed by, 199; in Young Americans for Freedom split of 1969, 260–61
Trager, Frank, 216
troop withdrawal. *See* withdrawal of U.S. troops
"Trouble on the Right" (Buchanan), 147, 152

INDEX

Truman, Harry, 11, 18, 27, 32, 66, 140, 347n32
Turner, Robert F., 250–52, 266, 270
Twining, Nathan, 82

Uniformed Firefighters Association, 193
unions. *See* organized labor
United Automobile Workers (UAW), 202
United Nations, 22, 173, 251, 329
United States Information Agency, 146, 166, 356n99
United We Stand, 229–30, 234
Unknown Soldier of the Vietnam War, 341

Vandenberg, Arthur, 11
van den Haag, Ernest, 176
Vanik, Charles A., 290–91
Veterans Day, 63, 190, 194–96
Veterans of Foreign Wars (VFW): on Cambodian invasion of 1970, 134; Colson on, 201; on domestic consequences of Vietnam War, 319; Honor America Week endorsed by, 193; Linebacker II bombings supported by, 318; in Nixon's flag-waving drive, 210; on Nixon's visit to China, 178; patriotic drives sponsored by, 7; positive means of seeing the war of, 189; and POW issue, 339; Reagan's 1980 address to, 1–3, 339; supporting-the-troops theme of, 56; welcome home parades organized by, 325; and "We Support Our Boys in Vietnam" parade in New York, May 13, 1967, 59
veterans' organizations: on anti-war movement as giving comfort to enemy, 201; bloodbath predicted by, 271; on Cambodian invasion of 1970, 133, 134; conservatives adopt methods of, 307; on December 1971 bombing campaign, 179; on domestic consequences of Vietnam War, 319; help popularize Nixon's efforts to secure troop withdrawal, 319; Linebacker II bombings supported by, 316;

members in John Birch Society, 56; minimal objective in Vietnam changes, 292–93; Moratorium opposed by, 211; National Unity and Honor America programs adopted by, 193; Nixon's "Silent Majority" speech rallies, 125; Operation Rolling Thunder supported by, 41; on patriotism and supporting the troops, 7, 55, 186, 240; in POW campaign, 161, 233, 340; pressure Nixon on Vietnam after election of 1972, 311; and Son Tay POW camp raid, 235; student pro-war groups contrasted with, 243; symbolic value of the war as emphasis of, 188; turn to promotion of patriotism, 262; Vietnamization supported by, 115, 124, 290; welcome home parades promoted by, 324–25. *See also* American Legion; Veterans of Foreign Wars (VFW)

VFW. *See* Veterans of Foreign Wars (VFW)
Vicites, Joseph, 201
Victory in Vietnam Association (VIVA), 271–82; Adoption program, 281; Coppin's support for, 273; founding of, 271; Freedom Tree project, 280–81; Goldwater adopts rhetoric of, 302; name changed to Voices Vital in America, 275; National League of Families of Prisoners of War and Missing in Action in Southeast Asia associated with, 278, 279; Nixon administration and, 244; Nixon commends, 276; Operation Mail Call, 274; Operation Ombudsman, 273–74; on Paris peace accords, 323; patriotism as focus of, 244, 286–87; positive programs emphasized by, 273, 277; in prisoners of war campaign, 277–81; Project Appreciation, 319; Project Education, 273; in pro-war movement, 16; Salute to the Armed Forces dinners, 273; speakers' bureau, 273; in Student Action Committee, 275–76; student radicals opposed by, 243;

VIVA (continued)
  Turner's "myths" published by, 252;
  Your Friendly VC, 274
Victory in Vietnam Marches, 198–201
Victory in Vietnam Week, 252–53
Viet Cong: Chinese aid to, 178; Kerry seen to have sympathized with, 224; sanctuaries for, 39; Soviet aid to, 50; Victory in Vietnam Association's Your Friendly VC program, 274; Young Americans for Freedom burn flag of, 249, 257
Vietminh, 76
Vietnam. *See* demilitarized zone (DMZ); North Vietnam; South Vietnam; Vietnam War
Vietnam: The Situation and Alternative Strategies (Johnson administration), 95
Vietnam: A Television History, 325
Vietnam Fact Day (University of Houston), 274
Vietnamization: airpower and, 112, 124; as ambivalent, 107, 108; American Conservative Union on, 115, 124, 139, 153, 156, 159; Buckley on, 127, 141, 159, 296, 299–300, 317, 334; and Cambodian invasion of 1970, 135, 138, 139, 144; CBS editorial on, 215; change in tone regarding, 296; Citizens Committee for Peace with Freedom in Vietnam on, 214; College Republican National Committee supports, 284–86; conservatives on, 113–14, 129–30, 140, 141, 148, 159–60, 175, 178, 239, 262, 268, 303–4, 306, 327, 334; détente associated with, 182, 289–91; domestic policy advisers urge quicker implementation, 138; emergence of, 102–3; and escalation, 127, 132, 139, 141; factors in sustaining popular support for, 183; Goldwater on, 127–28, 140, 183, 306, 308, 334; growing disillusionment with, 176; *Human Events* on, 123, 124, 130, 302–3; Johnson and concept of, 116; Laird on, 102, 103, 121; and Lam Son 719 operation, 154, 155, 157; Lane's assessment of, 114; Linebacker II bombings as boon to, 315; militarization of, 114–24; *National Review* on, 124, 153, 159, 179, 182, 333; National Student Association on, 268; and Nixon Doctrine, 108–9, 122, 124, 130, 285; and Nixon's China initiative, 175; in Nixon's 1968 presidential campaign, 85; original conception of, 103; patriotic organizations support, 124, 290; and peace proposal of January 1972, 182; and POW issue, 228, 236, 238; pressures to hasten, 289; pro-war movement on, 120, 138, 139; Reagan on, 159, 334; Republican Party on, 153; resembles unilateral retreat, 15–16; seems to imply saving of America's honor, 319; seen as enabling more conventional form of warfare, 145; "Silent Majority" speech establishes, 122, 125; Student Coordinating Committee for Freedom in Vietnam and Southeast Asia supports, 266–67; support for Nixon related to, 187; supporting the troops and support for, 187; Michael Thompson opposes, 263; Robert Thompson supports, 111, 156; Thurmond on, 155–56; veterans' groups support, 115, 124, 290; Vietnam Veterans for a Just Peace on, 223–24; Young Americans for Freedom on, 133, 258
Vietnam lobby, 31, 54–63
Vietnam syndrome, 334, 342
Vietnam veterans: bipartisan concentration on honoring, 339; Carter on, 340; National Student Coordinating Committee for Victory in Vietnam contacts returning, 253; Nixon on, 202; shameful treatment of, 3; welcome home parades for, 189, 324–25; in Young Americans for Freedom, 264–65; in Young Americans for Freedom's Tell it to Hanoi campaign, 257

Vietnam Veterans Against the War (VVAW), 223–26, 325
Vietnam Veterans for a Just Peace (VVJP), 223–26
Vietnam Veterans Memorial (Washington, D.C.), 3, 342
Vietnam War: American Conservative Union plan to win, 45–48; anticommunism associated with, 5, 14, 18–19, 21, 30, 59, 65–66, 240, 300; anxieties over apparent brutality of, 52; beginnings of, 17–42; both parties lose interest in, 291; civil war characteristics of, 33, 99, 275, 296; Cold War context of, 2; conservative acceptance of final settlement of, 16; conservative influence on policy for, 9–10; conservative movement changed by, 10; conservative postwar foreign policy views influenced by, 331–42; conservatives and, 1–16; conservatives' failure to serve, 264–65; continues after Paris peace accords, 328–29; de-Americanization of, 102, 115, 121, 265; debate over means for ending, 292; defining, 328–42; development of Nixon's policy, 97–114; discontinuing funding for, 136, 305, 314, 318, 323; divisions among conservatives over, 13–14; domestic disorder associated with, 87–88; domestic issues influence policy for, 10–12; elites begin to question, 185–86; ending of, 289–327; fall of Saigon, 330; Johnson's personal commitment to, 44; as Johnson's war, 19, 36; Kissinger's commitment to, 99; lessons of, 331, 334, 342; Linebacker II bombings, 313–19; in Manhattan Twelve's list of demands, 174–75; My Lai massacre, 221–23; Nixon's secret plan for ending, 83, 88, 104; Nixon's triangular diplomacy and, 177, 179, 294; North Vietnam's Easter 1972 offensive, 201, 292, 294, 300, 301; opposition to anti-war movement as implicit sanction of, 186; organized labor's association with, 67, 90–91; and overall U.S. foreign policy, 106–7; partisan politics and, 12; patriotism associated with support for, 9, 185–86, 188, 197, 198, 207, 208, 211, 239–41; popular frustration with progress of, 53–54; popular support for, 184–241; popular war weariness, 7, 16, 136, 145, 161, 168, 224, 225, 240, 292, 318; the postwar challenge, 324–27; POW issue changes meaning of, 227, 236; push for victory, 1965–1968, 43–71; rallies in support of, 5; Reagan on, 1–4, 15; Republican Party offers little opposition in 1964 and 1965, 18; residual U.S. forces, 105, 148, 160–61, 182; revisionism regarding, 4; seen as Soviet-engineered distraction, 35; seen as test of American will and credibility, 35; symbolic value of, 4–5, 175, 181, 186, 188; Tet offensive, 69–70, 226, 351n58; as unifying force for conservatives, 13; U.S. domestic politics, 1968–1969, 72–124; U.S. goals in, 57, 59, 216; U.S. push into Southeast Asia, 31–42; and U.S. electoral politics in 1968, 87–97; young conservatives serve in, 244. *See also* anti-war movement; bombing North Vietnam; Cambodian invasion of 1970; end-the-war amendments; escalation of Vietnam War; limited war policy; no-win policy; prisoners of war (POWs); pro-war movement; supporting the troops; "win the war" strategy; withdrawal of U.S. troops
VIVA. *See* Victory in Vietnam Association (VIVA)
Voices Vital in America, 275. *See also* Victory in Vietnam Association (VIVA)
VVAW (Vietnam Veterans Against the War), 223–26, 325
VVJP (Vietnam Veterans for a Just Peace), 223–26

Wallace, George, 79–80, 86, 199, 223
war crimes, 221, 222, 225

Ward, Chester, 38
Ward, William, 215, 216
Warner, John, 230
War Powers Act, 304–5, 329
wars of national liberation: American Conservative Union on, 46; conservatives on U.S. fighting, 18–19, 66; *National Review* on U.S. involvement in, 30; in *National Review*'s fake secret documents, 165. *See also* Vietnam War
Washburn, Abbott, 217–18
Washington Campus News Service (WCNS), 285
Washington Special Actions Group (WSAG), 136, 144
Watergate scandal, 326, 328
Wattenberg, Ben, 284
Wayne, John, 62–63, 79, 123, 337
Wedemeyer, Albert, 38
Weinberger, Caspar, 332
Weiss, Nora, 236–37
Welch, Robert, 25–26, 55–56
Welcome Home Parade (New York City, 1973), 8–9
welcome home parades, 189, 324–25
Westmoreland, William, 8, 111, 149, 196, 313–14
"We Support Our Boys in Vietnam" parades: American Legion support for, 57, 58, 59, 60, 340; conservatives focus on ideals of, 326; parade of May 13, 1967, 8, 57–61, 63, 191, 207, 209, 350n40
Whalen, Richard, 73
"What Is Conservatism?" (Meyer), 23
Wheeler, Earle, 92, 93–94, 117
White, F. Clifton, 83, 284
White, William Allen, 219
Why Vietnam? (documentary), 253
Wiley, Charles, 191–93, 330
Wills, Garry, 141–42
Wilson, Robert, 18
Winter, Tom, 170
"win the war" strategy: of American Conservative Union, 38–39; American Conservative Union on popular support for, 126; bombing North Vietnam in, 140; Broomfield's resolution supporting, 36; conservatives on Johnson's failure to pursue, 2, 53, 93; conservatives on victory of withdrawal, 35; December 1972 bombing seen to confirm, 324; Goldwater on no substitute for victory, 36, 37; Laird on "win or get out" strategy, 96; National Student Committee for Peace with Freedom in Southeast Asia on, 250; postwar acceptance of, 331; "supporting the troops" theme replaces, 135; Thurmond supports, 117; Victory in Vietnam Marches urge, 198, 199; Young Americans for Freedom supports, 60, 259, 261, 263
withdrawal of U.S. troops: from Cambodia, 144; ceasefire before, 310; Citizens Committee for Peace with Freedom in Vietnam on, 115–17; conservatives become unable to mount concerted challenge to, 293; conservatives on criteria for, 113–14; continuing war by alternative means after, 108; deadline for, 145, 151, 154, 181, 218, 236, 237, 268; Eisenhower on consequences of, 77; escalation versus, 7; fifty thousand troops after Cambodian invasion, 143; Goodell Resolution on, 120; grassroots activists call for victory or, 35; immediate, 7, 142, 211, 214, 218, 238, 263, 285; January 1972 announcement of, 183; in Johnson's September 1966 peace proposal, 105; June 1969 plan for, 113, 116; Laird on, 89, 110; Lane on, 112; making peace with, 1969–1972, 125–83; Mansfield amendment on, 168, 181; in May 1972, 307; McGovern–Hatfield amendment on, 136, 217, 218–19, 220; mutual withdrawal of troops, 149, 313–14; *National Review* on, 104, 182; negotiation as alternative to, 149; Nixon announces at Midway Island in June

1969, 107–8; in Nixon's May 1969 peace proposal, 104, 106; 150,000 announced on April 20, 1969, 130; in option to the right, 145; in Paris peace accords, 319–24; phased, 15, 104, 107, 123, 128, 142, 161, 179, 202, 203, 299, 304; POW issue and, 159, 161, 228, 234, 237, 280, 305, 319; precipitate, 116, 232; prisoners of war associated with, 159, 161, 305; pro-war demonstrations allow it to proceed, 209; public opinion favors, 121, 151; takes precedence over success, 301; twenty-five thousand beginning in July 1969, 107, 113, 118; unilateral, 15–16, 68, 89, 103, 104, 108, 149, 159, 183; U.S. role in Southeast Asia after, 286; Wills on, 142. *See also* Vietnamization

women in conservative movement of 1960s, 26

working class: Middle America Group engages, 211; support for Vietnam War in, 202–4. *See also* organized labor

World Anti-Communist League, 129

World Youth Crusade for Freedom, 63, 253

YAF. *See* Young Americans for Freedom (YAF)

Yarmolinsky, Adam, 100

YES-IN, 272

Yorty, Sam, 272, 273

You Can Trust the Communists (To Be Communists) (Schwarz), 35

Young Americans for Freedom (YAF), 245–65; Abate joins, 285–86; allied with American Conservative Union, 23, 245, 246; allied with *National Review*, 245, 246, 287; anticommunism of, 63–64, 65, 247; anticommunist guerrilla groups urged by, 51; anti-war movement opposed by, 242, 246–47, 249, 258, 259–60; breaks with Nixon, 158–60, 285; California YAF (CalYAF), 246–47, 260, 272; on Cambodian invasion of 1970, 133, 259; campus activism of, 5, 63–65, 246, 263, 264; Citizens Committee for Peace with Freedom in Vietnam contrasted with, 68; on Communist massacres in Vietnam, 242, 247; contradictory position of, 261, 264–65; East-West trade opposed by, 64, 245, 248; on educating Americans on real meaning of Vietnam War, 57; and Frank, 272; and Goldwater, 245, 259, 294; Independent Sector campaign, 248; at July 26, 1971, conservative meeting, 170; Keene as chair of, 243; on Kent State University shootings, 260; limited war policy opposed by, 245; long-term influence sought by, 249; Majority Coalition program, 248, 249; as mass membership group, 245; means of communication of, 245–46; as middle-class organization, 205; Moratorium opposed by, 254–57, 258; national board of, 245, 249, 287; National Student Coordinating Committee for Victory in Vietnam founded by, 250; on Nixon administration attempts to control pro-war message, 226; Nixon administration's relations with, 244, 259; Nixon endorsed in 1968, 86; on Nixon's China policy, 271; Norton's memorandum to Teague, 261–64, 265; origins of, 245; on Paris peace accords, 323–24; patriotism as focus of, 244, 287; People's Peace Treaty opposed by, 269; petition to Paris peace talks, 133, 258; polarization caused by, 245; on pro-Nixon stance as only option by late 1970, 264; "Rally for Freedom in Vietnam and All the World" publicized by, 195; speakers' bureau, 273; split at national convention of 1969, 147, 260–61; and split over Ashbrook's presidential campaign of 1972, 294; and Student Coordinating Committee for Freedom in Vietnam and Southeast Asia, 266, 271; on

YAF (*continued*)
　　student radicals, 204–5; Students for a Democratic Society opposed by, 64, 247, 260; supporting the troops by, 259, 264, 265; on teach-ins as unpatriotic, 62; Tell it to Hanoi campaign, 242, 256–58, 259, 262, 287, 326; tenth anniversary celebrations, 147–48; as vanguard of pro-war student activism, 16, 245; on Vietnamization, 133, 258; Vietnam veterans in, 264–65; Vietnam visit of April 1970, 259; violence by, 247; and "We Support Our Boys in Vietnam" parade in New York, May 13, 1967, 60; "Young America's Freedom Offensive," 247–49, 254, 255, 265

"Young America's Freedom Offensive," 247–49, 254, 255, 265

Young Republican National Federation, 282

Your Friendly VC, 274

Zaretsky, Natasha, 336
Zelizer, Julian, 11, 12
Ziegler, Ron, 137

www.ingramcontent.com/pod-product-compliance
Lightning Source LLC
Chambersburg PA
CBHW031410230426
43668CB00007B/265